D1505988

NOV 2 8 2005

CODE

LEONARDO

Roger F. Malina, series editor

CODE

Collaborative Ownership and the Digital Economy

Edited by
Rishab Aiyer Ghosh

The MIT Press
Cambridge, Massachusetts
London, England

© 2005 Massachusetts Institute of Technology

All rights reserved. No part of this book may be reproduced in any form by any electronic or mechanical means (including photocopying, recording, or information storage and retrieval) without permission in writing from the publisher.

MIT Press books may be purchased at special quantity discounts for business or sales promotional use. For information, please e-mail <special_sales@mitpress.mit.edu> or write to Special Sales Department, The MIT Press, 5 Cambridge Center, Cambridge, MA 02142.

This book was set in Bell Gothic and Garamond 3 by SNP Best-set Typesetter Ltd., Hong Kong. Printed and bound in the United States of America.

Library of Congress Cataloging-in-Publication Data

CODE: collaborative ownership and the digital economy / edited by Rishab Aiyer Ghosh.
    p.   cm.—(Leonardo)
Includes bibliographical references and index.
ISBN 0-262-07260-2 (hc. : alk. paper)
1. Electronic commerce—International cooperation. 2. Strategic alliances (Business) 3. Intellectual property—Economic aspects. 4. Group decision making. 5. Common good. I. Ghosh, Rishab Aiyer. II. Leonardo (Series) (Cambridge, Mass.)
HF5548.32.C62 2005
302.3—dc22
                                                          2004058786

10 9 8 7 6 5 4 3 2 1

Contents

Series Foreword

The cultural convergence of art, science, and technology provides ample opportunity for artists to challenge the very notion of how art is produced and to call into question its subject matter and its function in society. The mission of the Leonardo Book Series, published by The MIT Press, is to publish texts by artists, scientists, researchers, and scholars that present innovative discourse on the convergence of art, science, and technology.

Envisioned as a catalyst for enterprise, research, and creative and scholarly experimentation, the book series enables diverse intellectual communities to explore common grounds of expertise. The Leonardo Book Series provides a context for the discussion of contemporary practice, ideas, and frameworks in this rapidly evolving arena where art and science connect.

To find more information about Leonardo/ISAST and to order our publications, go to Leonardo Online at <http://mitpress.mit.edu/e-journals/ Leonardo/isast/leobooks.html> or send e-mail to <leonardobooks.mitpress. mit.edu>.

Joel Slayton
Chair, Leonardo Books Series

Book Series Advisory Committee: Annick Bureaud, Pamela Grant Ryan, Craig Harris, Margaret Morse, Michael Punt, Douglas Sery, Allen Strange.

Leonardo/International Society for the Arts, Sciences, and Technology (ISAST)

Leonardo, the International Society for the Arts, Sciences, and Technology, and the affiliated French organization Association Leonardo have two very simple goals:

1. Document and make known the work of artists, researchers, and scholars interested in the ways that the contemporary arts interact with science and technology, and
2. Create a forum and meeting places where artists, scientists, and engineers can meet, exchange ideas, and, where appropriate, collaborate.

When the journal *Leonardo* was started some thirty-five years ago, these creative disciplines existed in segregated institutional and social networks, a situation dramatized at that time by the "Two Cultures" debates initiated by C. P. Snow. Today we live in a different time of cross-disciplinary ferment, collaboration, and intellectual confrontation enabled by new hybrid organizations, new funding sponsors, and the shared tools of computers and the Internet. Above all, new generations of artist-researchers and researcher-artists are now at work individually and in collaborative teams bridging the art, science, and technology disciplines. Perhaps in our lifetime we will see the emergence of "new Leonardos," creative individuals or teams who will not only develop a meaningful art for our times but also drive new agendas in science and stimulate technological innovation that addresses today's human needs.

For more information on the activities of the Leonardo organizations and networks, please visit our Web site at <http://mitpress.mit.edu/Leonardo>.

Roger F. Malina
Chair, Leonardo/ISAST

ISAST Board of Directors: Martin Anderson, Mark Resch, Ed Payne, Sonya Rapoport, Stephen Wilson, Lynn Hershman Leeson, Joel Slayton, Penelope Finnie, Curtis Karnow, Mina Bissell, Beverly Reiser, Piero Scaruffi.

Acknowledgments

I would first like to thank all the distinguished contributors to this volume, who have shown a remarkable openness in pooling together their expertise and experience in diverse disciplines into this combined—*collaborative*—effort. This book is based substantially, in its conception as well as in terms of specific chapters contributed, on the CODE—Collaboration and Ownership in the Digital Economy conference at Queens' College, Cambridge, United Kingdom in April 2001. Many of the contributors to this volume were speakers at this conference, initiated by Bronac Ferran, Arts Council England, working closely with Alan Blackwell, Michael Century, Professor Bill Cornish, Peter Colyer, and John Howkins. The conference was a partnership between Arts Council England, Academia Europaea, and the University of Cambridge England's Intellectual Property Unit, University of Cambridge Computer Laboratory and Crucible Research Network. It was funded by Arts Council England, the Center for the Public Domain, the Daniel Langlois Foundation, East England Arts, the Rockefeller Foundation and the UK Engineering and Physical Sciences Research Council. An edited archive of presentations at the conference can be found at <http://www.artscouncil.org.uk>.

This book has also drawn on several contributions from the first workshop of the new Intellectual Property, Markets, and Cultural Flows program of the Social Sciences Research Council in New York, October 2003. The workshop was organized by Joe Karaganis at the SSRC, and funding for the SSRC program is provided by the Knowledge, Creativity, and Freedom program of the Ford Foundation and by the Rockefeller Foundation.

I would like to thank the organizers and sponsors of both these events for the opportunity to invite contributions for this volume; Michael Century for introducing me to MIT Press and bringing me on board as editor, and Doug Sery and Valerie Geary at MIT Press who have been most helpful and patient. This book would not have been possible without the assistance provided by Kirsten Haaland at MERIT, the University of Maastricht, who worked tirelessly and efficiently on the draft manuscripts, proofreading the text, and helping with the extensive revisions required to convert papers and presentations into chapters suitable for this volume.

Finally, I would like to thank my wife Kamini, who was always there for me, full of encouragement and support.

Maastricht, March 2004

CODE

1

Why Collaboration Is Important (Again)

Rishab Aiyer Ghosh

No matter how business-like and pragmatic one is, when describing open source software to a layman, after you get past the initial scepticism—"surely such a disorganized system can't work"—there is always a sense of wonder in the listener. It is fascinating, and somewhat mysterious, how a supposed "bunch of hackers" who have never met and are not formally organized have managed to come up with such a powerful system of creating software. Thousands of people organize informally to create single works that can hold their own against the assembly-line software produced by large multinational companies. It seems important to know that this is possible, but it still seems out of the norm, exceptional—as if people would only collaborate in this way for a *reason*, for some *ideology*.

Of course, there often *is* an ideology. Free software, the original term for open source, gets its name not for the price tag but for the freedoms that many software developers believe should adhere to software. But collaboration need not be driven by ideology, and the common, romanticized notion that collaborative ownership and creativity on a large scale requires the involvement of idealists is, to me, rather sad. Humans are social creatures, and our greatest achievements have been collaborative efforts, often vast ones—especially in the realm of knowledge and the mind. That most of us assume creativity as necessarily individual, private and subject to the creative inputs of others only under commercial conditions, is a symptom of the conversion from knowledge and art—whether closely guarded secrets or widely published—to "intellectual property."

"Intellectual Property" versus Creative Collaboration?

The economic basis for intellectual property is nonobvious, to say the least. Unlike most forms of property, intellectual property is almost unique in requiring state support for its very existence. While it is helpful to have state protection for a plot of land, it can also be protected by, for instance, putting a fence around it, and a chair can be protected by sitting on it. Such acts of protection express your possession of your property. Information is not just an extreme nonrival good, in that many people can enjoy its benefits at the same time; information is also unusual in that ownership over it cannot be expressed through a public act of possession. You can possess information if you keep it to yourself—in which case it remains private, and nobody knows what it is that you possess. As soon as you make public the information you claim to own, it is public information that everyone can access since you no longer have any natural control over it. The extreme nonrival nature of information means that any expression of possession you make over it, after publishing it, is impotent, and your "ownership" of published information can only be guaranteed through external support, such as by the state. With more tangible, physical goods, you express your possession over your property by preventing others from taking it from you. After all, when they take your property you don't have it any more. With information goods, your "property" can be secret and only possessed by you. However, if published—if distributed even to one other person—that information is no longer within your control and is available to everyone.

The external protection of such a hard-to-possess form of property also runs against the gradient of economic sense. Information can be reproduced infinitely with no inherent marginal cost of reproduction—any cost is solely related to the medium of production. Since something with a zero marginal cost of reproduction is clearly not scarce, it also has no value that can be naturally protected. Infinitely copied goods have no inherent value, and even though a single copy may have a value to a single recipient of such goods, there is no rational economic incentive for a recipient to pay for a single copy of information when it is clear that producing that copy cost nothing. I called this the problem of infinity,[1] and its sustainable solution cannot be to use laws and the power of the state to distort the natural functioning of a free market. Despite all the colourful imagery comparing copying information at no cost with piracy—murder on the high seas—implicit violations of intellectual

Rishab Aiyer Ghosh

property claims in fact outnumber violation of property claims of other sorts by orders of magnitude. Indeed, in most parts of the world, *respecting* intellectual property claims is the exception rather than the norm (while taking over someone's house is abnormal anywhere).

The various legal instruments of state protection lumped casually under the term Intellectual Property Rights (IPRs)—copyright, patent, trademark, and others—were developed with the primary justification of increasing human creativity, increasing the public's access to this creativity, and increasing collaborative creativity—Newton's "standing on the shoulders of giants." However, the single-minded push we see in policy decisions around the world today to strengthen intellectual property rights and make knowledge and art more and more like the physical forms of property they least resemble threatens to undo the very basis for these rights. It threatens to decrease creativity, decrease the public's access to creativity, and worst of all, to decrease collaborative creativity. Newton should have had to pay a license fee before being allowed even to see how tall the "shoulders of giants" were, let alone to stand upon them.

The Exciting Novelty of Collaboration

This is the context in which collaboratively creating knowledge, something inherently human, comes to be seen as a novelty. Yet novelty excites, and the headlines grabbed by the open source and free software movement have resulted in a renewed public interest in collaborative creation as a whole. Businesses are looking at collaboration, not just in open source software, where the likes of IBM, Oracle, and Sun—otherwise holders of vast intellectual property domains—have investment plans of billions of dollars. The pharmaceutical and biotechnology industry has organized consortiums for genetic information, where individual discoveries are shared in a common pool rather than—as used to be the norm—secretly squirreled away in in-house labs for further commercial exploitation. Commerce matters, for free software has shown that collaboration can be profitable simply by virtue of leading to greater human creativity.

This novelty stems partly from the tools of the free software movement that have been not just technical but legal—the General Public License, or GPL, the most common free software copyright license, requires redistribution of copyrighted free software to be on the same "share-and-share-alike" terms as the original software. This twists the fences of intellectual property around so that rather than enclosing private spaces out of the commons, the GPL protects the commons and prevents private appropriation.

Novelty is good for exciting interest, and it would be positive indeed if this interest leads to a greater awareness of the importance of collaboration in creativity in all areas of activity. But the novelty itself is misplaced. Humans have been collaboratively creating and owning knowledge for as long as we've been able to communicate, and such knowledge forms the basis of our ability to function as societies today in more or less every field of endeavor one cares to examine.

In this volume, the highly distinguished contributors examine a few such fields. The first part, "Creativity and Domains of Collaboration," aims to show that collaboration is not so novel after all, and looks at creativity and the collaborative ownership of knowledge in different times and places. Anthropology is one focus here, and the initial chapters look at approaches to collaborative ownership in traditional societies, while the final chapter by Paul David shows how collaborative creativity became an essential in the tradition of academic science, thus underpinning modern civilization.

The second part, "Mechanisms for Collaboration," examines some of the mechanisms through which collaborative creation of knowledge is taking place today, and the new mechanisms emerging for the study of such large-scale—indeed, industrial—collaborative efforts. The section begins with a look at how benefits are shared when contributors to knowledge do not have control over their implicit collaborative role—as when pharmaceutical firms commercialize traditional knowledge about medicinal plants—and then the issues of identity and trust, so crucial to the "virtual" relationships that are the basis for much collaboration in the age of the Internet. My own contribution and that of Yochai Benkler provide models by which new forms of online collaboration can be studied and explained and—important from an economic point of view—even measured. The final chapter in this section, by Tim Hubbard and James Love, also has an economic approach to a real social problem—how to fund creativity, especially in the area of research and development of medicines where IPRs pose a clear threat to public health in many parts of the world, but abolishing them outright wouldn't solve anything.

The last part examines the more philosophically resonant issues of "Ownership, Property, and the Commons"—which are causes as much as consequences of collaborative creativity. Just as the first section of this volume describes how collaboration has worked, and the second describes how collaboration's new forms are taking shape today, this third and final section provides visions for the future, and how it may be worse, or hopefully, better, than the past. With the increasingly demanding application of the language of property rights to knowledge and creativity, are we witnessing a second enclosure movement—this time, as James Boyle suggests, an enclosure of the mind? Or might, as John Clippinger and David Bollier argue, the worldwide acclaim for free software signify a renaissance of the commons? The final chapters by Philippe Aigrain and Richard Stallman bring us "down-to-earth" with concrete proposals for a new system of "positive rights" for information, and the very real threats being posed to the knowledge commons and the future of collaboration by current international trade policy.

Open Source Editing

I have taken an "open source" approach to editing this volume. A free software project relies on individual contributions being made by contributors who are good at what they do. With a bit of glue to stick things together, this leads to a combined software system of high quality, even if the individual components are very different—and require very different skills to create. The test of the open source process is if the software that emerges at the end works.

The contributors to this volume are extremely distinguished in their own subject domains, but these domains are so different from each other that their names rarely appear together, let alone all in one volume, to be read together as one work. The contributors' expertise ranges from anthropology via economics and law to software development. They are clearly very good at what they do. My commentary at the beginning of each section is meant to provide the right sort of glue to put each chapter in a common context. I hope you find that the resulting combination of very different components works.

Note

1. Ghosh, R. A., "The Problem of Infinity," *Electric Dreams* 63 (June 1995), available at <http://dxm.org/dreams/>.

I

Creativity and Domains of Collaboration

Many descriptions of the free software community, and other collaborative but nonmonetary production on the Internet, borrow the notion of "gift-giving" that (hypothetically) occurs in "tribal" societies. An assumption is that free software production is similar to supposedly primitive forms of interaction involving the generous contribution of gifts with no expectation of returns—altruism in the sense that economists use the term.[1] Whether this similarity is a sign that free software production is destined to be marginalized and unsustainable, or the beginning of the end of capitalist production, depends on the ideology of the discussant. Oddly enough, altruistic gift-giving is rarely a notion brought forth by anthropologists, whom we may imagine to be in more immediate contact with hypothetically gift-giving tribes than most people. Tribal societies do in fact engage in nonmonetary or nonproprietary production and flows of exchange, but they build complex webs of reciprocal obligation that bind them just as money might in a price-based society. The giving of gifts in tribal societies is, in reality, an action performed within the context of reciprocity and expectations of returns—status, rights, or more gifts. There are indeed similarities between collaborative production and non-monetary exchange in tribal societies and collaborative ownership in the digital economy, notably free software: both are based on the self-interested participation of individuals and communities linked by a complex web of rights and obligations.

This is highlighted first by Strathern, who offers a comparative perspective on nonproprietary forms of ownership. She describes how the notion of collective ownership—by humanity of the gene, for instance—is transformed into an *imagined collective* when applied to certain communities of Papua New Guinea. This represents not true collective ownership as much as multiple authorship or multiple ownership, where each "owner" lays claim to a certain definable but inseparable part of a collectively owned whole.

Leach makes explicit the location of this form of ownership somewhere between individual appropriation (individual works map to individual authors) and the commons (the entire work maps collectively to the entire set of authors). Leach details how the nature of ownership is necessarily based on the nature of creativity and mode of production. It depends on the process of creation and the coherence of the created; in an environment of collaborative creativity—Papuan Tambarans described by Leach, or the source code of the Linux Kernel—individual contributions have no value independent of the context of the whole (collaboratively produced) work of which they form a part. Yet, individual contributions can be clearly identified. In the case of the Linux Kernel, each individual line of source code is "owned" by its individual creator (thanks to copyright law, which makes explicitly claiming ownership unnecessary) and also identifiably associated with its creator (thanks to the version-control tools used to enable collaborative development of Linux). Under copyright law, the Linux is not *collectively* owned by any means; no single group owns the copyright to the entire work.[2] Nor, however, is it in the public domain, or even in a commons—each individual contribution can be associated with its individual contributor who, in terms of copyright law, owns it. However, the individual and individually owned contributions only make sense, and have any value, in the context of the combined whole—which is, hence, *multiply* owned. As Leach shows, free software is by no means the first domain in which multiple ownership is common.

Myers shows how ownership and identity are not only strongly associated with each other, in that people identify themselves on the basis of what they own as much as objects' ownership is defined on the basis of the identity of their owner (or owners). Ownership and identity are also closely linked to *negotiated exchange*—collaboration and participation within a web of relationships takes place through the merging of ownership over objects, and this in turn affects the sense of identity, placing autonomous entities within their social framework. He illustrates how Australian aborigines distinguish the ownership over an *idea* or *design* and share ownership (granting "licences") by allowing others to express the design and thus participate in the rights—and identity—enabled by the ownership of such intangible objects.

Boateng notes that the "mainstream Intellectual Property Rights (IPR)" framework is a result of a political and economic power play, and is unique to a particular space and time; it is not an obvious or necessary framework, let alone a universal one appropriate to all creativity in all contexts. She shows how collaborative ownership is seen as "a problem," using the example of Ghanaian textile patterns but this is equally applicable to, say, collaboratively owned open source software that some of the wilder defenders of the IPR orthodoxy have even accused of being "unconstitutional." However, collaborative ownership is only a problem when intellectual property law assumes that ownership and creativity is necessarily individual. This assumption is natural for those who build (and benefit from) the mainstream IPR system, and Boateng shows how this assumption is used in order to invalidate property claims to valuable—collaboratively produced and owned—traditional knowledge while seeking to enforce their own claims to works derived from such traditional knowledge resources.

Seeger looks at how ownership and creativity in the domain of music has been defined by the Western notion of copyright that ignores the collaboratively produced and owned nature of the majority of music not generated by the recording industry in Europe and America. Like Boateng, he argues that many creators of works in a collaborative framework use a metaphor of ownership that is not compatible with the framework of individual copyright. He shows how communities that have traditional ownership over songs not only cannot assert this ownership in a copyright framework, but that when he publishes such a song (originating in native communities in the Mato Grosso, Brazil), he gains copyright and ownership—as an individual identifiable in law with the published work—although he had nothing to do with the song's creation. And the originating community loses whatever implicit rights they had over it.

It is not only non-Western cultures that have a long tradition of collaborative production of knowledge. Nonproprietary, collaborative production and ownership has an extensive history in scientific communities of the West, and just as we enter a period of increased pressure from policymakers and industry against the "open science" tradition, Paul David describes that scientific research was not always an open process. Historically, "science" was the process of discovering (and keeping) "Nature's Secrets." This was similar to the knowledge systems of many other traditional societies described by, say, Strathern and Leach, where although the concept of proprietary ownership of knowledge is rare, it is often seen as something to be kept secret rather than publicly shared. In "modern" industrial IPR terms this is similar to trade secret law—once knowledge is shared, it is public and unprotected, so creators (or discoverers) try to exercise their "ownership" of such knowledge by keeping it secret as long as possible and controlling who has access to it, binding those with whom knowledge is shared with the ties of custom, professional honor (the mediaeval system of guilds), or trade secret and contract law.

David explores how the increasing complexity of scientific discovery and in particular the increasing reliance on mathematical techniques resulted in individual "star scientists" patronized by one or another court having to pool their expertise together, to collaborate in order to move forward. This complexity also resulted in the development of a peer-review system, since enthusiast patrons were no longer able to determine, on their own, the scientific caliber of those they wished to support. The need for peer review and collaboration led directly to the "open science" of publication and the borrowing of ideas that has been the mainstay of scientific development since the eighteenth century, and is under threat from strong-IPR advocates today.

Even as "open science" faces the threat of being closed—especially in fields prone to quick commercial exploitation such as biotechnology and genetics—software engineering shows a movement in the opposite direction, from closed, "secret" source code hidden behind the binary-only distribution of proprietary software products to an open, freer distribution of the secret sources. The underlying reasons for this bear a striking similarity to what made science change a few hundred years ago—software is increasingly more complex (and insecure), and developers, whether individual or corporate, benefit from collaboration. Open, peer review is seen widely—especially in the cryptography and security community—as the only way of ensuring quality and reliability, just as it has for scientific developments over centuries.

Notes

1. For instance, if a software developer contributes a program for free to the community with an expectation that this contribution will lead to recognition of his programming skills, this is not altruism in economic terms, but rational self-interest: the

programmer is using his contribution to "signal" his skill—see Josh Lerner and Jean Tirole, "Some Simple Economics of Open Source," *Journal of Industrial Economics* 50, no. 2 (2002): 197–234.

2. This is a major guarantee of the sustained "freeness" of Linux, as there is no single—individual or collective—owner able, for example, to sell the rights to Linux to a commercial entity that could make it no longer free software. Contrast this with a scientific paper where all joint authors collectively own the entire paper.

2

Imagined Collectivities and Multiple Authorship

Marilyn Strathern

Turning to the kind of society where Westerners often imagine they will find collective ownership, the anthropologist finds that it offers little purchase on the idea of free access but considerable purchase on questions of authorship and creativity. "Authorship" is a collaborative effort, yet it can involve trans-actions over claims to manifestations of the person that appear thoroughly materialistic. "Creativity" is a kind of distributive virtue, yet its free expression runs up against the need for validation. Are there issues here of interest to the digital economy? Consider these two descriptions.

First (I paraphrase): The [network] as a concept is fundamentally collective in nature. Though it is true that each individual human has its own unique [network], the [total network] as we are discussing here refers to a population. In this conception, each individual [network] is best thought of as a node in an overall hereditary web. Linking the nodes within that web there are kin relationships among members of a generation and also between succeeding generations. (Grobstein 1990)

In these dispersed linkages across time and space, the writer could be talking about flows of information, and in a way he is. However this is not informatics but genetics—where I put "network," the writer had "human genome." An embryologist by training, he continues with reference to a (then) current debate on germ-line therapy (his words):

It is the substance of the web of linkages with which we are concerned when we consider the implications of gene transfer to germ-line cells. That substance is the collective human genome . . . looking at individual human genomes within our species, commonness rather than difference is overwhelming. It is this commonness that is our collective heritage and property as human beings. And it is about possible changes in this collective property, which is both a characteristic of the human species and something that is commonly "owned," that all human beings have a right to be consulted. (Grobstein 1990, 20)[1]

A dream of a network owned! It is, he suggests, by virtue of substantial connection, of kinship, that humankind as a species possesses the genome in common, since we are all parts of a web that belongs to us as a collectivity. It is a collectivity imagined, strikingly, in terms of property ownership.

Second: another description of kinship that is about flows of information. Here, substance is handled quite differently. To commemorate a death a sculpture is commissioned by the dead person's relatives, often carved, but in the instance of a particular one made in 2000 to which I refer, plaited with fibre, the size of a man. It is called a *Malanggan*. This one took weeks of preparation, ropes first being flattened and then knotted to produce a huge disclike shape. Knotting is likened to quickening, as when bodily substances come together to form a child, while the plaiting evokes long-dead ancestors and the binding of the plaits makes the Malanggan into a body. All kinds of memories were being brought together in this form. At the center was a hole referred to as the eye, or a vent in the ground, or a whirlpool, full of movement as the eye is always in movement. Finally the figure was painted to make it "hot":

Its work is to reflect, bending light from beyond into the eyes of those who have come to view it. When it has been seen, it is common for the viewer to look quickly away, averting the eyes and registering the image against the eyelids. They see it again there, being able to return to that image in memory. In years after they come to want its material forms for themselves. Images do not leave the minds of those who see them. (Sykes n.d.)

Once displayed, people placed contributions of shell money at its base. It was then doused with kerosene and burnt.

The Malanggan that had just been made was in fact a model of one that existed on another plane: the image lodged in the memory. When it is given new form, as at a funeral feast, it embodies other images as well. There are no claims to collectivity or to shared substance here. Instead we might almost talk of multiple authors, for its value lies in its derivative nature. The person sponsoring its manufacture thinks he or she is replicating an image seen many years before—shell money will have been paid for the privilege of seeing it. In turn the image is now dispersed among a new generation, and they carry it off in their mind's eye. A network, we might say, is established through payment. For the transactions are transformative: they separate form from image. The form (in this case a woven figure) is destroyed while the design is kept in the mind, and in the mind can travel over the times and spaces that people traverse in their lives.

The embryologist opposed sharing to individual appropriation, the basis for sharing lying in what we, the human species, have in common. The assumption is that common property confers rights, above all, rights to knowledge as in case of making decisions about the human genome. Note that he could either have said no one owns the human genome or (as he did) everyone owns it. The ambiguity is thoroughly appropriate for a property-based system. Where it is possible to turn resources of all kinds into property which carries rights that individuals can exercise against others, one can either acknowledge those resources which are not appropriable (no one owns them) *or* suggest that they are owned by a collectivity and not divisible into individual lots (everyone owns them). Either formulation is powerful, and each has its place. But in the spirit of the present endeavour I want to explore what we may learn from nonproprietary regimes. So I welcome the invitation to go cross-cultural.

I am going to draw my examples from a part of the world recently signed up to the World Intellectual Property Organization (WIPO) one that has put Trade-Related (Aspects of) Intellectual Property Rights (TRIPS) legislation into place: Papua New Guinea. Papua New Guinea includes the islands of New Britain and New Ireland, and Malanggan comes from New Ireland. Colonized in the nineteenth century, globalized in the twentieth century, these people with their clan groups and face-to-face interactions are typical of the kinds of places where one might expect to find undifferentiated collectivities and the communal ownership of resources. In fact we find nothing of the kind. Indeed in the history of European contact it is interesting that when communal forms of social life are *not* found, the stereotypes often go completely the other way: the indigenes are presented instead as a mercenary, overindividualistic lot. However, that does not quite get to the heart of the matter either.

The two descriptions are radically different but together they prompt us to look more closely at notions of collectivity and the nature of individual claims. For the genome is being imagined both as a collective network *and* as property. It is just the scale that confuses, since it is meant to embrace all the human world.[2] This property is not, of course, marketable or transferable as such: rather, claims of common ownership are prompted by the possibility of individual persons or corporations turning portions of it into disposable resources for themselves by asserting private property rights. The collective interests are interests that remain undivided, undifferentiated, and only passively utilizable. By contrast, the Papua New Guinean systems that produce artefacts such as Malanggan discriminate between different claims all the time. But private property is not the mode through which this is done. Everything may be differentiated minutely in the way entitlements between persons are worked out, yet claims are understood as embracing multiple, rather than individual, interests.

And the digital economy? I take my cue from Michael Century's (2000) statement in which he suggests that the open source software movement is proof of the creative potential of networks for collaboration. In other words, *techniques of distribution do not just disseminate what has been created elsewhere, but have themselves a creative or productive potential.* Interdigitating creation[3] and dissemination is at the core of the nonproprietary regimes noted here. I bring these forward in turn in the spirit of finding creative analogies—suggestive counterworlds—for how we might think of claims over software inventions; to do *their* creative and suggestive work as analogies, the examples require some spelling out.

Materializing Forms

In a manner rather similar to the ease with which private property is amenable to commodification—its alienability means that it can flow between persons through transfer of title via purchase—people in many societies of Papua New Guinea have an interest in keeping up the flows of assets. They do so through payments. There are numerous occasions on which people pay for things, and things of all kinds, tangible and intangible; moreover, as new assets are defined through new demands they often bring considerable innovation and inventiveness to the occasion.[4] Included here may be payments for knowledge or artistic expertise (Harrison 1992, 1995). Yet despite this surface similarity with the transfer of commodities, there are some quite distinct consequences. The act of "purchase" in a nonproperty context is doing very different work, and invites us to separate out such transactions from commodity exchange (Radin 1996).

In Papua New Guinea, not only is great interest often put on things acquired through transactions but explicit value is put on maintaining the flow itself. This was notably enunciated by Nick Araho (2000, 186–188) in his summary of a discussion at a seminar on intellectual, biological, and cultural property held in Port Moresby in 1997:

Borrowing information between groups characterises Papua New Guinea; nobody should interfere with that. The sharing of information . . . only requires permission or the exchange of certain gifts. Thus, no actions should be taken that might stop the flow of information exchange through traditional channels.

Borrowing, sharing, and exchanging are all effected *through* payments. Moreover, keeping the flow going has generative connotations of its own.

We have a glimpse of that in the case of the woven Malanggan described by Karen Sykes, from Lelet, New Ireland. Recall that payment is made at the point when the figure is brought into public view. Recall also that those who make the payment keep the image in their mind's eye and are then entitled to reproduce what they have seen.[5] Others cannot. And this restriction has introduced a modern vocabulary of rights. "Rights" asserted over the designs have been generally referred to in the anthropological literature on New Ireland as "copyright." However, while such rights can be stolen, they cannot be sold. One person may accuse another of incorporating in a new Malanggan designs they have no claim to, yet the owner of the design cannot dispose of it him- or herself since its power (its value) is effective only for the owner. This "right", if we call it that, is less a right to a disposable possession than a right to protect *an enablement*. That in turn entails an ancillary right: the owner might not be able to sell it but is able to pass it on, and the value of this is bound up with the general value put on keeping powers and energies flowing.

The purchasers acquire the creative power to produce the design again. Literally, they take the image into their body through the eye, and years later—

a generation or so—can instruct a weaver or carver to once more give it form. This reproduction or procreation is a collaborative effort in two senses. First, the image (the Malanggan) is held by one person but expressed in a particular form (the carved or woven figure) by another. People do not, so to speak, materialize their own images. Every figure is the result of a joint enterprise. The roles of the joint creators, that is, the sponsor and the maker of the figure, can never exist in the same person. Indeed Sykes (n.d.) states that for the sculpture to be completed such interests *must* coexist as two distinct manifestations of creativity. Second, there is collaboration over a long time span, since the person who claims the image is, in fact, recalling the earlier occasion on which it was displayed. This results in a kind of delayed collaboration between the two makers, then, insofar as the original maker—or his clan—will only know the effect of the form when the figure is reproduced by another years later. The latter's acknowledged derivation from that earlier display validates its new appearance. At the same time each Malanggan will incorporate elements unique to the relationships of the person who is now having it made, and no two weavings or carvings are identical.

The time scales are significant. The public appearance and transfer of the image is over in a flash—a few hours or days. It is then retained out of sight for years until its next appearance. In other words, the moment of transaction is definitive, for it guarantees the Malanggan future life as a further memory in the minds of others.[6] It is a creative, procreative, act. This is comparable to those Papua New Guinean exchange regimes where it is the display of wealth items that is the definitive, ceremonial moment, by contrast to the long periods in between when the items are kept hidden from public view.[7] The rhythm is that of display and concealment or, in Kirsch's (n.d.) terms, flow and stoppages.

Now the flow may well result in components of the Malanggan design being dispersed in the minds of people over time, and over space. A design brought into material being will at that point be combined with new motifs and with elements from elsewhere, so when a person realizes a new form, it will be the form to which they alone are wholly entitled. In Gell's (1998) words, the Malanggan image is a "distributed object." And it is a distributed object twice over. Each figure gathers within itself the dispersed identities of the deceased in a fabrication that brings past memories together; it is then redispersed across a new generation, a network of persons created no longer through their interactions with the dead person but through their viewing of the image. The relevant distinction here is not between individual and collective but between those moments where identities are dispersed and those moments where identities are condensed or brought together.

The idiom of interpersonal relations aside, is the Malanggan doing with persons what the open source model seeks to do with software? Malanggan get themselves reproduced through persons scattered across time and space; open source is about energizing the contributions of dispersed individuals, about the distribution of a facility. But for the facility to reproduce itself, that is, be put into practice *as* a facility (to do its job as an enablement), it has to be given a form, to materialize, to appear as a technique that a user uses. The user creates that moment by bringing together the software, his or her own intentions for it, a particular agenda and so forth—uniquely combining a diversity of elements.

From the viewpoint of open software distribution, the user as such is a hidden element—not known, so to speak, until the moment when she or he is galvanized into (re)producing the facility in intelligible (readable) though highly transient form. In a property-based economy one might want to recognize those as moments of appropriation.

Collaborative Creativity

Two things are hidden in the Lelet Malanggan before it is displayed. First, the image is behind the eyelids, not in front, and viewable only by the holder(s) of the memory of it. But, secondly, all the work that went into creating the sculptural form is hidden—for once the image is passed on in its virtual form only the design is recalled. Sykes suggests that New Irelanders recreate the loss of the deceased in losing, through the destruction of the material figure, the work that created it.[8] We in turn might recall Century's comment about the hidden work of the open source editor, a vital but invisible creativity. Editorial steering is as essential, he says, as in the production of a scholarly work. Creativity is not only in one place, and there are many ways of both revealing and concealing.

In the Papua New Guinean rhythm of display and concealment, or flow and stoppages, the stopping point may hold everything in suspension, as retaining the image of the Malanggan does. But the period of concealment may also be highly productive: what is often out of sight is growth (e.g., Biersack 1982). This is where innovations get hatched. But there is an interesting interplay between appropriate and inappropriate innovations.

James Leach (2000) describes what happened when, in 1998, people of a village from the Madang area (mainland Papua New Guinea) decided they wanted to purchase the tune, words, and carvings of a particular Tambaran spirit from their neighbors.[9] The descendants of the originator of the spirit voice, ten men, lined up to receive the payment. One of the purchasers called each by name, placing in their hands money and other items. A live pig was also handed over, which the men took back to their village to cook and distribute among everyone there. Thus the transfer of the spirit voice was made public.

The transaction enabled the members of the purchasing village to sing and dance in the name of this spirit. Moreover since they had made a payment, they were also entitled to pass it on in turn, and profit from the payments it would bring them. This contrasts with those situations where someone may ask permission to use a song or dance but acquires only use-rights, and cannot really refer to themselves as the "owner" as the purchasers were entitled to do. In this process the descendants of the original "author" of the spirit voice lost nothing: they could still use the Tambaran [spirit] voice for their own celebrations—but its reach had now been extended to the neighboring village as well. What is important is that the songs should be rendered in a way that keeps their integrity. They evoke memories of the dead and are highly charged for their original owners. The new owners should do nothing to defame or mock the Tambaran spirit. At the same time, the spirit is now lodged in another network of people and, hidden from view, people may dream of new designs or forms for it.[10] Although an innovation may have a single creator, it is multiply owned by the residential group, who would together be paid if it were transferred to another. This social boundary has an interesting effect. If the power to deploy the Tambaran comes to be owned by a group of coresidential villagers, then they proceed to engage their own particular relationships with their ancestors and the spirit world, and these in turn enable them to subject the Tambaran forms to creative elaboration. The enablement, we may say, is "hidden" within these relationships. The knowledge is not public; only the (re-created) form is brought out to be sung or danced when the occasion demands.[11]

For these people in the Madang area, then, both growth and creativity—the time when people hatch innovations for the designs they own—come from experiences that occur out of public view. The form that is eventually displayed may thus be *an original and a derivative at the same time.* What is important is that the new owners acknowledge the source from which the Tambaran voice came. It is a Tambaran that originated at a particular place that they dance and sing. Transactions at the moment of transfer not only secure the release of the knowledge for use but also lock the form into a collaborative venture, making multiple "originators" evident. However there is an interaction here beyond authorship: what is also brought into being are multiple *destinations* for the creation, in the people who will witness the display. We are dealing with the propagation of objects as they become attachable to new people (Demian n.d.).

The very process of deriving a performance from an earlier one is what gives its new appearance validity. In fact, despite infinite room for variation, people may insist, while producing something somewhat new, that they are reproducing the same (rather than reproducing the same while claiming it is novel). *Derivation as such has value.* Here, the Papua New Guinean lawyer Lawrence Kalinoe (2004) notes complexities that copyright threatens to introduce in this field. When contemporary artists draw on traditional art forms, such as the Tambaran songs, they may be able to copyright their artistic expressions. Copyright thus declares the originality, but it cannot deal with the other side of the equation—the simultaneously derivative nature of the work.

The value of the derivative element comes precisely from the fact of what we might call "multiple authorship" (I leave aside the question of whether authorship is the right term). There is value in the very fact that an item has passed from one person to another. In some Papua New Guinean traditions this becomes an explicit technique in the transmission of knowledge. As it has been described for the Mountain Ok region of Papua New Guinea (Crook 2004), people are told half a story, and have to find the other half from within themselves—or from somewhere else. This is a much more specific demand than the Euro-American notion that an audience completes a performance or a reader is required for a book (e.g., Woodmansee 1984, 26–27). The very imagery, narrative, or design of the tale may make little sense freestanding: it has to be complemented by another tale. In this mode of "collaboration," one knows that only part of the form has been revealed—but the concealed bit is not simply held back by the storyteller; it lies also within the listener. It is the person hearing the tale who puts the other half into place. In short, a relationship is established out of which the knowledge is created.

Transmission thus becomes instrumental to the creation. But here the creation is never fully revealed in public; one always imagines that there must be some other, hidden side.

There is an interesting corollary to the fact that what is kept hidden may be as loaded with value as what is brought into the open.

Intellectual property rights regimes use monetary reward as a justifying motivation for creativity: the inventor's company that profits from his invention, the author who profits from her book. This assertion of exclusive rights is, we know, frequently counterposed to the idea of common availability. But there is, of course, a secondary justification for asserting intellectual property claims—the desire to make information or works of art publicly available, even though others should not profit from them until the originator has had a chance to. So products or information are made available for use (at a price) but not for reproduction. With that caveat on the manner of its circulation, IPR puts arts and inventions into the public domain. What the open source software movement seeks to lift is that very qualification, so that facilities transferred without profit are also seen to flow without restriction. Here the public domain may be invoked, as in comparable debate over the human genome sequencing. It is of course an imagined domain, like the collectivities imagined for indigenous peoples.

It is therefore exceedingly interesting that one reason given by Papua New Guinean colleagues for avoiding the IPR route in the protection of cultural property, and it is one offered for example by Kalinoe (2004), is precisely because IPR brings things into the public eye. The limited restriction guaranteed by IPR protection is nothing compared to the long-term publication entailed when the copyright (say) expires. He is thinking of items that are identified with particular groups—perhaps secret "property" in that sense, not unlike the Tambaran songs described by Leach—which should only be revealed under controlled conditions, when the moment for their reproduction is ripe. It is the public domain aspect of IPR that causes problems for this kind of resource.

This is not to overlook the public aspect to such moments of reproduction themselves. Those payments are not only securing release, not only locking the form into a collaborative venture, but they are also broadcasting their value—*validating them*—and a public is needed to register the transaction. The validation is (so to speak) of work already done, of the design well remembered, of the song that has grown with secret embellishments, and above all, the claims based on existing relationships. This implies a boundary between growth and product (Hirsch 2004). Without a division between the time of flow and the time of stoppage, between revelation and concealment, there would be no alterity to structure the moment of validation. As in the differentiation of participants into sponsors and audience at a Malanggan performance, the producers of creations need witnesses to confirm their value.

End Note: Validation

That an item can be validated at all becomes part of its value. And in the Papua New Guinean contexts that frequently involves underlining its derivation—publicizing where it has come from (cf. Woodmansee 1994, 17). If the source is highly relevant, so—I have suggested—is the destination, not just where it has come from but to whom it is going. Making (this kind of) collaborative enterprise visible is part of the validation process. That is, engaging the attention of the witness to the performance mirrors for the future what the performance itself encapsulates from the past in its own attention to an antecedent performance.

I offer the observation because of an issue to do with the circulation of information in Euro-American mode in which software is caught up. This rests in the twin dimension of validation: reliability and responsibility. The case has been argued for scientific authorship (for instance Biagioli 2000; Biagioli and Galison 2003). Validating data enables one to turn information into knowledge; it also enables a critical stance. Here I see the need for a network that knows itself as a social community of sorts. For perhaps a community defined by its freedom of access to sources, that is to one another's works, also needs, some of the time, to be a community defined by knowledge of its sources. I don't know what kind of contribution the open source software movement might make, but end with Century's (2000) provocative remark about the massiveness of data in circulation, where the politics of access shift from mere indexing to social forms of filtering, and (he says) "communities of interest help sort out what is meaningful."

Acknowledgments

I have synthesized the work of several colleagues on a project (PTC: Property, Transactions and Creations: New Economic Relations in the Pacific) funded by the U.K. Economic and Social Research Council between 1999–2002 to whom grateful acknowledgment is made. My co-convener was Eric Hirsch; members included Tony Crook, Melissa Demian, Andrew Holding, Lawrence Kalinoe, Stuart Kirsch, James Leach, Karen Sykes. [See Hirsch and Strathern (eds.).] I am especially grateful to Demian, Kirsch and Sykes, who contributed to a panel on Intellectual and Cultural Property Rights, at the 2001 ASA conference *Rights, Claims, and Entitlements*. I have drawn both inspiration and substance from their unpublished papers and thank Karen Sykes for her detailed comments.

Notes

1. Grobstein was writing a decade before the decoding of the human genome and the controversy over how information about the sequencing was to be released into the public domain.

2. A note on scale: speaking of the amalgam of contributors who compile (for example) a telephone directory, Jaszi (1994, 39) says that there may be "sufficient reason why such data should be placed firmly and irrevocably in the 'public domain.' Indeed, the very multiplicity and interdependency of their 'authors' may explain why we should treat name/address listings as common property."

3. I speak of creation rather than creativity, since it by no means follows that those who bring new forms or new life into existence imagine themelves as original authors. Malanggan-makers are inspired, but do not particularly value inventiveness; indeed, they regard themselves as copying what has gone before. "Procreation" would be an apposite term.

4. Which new sources of money have increased (e.g., Strathern 1999, 93–98)? The very possibility of finding new sources introduces minute distinctions in the jobs people do for one another as the basis for new claims for payment.

5. This will depend on other factors, too, including their relationships with the sponsors of the sculpture. Sykes makes reference to Susanne Küchler's work (1987, 1992), an important antedecent in this area, and one from which much of my own understanding derives. (Küchler 2002 discusses the implications for IPR; see also Lincoln 1987.)

6. "The material object is merely a transitional phase in the biography of a Malangan, most of whose existence is as a memory trace" (Gell 1998, 228); however, its occasional appearance is essential to its perpetuation.

7. Strathern (1999, passim). Exchange involves reciprocity—that is, payments for payments—with the proviso that one pays off one's debts with new wealth (one never returns the same objects, whether it is pigs or shells or money, that were given in the first place). In a property system or "commodity economy," the temporal movements of commodities are often different from those of other forms of property. On the one hand, in the circulation of commodities, the flow may be constantly speeded up, speed itself enhancing value expressed in terms of production and distribution time (cf. Brennan 2000). On the other hand, it may well be the possession of a thing that is valued, while its eventual disposal (or the possibility of it) is a kind of of limiting case, the point at which its value is realized in relation to others.

8. "In making the Malanggan, those participating in the production come to possess the network by which it came about. That network does not constitute itself as owners of the material form, because they dispose of it in a fire. The network is redundant as an enduring collective. That is, instead of possessing the material form collectively, the makers of Malanggan possess the network needed to describe [a] form of owner-ship which is neither personal nor collective" (Sykes n.d.).

9. As presented by James Leach to a conference held in Port Moresby in 2000, "Tra-dition, knowledge and ownership: Transaction and protection." The same example is used in a rather different context in Strathern (in press).

10. "Tambaran [spirit] songs are being innovated all the time" and this includes the dreaming of new Tambaran, which are made public with the distribution of pork everyone can eat, that is, among the villagers who are already/become co-owners of the Tambaran (Leach n.d.).

11. Leach contrasts this with the world of local business and marketing enterprises where no one owns the innovations people try out, and everyone rushes to imitate other people's little inventions. Villagers complain that as soon as anyone has a lucra-tive idea, everyone else follows suit!

References

Araho, Nick. 2000. Presentation of Discussion Group 2. In Kathy Whimp and Mark Busse (eds.), *Protection of intellectual, biological, and cultural property in Papua New Guinea*. Canberra and Port Moresby: Asia Pacific Press at the Australian National University and Conservation Melanesia Inc.

MALASPINA UNIVERSITY-COLLEGE LIBRARY

Biagioli, Mario. 2000. Right or rewards? Changing contexts and definitions of scientific authorship. *Journal of College and University Law* 27: 83–108.

Biagioli, Mario, and Peter Galison. 2003. *Scientific authorship: Credit and intellectual property in science*. New York: Routledge.

Biersack, Aletta. 1982. Ginger gardens for the ginger woman: Rites and passages in a Melanesian society. *Man* (NS) 17: 239–258.

Brennan, Teresa. 2000. *Exhausting modernity: Grounds for a new economy*. New York: Routledge.

Century, Michael. 2000. Open code and creativity in the digital age. Available at <http://www.music.mcgill.ca/-mcentury/Papers/Code.html>.

Crook, Tony. 2004. Transactions in perpetual motion. In Eric Hirsch and Marilyn Strathern (eds.), *Transactions and creations: Property debates and the stimulus of Melanesia*. Oxford: Berghahn.

Demian, Melissa. n.d. Claims without rights: Stable objects and transient owners in Suau. Paper delivered to panel on Intellectual and Cultural Property Rights, ASA conference 2001 on *Rights, Claims, and Entitlements*, Sussex.

Gell, Alfred. 1998. *Art and agency: An anthropological theory*. Oxford: Clarendon Press.

Grobstein, Clifford. 1990. Genetic manipulation and experimentation. In David R. Bromham, Maureen E. Dalton, and Jennifer C. Jackson, (eds.), *Philosophical ethics in reproductive medicine*. Manchester: Manchester University Press.

Jaszi, Peter. 1994. On the author effect: Contemporary copyright and collective creativity. In Martha Woodmansee and Peter Jaszi (eds.), *The construction of authorship: Textual appropriation in law and literature*. Durham, NC: Duke University Press.

Harrison, Simon. 1992. Ritual as intellectual property. *Man* (NS) 27: 225–244.

———. 1995. Anthropological perspectives on the management of knowledge. *Anthropology Today* 11: 10–14.

Hirsch, Eric. 2004. Boundaries of creation: The work of credibility in science and ceremony. In Eric Hirsch and Marilyn Strathern (eds.), *Transactions and creations: Property debates and the stimulus of Melanesia*. Oxford: Berghahn.

Hirsch, Eric, and Marilyn Strathern, (eds.) 2004. *Transactions and creations: Property debates and the stimulus of Melanesia*. Oxford: Berghahn.

Kalinoe, Lawrence. 2004. Traditional knowledge and legal options for the regulation of intellectual and cultural property in Papua New Guinea. In Eric Hirsch and Marilyn Strathern (eds.), *Transactions and creations: Property debates and the stimulus of Melanesia*. Oxford: Berghahn.

Kirsch, Stuart. n.d. Regulating cultural traffic: A strategic review, paper delivered to panel on Intellectual and Cultural Property Rights, ASA conference 2001 on *Rights, Claims, and Entitlements*, Sussex.

Küchler, Susanne. 1987. Malanggan: Art and memory in a Melanesian society. *Man* (NS) 22: 238–255.

———. 1992. Making skins: Malanggan and the idiom of kinship in New Ireland. In Jeremy Coote and Anthony Shelton (eds.), *Anthropology, art and aesthetics*. Oxford: Clarendon Press.

———. 2002. *Malanggan: Art, memory and sacrifice*. Oxford: Berg.

Leach, James. 2000. Multiple expectations of ownership. *Melanesian Law Journal* 27: 63–76.

Lincoln, Louise (ed.). 1987. *Assemblage of spirits: Idea and image in New Ireland*. New York: George Braziller, in association with the Minneapolis Institute of Arts.

Radin, Margaret J. 1996. *Contested commodities: The trouble with trade in sex, children, body parts, and other things*. Cambridge, MA: Harvard University Press.

Strathern, Marilyn. 1999. *Property, substance and effect. Anthropological essays on persons and things*. London: Athlone Press.

———. In press. Divided origins and arithmetic of ownership. In James Ferguson (ed.), *Futures of property and personhood*. Irvine: University of California, Critical Theory Institute.

Sykes, Karen. n.d. Malanggan possessed and re-possessed: How knowing knots transforms the net of sociality. Unpublished paper delivered to panel on Intellectual and Cultural Property Rights, ASA conference 2001 on *Rights, Claims and Entitlements*, Sussex.

Woodmansee, Martha. 1994. On the author effect: Recovering collectivity. In Martha Woodmansee and Peter Jaszi (eds.), *The construction of authorship: Textual appropriation in law and literature*. Durham, NC: Duke University Press.

3

Modes of Creativity and the Register of Ownership

James Leach

Introduction

In a recent popular newspaper article, the Director of Papua New Guinea's National cultural Commission wrote of the appropriation of Papua New Guinea's Cultural properties.[1] The Director, Jacob Simet, was trained as an anthropologist. While his article resonates with a popular impetus among activists to make property out of cultural productions, Simet's letter actually points out the myriad difficulties of assigning rights to a nation, a group, or individuals, in the Papua New Guinean (PNG) context.[2] His stated concern, shared with others, is with those in that country who think they can, "use indigenous people's cultural property whether they are in a position of 'ownership' or not" (Simet 2003). He points out that it is often those within the nation who disregard the restrictions their fellow citizens may place upon their cultural productions.[3] Simet's piece simultaneously illustrates the tendency to seek protection from property regimes, and the complications involved for indigenous peoples in doing so. Even if the issue were merely that of applying Intellectual Property (IP) as it stands to cultural and biological knowledge, the individual/communal divide is an inadequate mechanism through which to do so. The kinds of complex collectivities responsible for the creation of value that are apparent in Papua New Guinea, and as this book demonstrates, elsewhere, cross-cut some of the core logics of Intellectual Property. Collaborative, or distributed forms of creativity do not sit easily alongside the appropriative and individualistic terms it enshrines.

Another Papua New Guinean colleague recently reported a growing concern among craftspeople, and others, in the capital city of that country (Port Moresby). People there fear that the recent introduction of law governing copyright will have the unintended consequence of establishing a new significance for (and bounded-ness to) ethnic identity.[4] Craft producers have regularly borrowed styles of carving, or of looping string bags, for example, from other parts of the country. Thus women from the Highlands area loop string bags in the style used by women from the Sepik River on the North Coast, or male Sepik carvers copy the style of storyboard associated with people from the Gulf area on the Southern Coast. It is quite usual to see such items for sale in the city's markets and tourist areas. And indeed, as others have pointed out (Araho 2000), such borrowings and adoptions have been central to the diversity and creativity of indigenous cultures in the region: borrowing did not begin with tourist art.

What would the act of copyrighting do in such a situation? And if such "styles" could be owned, then what would the "owner" look like? The fear is that the owner would be a kind of collectivity based upon an ethnic or tribal identity. In PNG this would be inappropriate, it is thought, because of the history of borrowing, modification, and transformation referred to before. The creativity of flows could be lost (and see Vaidhyanathan 2001). Moreover, the strengthening of bounded ethnicities, as background to bounded cultural styles (Stolcke 1995) is imagined as a potential outcome. Control over external property (a style embodied by made objects) would be linked to internal properties (those given by tribal, or even ethnic/racial, identities). The dangers of linking ownership of resources to race need not be spelled out here. Whether these imaginings actually have any basis in what is justiciable or not, it should be no surprise that the promise of property, a promise that seems to exercise such a strong hold over imaginations everywhere, prompts visions of boundaries, exclusivity, and control.

Creativity and Appropriation

With the increasingly obvious value of intellectual property, people across the world express growing interest in protecting or transacting intellectual and cultural productions. There is an assumption of creativity, and of the value of creativity, written into attempts to protect cultural property, as well as other kinds of intellectual property. Creativity is the source of aesthetic pleasure and cultural value, as well as of economically valuable innovation. One (the dominant) model of creativity relies upon a kind of appropriation and enclosure, just as imagined in the scenario referred to previously. Creativity in this model is an individual activity, and the rights over its outcomes are clearly attached to the individual whose labor (mental creativity) is apparent in that outcome. In the case of tribal groups, this has been imagined simplistically as a form of communal production, making cultural resources something resembling a tribal commons. In reality, things are far more complex.

The impetus for this volume, and the conference that gave rise to it, has been technological and media developments that make collaborative endeavor central to contemporary economies. The emergence of digital information and communication technologies and the possibilities they provide for new combinations of knowledge, and indeed for new working practices and collaborations, are obvious. But how these changes effect, or are effected by ownership regimes, is a real issue.

This is why I focus on creativity in relation to ownership. A particular conception of the person, and of where the boundaries lie, figures into Intellectual Property. Long ago John Locke pointed out that natural reason demands that the person, as possessor of him- or herself, is also the rightful possessor of things from the commons that they modify through their labour (Locke 1966). There is a natural connection between the producer and the things they produce (that is, objects that demonstrate labor and intent). There is a ready-made location for creativity here—the kind of person whom we call a "possessive individual." A person, through mixing their labor with nature, or commonly owned resources, makes something his or her own. Intellectual Property is property in exactly this way. Something is appropriated from a common pool of ideas, and transformed though the labor of the mind. This transformation connects the creator to creation through the linkage of (mental) labor. But this formula is a culturally, and indeed historically, specific construction. I think it presents us with a problem. These notions of mental creativity, the person, and how they come to own things, make problematic the recognition of something we might want to label a collaborative or "distributed" creativity (Leach in press).

In other words, there are other models of creativity, and ownership that accompany them, that far from being secondary to cultural production (as in the aim of owning or protecting existing items after their appearance) facilitate a kind of network activity that is central to certain forms of cultural production in the first place. Ownership connects people and things in vitally different ways. Vital for creative endeavor itself, not just for post hoc reward and attribution.

It has been my argument in a number of writings (Leach 2003a, in press) that one can find a mode of what we can rightly call "creativity" in PNG that at one and the same time contains familiar elements, and yet relies upon different premises from the kind of creativity that is recognizable under IP law. By uncovering the specificities of kinds of creativity, I have been looking to highlight how the concept of intellectual property is embedded in a matrix of Euro-American thinking, in suppositions about being and doing, subjects and objects, agency and personhood. It seems that it is these suppositions, and how their logic conflicts with much of what we observe as creative endeavor in the contemporary world, that has caused critiques to appear from as diverse sources as advocates of traditional knowledge (e.g., Greaves 1994; Posey and Dutfield, 1996), and open source software developers (Stallman 1999).

If this is the case, we must ask how the assumptions about creativity built into IP law structure or restrict the conditions in which creativity will have an effect. That is, how a particular register for creativity, and assumptions about it as a process, might be responsible for undermining forms of creativity that do not neatly register in its terms. One such limitation may be the notion of the individual author (see Strathern, this volume) with all that this implies about creativity as an internal, mental activity. In this chapter, I highlight different modes in which creativity operates, and show how this can be linked clearly to how ownership acts to connect people to what they produce.

The advancement of IP regimes in the interests of developed nations and powerful corporations through WTO/TRIPS (World Trade Organization/ Trade-Related Intellectual Property) has understandably elicited a counternarrative in places such as PNG. The possibilities provided by the Convention on Biological Diversity apparently legitimate the application of established property regimes to protect and ensure recompense for biological and cultural knowledge at a national level (Hayden 2003). Happily however, many are aware of the shortcomings of property itself in that context,[5] and of the difficulties that arise when complex cultural productions are made to appear simple in origin by the attribution of private property.

I focus first on how value is produced, and thus how creativity operates in the Papua New Guinean context. I begin with some contemporary examples of ownership expectations from Madang Province, Papua New Guinea, which serve as background to the discussion of ownership, and creativity, which are the focus of this study. The detail of the material is a springboard for wider conclusions.

Multiple Ownership of Spirits and People[6]

Some people in the Madang area of Papua New Guinea (where I have undertaken long-term field research[7]) have attempted to introduce new forms of individual ownership (private property), which they see as relevant to production for the cash economy. However, in calling upon the aid of kinsmen as labor for their endeavors, they generate expectations of a different, or what we might term "multiple" (not common) system of ownership. Expectations of multiple ownership, based on customary principles of shared interest in the products of people's labor, conflict with a convenient reading of capitalism on the part of the organizers of business. This reading places all power and resources in the hands of the capitalist—they are his "property." Convenient, because at the same time, the entrepreneur appeals to customary authority and multiple interests, rather than wage-labor payments, to recruit their major resource (labor). Development fails all too often in the area because of this tension.

This region, for various historical reasons,[8] has maintained an interest in *kastom*[9] that is more than just rhetoric. The spiritual life of many people there is consciously understood as an alternative to Christianity, and is a living contemporary form. In the lingua franca, such religion is known as Tambaran, and covers a complex kaleidoscope of practices and understandings that generate growth and change. One aspect of Tambaran is a male musical cult with secret ritual paraphernalia. The tunes and designs used by this cult are associated with particular people, are owned by them (Leach 2000a), and handed down as heirlooms. That is, they have a named owner. Yet this ownership does not give the right of disposal. They are not "property," yet they are transacted.

Spirit songs are being innovated all the time. There is a stock of ancestral songs for each residential group, but new spirits are coming into being today. Powerful men dream new tunes, and compose words to accompany them. It is said that spirits of the particular places that men reside give them thought, and generate spirit children in the form of voices (tunes) and accompanying designs in their dreams. The spirit itself reproduces in the mind of a man. A man who has become aware of a new spirit in this way must cook pigs, and give people cooked food with the pork, in order to unveil the new creation. Having done so, he is known as the owner of this spirit voice. However, far from having all rights in the creation invested in him as an individual, there is a requirement for all members of a residential and family group to discuss the transaction of such an entity. Old and new spirits have exactly the same conditions attached.

In a similar vein, innovation in the carved designs (*torr*) displayed to accompany spirit voice renditions carry the same restriction. A recent innovation in the carved designs displayed to accompany spirit voice renditions was shown in 1999. It came into being when an elder saw a snake twined around a tree in the sacred grove of a particular spirit. When he cooked pigs for a life-cycle payment, he unveiled this new design. Yet such an originator has no right to dispose of this design. In the same way as a new Tambaran song has a single creator, yet is owned multiply by the residential group that its creator belongs to, so a design is multiply owned by a residential group. Why should this be so?

Looking at conflicts over ownership of spirit voices is revealing. The misuse of spirit voices and/or designs are offenses that incur fines among Nekgini speakers. These fines are specifically of valuable items that are used in bride and child payments. In essence, making payments in the currency of kin transactions establishes the inclusion of the wrongdoer in the kin group of those he has wronged through payments that link him, as kin, to those people. Theft, or even appropriation is not really the right gloss for this, then. Claims of inclusion might be a better explanation for what has happened when a spirit is used without authority (Leach 2000a). The consequence is a call by those who do have authority for the person to establish his connection to them. This can be done in retrospect through work,[10] though making presentations that do include him within the generative, kinship relations that have as one of their nodes, particular spirits, songs, or designs. It is this inclusion in the network—spirits and people *belong* to one another—that gives authority/influence over any one of its nodes (people or spirits). It looks like spirits and persons are substitutable. They constitute one another's existence and identity, and so these items are not primarily mental abstractions, but elements in the relational constitution of persons. As family members are also nodes in this network, they all belong to one another.

To examine authorship in this context is to discover that a spirit can reproduce itself. It is not a mental addition or creation in the thought processes of the person who dreams the thing. The authors of new spirit voices are parties to, or facilitators of, the reproductive potential embodied in the image/song/artefact *itself*. Thus the significant point about such things is not their status as things in the mind, but their analogy with and positioning within, the reproductive capacity of relationships between persons.

The forms of the carved designs (*torr*) must not be copied exactly. Reproducing the same combination of images and figures is seen as shameful by the owners, and as inappropriate copying, by others. Each element that goes to make up a *torr* (particular snakes or lizards, particular designs) are owned by kin groups. The elements are held in the memories of men from these groups, and combined in new forms for each occasion. It is these memories of *torr* that allow carvers to make new ones. There is a novel combination of elements, which to Euro-Americans looks remarkably like the operation of intellectual creativity. And the restrictions on others copying the images seem to confirm this (in the model of copyright). But, as I pointed out, it is not the novel combination (as a mental appropriation from a common pool) but the elements themselves that belong in certain networks of relations. While those who are part of this network may make new combinations using the elements, even they may not copy the combination of images from any previous post, be that of their own creation, or of others.

This, then, is nothing like copyright, where the original idea is instantiated in material composition, and then the rights to copy that composition are attached to the originator of the idea. Here no one can copy the specific forms (i.e., combinations) of *torr* posts. The images that are combined are kept separately available for new creative projects. It is not then a particular instantiation and material realization of ideas that is valued, but the elements, which are valued as instruments for future action.

People do own images, and ideational forms, but these are not owned in objects. In other words, they do not rely on the separation of mental/ideational creativity from its instantiation in an object that can then be owned as property. The same goes for people themselves. They, too, have reproductive potential because of their constitution in the work of others. They can be owned and transacted, but not as property, rather as elements in other's projects.

From the ethnography of transactions and the complaints that arise in the context of those transactions, we can see that the songs and designs that are generated in family relationships are seen as a resource—a powerful one as they elicit the currency of kinship, the currency through the exchange of which, new persons are created. But because of the kind of resource that they are—a resource commensurate with other aspects of creativity, understood as the regeneration of people and places through the work of family groups—it is inappropriate for any one person to claim (as an individual idea), even though the new song or design originated in their mind. Such things are multiply owned. And here we come to the complex collectivities to which Simet referred.

Common property is not an acceptable gloss of such a complex either. There is an explicit equation of such resources with persons—the commensurate product of other creative work—and persons are not communally owned. Children, like spirit designs, are generated in the specific productive partnerships of kin groups. They belong to certain people, but these people are differentiated by their input. A maternal uncle is not the same as a father, and each receives a different kind of recompense accordingly. Kin is not a simple designation as it also includes entities such as spirits. Peoples' obligations to one another (and their ownership of one another), are due to this multiple endeavor in the production of families. People achieve prominence and authority through association with powerful spirits, and other persons, but they do not achieve exclusive control over them.

Property

In a telling contrast, innovations in the sphere of business (new ideas that make money) do not generate ownership at all. As someone recently told me, "whatever you find through your own endeavor in the arena of the spirit cult belongs to all of us as a family. It is for us all to generate a name for ourselves and consume [wealth] on the basis of this name. But whatever innovations you accomplish on the side of business, you cannot claim the idea behind it."

When questioned about someone copying their business idea, people reply that everyone wants to make money, and it is open for anyone to try any way they can think of to do so. Business is novel, but it is public new knowledge. What is not public in this part of Madang is the particular creativity that is understood to be part of a family and its interactions with its ancestors, spirits, and lands. This form of creativity is based in particular groups of people, we might say particular relationships. Where it is assumed that ownership of a kind envisaged by Western property regimes is appropriate, as in the convenient mixture of familial obligation to assist in familial enterprise, and capitalist appropriation of profits with no regard to family obligation, we see development failing.

There is a wider lesson about IP. It is clearly the inappropriate assumptions about the disposal of the products of resources by a single individual, once those resources appear in the form of money, that is behind the failure of business enterprise in the region.[11] Money is consumed by the individual without reference to the long-term relationships that people are engaged in to be productive. The notion of individual authorship, and specifically intellectual work in the attribution of copyright, would perform a similar distortion in the realm of *kastom*.

Preservation of materials is one (important) thing, but it seems to me that of more basic importance is the preservation of the social conditions of creativity itself. Laws that take such property relations as their baseline inhibit the utilization of indigenously appropriate mechanisms for the control, distribution, and protection of indigenous resources. In other words, it is not just the material expressions (object outcomes of creative work), but the actual form of social relations, which must be considered in a discussion of protection or attribution.

We can see that "attempts should be made to develop new exchange taxonomies by analyzing transactions in the light of social relations of which they are a part" (Gregory and Altman 1989, 203). This focus makes clear that it is not just the material, but the actual form of social relations that must be considered. One way of achieving this may be to develop the concept of multiple ownership).

In Madang, persons and spirits are multiply owned because they are the product of creativity, and this by definition does not belong to any one individual. Western capital-based property relations separate through ownership. One might say that this Melanesian economy connects through ownership (cf. Strathern 1996). These principles point to very different modes of creativity.

Valuing Process or Outcome?

Madang people's valuation and validation of "*kastom*" contrasts sharply with notions of heritage and cultural property as they are articulated in a current and prominent view of culture, and one relied upon by the United Nations Educational, Scientific, and Cultural Organization (UNESCO) for example, in formulating recommendations for the return of cultural property.[12] This in turn rests upon a contrast in assumptions about the relationship between objects and persons.

Value, in the Lockean tradition, passes from the labor power of the producer into the thing itself. It is this transmission that makes an apparently natural connection between the producer and the object they produce. This is, in turn, based on a notion of the individual as possessor of her- or himself, and thereby, by extension, the products of her or his own labor. But by locating value in productive relationships (that they call *kastom*), and not in things, people in Madang have a different interest. The contrast is between the valuation of culture as tradition and heritage, embodied by objects or sites, and notions of culture that appeal to the inherent and ongoing creativity of human engagement (Kirsch 2001). It is our focus on the thing itself as the locus of value that confuses us here. It means we assume that granting cultural property is the granting of property rights over objects.

In a striking parallel, one that emphasizes the current connections between apparently different worlds and concerns, the ground for the success of open source software lies as much in the way a community and ethos has developed as it does in the brilliance of its prime movers (individual authors). In other words, there are conditions for creativity here in which value is generated without that value being realized by individuals as private property.

The parallels with the preceding PNG example are many. For example, in the development of the Linux operating system, each contributor's work is individually owned; they are identified with that work, and retain ownership. However, the work of one person is only coherent and valuable as a combined work that is *multiply owned* by all contributors. Creativity operates as a distributed process, not as individual appropriation. This is neither collective/communal ownership, not private property. The willingness of contributors to have their work included in the overall outcome is partly to do with the coherence of the combined work, and with the fact that no one else can appropriate it for her- or himself. There are conditions for creativity here, which are not based upon the logic of motivation and reward in IP, just as the creation of new designs and spirits, and of new persons, are based on an alternative register in the Madang examples I have outlined.

Collaboration, then, is essential in both cases, and relations are not built as external to creations (rights attached to things and individuals), but are already present within them. It is what they do that tells one about one's own capacities. The logic of private property renders relating it as an option, and a conscious effort, because of the insistence that relationships are things that have to be made, and exist as external elements of persons. If one saw Linux as a kind of person on the Madang model (that is, made up of many people's inputs, each element ultimately available to its contributor for future projects) it would be clear that in the construction of Linux relating is not an option. Without the network, it would not exist. But the IP model of creativity and its workings locate the capacity not in relationships between people, but in individual mental work. The intellect is seen as the source and engine of creative endeavor, not the network of relations from which value emerges.

So we have a mode of creativity tied to a regime of ownership here. Creativity occurs within the individual mind. Its effects are a result of the will, of agentive appropriations from, and subsequent interventions in, the world that exists beyond the person. It is as if the person, through their creative work, remakes or refashions their relationship to others and the world through the mediation of the objects they create. The idioms we have for authorship, ownership, and credit for creativity insist on seeing relations as external to any single entity. Remember Locke. A person is the rightful possessor of anything from the commons that they modify through their labor. There is a natural connection between the producer and the things they produce (that is, objects that demonstrate labor and intent). In PNG, this kind of attachment is very weak. Identity is not in objects attached to the producer, but is seen and known in how others act and respond to one. Dispersal of agency and creativity results.

Now the thing about a dispersed creativity is that its effects can only show in particular people. This is true both in PNG, and here. The vital difference is in the way effects are registered, and how this leads to reward, recognition, and claims. In one case, that operating in the mode of creativity and its register for effect in IP, the register is in the material, object world, and thus external to the person. Property logics make a relation between subject (producer) and object. Property looks like a relationship between people and things, even though it is in fact a relation between persons. In PNG, work is apparent in others' bodies and capacities. When these are demonstrated, claims are admissible.

My argument, then, has been that in the particular conception of creativity we operate with in the West, one based upon the individual mind as the location of creative effort, we have difficulties registering exactly the kind of dispersed creativity that collaborative endeavor exhibits. New possibilities for combinations of images and previous work afforded by technical developments pose the same issues. These are arenas in which creativity lies in the relationships between persons, and between knowledge practices. When these elements are encompassed by any single mind, which they must be for the identification of an author, and therefore property rights to occur, it looks as if they have been appropriated. This impression is made real by the workings of Intellectual Property, which operate to make objects out of ideas, and then attach them to individual (or communal) producers.

Conclusion

This chapter has two linked points. First, I argued that it is important to understand the essentially distorting nature of private property itself as a form of ownership when introduced in places such as Papua New Guinea (PNG). The distortion is to forms of social relation that lie behind cultural production there. Among other things, the concept of intellectual property sustains assumptions about the individual author and exclusive access that are inappropriate to the kinds of processes people understand as creative. But I do not mean for this observation to be taken as relevant only in Papua New Guinea. Collaborative and multiauthored creations are highly significant globally. Alternative models of ownership, as registers for creative endeavor that acknowledge multiple and differentiated inputs, seem vital in such a world. An understanding of the nature and specific form that creativity and value generation take, in particular circumstances, is essential if the property logic inherent in IP regimes (and based on these two aspects) is not to undermine the very forms of sociality that result in cultural productions in the first place.

Second, I pointed out that creativity itself is not something that can be addressed through current IP law. Instead, a focus on the products of creativity substitutes by making property out of objects. It is through control over these objects that creators realize reward from their creativity under IP regimes as they stand currently. This may have the effect of bypassing the value-generating practices of peoples, and making what they own into tradition or heritage (that is, objects that can be attached to communal/tribal groups).[13] The rhetoric of IP has always been about facilitating the circulation and creative modification of others' creations (in other words, about flows). There is a danger in current versions of cultural property regulation of obviating innovation among those with culture to protect (Weiner 1999). This in turn reinforces a stereotypical divide between traditional culture (valued as heritage, but a barrier to innovation) and modern (no heritage value, but reliant upon innovation) that in turn feeds an impulse to appropriate and make value from traditional knowledge or resources by institutions and industries in developed nations.

For there to be creativity, there has to be a recognition that something has happened, or that a novel entity has come into being (Hirsch in press). And flows are also dependent upon recognition. In other words, a register for effect is required. The dominant register we have available is reward (ownership) through property logic. The logic of ownership inherent in this register does not succeed in accommodating modes of creativity based upon multiple and differentiated inputs, and thus we must find registers for creative work that do not rely upon the appropriation of common resources by individual authors if we are to recognize a significant contemporary form of value creation.

Notes

This chapter draws together material also discussed in other writings, notably Leach (2000b in press). The term ownership is used here to indicate a wider set of conceptual referents than "property," which I use as shorthand for the kind of rights that private property, and particularly the private property granted through current Intellectual property laws, imply. Ownership here is intended to cover the multiple ways in which people feel attached to what they, and others, do, produce, have responsibility for, and so forth. Private property, then, is one of many forms that ownership may take. The fact it is the dominant model in IP law reveals assumptions that many in Europe and America have about the nature of the intellect, of creativity, and of the person. It is part of the intention of this paper to make some of these assumptions apparent through the description of modes of creativity that do not rest upon these assumptions, and thus which highlight the need for theorising alternative models of ownership.

1. "Who Appropriates PNG Cultures?" *The National*, September 25, 2003. Sent around expatriate and scholarly list-serves as well as generating interest with PNG.

2. That is a context with many language groups and cultures. Finding common principles on which to assign rights over intellectual and cultural property among this diversity has proved tricky (see Kalinoe 2000).

3. This construction makes obvious the inherent conflict in nation states when certain groups (on the basis of ethnic or religious identity) claim sovereignty over their own culture (and see Brown 2003). In this case, Simet argues that those who originate cultural productions should be consulted before others use (appropriate) them.

4. Andrew Moutu, personal communication.

5. See Simet article mentioned previously, for example, or Kalinoe in Kalinoe and Leach (2004).

6. This material is also discussed by Strathern (in press).

7. Research undertaken among Nekgini speaking people on the Rai Coast, 1993–1995, 1999, 2000–2001.

8. See Lawrence (1964) and Leach (2003a).

9. Local customs, and much more besides.

10. "Work" is the local idiom for any ceremonial presentation. Work is thus both the combined labor of all those who assist in production, and the transformation of this effort into a form to which others must recognize and respond.

11. For more detail, see Leach (in press).

12. See Leach (2003b).

13. See Leach (2003b).

References

Araho, Nick. 2000. "Presentation of discussion group 2." In Kathy Whimp and Mark Busse (eds.), *Protection of intellectual, biological and cultural property in Papua New Guinea*. Canberra and Port Moresby: Asia Pacific Press at the Australian National University and Conservation Melanesia Inc.

Brown, Michael F. 2003. *Who owns native cultures?* Cambridge, MA: Harvard University Press.

Free/Libre and Open Source Software (Floss). 2002. Final Report. International Institute of Infonomics. The Netherlands: University of Maastricht.

Greaves, Tom. (ed.). 1994. *Intellectual property rights for indigenous peoples: A sourcebook*. Oklahoma City: Society for Applied Anthropology.

Gregory, C. A., and Jon C. Altman. 1989. *Observing the economy*. London: Routledge.

Hayden, Cori. 2003. From market to market: Bioprospecting's idioms of inclusion." *American Ethnologist* 30(3): 1–13.

Hirsch, Eric. in press. Boundaries of creation: The work of credibility in science and ceremony. In Eric Hirsch and Marilyn Strathern (eds.), *Transactions and creations: Property debates and the stimulus of Melanesia*. Oxford: Berghahn.

Kalinoe, Laurence K. 2000. Accessing indigenous intellectual and cultural property or traditional knowledge in Papua New Guinea: Legal options. *Melanesian Law Journal* 27: 86–95.

Kalinoe, Laurence, and James Leach. 2004. *Rationales of ownership. Transactions and claims to ownership in contemporary Papua New Guinea*. Oxford: Sean Kingston Publishing.

Kirsch, Stuart. 2001. Lost worlds: Environment disaster, "culture loss" and the law. *Current Anthropology* 42(2): 167–198.

Lawrence, Peter. 1964. *Road belong cargo*. Manchester: Manchester University Press.

Leach, James. 2000a. Situated connections: Rights and intellectual resources in a Rai Coast society. *Social Anthropology* 8(2): 163–179.

———. 2000b. Multiple Expectations of Ownership. *Melanesian Law Review* 27: 63–76.

———. 2003a. *Creative land. Place and procreation on the Rai Coast of Papua New Guinea*. Oxford and New York: Berghahn Books.

———. 2003b. Owning creativity. Cultural property and the efficacy of Custom. *Journal of Material Culture* 8(2): 123–143.

————. in press. Modes of Creativity. In Eric Hirsch and Marilyn Strathern (eds.), *Transactions and creations: Property debates and the stimulus of Melanesia*. Oxford: Berghahn Books.

Locke, John. 1966. *Second treatise of government*. Oxford: Blackwell.

Posey, Darrell, and Graham Dutfield. 1996. *Beyond intellectual property: Toward traditional resource rights for indigenous peoples and local communities*. Ottawa: International Development Research Center.

Simet, Jacob. 2003. Who appropriates PNG Cultures? *The National* (Papua New Guinea), September 25, 2003.

Stallman, Richard. 1999. The GNU operating system and the free software movement. In Chris DiBona, Sam Ockman, and Mark Stone (eds.), *Open sources. Voices from the open source revolution*. Sebastapol, California: O'Reilly.

Stolcke, Verena. 1995. Talking culture: New boundaries, new rhetorics of exclusion in Europe. *Current Anthropology* 36: 1–24.

Strathern, Marilyn. 1996. Cutting the Network. *Journal of the Royal Anthropological Institute* (NS) 2: 517–535.

————. in press. Divided origins and arithmetic of ownership. In J. Fergusson (ed.), *Futures of property and personhood*. Irvine: Critical Theory Institute.

Vaidhyanathan, Siva. 2001. *Copyrights and copywrongs: The rise of intellectual property and how it threatens creativity*. New York: New York University Press.

Weiner, James F. 1999. Culture in a sealed envelope: The concealment of Australian Aboriginal heritage and tradition in the Hindmarsh Island Bridge affair. *Journal of the Royal Anthropological Institute*, 5(2): 193–210.

4

Some Properties of Culture and Persons

Fred Myers

Ownership gathers things momentarily to a point by locating them in the owner, halting endless dissemination, effecting an identity. (Marilyn Strathern 1999, 177)

Culture, Knowledge, and Identity

Anthropologists have, for some time, been interested in culture as being something—an "object"—over which people have rights, and we have been interested in what it might mean to have "possession" of culture (Handler 1985). In the contexts of liberal, multicultural states, such as the settler nations of Australia, the United States, Canada, and New Zealand, issues of cultural identity and assimilation have led to a related but distinct politics of culture exemplified by contests over the right to represent or speak on behalf of cultural identities other than one's own.

At a small conference on Native American art history held a few years ago, the Haida art historian Marcia Crosby confronted—perhaps confounded—the non-Native people with her question about who they were. "We want to know," she said, "who you are, why you want to study us? We don't know you." At least one of the senior non-Native participants misread the implications of this question, defensively perceiving it to be an exercise in boundary maintenance or essentialism. He denounced the question in liberal terms—as ghettoizing, as leading to the converse claims of white rights and white exclusivism, which he deplored. If Native people want to close themselves off and say only Native people can learn their traditions, what would be wrong with whites claiming similarly?

Apart from the power issue, he misread the question as if Native identities could be conceived in terms of "possessive individualism," as something one *has*. At any gathering, Native people typically identify themselves positioned in relation to their work, as coming from some or another community—as do Aboriginal Australians. They do so, not to claim themselves abstractly as indigenous in a legalistic manner; rather, this identification announces their accountability to a community—that their representations and actions are rooted in commitments to a recognized body of Native people. In Australia the question is also one of accountability—of the answerability of one's representations to a community, of being recognized and responsible for what one does. This is a concern they felt non-Natives working in their communities need to address as well—as part of their social obligation and relationship.

With culture itself the most expansive object of shared identity in contemporary formulations, Marcia Crosby's intervention had offered a way of crossing boundaries—had the academic recognized the potential of diplomacy rather than "freezing into categories what Native peoples find flowing in relationships" (Coombe 1997, 92). The defensive reply had assumed the permanence of racial categories as defining the relationships available.

These are among the circumstances that define many anthropologists' approach to intellectual and cultural property. My own interest in Intellectual Property frameworks is a product of ethnographic research with a Western Desert Aboriginal people in Australia since 1973, and this research suggests that culture can be understood as a medium of exchange, where rights over culture—or particular cultural objects—provides a basis for establishing relationships of shared and distinctive identities. The question of how this object-ideology—as I might call it, this attitude to the potentials of "objects" (understood very broadly so as to include even the most evanescent forms of culture)—can be articulated with Intellectual Property regimes of regulation is a basic one that I share with many concerned with indigenous points of view (see Brush 1996; Warren 1999; Tsing 2003).

In my first study of a traditional indigenous system of knowledge, landownership, and identity, it became clear that custodianship of elements of a complex of knowledge—myth, ritual, and song related to and constitutive of places—was central to the organization of social life and the relationships among people (Myers 1991). In this sense, cultural knowledge was a kind of property formation, but one that might be understood less as a commodity to be exchanged and more as an objectification of relationships around which personhood was defined and from which persons could project themselves. In order to sustain their effectiveness in social life, their control and display—their circulation and visibility—was regulated. From this point of view, too, the material properties of different cultural objects (myth, ritual performances, land, designs, names, and subsequently motor vehicles, etc., as well) were significant in terms of their ability to sustain various kinds of social relationships (Myers 1988).

Collaborative Ownership: A Western Desert Aboriginal Case

The argument I have made is that "things" (objects, rituals, land, knowledge, prerogatives, duties) have meaning or social value for Pintupi people largely as an expression of autonomy and "relatedness" (by which I refer to shared identity), a basic issue at all levels of indigenous social organization. What has been most impressive to me about the Western Desert understanding of such objects is the continual negotiation about relationships to them and a willingness to include others as what, for want of a better heuristic term, I call "co-owners." These relationships of what might be understood as "collaborative ownership" are not given, but must be worked out in a variety of social processes whose roots lie in the emphasis placed on shared identity with others as a basis for social interaction.

In this system of practices, rights over the expression or transmission of marked forms of knowledge are essential to and constitutive of vital forms of social identity.[1] Correspondingly, such forms of knowledge objectify these identities and make them available as meaningful social positions. Their value lies, therefore, substantially in their capacity for personification—a process by which the consumption of things is turned to the production of (cultural) human beings.

Thus, analysis of the cultural relationships between persons and objects begins with local ideas of ownership—a conception better translated as one of "identification." The Pintupi words most closely approximating "property" in English are *walytja* or *yulytja*. While the former may be translated as "relative(s)" or as "one's own personal effects" (see Hansen and Hansen 1977, 152) and the latter as "baggage and personal effects" (ibid. 190), the significance of identification is clearer when one understand the entire semantic range of walytja. In addition to objects associated with a person, it can refer to "a relative," to the possessive notion of "one's own" (such as "my own camp" [*ngayuku ngurra walytja*]) or "my own father" [*ngayuku mama walytja*], or to reflexive conceptions like "oneself" (such as, "I saw it myself" [*ngayulu nyangu walytjalu*] or "He sat there by himself" [*nyinama walytja*].

There is an ambivalence or ambiguity about Pintupi relationships to objects. There is clearly a sense that objects might "belong to" to someone— the idea that X is the walytja of a person contrasts with the idea that an object is *yapunta*, a word whose literal meaning is "orphan," without parents. To pursue the linguistic usage further, one's parents are said to *kanyininpa* one, meaning "to have," "to hold," or more loosely "to look after one." Thus an object that is yapunta does not belong to anyone, but it appears that this might mean also that it has no one who is holding or looking after it. The question remains of what it means for something to belong to—to be walytja of—someone. An object becomes yapunta when it is no longer "held" but has instead been *wantingu*, "lost" or "relinquished," released from an active association with a subject. For objects to belong to someone means as much that they are expressive of that person's identity as it does that they are simply identified with or related to that person. To say that something is "one's own" implies that one does not have to ask (or defer to) anyone about its use.

Leaving aside for a moment the issue of co-owners, the right to use an object without asking—even the claim that it is "my own"—expresses one's autonomy. By "autonomy" I mean self-direction, although local ontologies of the person mean that this is not necessarily self-created. In contrast, rights to objects that might be regarded as personal effects still seem less exclusive than Americans would tolerate. The very notion of ownership as identification provides also a sense that rights to objects can, and should, be more widely distributed, a willingness (not always ungrudging, of course) to include others with one's self as co-owners.

Rights to objects—and preeminently knowledge of ritual, myth, and land—enter into a system of exchange that constantly negotiates the relationships of shared identities among persons. The negotiation of the meaning of ownership rights moves within a dialectic of autonomy (as in the right to be asked) and relatedness (exemplified in the tendency to include others and to share rights with others who one recognizes as identified). In this sense, "property" potentially provides a temporally extended objectification of shared identity.

To make this discussion more concrete, let me provide an account of the tendency to inclusion and proferring of shared identity in rights to "sacred objects" (*turlku*), the sort of objects referred to by Strehlow (1947) for the Arrernte as *churinga*. A class of objects restricted to possession and control by initiated men, *churinga* were a vital component of the revelatory regime of value, also pursued for collections, and have since become a significant concern in terms of their display, ownership, and repatriation.[2] These objects have often been understood as constituting title deeds for rights in land, although they are not reducible to this. Throughout Central Australia, sacred boards represent, for men at least, the epitome of value, objects said to be "left by the Dreaming" (although fashioned by men), which men are permitted to know about and view only after initiation. Individual boards are always associated with particular Dreaming stories and usually with one or more named places created by that Dreaming-ancestor. Rights to such objects, as to songs and stories, are part of the estate associated with mythologically constituted places. Presumably, a man has rights to manufacture and/or possess boards related to his *own* Dreaming, determined by his place of conception.

The value of such sacred objects is constituted by their imputed indexical relationship to the Dreaming, by the restrictions on knowledge about them, by the difficulty of acquiring them, and by their historical associations with the subjectivity of people who once held them and have since died. Pintupi men often emphasized how such objects were held by people who are now dead and how seeing the objects makes men "sorrowful" and the objects "dear." In some sense, a sacred object is a powerful representation of one's identity, something hidden from the sight of women and children and shown only to initiated men of one's choosing. A man keeps his sacred objects in several places, many of them being held jointly with other men in one place or another. Only authorized men can manufacture a sacred object; that is, only a person who has passed through all the stages of initiation and has been granted ("has been given" [*yungu*]) the right to make a board for a particular site by being taught the design by a legitimate custodian.

Knowledge of such matters, as with much of religious life, is restricted in access, not only difficult to learn about but also problematic for publication because of the desire for secrecy.[3] Nonetheless, it is clear that the exchange and circulation of these objects is a matter of intense interest and concern among men. Indeed, while such boards come "from the country," more or less representing the country, as it were, they are detached from it and movable.

In this detachability lies part of their power. Their exchange among men who may live far apart constitutes a distinctive level of organization, one that transforms other relationships of marriage and ritual exchange through another medium (the boards) that has the capacity to constitute a common identity among those not in daily contact. While it is much like these other "levels" of exchange, the negotiation of identity through sacred objects has distinctive qualities.

Among the Pintupi, boards are frequently exchanged as a result of bestowals between a man and his male in-laws, sometimes as a result of initiation, and sometimes to settle long-standing disputes (such as murders). Obviously, access to sacred boards is an important precondition for a person to attain and enact autonomy and equality with other men. A young man must, consequently, rely on elder male relatives to supply him with sacred objects for marriage and for fulfilling his social obligations. Levi-Strauss (1966) likened the exchange of such objects to the lending of one's basic identity to the care of another group, the ultimate sign of trust.

Having said this, the first point I would like to make is that a Pintupi man has rights to more than one sacred board. His total identity is not wrapped up in one. Second, it was always difficult to find out who were the owners of the sacred boards I was shown. This is not only because of the secrecy surrounding boards, I think, but it reflects the fact that boards are rarely owned by a single person. A man would tell me, typically, that this one belonged to him and also to such and such other men, that another one belonged to him, and X, and so on. Frequently, a group of brothers (rarely genealogical brothers, however) held boards in common. The way in which I was told made me feel that there is a tendency for individuals to extend ownership of sacred objects to men with whom one identified. This is consistent with the Pintupi stress on the enormous dangers involved if one should try to make a sacred object by oneself. To do so, I was told, would inevitably arouse the jealousy of other men who would kill him. Making a sacred object oneself, it would appear, is to assert one's total autonomy, to deny other people's relationships to oneself and to the object. One should have shame or respect (*kunta*) for others.

Thus, Pintupi are inclined to share out ownership of and responsibility for sacred objects with men they regard as close. Conversely, their planning of and participation in cycles of exchange with other men always involves a set of men who cooperate as brothers as a node in the exchange, just as a group of brothers will stand as a party in arranging marriage bestowals. Joint participation in exchange, then, constitutes an identity among the men who jointly accept a responsibility: the boards they possess in common are an objectification of their shared activity, their joint responsibility, of who they are. Failure to fulfill one's obligations in a board exhange is described as "having trouble" (*kununkarringpa*, i.e., being under threat of revenge and retaliation); fulfilling one's obligations is described as "clearing oneself" (*kilininpa*) or being free. Joint participation may reduced the danger of failure.

What happens in the exchange itself is equally illuminating. Men often described to me, for instance, how they had lived in other people's country for some time (as young novices or in bride service), and when they made ready to return to their own country, "owners" of the host country "gave" them sacred boards. What they meant by this, they explained, was that the owners drew designs on a fashioned board that a young man then carved; he then took his finished object back with him to his own country. Effectively, he had been taught the design and given the right to reproduce it, although (it appears) not the right to teach other people. His possession of the board from the host country recognizes his prolonged residence and (therefore) shared identity with other owners of that country, converting residence and everyday cooperation through time into an identity projected into the more enduring medium of land ownership (signified by the board). It is important to recognize also that in "giving" the board, the original owner had not actually lost it, indeed, had not lost anything. While he recognized or granted to another rights in the country and shared identity as embodied in that object, he still retained his own identification with the place.

Intercultural Exchange: Knowledge Across the Boundaries

There is something like a political economy of knowledge here. In this vein, Basil Sansom (1980), writing about fringe-dwelling Aboriginal people in Darwin, described them as people without property and emphasized that the rights to tell stories (ownership of stories, surely a rather evanescent object) provided a fundamental organizational feature of their lives. Relatedly, these local and long-standing concerns with control over the circulation and display of culture—with the politics of representation and voice (as central to their own knowledge regime)—were also understood to extend to relationships with outsiders. Among the issues of concern to Western Desert people is the accountability of those who spoke on their behalf—their willingness to be actively answerable to those they represent. As a form of exchange, the giving of knowledge, then, is understood to activate and sustain a relationship—a kind of identity—between the giver and the recipient. My more recent study of Western Desert painting in the (introduced) medium of acrylic and canvas presents these activities as a significant articulation of the local regime with a formative stratum of the Australian nation (a "taste-class" in Bourdieu's terms (1984)) and what Terence Turner (1999) described as a global cultural conjuncture (of NGOs and consumers) that has valorized indigenous identities (Myers 2001). Along with other work on the emerging "traffic in culture" (Marcus and Myers 1995; Phillips and Steiner 1999), many anthropologists explored the intensified engagement of local art forms with globalizing processes of cultural circulation, and a special, anxious focus of this work is the problematic transformation of culture into commodity. Various commentators on and critics of the developments in Aboriginal art have been concerned or anxious about the effects, opportunities, and means of managing intercultural circulation as these might depart from or preserve expectations of cultural exchange, leading to indigenous empowerment or cultural loss (Benjamin 1989; Fry and Willis 1989; Michaels 1988; Johnson 1996; Merlan 2001; Coleman 2004). Indigenous art objects, in this context, can be understood not just as something taken by Western consumers, but equally and more complexly as extensions of the agency of their makers (Gell 1998) and even the basis for the formation of new networks of identity.

As a compelling example, in the early 1970s, the Aboriginal artist and activist Wandjuk Marika asked the Australian government to investigate the unauthorized use of Yolngu clan designs on a variety of commodity forms, inaugurating a process of recognizing indigenous "copyright" for such designs. Copyright, famously, is known to involve a particular formulation of materiality, distinguishing idea from concrete expression, with only the latter being subject to ownership rights as a form of property (Vaidhyanathan 2001). However sympathetic to indigenous concerns over controlling their culture, this treatment of design—and culture—as a form of property involves understandings and practices of materiality and subjectivity that are different from indigenous Aboriginal relationships to cultural production and circulation. In exploring the significance of recent work on and events in the development of notions of cultural property, one of my main concerns has been to emphasize the relevance of local understandings of objectification or "objectness" and human action—as embedded object-ideologies. I am inclined to emphasize the limits of legal discourses of cultural property to capture and reflect indigenous Australian concerns about their relation to culture, to creativity, and to expression.

In a theoretical sense, the project of studying the circulation of Aboriginal art has been concerned with the materiality of representations, of indigenous knowledge and of representational practices, and it has been an extension of an earlier study that explained how a sphere of traditional religious/mythological knowledge and practice constitutes a regional system of producing and distributing identity. I focused on a range of media (religious knowledge, ritual practice, land, names, etc.) as forms of "property" understood not so much as possessions but as bases for the objectification of shared identity and distinctions of identity.

Western Desert Aboriginal people continue to insist that what Westerners might call "traditional knowledge" defines the core of their identity, and this is a central issue in their art (painting in the introduced medium of acrylic and canvas), which I understand as a significant articulation of the local regime and an emerging, global "traffic in culture." My interest is in the articulation or lack of it between a system of indigenous knowledge and other regimes of value, what I observed as Indigenous Australian paintings and designs move through the Western art-culture system and the Western concept of property and as different object-ideologies meet. The contemporary situation extends Aboriginal concerns over the control of socially valued knowledge and its dispersal—through practices of secrecy, exchange, invisibility, and immateriality into new relations. These practices clearly depended on the materialities of producing and circulating knowledge through voice, ritual, and object-presentation and equally certainly did not anticipate the materiality of mechanical and digital reproduction. Ultimately, I see this study as one consideration of what happens when "culture" (knowledge) takes on new and varied forms of materiality and as it enters into historically specific forms of circulation as a commodity. The issues of performance, possession, and display take on new forms.

I have been very taken by the contrasting positions that have emerged among those theorizing intellectual property. For example, Vaidhyanathan's (2001) concern about the intensification and expansion of property controls over culture and their impact on creativity and democracy suggests a position of limiting group rights, agreeable to liberal thinkers like Michael Brown, who have expressed concern over the "copyrighting of culture," in his well-known article (1998) and new book (2003). While I am persuaded by Vaid-hyanathan's concern that corporations threaten to restrict access to what should be the basis of further creativity, I believe another position of equal value is articulated in the concerns of Indigenous people. The latter see control over their own culture as a political issue, a remedy for historical loss, and a necessity for survival as a people, for survival as a culture. This is in accord with some recent considerations in the UN declarations of Human Rights. As Tressa Berman (n.d.) has objected in a reply to Shweder's (2003) review of Brown's new book,

The fact that Native peoples seek just compensation for these takings is less about "liberal pluralism" (as Shweder suggests), and more about acknowledging how the origins of "property" loss flow from the dispossession of Native title itself—whether in North America, Australia or New Zealand, all settler colonies subjected to British Common Law.

Berman argues that that Brown's work "caters too much to a laissez-faire view of protectionism." The more compelling issues involve the international law that Native people now invoke with respect to human rights and moral rights, which include legal grounds of cultural harm.

Questions

Given the cultural location of intellectual and cultural property discussion in Western institutions, and given what I have learned about the different commitments to understandings of persons and objects in the world, I think anthropological attention is being directed usefully toward the emerging discourses and activities shaping the contentious field of cultural property. Among the topics of study appropriate to the politics of cultural property, I would include questions of material circulation, appropriation, authenticity, and commodification as they relate to the objectification of indigeneity and identity. How are claims and counterclaims to legal, moral, ethical, political, and intellectual heritage rights being asserted? How do assertions of cultural property engage global circuits and markets of material culture, and how this does this concept itself shape objects and knowledges today?

Concomitantly, recognizing that the articulation of property formulations takes place in a complex social space, it can also be seen as constitutive of new social formations—the kind of actor-network forms described in science studies. It would be worthwhile to explore the emergence and constitution of forms such as copyright advocacy groups and mediating institutions, among the range of stakes-holders, as well as those of anthropologists and others involved in representational practice. A variety of issues are circulating generally in the discipline of anthropology and more specifically in its subareas, among archeologists, biological anthropologists, ethno-botanists, legal anthropologists, applied anthropologists, cultural anthropologists, anthropologists working as/for NGOs, etc. Discourses on antiquities, heritage, preservation, looting, and exhibiting should be considered alongside those of genome research, bioprospecting, ethno-pharmacology; human rights, local and international law, ethnical, advocacy, and indigeneity politics, alongside those of media (film and video), appropriation, and representation. Bringing these different practical constituencies into the same overall framework is one of the most compelling advantages of thinking about cultural circulation as a question of cultural and intellectual property.

There are, from a classical anthropological point of view, fundamental questions about exchange that might underlie the discussion of intellectual and cultural property (see Strathern 1999). How do things become objects? How does culture become an object? What are the connections between these kinds of objectifications and the (cultural) construction of cultural "property?" How are understandings of consumption and commodification critical to understanding cultural property and vice versa? What are the specific implications for material culture, and particularly those kinds of material culture that come to be constructed, objectified, or commodified as "art" works in larger worlds? What connects objects and persons? Have specific cultural modes of sociality (specifically Melanesian notions around exchange, reciprocity, emotionality, wealth, the person, objects, and memory) played a distinctive role in these conversations?

Finally, where are the major developments and cases occurring in IP? For example, case studies from Australia would be prominent in understanding control of objects and knowledges, specifically linking persons, land rights, and arts. I have found that the distinctive cultural and historical character of the Australian material highlights a link between two levels of cultural property discourse. One level concerns how persons, knowledge, and rights are constituted *in* Aboriginal communities. Another level concerns how these senses of personhood and society are revealed in acts that assert, contest, and police identity and ownership, particularly in the areas of land rights and arts.

Another area of great concern must be the contemporary music industry. While others are better suited than I to consider these, one must ask what the controversies about "piracy" tell us about what Steven Feld (2003) calls "the anxious space of containing music in the physical and legal discourses of (cultural or intellectual) property." How are these very contemporary debates themselves replaying, repeating, and respinning ones like them that have happened since the invention of the phonograph? What distinct forms do they take as a result of the extensions of the rule of literary copyright into musical copyright? Theorizing the relationship of circulation/circulatory economies to the role of mimesis in shaping sound as cultural property, Feld suggests that music is both the most and least controllable and policeable kind of property (see Feld 1994, 1995). The history of what he calls "pygmy POP" (Feld 1996) he describes as a distinctive global microcosm of sonic property both as capitalist triumph and cultural humiliation.

Both the cases of music and that of indigenous art suggest not only the ethnocentrism of current IP formulations (see Warren 1999; Tsing 2003). They also suggest the centrality of inequalities of power that might enter into the way such formulations are enacted in complex, differentiated social fields. And it is on these grounds, that the arguments of Vaidhyanathan (2001) about restricting IP regulations and those of indigenous activists for restricting access to culture surely begin to coincide in asking how the circulation of culture might contribute to or detract from the sustaining of valued identities and activities.

Acknowledgments

This essay was originally developed for the Social Science Research Council Conference, "Intellectual Property, Markets, and Cultural Flows," October 23–25, 2003, New York University City. In writing it, I have drawn on two other essays that should be acknowledged: "Ontologies of the image and economies of exchange," *American Ethnologist* (2004): 31(1); "Some properties of art and culture," in *Materiality*, Daniel Miller (ed.), Durham, NC: Duke University Press (in press).

Notes

1. For simplicity's sake, I will characterize these marked forms as comprising "totemic knowledge." By this trope, I refer to the fact that the restricted forms of knowledge are those associated with the land-based socioreligious complex known as The Dreaming (*tjukurrpa* in Pintupi). In this system, persons and groups are identified and differentiated by their relationships to distinctive sites on the land, "places" that are believed to have been brought into being by the activities of powerful ancestral beings. These ancestral beings left part of their essence at these places—not only as "spirits" that could be reborn but also as rituals, songs, designs, and other objectifications that now comprise an "estate" that is managed—"held" and "looked after"—by contemporary custodians. The custodians are also responsible to a larger society for managing them properly, and just as their identity is expressed in their performance of these prerogatives, their own esteem and social value flows from their capacity to carry this burden.

2. In 1994, a stone churinga appeared on the cover of Sotheby's catalog as the lead element in their tribal art auction. After protests by Aboriginal people in Australia, the photograph was removed from the cover but the object was still up for sale, not subject to Australian law because it was outside the country. Having obtained funds from the sympathetic Minister of Aboriginal Affairs, the Central Land Council faxed me and asked me to bid on the churinga—with the hopes of acquiring it for repatriation. Our bid fell far short of its final sale price, $34,000, to an unknown telephone bid.

3. Indeed, in this sense, knowledge of sacred objects and its control represents an area of indigenous intellectual property concern. Aboriginal people have attempted to reproduce and extend their system of controls over objects and knowledge that might circulate in museums, films, or books. They have asked that sacred objects be removed from public display, that films of ritual be removed from distribution, and that books limit their discussion and photographic depiction of restricted concerns.

References

Benjamin, Roger. 1989. Aboriginal art: Exploitation or empowerment? *Art in America* 78(July): 73–81.

Berman, Tressa. n.d. Unpublished letter to *New York Times*, in reply to Shweder's review (2003) of *Who Owns Native Culture?*

Bourdieu, Pierre. 1984. *Distinction: A social critique of the judgement of taste*. Cambridge, MA: Harvard University Press.

Brown, Michael. 1998. Can culture Be copyrighted? *Current Anthropology* 39(2): 193–222.

———. 2003. *Who owns native culture?* Cambridge, MA: Harvard University Press.

Brush, Stephen. 1996. Whose knowledge, whose genes, whose rights? In Stephen Brush and Doreen Stabinsky (eds.), *Valuing local knowledge: Indigenous people and intellectual property rights*. Washington, DC: Island Press.

Coleman, Elizabeth. 2004. Aboriginal art and identity: Crossing the borders of Law's imagination. *Journal of Political Philosophy* 12(1): 20–40.

Coombe, Rosemary. 1997. The properties of culture and the possession of identity: Postcolonial struggle and the legal imagination. In Bruce Ziff and Pratima Rao (eds.), *Borrowed power: Essays in cultural appropriation*. New Brunswick, NJ: Rutgers University Press.

———. 1998. Introduction: Authoring culture. In Rosemary Coombe (ed.), *The cultural life of intellectual properties*. Durham, NC: Duke University Press.

Dove, Michael. 1996. Center, periphery and biodiversity: A paradox of governance and a developmental challenge. In Stephen Brush and Doreen Stabinsky (eds.), *Valuing local knowledge: Indigenous people and intellectual property rights*. Washington, DC: Island Press.

Feld, Steven. 1994. Notes on World Beat, Public Culture 1. In Charles Keil and Steven Feld (eds.), *Music grooves*. Chicago: University of Chicago Press.

———. 1995. From schizophonia to schismogenesis: The discourses of world music and world beat. In George Marcus and Fred Myers (eds.), *The traffic in culture*. Los Angeles: University of California Press.

———. 1996. pygmy POP: A genealogy of schizophonic mimesis. *Yearbook for Traditional Music* 28: 1–35.

———. 2000. A sweet lullaby for world music. *Public Culture* 12(1): 145–171.

————. 2003. Personal Communication.

Fry, Tony, and Anne-Marie Willis. 1989. Aboriginal art: Symptom or success? *Art in America* (July): 109–117, 159–160.

Gell, Alfred. 1998. *Art and agency*. Oxford: Oxford University Press.

Handler, Richard. 1985. On having a culture. In George W. Stocking (ed.), *Objects and others*. Madison: University of Wisconsin Press.

Hansen, Ken, and Leslie Hansen. 1977. *Pintupi-Loritja dictionary*. Alice Springs, NT: Institute for Aboriginal Development.

Johnson, Vivien. 1996. *Copyrites: Aboriginal art in the age of reproductive technologies*. Sydney: National Indigenous Arts Advocacy Organization and Macquarie University.

Levi-Strauss, Claude. 1966. *The savage mind*. Chicago: University of Chicago Press.

Marcus, George, and Fred Myers, eds. 1995. *The traffic in culture: Refiguring art and anthropology*. Berkeley: University of California Press.

Merlan, Francesca. 2001. Aboriginal cultural production into art: The complexity of redress. In Chris Pinney and Nicholas Thomas (eds.), *Beyond aesthetics: Art and the technologies of enchantment*. Oxford: Berg.

Michaels, Eric. 1988. Bad Aboriginal Art. *Art and Text* 28: 59–73.

Myers, Fred. 1988. Burning the Truck and Holding the Country: Property, Time, and the Negotiation of Identity among Pintupi Aborigines. In Tim Ingold, David Riches, and James Woodburn (eds.), *Property, power and ideology in hunting and gathering societies*. London: Berg.

————. 1991. *Pintupi country, Pintupi self: Sentiment, place and politics among Western Desert Aborigines*. Berkeley: University of California Press.

————. 2001. "Introduction." In F. Myers (ed.), *The empire of things*. Santa Fe: School of American Research Press.

————. 2003. *Painting culture: The making of an Aboriginal high art*. Durham, NC: Duke University Press.

Phillips, Ruth, and Christopher Steiner, eds. 1999. *Unpacking culture: Art and commodity in the Colonial and Postcolonial Worlds.* Berkeley: University of California Press.

Sansom, Basil. 1980. *The camp at Wallaby Cross.* Canberra: Australian Institute of Aboriginal Studies Press.

Strathern, Marilyn. 1999. Potential property: Intellectual rights and property in persons; What is intellectual property after? In Marilyn Strathern (ed.), *Property, substance and effect.* London and New Brunswick: Athlone Press.

Strehlow, T. G. H. 1947. *Aranda traditions.* Melbourne: Melbourne University Press.

Tsing, Anna Lowenhaupt. 2003. Cultivating the wild: Honey-Hunting and forest management in Southeast Kalimantan. In Charles Zerner (ed.), *Culture and the question of rights.* Durham, NC: Duke University Press.

Turner, Terence. 1999. *Indigenous and culturalist movements in the contemporary global conjuncture.* In Francisco F. Del Riego, Marcial G. Portasany, Terence Turner, Josep R. Llobera, Isodoro Moreno, and James W. Fermandez (eds.), Las Identidadesy las tensiones culturles de modernidad. Santiago de Compostela: Federacion de Asociaciones de antropologia du Estado Espanol.

Vaidhyanathan, Siva. 2001. *Copyrights and copywrongs: The rise of intellectual property and how it threatens creativity.* New York: New York University Press.

Warren, Karen J. 1999. A philosophical perspective on the ethics and resolution of cultural properties issues. In Phyllis Mauch Messenger (ed.), *The ethics of collecting cultural properties,* 2nd ed. Albuquerque: UNM Press.

Ziff, Bruce, and Pratima V. Rao, eds. 1997. *Borrowed power: Essays on cultural appropriation.* New Brunswick, NJ: Rutgers Press.

5

Square Pegs in Round Holes? Cultural Production, Intellectual Property Frameworks, and Discourses of Power

Boatema Boateng

In 1985 Ghana revised its copyright law and, for the first time, included folklore in protected creative works. In defining folklore the law followed the Model Provisions for National Laws on Protection of Expressions of Folklore Against Illicit Exploitation and Other Prejudicial Actions produced (also in 1985) by the United Nations Educational, Scientific, and Cultural Organization (UNESCO) and the World Intellectual Property Organization (WIPO). Thus folklore was defined very broadly in the Ghanaian law to include items ranging from oral narratives to textiles. Of particular concern were Ghanaian adinkra and kente cloth[1] that were being mass-produced by factories outside Ghana for both local and foreign markets. The official view was that these textiles and other kinds of folklore were part of Ghana's cultural heritage and therefore must not be exploited for profit without consent—or royalty payments.[2] When Ghana revised its intellectual property laws in 2000, in response to the World Trade Organization's (WTO) requirement that its member states align their laws with the provisions of the Agreement on Trade Related Aspects of Intellectual Property Rights (TRIPS), the copyright protection of folklore was retained, even though such protection is not universally recognized as a principle of intellectual property law.

In protecting this kind of cultural production under copyright law, Ghana is part of an emerging movement of indigenous peoples and Third World nations[3] that has grown as forms of knowledge[4] commonly referred to as "folklore" and "indigenous knowledge" have been drawn into the global economy on an intensified scale. Very often the entry of these cultural goods into global markets occurs through their appropriation by parties outside originating communities, with little or no compensation to such communities. Further, the norms that guide the ownership and circulation of these products in their locations of origin hold little force in the formal legal context at national and international levels. In the case of Ghanaian adinkra and kente cloth, for example, craftsmen[5] acknowledge multiple owners of their cloth and designs. These owners may include living and deceased craftsmen, royal patrons, and entire communities. In the case of certain forms of indigenous music, communities of musicians may acknowledge both individual and group ownership of their songs.[6] In other cases, communities may perceive their relationship to their cultural production as one of custodianship rather than ownership.[7] Despite the differences between such ownership norms and the principles of orthodox intellectual property law, the latter has become the framework of choice for many groups and nations seeking to regulate the appropriation and global circulation of their cultural production.

At the same time, cultural goods, in general, have become increasingly important in the global economy. Such goods include computer software and pharmaceuticals and as their protection has become a matter of growing economic concern, intellectual property regulation has gained unprecedented significance as a branch of international trade policy. A key indicator of this development is the shift from the WIPO-mediated regulatory framework of the United Nations to the WTO's TRIPS Agreement as the primary context for international intellectual property regulation.

The encounter between intellectual property and cultural property is therefore closely bound up with globalization, characterized by the accelerated expansion of capital and intensified commodification of culture. That encounter is also connected to the exercise of power within the global economy since decision making within the World Trade Organization is linked very closely with economic power of member states, in contrast with the relatively egalitarian one nation, one vote principles of the United Nations. That power is particularly apparent in attempts to set the terms for the circulation of cultural goods such as medicines and seeds developed over generations within local communities, or forms of aesthetic expression that embody the beliefs of such communities. In the encounter with intellectual property law these newer and rather unorthodox candidates for protection are rendered marginal in comparison with other forms of cultural production.

Although it can be argued that intellectual property law is inappropriate for the protection of such cultural production, and the focus must therefore be on developing alternative regimes, the encounter is worth examining for a number of reasons. Despite its limitations, intellectual property law is still used by a number of nations and groups to protect their cultural production. Further, the appropriation of such cultural production is often justified by means of intellectual property law. Appropriating individuals and groups classify such knowledge under the intellectual property category of the public domain, thereby justifying its appropriation. However once they have processed appropriated cultural production into mass-produced textiles or drugs, they claim ownership of these products through the mechanisms of intellectual property law.

Against this background, this chapter examines the power implications of the encounter between the cultural production of indigenous peoples and Third World nations, on the one hand, and intellectual property regulatory frameworks on the other. The main argument here is that when the cultural production of such groups becomes a matter of intellectual property protection, it tends to be discussed in terms that pose its difference from orthodox conceptualizations of intellectual property as a matter of lack and deficiency. In the encounter with intellectual property regulatory systems, therefore, such cultural production is ranked at the lower end of a scale that places scientific inventions and formulae as well as artistic manuscripts and compositions at the higher end.

The ordering of knowledge through such terminology makes it clear that the exercise of power around intellectual property regulation is not only structural, in the form of policymaking bodies but also discursive. By examining the contingency of the categories that distinguish between different kinds of knowledge, the chapter shows that such categories are not neutral descriptors but are often bound up with relationships of power. Thus even when they are used in measures like Ghana's copyright law to change the status quo, ultimately they only reinforce it. This argument is similar to those made in critiques of mainstream (and dominant) epistemologies by scholars from a range of disciplines. The discussion that follows draws, in particular, on the insights of feminist standpoint epistemology and critical discourse analysis.

Standpoints, Discourse, and Power

Feminist scholars in different locations have long asserted that claims about what is worth knowing are bound up with the identities and social location of those making such claims.[8] They show how accounts of reality that differ from the mainstream have routinely been denied legitimacy in the academy. Patricia Hill Collins identifies two political criteria guiding the validation of knowledge in the academy. The first is that the experts who evaluate knowledge "represent the standpoints of the groups from which they originate." The second is that those experts must maintain their credibility according to the criteria of their groups of origin rather than in opposition to them. She notes that, as a result, "(w)hen elite white men or any other overly homogenous group dominates the knowledge validation process, both political criteria can work to suppress Black feminist thought" (Collins 2000, 253).

In highlighting the ways in which the elements of race, class, and gender are interrelated in the production and validation of different kinds of knowledge, Harding notes that Hill Collins illuminates the standpoint feminist argument that ". . . not just opinions, but a society's best beliefs—what it calls knowledge—are socially situated" (Harding 1991, 119). Thus scientific knowledge, for example, which is generally regarded by its producers as being neutral, is in fact as culturally specific as knowledge that is deemed to be nonscientific.

Scholars of discourse and power have also shown that particular accounts of reality are not only legitimized and made dominant through the identity of their proponents. When they gain wide acceptance, such accounts function as discourses or representations whose dominance precludes alternative accounts of reality. Such representations do not necessarily derive their power from any acts of coercion but from the taken-for-granted status that makes them seem obvious and inevitable—even in cases where they function oppressively (Foucault 1972; Hall 1992; van Dijk 1993).

Square Pegs in Round Holes?

When one applies a similar analytical perspective to intellectual property regulation, treating it as a historically and culturally contingent set of practices, the bases for its treatment of different kinds of knowledge begin to crumble; the shapes of the pegs of cultural production and the holes of intellectual property law begin to look a lot less distinct. This is because some of the basic principles of intellectual property law, such as individual creativity and ownership, are neither self-evident nor universally agreed upon. Rather these principles have emerged out of struggles between competing notions of the nature of property rights in cultural production. For example, there is lack of agreement over whether such "rights" are indeed rights or privileges. Intellectual property law also goes back and forth between favoring publishers (or owners) over creators and vice versa. In yet another example, there has always been disagreement over which cultural goods must be regarded as part of a universal "commons" that should be accessible to all, and which ones must be restricted in their circulation.

Such disagreements arise out of philosophical, economic, and cultural sources. Thus the question of whether intellectual property rights are inherent in the person of the creator or in the power of the state to grant and withhold privileges is both a philosophical and economic one. The view that created work is inextricably bound up with the person of its creator and therefore inseparable from the latter gives rise to the "moral rights" principle whereby a producer of creative work can continue to exercise control over the work concerned—even after ownership has been formally transferred. This position is closely allied with the Lockean "natural rights" principle of property where combining one's labor with resources existing in nature gives one the right of ownership over the results of that combination. When the view is that property rights are not inherent in producers but are privileges granted by the state, the rights of creators to what they create are much more limited. In such cases, the grounds for granting such rights are that they compensate creators for their work and provide them with an incentive for further creative work; the mere act of creating does not necessarily translate into entitlement.

An economic source of disagreement over whether cultural production must be perceived as a "commons" or as private property is evident in the differing views of industrialized and Third World nations on the conditions under which the technological knowledge of the former can be obtained by the latter. The position of Third World nations has often been that their access to industrial property must be facilitated in order to achieve the technology transfer necessary for industrialization.[9] On the other hand, much cultural production that Third World nations and indigenous peoples seek to protect is deemed by mainstream intellectual property law to reside in the public domain and therefore is legitimately open to exploitation by all and sundry. These positions are related to deep-seated differences over the terms by which the world's resources should be distributed. Rather than being absolute and universal, therefore, the basic premises of intellectual property law have emerged in a process of struggle between different positions and through the reiteration and reinforcement of those positions that win out in the process.

When the property rights of indigenous peoples and local communities are raised in terms of intellectual property, the question often becomes one of the degree to which the cultural production of such communities fit into intellectual property law. For example, the premise of individual authorship and ownership in intellectual property law converts communal or multiple authorship of the kind described in the case of adinkra and kente into a problem. Similarly, knowledge that has not been produced according to the conventions of Western science is not treated as worthy of protection even if it includes medically and agriculturally efficacious knowledge that is developed and applied by specialists within the originating community.

The issue is seldom perceived as one of mediating between different systems of authorship, ownership, and knowledge production. Therefore the fact that similar objections can be raised about forms of scientific and artistic cultural production that are considered legitimate candidates for intellectual property protection, is routinely obscured. For example, such cultural production occurs within communities of art or science according to established traditions that are upheld by the community. However the Western Enlightenment focus on the individual leads to a focus on the latter rather than on the community and tradition in which she or he operates. The same focus leads to an emphasis on the individual author, creator, or inventor in intellectual property law.

These observations are not made in order to propose a system of regulatory relativism in which all cultural production is regarded as equivalent and interchangeable. Rather they are intended to show that the objections that are often raised against the intellectual property protection of indigenous knowledge are only tenable if the contingent and partial nature of intellectual property law is denied. Further, the ability to evaluate whether or not certain kinds of cultural production fit into established conventions of intellectual property law, and to accord or deny protection translates into the exercise of power over such production.

In contrast to the obscured communal sources of artistic and scientific creative work, folklore is communal by definition, given its direct reference to "folk" or "people." Further, the history of the term includes its use for the dismissive categorization of the cultural production of non-Western subjects of anthropological study. It is therefore opposed to science not only by definition but also in its use to denote cultural production considered inferior to that of the West. An additional contrast occurs between the perceived informality and imprecision of folklore compared to the purported rigor and systematic nature of science. This is particularly evident in the view that folklore is not learned (Kuruk 1999). Similarly, the term "indigenous knowledge" refers to cultural production that is very location-specific, in contrast with the presumed universality of science. Accordingly, it becomes difficult to conceive of such knowledge assuming any significance or legitimacy beyond its location of origin.

For these reasons scholars and activists have sought to change the terminology used to describe the cultural production of "indigenous people" and "local communities." In place of "indigenous knowledge" and "folklore," therefore, they have sought to substitute "traditional resources" and "traditional knowledge." The question that arises here, however, is what makes such knowledge traditional when tradition can be said to exist everywhere? How is tradition in traditional knowledge different from tradition in science? The essential difference is that between tradition and modernity, and "tradition," in this sense, has connotations as problematic as those of "folklore" and "indigenous knowledge," for when tradition and modernity are posited in contrast to each other, modernity is invariably held to be superior. Thus modernization theorists speak of the need to move Third World societies from conditions of tradition to those of modernity—indeed one early and extremely influential text in this area was Daniel Lerner's *The Passing of Traditional Society: Modernizing the Middle East* (1958). Tradition is thus a state of being that must be superseded by modernity.

The word "traditional" is therefore not only an index of the nature of the knowledge in question but also points to what such knowledge is *not*; that is, it simultaneously indicates that such knowledge is not modern. Tradition further tends to be perceived as static and frozen in time, in contrast to the dynamism and ever-advancing nature of modernity, reinforcing the perception that the former is inferior to the latter. In fact, as Ghanaian lawmakers claim in defending the copyright protection of folklore, traditional knowledge is dynamic. While the Ghanaian law is somewhat contradictory on this point—asserting that "folklore" is dynamic but at the same time seeking to preserve it—the fact remains that the cultural production denoted by traditional knowledge is not hermetically sealed off but developed applied under constantly changing conditions that shape it.

Ghanaian kente cloth, for example, has changed continually in its encounter with global markets. These changes go back to the era of mercantile capitalism during which colored silk yarns were introduced into the local cloth-weaving economy from Europe. This enabled weavers to extend their palette beyond the white of raw cotton and blue of indigo dyes. The distinctiveness of the resulting strikingly colored cloth translated into a source of prestige for local communities and centers of power rather than any sense that the purity of indigenous tradition had been diluted. For producing communities, there was no contradiction in the incorporation of foreign yarn into local cloth production. References to Europe were retained only in narratives of origin that related how color was introduced into cloth weaving, and in the reference to silk in some indigenous names for kente, for example, the Asante *serekye nwentoma* or silk woven cloth. More recently, adinkra cloth producers have substituted cotton produced in local and foreign factories for the handwoven cotton on which they stencil the distinctive patterns of the adinkra symbolic system. It is therefore evident that the word "traditional" is often a misnomer and as problematic as the terms "folklore" and "indigenous knowledge" that it replaces.

Discourse and Power in Intellectual Property Regimes

The problematic nature of terms such as "indigenous knowledge," "folklore," and "traditional knowledge" is reinforced by their association with groups and nations that occupy positions of limited power within the global economy. Through the use of such terms, the cultural production of such groups and nations becomes an additional means by which they are marked as not only marginal but also as "Other," distant, strange, and inferior. Yet, in a description of Western science, Sandra Harding shows that scientific knowledge can seem equally strange. She states:

The "indigenous peoples" of the modern West . . . have culturally distinctive belief patterns in which scientific rationality plays a role. These "natives," like all others,

have trouble even recognizing that they exhibit culturally distinctive patterns of belief
. . . From an anthropological perspective, faith in scientific rationality is at least partly responsible for many of the Western beliefs and behaviors that appear most irrational to people whose life patterns and projects do not so easily fit with those of the modern West. From the perspective of women's lives, scientific rationality frequently appears irrational. (Harding 1991, 3)

This description of science is significant not only in drawing attention to the partiality of scientific perspectives that claim to be value-neutral, but also for the crude anthropological terms used. The application of such language to Western science undermines its claims to universality and renders it almost as marginal as the non-Western "Others" to whom such terms are routinely applied. It is only when the practices around the production and protection of art and science are posed in terms like this that the cultural specificity and resulting partiality of the premises of intellectual property regulation begin to emerge.

The description of certain kinds of cultural production as "indigenous," "folkloric," and "traditional," when they occur outside the norms and institutions of Western "art" and "science," translates into discourses of power over such cultural production, for it justifies the treatment of such production as inferior rather than different. Through such discourses the characteristics that are common to these kinds of knowledge production and Western art and science are emphasized in the case of "indigenous knowledge," and obscured in the case of "science" justifying policy treatment that devalues the former and validates the latter. Tied into these discourses are principles of intellectual property protection that stress certain aspects of knowledge production and dismiss others. The result is that while scientific products are perceived as legitimate subjects for intellectual property protection, "folkloric" ones are not—a fact that is vividly illustrated by the following quotation:

Cultural forms, dances, patterns, traditional medical knowledge, genetic information from the plants of the rain forest, or from peasant-cultivated seed varieties, all flow out of the developing world unprotected by property rights. In return, the developed countries send their cultural forms—Mickey Mouse, the X-Men, Pearl Jam, Benetton, Marlboro, and Levi's. The developed world also sends in its wonderful medicines—Prozac and Tagamet—its computer programs—WordPerfect and Lotus 1-2-3—its novels and its industrial designs. Almost all of *these* things, of course, are well protected by intellectual property rights. (Boyle 1996, 141–142, emphasis in original)

As Boyle argues further, these different cultural forms are not necessarily equivalent. However the extreme disparities in their policy treatment reinforce and perpetuate the inequities between the Third World and industrialized nations. The interrelated nature of power imbalances between world regions and the discourses that justify the disproportionate exploitation of the cultural production of some regions mean that any solution must entail more than mere changes in terminology. Unless the premises of intellectual property law can be changed to include the principles underlying other kinds of cultural production, alternative terminology merely perpetuates the status quo—especially when such terminology emphasizes difference in ways that bear connotations of inferiority. In the absence of such changes in the premises of intellectual property law, its use in protecting the cultural production of indigenous peoples and Third World nations is very uneven in its effectiveness. For example, while the indigenous people of Australia have had some success in using copyright law to protect their art, the Ghanaian state has failed dismally in gaining similar protection for its folklore.

In seeking to assert their ownership rights over cultural production within the global economy, indigenous peoples and nations such as Ghana have limited options for changing the terms on which protection can be secured. Yet such changes are essential in addressing the inequities in global cultural flows and distribution of resources, and must entail challenges to both the discourses and institutions of mainstream intellectual property law.

Conclusion

Intellectual property law is a set of practices based on principles that have gained their legal force through a process of contest, accretion, and reiteration. These power struggles continue as regulators seek to determine what ownership rights can and cannot be protected under the law. Within these debates, however, indigenous peoples of Third World nations find themselves operating from a position of disadvantage. That disadvantage stems from a number of sources.

First, the categories of intellectual property law and the kinds of cultural production that it protects are treated as absolute rather than contingent.

Second, the kinds of cultural production over which such groups and nations seek to assert ownership rights are conceptualized in terms that render them inferior to other kinds of cultural production. Third, indigenous peoples' and Third World nations' relative lack of power within the global economy provides them with limited scope for insisting that the terms of the debates around the protection of different kinds of cultural production be changed. This is especially so in the current WTO/TRIPS era, where the ability to participate in international intellectual property policymaking is closely bound up with economic power. These factors combine in interrelated structures and discourses of power in which Third World nations and indigenous peoples are often as complicit as they are resistant.

This state of affairs presents a challenge to international property law as a key regulatory mechanism of the global economy. That challenge is to rethink and reform the basic premises of such law so that its encounter with all forms of cultural production works to reduce the disparities in power that make it possible to cordon off and dismiss certain kinds of knowledge and the communities that produce them.

Notes

1. Adinkra cloth is produced by stenciling motifs with symbolic meanings onto cloth using a black dye. Kente cloth is made from strips woven with motifs arranged in alternating blocks such that when the strips are stitched together, the overall design resembles a checkerboard.

2. In its November 4–10, 1996, edition, *Public Agenda*, a Ghanaian newspaper, reported that imitations of Ghanaian kente cloth were being mass-produced by Korean and Chinese textile companies without any payment of royalties to the originators of the designs. The article quoted the director of the country's Copyright Administration who stated that royalties paid for such folklore must accrue to the state "on behalf of the unknown creators of the ancient kente designs or drum rhythms, traditional tunes, etc."

3. Indigenous peoples are groups of people who have endured settler colonialism, have resisted integration into the dominant culture, and are not organized into nation-states that represent their interests internationally. Some scholars (for example, Greaves 1994) therefore distinguish between them and the people of Third World countries who are perceived to be more integrated into the global economy and who may not have experienced colonization at all or have gained independence—at least nominally.

4. "Knowledge" and "cultural production" are used interchangeably in this chapter to refer to all products of the mind that have social meaning—whether they are produced communally or individually.

5. These textiles are produced predominantly by men. Their views were obtained through life history narrations conducted in Ghana in 1999 and 2000.

6. Tsikata and Anyidoho (1998).

7. The Working Group on Traditional Resource Rights uses the concept of "resources" in place of "property because ". . . property for indigenous peoples frequently has intangible, spiritual manifestations, and, although worthy of protection, is inalienable or can belong to no human being" (Posey and Dutfield 1996, 3).

8. For example, Hartsock (1983); Haraway (1991); Harding (1991); Hill Collins (2000).

9. Hamelink (1994); Ryan (1998).

References

Boyle, James. 1996. *Of shamans and spleens: Law and the construction of the Information Society*. Cambridge, MA: Harvard University Press.

Collins, Patricia Hill. 2000. *Black feminist thought: Knowledge, consciousness and the politics of empowerment*. 2nd ed. New York: Routledge.

Foucault, Michel. 1972. *The archaeology of knowledge and the discourse on language*. New York: Pantheon Books.

Greaves, Tom., ed. 1994. *Intellectual property rights for indigenous peoples: A source book*. Oklahoma City, OK: Society for Applied Anthropology.

Hall, Stuart. 1992. The West and the rest: Discourse and power. In Stuart Hall and Bram Gieben (eds.), *Formations of modernity*. Cambridge, UK: Polity Press.

Hamelink, C. J. 1994. *The politics of world communication: A human rights perspective*. London: Sage.

Haraway, Donna., ed. 1991. Situated knowledges: The science question in feminism and the privilege of partial perspective Simians. In *Simians, cyborgs and women: The reinvention of nature*. New York: Routledge.

Harding, Sandra. 1991. *Whose science? Whose knowledge? Thinking from women's lives*. Ithaca, NY: Cornell University Press.

Hartsock, Nancy C. M. 1983. The feminist standpoint: Developing the ground for a specifically feminist materialism. In Sandra Harding and Merrill B. P. Hintikka (eds.), *Discovering reality*. Dordrecht, The Netherlands: Reidel Publishing Co.

Kuruk, Paul. 1999. Protecting folklore under modern intellectual property regimes: A reappraisal of the tensions between individual and community rights in Africa and the United States. *American University Law Review* 48(4): 769–850.

Lerner, Daniel. 1958. *The passing of traditional society: Modernizing the Middle East*. Glencoe, IL: Free Press.

Posey, Darrell A. and Graham Dutfield. 1996. *Beyond intellectual property: Toward traditional resource rights for indigenous communities and local communities*. Ottawa, Canada: International Development Research Center.

Ryan, Michael P. 1998. *Knowledge diplomacy: Global competition and the politics of intellectual property*. Washington, DC: Brookings Institution Press.

Tsikata, Fuis S. and Kofi Anyidoho. 1988. Copyright and oral literature. In K. Anyidoho and K. Yankah (eds.), *Power of their word: Selected papers from Proceedings of the 1st National Conference on Oral Literature in Ghana*. Legon, Ghana: University of Ghana.

Van Dijk, Teun A. 1993. Principles of critical discourse analysis. In *Discourse and Society* 4(2): 249–283.

6

Who Got Left Out of the Property Grab Again? Oral Traditions, Indigenous Rights, and Valuable Old Knowledge

Anthony Seeger

In the front-page pandemonium over whose rights to music are being violated by whom and what software is being copied, little mention is made of those works that are excluded from consideration by the legislation itself. In the rapid adaptation of the concept of property to knowledge, some of the same patterns of exploitation found in earlier centuries repeat themselves in a new domain. In this chapter I describe some of the kinds of knowledge that are omitted from most existing copyright legislation, and why this should be considered a problem to be addressed by a broad constituency rather than ignored or left to legal specialists.

The rapidly expanding extension of capitalist and market procedures to all forms of knowledge and creativity has had a number of effects that deeply concern those of us who perform, study, publish about, and record musical performances in different parts of the world. Most of the legislation dealing with intellectual property has been created in Europe and the United States; a vast majority of the world's musical traditions are created in other places and the international legislation may conflict with local practice. Issues of power, piracy, and trade tend to dominate the examination of intellectual property today to the exclusion of all other perspectives. Different perspectives yield an abundance of other issues that are often forgotten in concerns over unlicensed copying.

Different Perspectives and Different Problems

Although I have written elsewhere about my multiple perspectives on music copyright (Seeger 1991, 1992), it is worth reviewing them here to illustrate how many different activities have been affected by the increasingly determined application of copyright legislation to creative activity.

As a musician I am concerned about future creativity. Increased litigation over the use of musical ideas, the extension of time limits for copyrights, and the expanding number of venues and performance types coming under the control of collection agencies may stifle the creative musical processes. Musicians have always used musical ideas they have learned from other musicians, but it can be very difficult to determine what is "new," and such issues are decided increasingly in courts. This can lead to considerable confusion. Anthony McCann has described how Irish musicians playing in pubs will sometimes suddenly stop and wonder aloud who might own the old tune they have been playing and whether it is copyrighted (McCann 2002). John Collins has described how a member of a family in Ghana may have to pay a tax to perform his own family traditions (Collins 2003). Even legislation written with the best of intentions—but without consulting the tradition bearers— can do much more harm than good to the creative processes that are at the heart of musical creativity.

As an ethnomusicologist I am concerned about the changing legislation and attitudes toward music that affect research. I am concerned that our audiovisual archives are filled with hard-to-access recordings. Archives hold millions of hours of unique recordings for which legal clearances were not obtained (no one imagined they would be necessary in previous decades). As a result, these recordings cannot be widely distributed even to the communities who originally performed them. Changing legislation and practices may impose a terrible burden on archives and those who wish to use them at a time when their collections could be widely accessible. Working with contemporary music is not much easier. Licensing difficulties make writing about popular music extremely difficult—permissions are hard to obtain and often expensive relative to the number of copies a scholarly book will sell. I am also concerned that my own students will be unable to obtain the rights they need from the musicians they study in order to publish the works that will contribute to the development of my field. Musicians are increasingly suspicious (with some justification) of people carrying tape recorders and video cameras. Ethnomusicologists are part of the very globalization processes they often criticize (Feld 1996; Zemp 1996)—but unless they learn how to manage intellectual property rights as well as they manage theories they may contribute to the problems they wish to resolve.

As a member of a family of songwriters, I sympathize with those who complain that indiscriminate file sharing and other unauthorized uses of copyrighted material affects more than large companies. My relatives have used the royalties they receive from their songs and recordings for important social and cultural causes. If use of these compositions without payment of royalties to songwriters is the first step toward socialism, then songwriters and performing artists should be able to look forward to adequate health care and retirement benefits from the grateful public in return. So far I have not seen any move in that direction—no alternative compensation has been proposed, at least in the United States. While I am concerned about creativity (as discussed before), I am also concerned about the livelihood of musicians—what are called the "tradition bearers." Will we develop new ways of supporting those who spend their lives creating music and other arts? Noble patrons are gone; state patronage is virtually absent in the United States of America, and if the market won't feed artists, who will?

As a record company director (I was Director of Smithsonian Folkways Recordings from 1988–2000) I would have been happy to increase royalties to artists, songwriters, and their communities. I wished to run an ethical enterprise that benefited both artists and consumers. But with a margin of only pennies on each CD sold (remember that distributors and stores keep more than half of the price of a CD), I could only do so if all companies agreed to make the additional payments. The record business is highly competitive and many companies have gone out of business or been absorbed by larger ones.

As Secretary-General of the International Council for Traditional Music, I am very concerned about how little the many other stakeholders in intellectual property have been involved in discussions of music copyright. Artists and communities around the world are being asked to change their practices to fit an imposed international standard, without much consultation about their existing practices. Legislation is usually created by those quite far from the artistic processes. The creators, performers, and consumers of music are rarely participants in discussions of legislative priorities and their implementation.

I am concerned that too few lawyers are artists. As others have observed, intellectual property is a subject that is too important to be left to lawyers, yet they have dominated the discourse on this subject. The legal profession is a classic guild. It licenses its own members, and has created its own language and its own rules that virtually require everyone else to use the services of its members. But many musicians and communities around the world have very different ideas. New ways of conceptualizing these issues will emerge if more perspectives are added to the debates.

The Property Grab Again

When the British colonized Australia, they did not recognize the land rights of any of the Aboriginal occupants. Instead, they declared Australia a *terra nullius*, legally empty, without owners. While they could have done this by might alone, their justification lay partly in the dramatic difference between British occupation of land and the Aboriginal occupation. The Aboriginal peoples did not have cities with permanent constructions, and many of them were seminomadic or transhumant. Many of them had a very evolved sense of place, however. Communities often "owned" spiritual centers to which they returned on a regular basis and about which they sang long song cycles. But such ideas did not resemble English real estate legislation. In the twenty-first century, some Aboriginal groups have been able to reclaim their rights to some of their territory, in many cases based on songs and stories that now are considered legal documents of possession.

Some of the same kind of self-interested blindness characterizes the exclusion of what is often called "folklore" and traditional knowledge from Intellectual Property (IP) legislation. Copyright laws evolved in Europe together with printing, which turned writing into a commodity. They are intimately linked to the figure of the "author," which was partly created by them. (A fascinating literature has developed on the history of copyright, which reveals it to be a very European institution that, like many other European developments, has been imposed on the rest of the world—for example see Woodmansee and Jaszi 1994.) Since the materials copyrighted were all, by definition, fixed in printed form, and since they were created, consumed, and regulated by members of the upper-class urban population of each country, little thought was given to creating legislation for unwritten and unpublished traditions. Not only were their performers illiterate, they were often lower class and in many cases distant—in other counties or colonies.

Ignoring the illiterate and dispossessed is nothing new in the history of humanity since writing was invented. In the current rush to stake claims to and defend existing intellectual property rights, scant attention is being paid to those who were deprived of them in the first place. In an age when non-print publications are so important, it is striking that copyright legislation continues to be based on a concept that evolved with print media in a very different era.

What Has Been Left Out?

Most intellectual property legislation excludes folklore and anonymous works from consideration. The same legislation usually (there are exceptions) fails to recognize collective ownership of knowledge. Folklore and anonymous works, along with works whose copyright terms have expired, are all part of what is called the "public domain," where they may be appropriated by anyone. One metaphor of the public domain is that of the English commons—a public grazing area. Another metaphor might be a deep well, from which anyone may take water. Once in the bucket the water has an owner for a fixed period, after which the water returns to the well. This leaves who owns the water in a bucket, and who may use it, to be resolved. What the combining of folklore and traditional arts with creations whose copyright terms have expired in the same public domain has meant in practice is that "traditional" blues performed by "traditional" musicians (water in the well) can be taken, arranged, and made into popular rock songs (water in the bucket) without recognition or payment to the original artists.

Musicians may adopt styles or songs directly from most oral traditions and turn them into property that yields a royalty to the arranger, but not to the source of their inspiration. Looking at the way some developed countries have appropriated music from less-developed countries, one finds a pattern similar to that of colonialism: raw materials are provided by colonies, taken to the mother country, and turned into products that are then sold back. In this case, oral traditional knowledge is the raw material that becomes property only when some literate individual converts it into a commodified product. But the people who had it in the first place often do not see their rights in the same way. They see ideas, styles, and even entire pieces they call their own used by others for profit with neither recognition nor payments coming to them. Where others see opportunity and inspiration, they see injustice.

Who Has Been Left Out?

The individuals and communities ignored by copyright legislation are the same ones that have been ignored before: indigenous peoples within nation states, the poor, the illiterate, and the already otherwise dispossessed. They are often unaware of the national laws and rarely in a position to hire lawyers to represent them. They are visited by ethnomusicologists, however, who inadvertently become involved (Feld 1996; Zemp 1996; Guy 2003).

Ethnomusicologists study musical traditions from all parts of the world. Many of us have worked with noncommercial music in distant places. The nature of our research brings us into close and prolonged contact with artists of many persuasions in many different communities. Although most ethnomusicologists have paid little attention to local concepts of music ownership, those that did encountered very different ideas and practices than those in international copyright legislation. One need not go to a distant jungle to find oral traditions affected by changing concepts of ownership, however. Anthony McCann has written an excellent dissertation on the effects of collection agencies on informal "sessions" in Irish pubs (McCann 2002).

My own research in Mato Grosso, Brazil, revealed a variety of concepts of ownership and control over music (Seeger 1987). In the native community I lived with for two years, all songs were said to originate with the spirits of natural species or with monsters or human enemies. The songs were introduced by people with special spiritual hearing who taught them to the rest of the village. Although they seem to be similar to composers, they were not considered to be so by the Indians, who did not usually remember who taught them which song. Once introduced to the community, a song could be "owned" and its performance controlled by an individual, a name group, a moiety (half of the men in the village), or by the community as a whole.

For example, the originator of the song might be a savannah deer, and the owner-controller is a group of names that remains the same even as the men who hold them change (a man gives his own names and ritual identity to one of his sister's sons who eventually replaces him). One savannah deer song was incorporated into a naming ceremony for young children. This ceremony may remain the same for hundreds of years, as long as there are men using those names and singing. There is no one in this process of song creation that resembles the European notion of a composer. It thus makes no sense to argue for rights for the lifetime of the nonexistent "composer" plus seventy years. If the song can be traced to anything, it is to the savannah deer spirit. What is the lifetime of a savannah deer spirit? Or, more generally, what is the lifetime of a god? Will legislation recognize divine authorship? Can legislation declare God is dead? Once learned, the Indians I studied placed no time limit on the control of the owner-controller over the piece. But they did have a kind of "public domain" or well from which all new songs came—the world of animal spirits, monsters, and enemies who are all considered powerful outsiders. Clearly the concepts about music, its origin and control are not the same as those found in international legislation.

Regardless of what the Brazilian Indian community thinks, however, once I published the song with the title "Savannah Deer Song" on a barely commercial ethnographic recording, the name group lost control from the point of view of the Brazilian copyright law then in effect. The piece is "Traditional" and what had been restricted to a single name group is now available for anyone to perform, adapt, and (after arranging) copyright in their own name.

Theories of individual creativity, concern over fencing in the commons of the public domain, and the frankly protectionist attitudes of current rights holders aside, the one-sided decision to leave traditional knowledge and oral traditions outside the definition of "intellectual property" looks a lot like declaring Australia "terra nullius" or sending all the native peoples in the United States to the west of the Mississippi. The same people dispossessed of their lands in previous centuries are today dispossessed of control over (and income from) their artistic life.

Woody Guthrie, a prolific songwriter of the mid-twentieth century, once wrote that while some people robbed you with guns, others robbed with fountain pens ("Pretty Boy Floyd" [Woody Guthrie, Folkways Music, Inc./TRO BMI]). That's true. And while armed robbers take all the money you have with you, those wielding fountain pens can take all the money you might make in the future and are the more dangerous to most individuals and communities around the world.

Who Does What about This?

Most developed countries have little interest in this problem, but instead focus on incursions on already established rights. Other countries, especially those with strong oral traditions, have begun to protest legislation that ignores oral traditions and other forms of intangible knowledge (Mills 1996). These countries often see their peoples' oral traditions as a source of income—often for the state coffers rather than local communities or artists. The United Nations Educational, Scientific, and Cultural Organization (UNESCO) and the World Intellectual Property Organization (WIPO) are both addressing these issues, and there is an active indigenous knowledge section of WIPO. Recommendations regarding the recognition of indigenous knowledge are frequently turned down by the developed countries. It is true that some of the recommendations have glaring conceptual problems and troubling implications that need to be discussed (see Brown 1998, 2003). That is not a suitable reason for maintaining an unsatisfactory status quo. In fact, a few countries have unilaterally created legislation protecting specific groups. Australia is working on legislation that will recognize community ownership of knowledge, rather than only individual ownership. Brazil passed indigenous knowledge legislation that appears to ensure profit from pharmaceutical uses of their knowledge for longer periods of time. The fate of such legislation within the framework of GATT is uncertain, but the attempts to address the issues are certainly to be praised.

One of the central issues in intellectual property is about power. Legislation like that governing copyright is a part of larger social and economic processes. The deliberations of scholars should extend beyond current definitions to the broader contexts in which the legislation is being formulated. Nor should the discussions be limited to scholars. The same activists who contest other aspects of international trade agreements such as the GATT should focus their attention on the injustices of the trade-associated intellectual property legislation. Indigenous peoples are already taking active steps to protect their cultural heritage, but do not always find support at the national level.

Not all knowledge is meant to be a commodity. Not all music is created for the pop charts and not all performers seek a paying public. Some music is the opposite of commodified—it cannot be heard by anyone except those born to the right. Some Australian Aborigines perform songs whose sole audience is members of the same clans as that of the performers. The purpose of the music is sacred rather than to go platinum. Unfortunately, legislation governing intellectual property began to take its modern form with commodification, and it is very difficult to remove that bias. It is especially difficult since trade and distribution issues have so dominated international legislation in recent decades.

We are faced with another case of cultural blindness. Just as the English did not recognize the Australian Aboriginal use of their lands (in spite of listening to their songs for many decades), so intellectual property legislation fails to recognize other musical intentions. Is there any way we can avoid repeating the power grabbing of previous centuries? Possibly—but only if we recognize existing legislation to be culturally biased and the creation of self-interested parties; only if more perspectives are brought to discussions of music and ownership; only if we listen to what others, very different from ourselves, have to say; and only if a diverse constituency is mobilized to insist on policy changes.

References

Brown, Michael F. 1998. Can Culture by Copyrighted? *Current Anthropology* 19(2): 193–222.

————. 2003. *Who owns native culture?* Cambridge, MA: Harvard University Press.

Collins, John. 2003. Unpublished manuscript on copyright legislation in Ghana.

Feld, Steven. 1996. pygmy POP. A genealogy of schizophonic mimesis. *Yearbook for Traditional Music* 28: 1–35.

Guy, Nancy. 2003. Trafficking in Taiwan aboriginal voices. In Sjoerd R. Jaarsma (ed.), *Handle with care: Ownership and control of ethnographic materials*. Pittsburgh: University of Pittsburgh Press.

McCann, Anthony. 2002. Beyond the commons: The elimination of uncertainty and the politics of enclosure. PhD Dissertation, University of Limerick.

Mills, Sherylle. 1996. Indigenous music and the law: An analysis of national and international legislation. *Yearbook for Traditional Music* 28: 57–86.

Seeger, Anthony. 1987. *Why Suya Sing, A Musical Anthropology of an Amazonian People*, with audio recording. Cambridge University Press. To be reissued in 2004 by University of Illinois Press.

————. 1991. Singing other people's songs. *Cultural Survival Quarterly* (Summer): 36–39.

————. 1992. Ethnomusicology and music law. *Ethnomusicology* 36(3): 345–360.

————. 2002. Intellectual Property and Audio Visual Archives and Collections. In *Folk heritage collections in crisis*. Washington, DC: Council on Library and Information Resources.

Woodmansee, Martha and Peter Jaszi eds. 1994. *The construction of authorship: Textual appropriation in law and literature*. Durham, NC and London: Duke University Press.

Zemp, Hugo. 1996. The/An ethnomusicologist and the record business. *Yearbook for Traditional Music* 28: 36–56.

7

From Keeping "Nature's Secrets" to the Institutionalization of "Open Science"

Paul A. David

Introduction

This chapter examines the economics of patronage and the roles of asymmetric information and reputation in the early modern reorganization of scientific activities, specifically their influence upon the historical formation of key elements in the ethos and organizational structure of publicly funded open science. The emergence during the late sixteenth and early seventeenth centuries of the idea and practice of open science represented a break from the previously dominant ethos of secrecy in the pursuit of "Nature's Secrets." It was a distinctive and vital organizational aspect of the Scientific Revolution, from which crystallized a new set of norms, incentives, and organizational structures that reinforced scientific researchers' commitments to rapid disclosure of new knowledge. The rise of cooperative rivalries in the revelation of new knowledge, is seen as a functional response to heightened asymmetric information problems posed for the Renaissance system of court-patronage of the arts and sciences; preexisting informational asymmetries had been exacerbated by increased importance of mathematics and the greater reliance upon sophisticated mathematical techniques in a variety of practical contexts of application. Analysis of the court-patronage system of late Renaissance Europe, within which the new natural philosophers found their support, points to the significance of the feudal legacy of fragmented political authority in creating conditions of "common agency contracting *in substitutes*." These conditions are shown to have been conducive to more favorable contract terms (especially with regard to autonomy and financial support) for the agent-client members of Western Europe's nascent scientific communities.

In the United States, indeed, throughout the community of industrially advanced nations, a sense of urgency has surrounded discussions and debates about the organization and funding of R&D by governments. Surely it is not entirely coincidental that such issues were broached for serious discussion in the United States during the late 1990s against the backdrop of unprecedentedly large contractions in the projected levels of real federal expenditures for both defense-related and civilian R&D during 1997–2002.[1] Lively debates concerning science policy have erupted in the United States on many previous occasions, but the most recent episode would seem to have been the first sustained that has seen a fundamental questioning of some of the infrastructure institutions and organizational commitments that have framed the nation's science and technology system—at least since the major restructuring initiated by the 1945 report of Vannevar Bush.[2]

Even when the federal funding picture seemed to improve for basic research, opinion leaders in the areas of science and education have continued to ask whether American universities should continue to be supported as the primary sites for conducting basic research in an "open" fashion that facilitates its close integration with teaching. Some are questioning whether the emphasis on research is healthy for undergraduate teaching. Others wonder whether an "academic research" environment is compatible with concurrent efforts to expand the sphere of collaborative R&D with industry, proactive forms of technology transfer, and to make more extensive use of intellectual property and other means of establishing a proprietary interest in the research activities of faculty, staff, and students. Might it not be better to hive off both basic and applied research into specialized institutes, thus resolving conflicts that arise between the universities' conduct of their traditional functions and the drive on the part of other organizations and agencies (both private and governmental) to control information flows in order to better exploit new findings? Issues similar to those concerning the future role of the university in the "national innovation system" also have arisen in discussions of moves toward privatizing other publicly funded research institutions such as the National Laboratories, and reorienting national research institutes toward commercial application of their research output.[3]

At a time when the reorganization of national science and technology systems are under active consideration and the fitness of recent experiments with innovations in institutional arrangements are undergoing reassessment, it may be especially useful to look backwards to the historical circumstances in which some of the basic institutions of science first emerged; and, equally, and to the economic, social, and political forces that have shaped their subsequent evolution. Economists quite rightly will wish to continue to probe for deeper understanding of the insides of the "black box" of technology (Rosenberg 1982). But, by comparison with what has been learned already concerning institutional arrangements and business strategies affecting corporate R&D investments, and the mechanisms enabling private appropriation of research benefits, it remains surprising that so much less is known about the economics origins and effects of the corresponding institutional infrastructures shaping the world of academic science, and about the organization of publicly supported R&D more generally.

The desirability of closing this particular lacuna in the economics and economic history literature has been just as evident to those who have noticed it within a broader framework of concern with the economic analysis of institutions, as to those who have begun to approach that task by bringing the perspectives and methods of industrial organization economics to bear in the area of science and technology studies.[4] Even before the "new economics of science" had begun to direct attention to such a program, Douglass North (1990, 75) saw a significant challenge and a promising opportunity in explicit exploration of "the connecting links between institutional structures . . . and incentives to acquire pure knowledge."

A variety of historical inquiries may be seen as responses to that challenge, by examining key episodes in the institutional evolution of public science and its complex and changing relationship with the other organizational spheres of contemporaneous scientific activity.[5] The latter include, of course, both those in which industrial research was conducted for private commercial gain under proprietary rules, and the defense-related pursuit of scientific and engineering knowledge under conditions of restricted access to information about basic findings and their actual and potential applications. Much fascination is imparted to the study of institutional evolution in that sphere by the complexity of the organizational details, and the high stakes attached to issues arising from the immediate entanglement of R&D programs and project with matters of national security; or, alternatively by the strategies and fortunes of business corporations that turn on the capabilities of their research organizations. Nevertheless, the historical emergence of the other, academic sphere of research poses a number of questions to which the answers seem less intuitively obvious and straightforward, and yet critically important as a guide in the formation of constructive science and technology policies.

Although the conceptualization of science as the pursuit of "public knowledge" and an object of public-minded patronage today seems a natural, even primitive notion, it is in reality a complex social contrivance. Moreover, open science is a social innovation of comparatively recent historical origin. This has afforded historians of scientific institutions the archival material to examine the evolution of its outward forms of support in considerable detail. But the circumstances and interests that gave rise to this innovation, and their relationship to the economic forces that have sustained and shaped its subsequent development have not received the attention that the importance of the subject in the modern world would seem to warrant.

Within university-based research communities, especially, there are recognized norms and conventions that constitute a well-delineated professional ethos to which scientists generally are disposed to publicly subscribe, whether or not their own behaviors always conform literally to its strictures governing the organization and conduct of research. The norms of "the Republic of Science" that have famously been articulated by the sociologist Robert K. Merton (1973, esp. Ch. 13; 1996, Pt. III) sometimes are summarized under the mnemonic CUDOS: communalism, universalism, disinterestedness, originality, skepticism. (See Ziman 1994, 177). The communal ethos emphasizes the cooperative character of inquiry, stressing that the accumulation of reliable knowledge is an essentially social process, however much individuals may strive to contribute to it. The force of the universalist norm is to render entry into scientific work and discourse open to all persons of competence regardless of their personal and ascriptive attributes. A second aspect of openness concerns the disposition of knowledge: the full disclosure of findings, and methods, form a key aspect of the cooperative, communal program of inquiry. Full disclosure, in turn serves the ethos legitimating and, indeed, prescribing what Merton called "organized skepticism"; it supports the expectation that all claims to having contributed to the stock of reliable knowledge will be subjected to trials of replication and verification, without insult to the claimant. The originality of such intellectual contributions is the touchstone for the acknowledgement of individual scientific claims, upon which collegiate reputations and the material and nonpecuniary rewards attached to such peer evaluations are based.

When did we come by this distinctive set of governance norms for the search for reliable knowledge? How did they become institutionalized as the legitimate ethos—even where they are not strictly adhered to in practice— among the class of academic organizations that flourish in the democratic societies of the modern world? These questions about the nature and origins of the fundamental lines of cultural and institutional demarcation that distinguish the sphere of open science activities—supported by state funding and the patronage of private foundations, and carried on in universities and public (not-for-profit) institutes—form the central substantive historical problem that I address in this study.[6] It will be seen that, in the particular answers to which I have been led, there also lies a broader message for contemporary science and technology policymaking.

The Problem: Why "Open Science"?

Judged by historical standards, open science is a comparatively recent organizational innovation. Accompanying the profound epistemological transformations effected by the fusion of experimentalism with Renaissance mathematics, the cultural ethos and social organization of Western European scientific activities during the late sixteenth and seventeenth centuries underwent a significant reorganization—departing from the previously dominant regime of secrecy in the pursuit of Nature's Secrets. This development should be seen as a distinctive and vital aspect of the Scientific Revolution, from which there crystallized a new set of social conventions, incentive structures, and institutional mechanisms that reinforced scientific researchers' commitments to rapid disclosure and wider dissemination of their new discoveries and inventions. Yet, the puzzle of why and how this came about has not received the notice it would seem to deserve, especially in view of the complementarities and tensions that are recognized to be present today in relations between the regimes of open and proprietary science.

Even superficial reference to the antecedent intellectual orientation and social organization of scientific research in the West suggests the utter improbability of the historical bifurcation that this involved. For, it saw it emerge alongside and in some sense in competition with the older, secretive search for "Nature's Secrets," a new and quite antithetical mode of conducting the hunt for knowledge. Virtually all of the intellectual traditions and material conditions in the medieval West inveighed against openness of inquiry and public disclosure of discoveries about the natural order of the world, let alone the heavens. Medieval experimental science was shaped by a political and religious outlook that encouraged withholding from the "vulgar multitude" arcane knowledge that might bring power over material things (see Thorndike 1950, vol. II; Eamon 1985, 1994). The imperative of secrecy was particularly strong in the medieval and Renaissance traditions of alchemy, where, indeed, it persisted side-by-side with the emergent institutions of open science throughout the seventeenth century and into the eighteenth century (see Dobbs 1975; Westfall 1980; Vickers 1984). Social and economic regulations during the Middle Ages, along with the relatively primitive and costly technologies available for scientific communications, also reinforced the moral and philosophical considerations arrayed against open disclosure of discovered secrets. Economic rent-seeking worked in the same direction: knowledge of recently discovered geographical secrets that were held to be of potential mercantile value, such as trade routes, would be kept from the public domain. Similarly, craftsmen normally held closely technological recipes, even when they were not compelled by guild restrictions to preserve the mysteries of the industrial arts.[7]

Why then, out of such a background of secrecy and obfuscation, should there have emerged a quite distinctive community of inquiry into the nature of the physical world, holding different norms regarding disclosure, and being governed by a distinctive reward system based upon priority of discovery? Why so? The question is striking especially in the modern context, where one may see that there is little, if any, difference between the methods of (scientific) inquiry used by university scientists working under the institutional norms of open science, and the procedures that they (or others with the same academic training) employ in the setting of a corporate R&D laboratory? Can the social organization of open science then be simply an epiphenomenon of the profound philosophical and religious reorientations that have been presented as underpinning the Scientific Revolution, if not the epistemological transformation the latter had wrought? Or, should the intellectual achievements of that epoch instead be read as consequences of what might be called the "Open Science Revolution"? To restate the problem, is it not plausible that these two discontinuities—the one taking place in the social organization of scientific inquiry and the other transforming its intellectual organization—were interdependent, and entangled with each other in ways that need to be more thoroughly understood?

A start towards answering this question is provided by considering the economic logic of the organization of knowledge-producing activities, for, it is possible in such terms to give a complete functionalist account of the institutional complex that characterizes modern science (see, e.g., Dasgupta and David 1987, 1994; David 2003). In brief, the norm of openness is incentive-compatible with a collegiate reputational reward system based upon accepted claims to priority; and it is conducive to individual strategy choices whose collective congruence reduces excess duplication of research efforts, and enlarges the domain of informational complementarities. This brings socially beneficial spillovers among research programs, and abets rapid replication and swift validation of novel discoveries. The advantages of treating new findings as public goods in order to promote the faster growth of the stock of knowledge, thus, are contrasted with the requirements of secrecy for the purposes of securing a monopoly over the use of new information that may be directly or indirectly exploited to produce goods and services, or further knowledge.

There is some explanatory insight in the latter, functional contrast between institutional arrangements that are well suited to maximize of the rate of accumulation of knowledge, on one hand, and, on the other, social arrangements that suited to maximize a society's extraction of economic rents from the existing state, or stock of knowledge. This juxtaposition suggests a logical basis for the existence and perpetuation of institutional and cultural separations between two normatively differentiated communities of research practice, the open Republic of Science and the proprietary Realm of Technology: the two distinctive organizational regimes serve different and potentially complementary societal purposes.

The foregoing, logical origins style of explanation for the institutions of modern science (and technology), however, is one in which all details of their historical evolution are ignored. Such a rationale would seem, at best, to presuppose a form of creationist fiction—namely that these arrangements were instituted ab initio by some external agency, such as an informed and benevolent political authority endowed with fiscal powers. That objection calls for an explicit examination of the historical origins of the institutions of open science, since these remain outside the set of logical origins that one arrives at by simply considering the present-day functional value of an already extant, cooperative mode of scientific research.

The Argument: Noble Patrons, Mathematicians, and Principal-Agent Problems

Rather than trying to construe the reorganization of scientific activities in early modern Europe as having somehow derived automatically from the intellectual changes represented by the new style of scientific activity, I contend that the historical emergence of the norms of disclosure and demonstration, and the rise of cooperative rivalries in the revelation of new knowledge, had independent and antecedent roots. These are to be found in the social and institutional contexts in which the new breed of scientists of that era were working. My central thesis here is that the formation of a distinctive research culture of open science was first made possible and, indeed, was positively encouraged by the system of aristocratic patronage in an era when kings and nobles (both lay and ecclesiastical) were immediately concerned with the ornamental benefits to be derived by their sponsorship of philosophers and savants of great renown.

To support this interpretation, I argue that the economic logic of the patronage system in post-Renaissance Europe induced the emergence and promoted the institutionalization of reputation-building proceedings, all of which turned upon the revelation of scientific knowledge and expertise among extended reference groups that included peer-experts. The mechanisms involved spanned the range from participation in informal networks of correspondence, to public challenges and contests, open demonstrations, and exhibitions and the certification of individuals by co-optation and election to "learned societies." Patronage, however, was an old system in the seventeenth century, and the sponsorship of intellectuals was a long-standing prerogative and responsibility of Europe's social and political elites. It is necessary, therefore, to explain why something new appeared on the scene; why some of the conventions and norms now associated with open science—in particular, the reliance upon peer appraisal and collective evaluation expressed through the formation of professional reputations—were induced in primitive form at this particular juncture in history. The key propositions for this part of my argument derive from first considering the economics of patronage in general, and then noticing the specific implications of the newly arising problems of "principal-agent contracting" that were created by the encounter of the late Renaissance patronage system with the new (mathematical) form of natural philosophy practiced by Galileo, Kepler, and their contemporaries.[8]

Paul A. David

Aristocratic patronage systems have reflected two kinds of motivation: the utilitarian and the ornamental. Most political elites, in addition to recognizing some need in their domain for men capable of producing new ideas and inventions to solve mundane problems connected with warfare and security, land reclamation, food production, transport facilities, and so forth, also have sought to enlist the services of those who professed an ability to reveal the secrets of Nature, and of Destiny. Kings and princes, and lesser nobles, too, sought to surround themselves with creative talents whose achievements would enhance not only their self-esteem, but also their public image—those aspects of grandeur and ostentatious display that might serve to reinforce their claims to rightful authority. Thus, poets, artists, musicians, chroniclers, architects, instrument-makers, and natural philosophers found employment in aristocratic courts, both because their skills might serve the pleasures of the court, and because their presence "made a statement" in the competition among nobles for prestige. These dyadic patron-client relationships, which offered the latter material and political support in exchange for service, were often precarious, uncomfortably subject to aristocratic whims and pleasures, and to the abrupt termination that would ensue on the disgrace or demise of a patron. Nonetheless, they existed in this era as part of a well-articulated system characterized by elaborate conventions and rituals that provided calculable career paths for men of intellectual and artistic talents (see Biagioli 1990, 1993; Moran 1991).

Those motives for entering into a patron's role that reduce to symbolic acts of self-aggrandizement are here subsumed under the heading "ornamental." Such reasons, however, should be understood to have been no less instrumental in their nature and roots than were the utilitarian considerations for the patronage of intellectuals. The public display of "magnificence," in which art and power had become allied, was a stock item in the repertoire of Renaissance statecraft (see Strong 1984). This is significant, because inventions and discoveries that met utilitarian needs in some instances would have to be kept secret if they were to be most useful, whereas it is in the nature of the ornamental motive that its fulfilment elicits the disclosure of new, marvelous discoveries and creations; that the client's achievement on behalf of the patron be widely publicized. Indeed, it was very much in the interest of a patron for the reputations of those he patronized to be enhanced in this way, for their fame augmented his own.[9] A second point of significance is that only some utilitarian services but most ornamental services had positional value from the patron's point of view. Although having a skilled artist or a clever astronomer in one's court was altogether a good thing; it was far better if such clients were personages of greater accomplishments and renown than those who happened to be in the service of a rival's court. The pressure on Europe's ruling families to have intellectuals of recognized eminence in their service was thus exacerbated by the existence of rival rulers and their courts, and so lent additional strength to the ornamental motives for their patronage of such clients.

Into this setting a new element had been interjected during the sixteenth century. The more extensive and rigorous use of mathematical methods formed an important aspect of the work of the new breed of natural philosophers.[10] But, one surely unintended side effect of this intellectual advance was to render the basis of the mathematically sophisticated savants' claims and reputations less immediately accessible for evaluation by the elites in whose service they wished to be employed. The difficulties thereby posed by the asymmetric distribution of information were rather unprecedented, not having been encountered to the same degree in the patronage of intellectuals and artists who followed other, less esoteric callings. The new breed of scientists, however, claimed to specialize in revealing the unfamiliar. Opportunities for charlatanry here were more rife, and so were the risks of embarrassment for the patron, should it turn out that one had sponsored a fraud—or much worse, a heretic. Thus, even where the services of the mathematically trained intelligentsia might be sought for essentially practical, utilitarian motives (such talents being useful in designing machinery for public spectacles, surveying and cartography, ballistics, and correct use of perspective in pictorial arts), the soundness of the candidates' qualifications had become more problematic and far from inconsequential.

In other words, this line of argument directs attention to the emergence of especially compelling reasons for noble patrons in the late Renaissance to delegate part of the responsibility for evaluating and selecting among the new breed of savants, devolving those functions upon the increasingly formalized communities of their fellow practitioners and correspondents. Except for those few who were themselves versed in mathematics or other experimental practices associated with the new learning, patrons were inclined to refrain from passing personal judgement on scientific assertions and involving themselves in substantive controversies (see Biagioli 1993). It was left to the initiative of the parties dependent upon such patronage to organize the production of credible testimonials to their own credibility and scientific status.

Paul A. David

Not altogether surprisingly, therefore, the mid-sixteenth century, which is frequently taken as the beginning of the era of modern mathematics, also witnessed the formation of active networks of correspondence among Europe's adepts in algebra, announcing newly devised techniques and results; this era initiated the modern tradition of publicly posing mathematical puzzles, issuing scientific challenges, announcing prizes for the solutions of problems, and the holding of open competitions to test the claims of rival experts in the mathematical arts (see e.g., Feingold 1984; Boyer 1985, esp., 310–312; Keller 1985). On the interpretation proposed here, the new practices of disclosure constituted a functional response to heightened asymmetric information problems that the mathematization of natural philosophy and the practical arts posed for the Renaissance system of court-patronage.

Rival Principals and Common Agency Contracting—The Legacy of European Feudalism

The conditions I have sketched regarding the late Renaissance and early modern system of court-patronage present a situation economists would describe as "common agency contracting" involving the competition among incompletely informed principals for the dedicated services of multiple agents. This correspondence suggests several noteworthy points about the economic organization of scientific activities in Europe during the late sixteenth and early seventeenth centuries.

First, since what the scientist-clients had to offer was novelty, at any point in time the welfare of several patrons could not be jointly advanced in the same degree. As a consequence of the dominance in the early history of modern science of patrons who were concerned with the ornamental rather than the utilitarian value of scientist-philosophers, the services a client provided to his several patrons were essentially "substitutes" rather than "complementary" commodities.

Second, in the majority of cases the material rewards offered to clients by any single patron were not sufficiently large and certain to free the former from the quest for multiple patrons. The situation typically being that of common agency, we may draw on Avinash Dixit's (1996) recent theoretical exposition to point out that in the absence of full information, and concerted action on the part of principals, the nature of the incentive contracts offered by the latter would reflect their awareness of the possibility that an agent/client could use the means provided by one patron to serve the ends of another. The resulting Nash equilibrium in the game among rival principals would then be a set of patronage-contracts that offered clients comparatively weak material incentives to devote their efforts exclusively to the service of any one patron. Such an equilibrium outcome, of course, would be consistent with the necessity of seeking to serve a number of patrons concurrently (however arduous and demeaning a scientist such as Galileo might feel that to be); it would thereby reinforce the choice on the part of would-be clients of research and publication strategies that would lead toward widening the circle of their repute.

Third, as has been shown by Lars Stole's (1990) analysis of mechanism design under common agency contracting, the equilibrium outcome in the case of "contract substitutes" is in general more favorable to the agent than is the case when the services performed for different principals are complements. In effect, the competition among patrons to command the faithful attention of an agent/client would lead to contracts that allowed the latter to retain more "rents" from the specialized information he possessed. This provided greater rewards for scientific activities than would have resulted otherwise, were there only a single possible patron on the scene, or had the patrons predominantly enjoyed positive externalities from others' support of the agent's efforts—the characteristic situation where there are significant "spillovers" of utilitarian benefits from new knowledge.

There is in the story related here an historical irony well worth remarking upon, especially as it serves also to underscore the tenacity of the past's hold on the incrementally evolving institutions that channel the course of economic change.[11] The nub of it is simply this: an essentially precapitalist, European aristocratic disposition to award patronage for the purposes of enhancing rulers' political powers symbolically (through displays of magnificence), came to confer value upon those who pursued knowledge by following the "new science" in the late sixteenth and seventeenth centuries. The norms of cooperation and information disclosure within the community of scientists, and their institutionalization through the activities of formal scientific organizations, emerged—at least in part—as a response to the informational requirements of a system of patronage in which the competition among noble patrons for prestigious clients was crucial.

Those rivalries, in turn, were a legacy of Western European feudalism: it was the fragmentation of political authority that had created the conditions of "common agency contracting in substitutes." An instructive contrast therefore might be drawn with the alternative circumstances of a monolithic political system, such as had prevailed elsewhere—as in the Heavenly Empire of China during an earlier epoch, to cite a well-known case of a society that clearly possessed the intellectual talents yet failed spectacularly to institutionalize the practice of open science.

Sequelae: Open Science in the "New Age of Academies"

The foregoing necessarily brief treatment of immensely complex matters has focused upon the economic aspects of patronage in the production of knowledge, and the influence of the latter upon the historical formation of key elements in the ethos and organizational structure of open science. Those developments preceded and laid the foundations for the later seventeenth- and eighteenth-century institutionalization of the open pursuit of scientific knowledge under the auspices of State-sponsored academies. The Royal Society of London was founded in 1660 and received charters from Charles II in 1662 and 1663, and within another few years, in 1666, the Académie Royale des Sciences was created on the initiative of Jean-Baptiste, Colbert, the French minister of finance under King Louis XIV. The activities of these two State foundations, and the ensuing formal institutional reorganization of science in Europe that they inspired, have received much attention from more than one generation of historians of science.[12] Although from some perspectives this concentration of scholarly focus might be judged inordinate, it may also be justified by the fact that another seventy officially recognized scientific organizations have been identified by McClellan (1985) as having been established between the 1660s and 1793, specifically on the models provided by those archetypal institutions.

Just as I have argued in the foregoing text that the intellectual reorientation represented by the scientific revolution cannot be held to have been a motor cause of the emergence of the open mode of searching for Nature's Secrets, so there are good grounds in the work of other scholars for resisting the interpretation of the "new Age of Academies" as constituting a radical organizational departure. Furthermore, there is reason also to contest the view that the so-called "New Age of Academies" had been called forth by the enlarged scale and costs of the new modes of scientific inquiry, and the supposed failures of private patronage in the mid-seventeenth century.[13]

The post-1660s phase in the evolution of the institutions of modern science is better viewed essentially as the continuation of a much broader cultural movement that had been taking place in Europe outside the medieval universities. One aspect of this movement manifested itself in the appearance, around the turn of the sixteenth century, of numerous privately patronized scientific societies and academies. Seventeenth-century science proper thus has been found to have played only a very minor part of that wider intellectual reorganization: of the 2,500 learned societies that are known to have been instituted in Europe between 1500 and 1800, at least 700 were formed during the sixteenth century alone. Although some among these organizations were scientific in purpose, they were not in the pre-1550 vanguard; according to McClellan (1985), the overwhelming majority were formed in response to interests broader than anything resembling the organized pursuit of science.

The following passage from the work of David Lux (1991) serves well to articulate the present state of understanding about the nature of the causal relationships in this complicated sequence of developments:

[T]he traditional points of departure for discussing organizational change in science—della Porta's *Academia Secretorum Naturae* [founded in Naples, 1589] or Cesi's Accademia dei Lincei [founded in Rome, 1604]—offer nothing to suggest the intellectual novelties of sixteenth-century science produced real organizational change. . . . Rather than producing organizational change, sixteenth- and seventeenth-century science followed other intellectual activity into new organizational forms. Indeed, in strictly organizational terms there is no obvious justification for attempting to isolate science from other forms of intellectual activity before the end of the seventeenth century. Nor is there any obvious justification for portraying science as honing the cutting edge of organizational change. Despite the literature's claims about novel science creating needs for new organizational forms, the institutional history of science across the sixteenth and seventeenth centuries actually speaks to a record in which scientific practice changed only after moving into new organizational forms. (pp. 189, 196)

Thus, the institutional context provided by the early academies had readily accommodated the needs for "social legitimization" and, for theatres for disclosures where patronage-seeking practitioners of the new natural philosophy might enhance their public repute. Subsequently, the institutionalization of the nascent open science mode of organization was carried forward upon an elevated stage under the aegis of the early modern state, where it mobilized augmented resources and applied the new methods of scientific inquiry on a scale that eventually altered the character of scientific practice.

In a still later era, beginning midway through the nineteenth century with the introduction of modern scientific research into the German state-sponsored universities, mimetic interinstitutional competition created a new set of academic market conditions that proved propitious for the establishment of research scientists, and graduate research seminars within the ambit of the university. In this new setting, the fundamental problems of reputation and agency—upon which the foregoing economic analysis has been focused—soon reemerged in different, but nonetheless recognizable forms.[14] Even today, university patrons, both private and public, along with academic administrators, and members of the professoriate find themselves confronted by informational asymmetries, agency problems, and reputational reward mechanisms that parallel in many respects those that once had characterized the system of European court patronage.

Some things change, however. As the ornamental value of supporting esteemed scholars and scientists has given way to the instrumental power of scientific knowledge, the ability of individual members of "the Republic of Science" to extract a large part of the "information rents" has been circumscribed. Correspondingly, there has been an enlargement of the relative share of the benefits that flow—in the form of knowledge spillovers—to the ultimate patrons of the publicly supported regime of open science. Yet, some continuities are preserved: in the modern system of devolved patronage of science, those having the responsibility for the management of academic institutions and nonprofit research institutes appear simultaneously in the roles of agents vis-à-vis the public, and principals vis-à-vis the research agents upon whose expertise they must rely. In their dual capacities the administrators of academic institutions (and the individuals who staff them) must continue to seek effective ways of mediating conflicts between the divergent interests of the principals and their respective agents. On the one hand, they are enjoined to seek the larger societal, public goals that are best served by preserving the organizational modes and norms open scientific inquiry; while, on the other hand, they are being encouraged to try to appropriate a larger portion of the "information rents" for use in more narrowly parochial institutional and private undertakings—even when to do so entails circumscribing open access to the new knowledge gained from the research conducted under their auspices.

Conclusion

The moral of all this goes further than merely providing another attestation to the truth in the aphorism that the more things seem to change, the more they stay the same. Some important part of the power of modern science today derives from the radical social innovation that the open science regime constituted. A corollary proposition, to which the historical experience recounted here also lends support, is that the methods of modern science themselves have not been, and still are not, sufficient to create the unique cultural ethos associated with the Republic of Science. Nor can they be expected to automatically induce and sustain the peculiar institutional infrastructures and organizational conditions of the open science regime, within which their application has proved so conducive to the rapid growth of the stock of reliable public knowledge, and all that flows therefrom.

Rather than emerging and surviving as robust epiphenomena of a new organum of intellectual inquiry, the institutions of open science are independent, and in some measure fortuitous social and political constructs. They are in reality intricate cultural legacies of a long-past epoch of European history, which through them continues to profoundly influence the systemic efficacy of the modern scientific research process.

Major features of the institutional infrastructure of public science, thus being to a considerable degree exogenous to actual scientific practice in the contemporary world, can be subjected to substantial amounts of experimental tinkering, and even major redesign, without jeopardizing the methodology of current inquiry. In one sense, the freedom this affords the manipulation of institutional incentives and constraints, as instruments of modern science and technology policy, can be read as "the good news."

It should be taken with a grave caution, however: wise policymaking in this sensitive area must pay special heed to those organizational instruments' own complex and contingent histories, and so respect the potential fragility of the institutional matrix within which modern science evolved and flourished. Along with a sense of awe and gratitude for the good fortune of having received this remarkable gift from the past, we shall do well to maintain a sobering awareness of the extent to which our future welfare has come to depend upon the continued smooth workings of an intricate and imperfectly understood piece of social machinery—one that need have no adequate capabilities for self-repair, but readily may be damaged by careless interventions.

Paul A. David

Acknowledgments

An earlier version of this paper was presented to the University of Sienna workshop, "Science as an Institution and the Institutions of Science," held at the Certosa di Pontignano (nr. Sienna), Italy January, 25–26, 2002. The author is grateful for the comments received on that occasion from Fabio Pammoli, the workshop's organizer, and from other participants, especially Richard Nelson and Keith Pavitt. Many other intellectual debts that were incurred in the course of research on the larger corpus of work upon which this study draws are acknowledged in David (2000).

Notes

1. See Boesman (1997), Koizumi (1997), and Mowery and Zredonis (1998).

2. On the Bush Report, the recurring issues in U.S. science policy debates, and the prelude to the recent discussions, see, e.g., David (1996), Boesman (1997), and references therein.

3. For entry points to the vast literature, see e.g., David, Mowery, and Steinmueller (1994) on university-industry R&D collaborations; Guston and Keniston (1994) on university relations with the federal government; Branscomb (1994) and Cohen and Noll (1994) on the National Labs.

4. Within the past decade the situation has begun to change. See Dasgupta and David (1987, 1988, 1994), David (1994), and the more recent surveys by Diamond (1996), Stephan (1996), and David, Foray, and Steinmueller (1997).

5. See, for a recent effort to bring this historical experience to the attention of economists, the special session in the American Economic Assocation *Proceedings* on "Clio and the Economic Organization of Science" (May 1998), which included brief, chronologically ordered contributions by David (1998), Lenoir (1998), Lécuyer (1998), and Blumenthal (1998).

6. This study draws upon David (2000), which should be consulted for fuller historical documentation and references to the relevant literature. Space there also permits proper acknowledgement of the help of Avner Greif, Mario Biagioli, Partha Dasgupta, Weston Headley, Scott Mandelbrote, Joel Mokyr, Noel Swerdlow, and many other colleagues, institutions and foundations who generously contributed both intellectually

and materially in support of my researches in the area since 1991. The present essay has benefited from the comments and suggestions by Kenneth Flamm, Zvi Griliches, and David Mowery, which could not be accomodated within David 1998—the very abridged version read at the January 1998 AEA Meetings in Chicago, and published shortly thereafter in the *AEA Proceedings*.

7. From the fourteenth century to the early eighteenth century in Europe, the issuance of "letters patent" and granting of royal "privileges" conferring monopoly rights in exchange for the disclosure of technological information was aimed primarily at effecting the transfer and application of existing industrial arts and engineering practices, i.e., techniques already known to master-craftsmen and engineers in other territories, not at inducing fresh inventive activity. Many early patent monopolies were, in effect, local franchises designed to shelter immigrating expert-practitioners from the subsequent competition of the apprentices and journeymen they were expected to train, or others who would try imitate them once their particular "mysterie" had been successfully established in the new cities and principalities to which they were recruited. See David and Olsen (1992), David (1993a), and sources cited therein.

8. Galileo's involvement in the system of court patronage in Italy, and his communications during 1610 with Kepler, then in the service of Emperor Rudolph II in Prague, is documented by Biagioli (1993), and further considered in David (2000, 32–36). The situations of many other notable scientific figures elsewhere in Europe also can be mentioned, e.g., as by Mokyr (1990, p. 73 on Leibnitz; p. 84 on Torriceli; p. 169 on Borelli.) See also the extensive discussions in Moran (1991) on the patronage of science and medicine in the court of Prince Henry of Wales (d.1612) at Richmond Palace, the Court of Rudolph II and the Habsburg circle in the mid-seventeenth century, the Munich Court of Ferdinand Maria, the Elector of Bavaria (r. 1654–1679), and elsewhere in Europe.

9. Galileo understood this well, as was evident from the adroit way in which he exploited his ability to prepare superior telescopes for the Grand Duke of Tuscany, Cosimo II de' Medici: he urged his patron to present these to other crowned heads in Europe, whereby they, too, might observe the newfound moons of Jupiter which the *Sidereus Nuncius* (March 1610) had proclaimed to be "the Medicean stars." See Drake (1957, 1978), Westfall (1985), and Biagioli (1990, 1993, Ch. 1).

10. Following the fusion of Arabic and classical mathematics, the significance of algebra, the geometry of conic sections, trigonometry, and still more esoteric developments was recognized and openly proclaimed in terms that drew upon a rhetorical tradition reaching back to the great Renaissance mathematician "Regiomontanus"—

as Johannes Muller of Konigsberg (1432–1476) styled himself. See Swerdlow (1993), Boyer (1985, Ch. XV) on Renaissance mathematics; Keller (1985) on the program and rhetorical developed on behalf of mathematical training during the 1570s and 1580s; Feingold (1984, Ch. IV), Westfall (1985), and Biagioli (1989, 1990, 1993) on the patronage of mathematicians.

11. On the theme of "path dependence" in the dynamics of economic systems, see, e.g., David (1988, 1993b, 1994, 2001).

12. See, e.g., Brown (1934/67), Orenstein (1963), Hahn (1971), Hunter (1981), and McClellan (1985).

13. See, e.g., Lux (1991) for discussion and references to the relevant literature.

14. See, e.g., Ben-David (1991, Ch. 8); Lenoir (1998) and references cited therein.

References

Arrow, Kenneth J. 1962. Economic Welfare and the Allocation of Resources for Inventions. In Richard R. Nelson (ed.), *The rate and direction of inventive activity: Economic and social factors.* Princeton, NJ: Princeton University Press.

Ben-David, Joseph. 1991. *Scientific growth: Essays on the social organization and ethos of science.* (Edited with an Introduction by Gad Freidenthal). Berkeley, CA: University of California Press.

Biagioli, Mario. 1989. The social status of Italian mathematicians. *History of Science* 27: 41–95.

———. 1990. Galileo's system of patronage. *History of Science* 28: 1–62.

———. 1993. *Galileo, courtier: The practice of science in the culture of absolutism.* Chicago: University of Chicago Press.

Blumenthal, Marjorie S. 1998. Federal government initiatives and the foundations of the information technology revolution: Lessons from history. *American Economic Review* 88(2): 34–39.

Boesman, William C. 1997. *Analysis of ten selected science and technology policy studies* [Library of Congress Number 97–836 SPR]. Washington, DC: Congressional Research Service.

Boorstin, Daniel J. 1984. *The discoverers: A history of man's search to know his world and himself*. New York: Random House.

Boyer, Cart B. 1985. *A history of mathematics*. Princeton, NJ: Princeton University Press.

Branscomb, Lewis M., ed. 1994. *Empowering technology: Implementing a U.S. strategy*. Cambridge, MA: MIT Press.

Brown, Harcourt. 1934/1967. *Scientific organization in seventeenth century France (1620–1680)*. New York: Russell and Russell.

Cohen, Linda R., and Roger Noll. 1994. Privatizing public research. *Scientific American* 271(3): 72–77.

Dasgupta, Partha, and Paul A. David. 1987. Information disclosure and the economics of science and technology. In George R. Feiwel (ed.), *Arrow and the ascent of modern economic theory*. New York: New York University Press.

―――. 1994. Toward a new economics of science. *Research Policy* 23: 487–521.

David, Paul A. 1988. Path-Dependence: Putting the past into the future of economics. Institute for Mathematical Studies in the Social Sciences (Stanford University, Stanford, CA) Technical Report No. 533.

―――. 1993a. Intellectual property institutions and the Panda's Thumb: Patents, copyrights and trade secrets in economic theory and history. In Mitchel B. Wallerstein, Mary Ellen Mogee, and Roberta A. Schoen (eds.), *Global dimensions of intellectual property protection in science and technology*. Washington, DC: National Academies Press.

―――. 1993b. Path-Dependence and predictability in dynamic systems with local network externalities: A paradigm for historical economics. In Dominique Foray and Christopher Freeman (eds.), *Technology and the wealth of nations: The dynamics of constructed advantage*. London: OECD and Pinter Publishers.

————. 1994. Positive feedbacks and research productivity in science: Reopening another black box. In Ove Grandstrand (ed.), *Technology and economics*. Amsterdam: Elsevier Scientific Publishers.

————. 1996. Science reorganized? Post-modern visions of research and the curse of success. *Proceedings of the 2nd International Symposium on Research Funding*. Ottawa: National Sciences and Engineering Research Council.

————. 1998. Common agency contracting and the emergence of open science institutions. *American Economic Review* (Papers and Proceedings) 88(2): 18–21.

————. 2000. Patronage, reputation and common agency contracting in the scientific revolution. Unpublished Working Paper, Stanford Economics Department Working Paper (March). Available at <http://www-econ.stanford.edu/faculty/workp/swp00025.html>.

————. 2001. Path dependence, its critics and the quest for historical economics. In Pierre Garrouste and Stavros Ioannidis (eds.), *Evolution and path dependence in economic ideas: Past and present*. Cheltenham, Glos.: Edward Elgar.

————. 2003. The economic logic of "open science" and the balance between private property rights and the public domain in scientific data and information: A primer. In J. M. Esanu and P. F. Uhlir (eds.), *The role of scientific and technical data in information in the public domain: Proceedings of a symposium*. Washington, DC: The National Academies Press. Available at <http://www.nap.edu>.

David, Paul A., Dominique Foray, and W. Edward Steinmueller. 1999. The research network and the new economics of science: From metaphors to organizational behaviors. In Alfonso Gambardella and Franco Malerba (eds.), *The organization of innovative activities in Europe*. Cambridge: Cambridge University.

David, Paul A., David C. Mowery, and W. Edward Steinmueller. 1994. University-industry research collaborations: Managing missions in conflict. Center for Economic Policy Research (Stanford University, Stanford, CA) Conference Paper, March 1994. (Reprint available from SIEPR, Stanford University—contact D. Baldwin at <http://siepr.stanford.edu>).

David, Paul A., and Trond E. Olsen. 1992. Technology adoption, learning spillovers and the optimal duration of patent-based monopolies. *International Journal of Industrial Organization* 10: 517–543.

Diamond, Arthur M., Jr. 1996. The economics of science. *Knowledge and Policy*, 9(2/3): 6–49.

Dixit, Avinash. 1996. *The making of economic policy: A transaction coast politics perspective.* Cambridge, MA: MIT Press.

Dobbs, Betty J.T. 1975. *The foundations of Newton's Alchemy, or "The Hunting of the Greene Lyon".* Cambridge: Cambridge University Press.

Drake, Stillman, ed. 1957. *Discoveries and opinions of Galileo.* Garden City, NJ: Doubleday.

———. 1978. *Galileo at work.* Chicago: University of Chicago Press.

Eamon, William. 1985. From the secrets of nature to public knowledge: The origins of the concept of openness in science. *Minerva* 23(3): 321–347.

———. 1994. *Science and the secrets of nature: Books of secrets in medieval and early modern science.* Princeton, NJ: Princeton University Press.

Feingold, M. 1984. *The mathematicians' apprenticeship: Science, universities and society in England, 1560–1640.* Cambridge: Cambridge University Press.

Guston, David H., and Kenneth Keniston. 1994. *The fragile contract: University science and the federal government.* Cambridge, MA: MIT Press.

Hahn, Roger. 1971. *The anatomy of a scientific institution: The Paris Academy of Sciences, 1666–1803.* Berkeley: University of California Press.

Hunter, Michael. 1981. *Science and society in restoration England.* Cambridge: Cambridge University Press.

Keller, Anno C. 1985. Mathematics, mechanics and the origins of the culture of mechanical invention. *Minerva* 23(3): 348–361.

Koizumi, Kei. 1997. R&D trends and special analyses. In *Intersociety working group, AAAS Report XXII: Research and development, FY 1998.* Washington, DC: American Association for the Advancement of Science.

Lécuyer, Christophe. 1998. Academic science and technology in the service of industry: MIT creates a "permeable" engineering school. *American Economic Review* (Papers and Proceedings), 88(2): 28–33.

Leff, Gordon. 1968. *Paris and Oxford Universities in the thirteenth and fourteenth centuries: An institutional and intellectual history*. New York: John Wiley & Sons.

Lenoir, Timothy. 1998. State-building and the nineteenth century reorganization of scientific activities in Germany: From research in the universities to the Kaiser-Wilhem-Gesellschaft. *American Economic Review* (Papers and Proceedings), 88(2): 22–27.

Lux, David S. 1991. The reorganization of Science 1450–1700. In Bruce T. Moran, (ed.), *Patronage and institutions: Science, technology and medicine at the European Court, 1500–1750*. Woodbridge, Suffolk: Boydell Press.

McClellan, James E., III. 1985. *Science reorganized: Scientific societies in the eighteenth century*. New York: Columbia University Press.

Merton, Robert K. 1973. *The sociology of science: Theoretical and empirical investigations*. Norman W. Storer, ed. Chicago: University of Chicago Press.

————. 1996. *On social structure and science*. Piotr Sztompka (ed.). Chicago: University of Chicago Press.

Mokyr, Joel. 1990. *The lever of riches: Technological creativity and economic progress*. New York: Oxford University Press.

Moran, Bruce T., ed. 1991. *Patronage and institutions: Science, technology, and medicine at the European Court, 1500–1750*. Woodbridge, Suffolk: Boydell Press.

Mowery, David C., and Arvids Ziedonis. 1998. Market failure or market magic? National innovation systems and the transfer of technology. *Science Technology Industry Review* 22: 101–136.

Nelson, Richard R. 1959. The simple economics of basic scientific research. *Journal of Political Economy* 67: 297–306.

North, Douglass C. 1990. *Institutions, institutional change and economic performance*. Cambridge: Cambridge University Press.

Orenstein, Martha. 1963. *The role of scientific societies in the seventeenth century*. London: Archon Books.

Rosenberg, Nathan. 1982. *Inside the Black Box: Technology and economics*. New York: Cambridge University Press.

Stephan, Paula. 1996. The economics of Science. *Journal of Economic Literature* 34(3): 1199–1235.

Stole, Lars. 1990. Mechanism design under common agency. Working Paper, MIT Department of Economics.

Strong, Roy. 1984. *Art and power*. Woodbridge, Suffolk: Boydell Press.

Swerdlow, Noel. 1993. Science and humanism in the Renaissance: Regiomontanus's oration on the dignity and utility of the mathematical sciences. In Paul Horwich (ed.), *World changes: Thomas Kuhn and the nature of Science*. Cambridge, MA: MIT Press.

Thorndike, Lynn, Jr. 1950. *History of magic and experimental science*. 2nd ed. New York: Columbia University Press. vol. 2.

Vickers, Brian, ed. 1984. *Occult and scientific mentalities in the Renaissance*. Cambridge: Cambridge University Press.

Webster, Charles, ed. 1970. *Samuel Hartlib and the advancement of learning*. Cambridge: Cambridge University Press.

Westfall, Richard S. 1980. *Never At rest: A biography of Isaac Newton*. Cambridge: Cambridge University Press.

———. 1985. Science and patronage: Galileo and the telescope. *Isis* 76: 11–30.

Ziman, John. 1994. *Prometheus bound: Science in a dynamic steady state*. Cambridge: Cambridge University Press.

II

Mechanisms for Collaboration

One of the principles that connect the diverse legal constructions lumped together as "intellectual property" is that those who create a work should benefit from it, if not exclusively, then at least predominantly. Such semi-exclusive benefit extends, but is not limited, to any profit that can be derived from the created work. When a work originates in not one but many creators who have contributed, deliberately or implicitly, to a combined work, these benefits are guaranteed to the creators only if they are collectively identified as the work's legal "owners."

Often, especially when a work draws on implicit collaboration, from a collective or "public domain" body of ideas, such collective identification is not possible. It is then up to legal or social constructions to determine how, if at all, the benefits from exploiting a work can be shared among all those who contributed.

One legal construction to ensure that benefits are shared among all contributors is "copyleft," reciprocal licensing schemes such as the General Public License (GPL). Most benefit sharing occurs through social standards or ethical motives—the urge in those who benefit from the efforts of a broadly defined community to "give back." This is a motive for many free software developers. Colin Needham, one of the creators of the very successful database, <imdb.com>—the Internet Movies Database (IMDb), the single biggest source of information on movies online—started it as a free collaborative project "just to put something back into the Internet community in one small way," contributing his programming skills to the community that provided him and others with a regular source of movie reviews.[1] The dozens of companies investing large sums of money in contributing to open source software communities have many sound business motives for doing so, but giving back to the community of independent software developers who create software for which the companies sell support is a very important one.

Cori Hayden discusses benefit sharing in the pharmaceutical industry, where the distance between those who implicitly contribute (native communities, individuals suffering from particular genetic conditions) and the large firms that commercially exploit the resulting drugs is greater, geographically, socially and economically, than in software. This is especially true in "bioprospecting"—the identification of potential commercial uses for plants and other materials based on their traditional use in local communities. While it may be in the (shortsighted) commercial interest of the pharmaceutical industry not to share benefits with the communities that originate and preserve knowledge without which it may be impossible to locate and identify subjects for new or commercial use, it is increasingly in their political interest to do so. Hayden describes the evolving global environment in which benefit sharing plays an increasingly important role, and the politics and ethics surrounding conflicting visions of intellectual property, from Trade-Related Aspects of Intellectual Property Rights (TRIPS) to the UN Convention on Biological Diversity.

Free collaboration and implicit relationships are all very well; how can they be studied in a structured way? Priced markets involving transactions of clearly demarcated, individually owned "property" certainly help answering the broad question of identifying *who* is doing *how much* of *what* with *whom*. This is much harder with collaborative production, especially when it is informal.

Christopher Kelty addresses head-on the worrying issues of identity, the collaborating "who" that we must understand. Without trust and security, collaboration—or any sort of interaction—across the large distances of the Internet is quite hard, if not impossible. Our conception of identity is dependent on the technology that mediates between social interaction, and defines the framework or "format" of collaboration that is possible. Kelty examines how technologies of authentication and anonymity affect the role of trust and identity in the social networks of today.

My own contribution and that of Yochai Benkler provide models by which new forms of online collaboration can be studied and explained and—important from an economic point of view—even measured. Since such creativity is typically unhindered by formalized monetary transactions, alternative methods of measuring how much, and what, is going on are crucial to a deeper understanding of the economic and social impact online collaboration will have.

My chapter describes how, even without clearly identified one-to-one transactions, which informal collaboration eschews, one can model participants in collaborative creation as working on balancing their *value-flows*. Self-interested people can continue contributing to a pool of creativity as long as they draw more from it in one way or another than they put in, allowing an analysis based on the "rational actors" favoured by economists. The benefits individuals draw from the common pool differ from person to person, but as long as the aggregate benefits are greater than aggregate costs of contribution, for each individual, it makes "rational, self-interested" sense to contribute.

As Yochai Benkler describes in much detail in this condensed version of a paper previously published in the *Yale Law Journal*, the Internet has made possible a system of collaborative production that can be sustained *regardless* of the motives of individual contributors. They may or may not be "rational" in a conventional sense, whether monetary or otherwise. But as long as *some* motive causes each individual to contribute, and technology allows the integration of very small contributions seamlessly into a larger combined work, this form of "peer production" is sustainable. Indeed, it may be more efficient than markets based on one-to-one transactions as they limit the scope of the collaborations that may be possible.

The final paper in this section, by Tim Hubbard and James Love, also has an economic approach to a real social problem—how to fund creativity, research, and development. In the various domains examined by this paper, from music publishing to medicine, knowledge goods that have significant public social value are strongly protected as intellectual property with increasingly Draconian enforcement. This protection is supposedly to ensure a monopoly stream of profits, which is the only way to fund the creation of this knowledge. But it results in a vicious circle where it inhibits collaboration between creators, thus driving up the costs of (necessarily duplicated) creativity, driving up the minimum level of investment required and thus further driving up the level of Intellectual Property Rights (IPR) protection demanded. This is especially and glaringly harmful in the field of medicine, where IPRs pose a clear threat to public health, and where abolishing them outright would simply dry up R&D funding. Hubbard and Love propose as a solution an alternative method of funding creativity where the funding is as collaborative as the ownership of the created works.

Note

1. Rishab A. Ghosh, "Cooking Pot Markets: An Economic Model for the Trade in Free Goods and Services on the Internet." *First Monday*, 3, no. 3 (1998). <http://www.firstmonday.org/issues/issue3_3/ghosh/index.html>.

8

Benefit-Sharing: Experiments in Governance

Cori Hayden

An Incitement to Share

The idea of benefit sharing has, over the past fifteen years, taken hold in several prominent arenas of research and development, from pharmaceutical, oil, and mineral prospecting to human genetic research. Broadly, the idea refers to a commitment to channel some kind of returns—whether monetary or non-monetary—back to a range of designated participants: affected communities, source communities or source nations, participants in clinical trials, genetic disease patient groups. Derived from stakeholder theory and postneoliberal attempts to harness market-based activity and intellectual property to social and environmental ends, benefit sharing is often framed simultaneously as a matter of justice, as a proxy for (or a swerve around) property rights, and as a nonmarket tool for both encouraging and redistributing value production.

The politics, ethics, and practice of benefit sharing have been elaborated most thoroughly (though not to particularly straightforward effect) in the realm of bioprospecting—the use of plants, microbes, insects, and (sometimes) traditional knowledge as leads for new pharmaceutical, agricultural, and biotechnological products. Here, the promise of equitable returns to source communities and source nations was institutionalized as a multilateral principle for the sustainable management of biodiversity in the 1992 UN Convention on Biological Diversity (CBD). In this arena, and increasingly in others, a broad commitment to benefit sharing is installed in and through a number of mechanisms. Licensing agreements and royalty-sharing contracts feature alongside academic research protocols, ethical guidelines for good practice, multilateral mandates, and government regulation and legislation.

At stake in ongoing experiments with this redistributive idiom is, in part, an as-yet unanswered question: what kind of entitlement *is* benefit sharing? What and who can guarantee it? In what idiom and with what mechanisms—ethics, legal rights, trade, contract—shall it be rendered in practice? One way to look for an answer to the question of what benefit sharing is, is to think about what it is not. In this vein, it may be productive to trace, in a few different registers, the relation between intellectual property and benefit sharing.

In many arenas, and certainly where biologicals are concerned, benefit sharing relies on but should not be confused with intellectual property rights per se. Indeed the relationship between an ethic and politics of benefit sharing and intellectual property is complex and under constant renegotiation. This chapter sketches out some dimensions of that relationship, with a pointed question in mind: what might the recent proliferation of benefit sharing suggest about the stability and legitimacy of intellectual property itself as a regime of governance?

International Frameworks, Competing Sovereignties

The 1992 UN Convention on Biological Diversity, ratified by all member nations except the United States, set forth a multilateral framework for harnessing the biotechnological, agricultural, and pharmaceutical value of biodiversity, and ensuring that some of the benefits of such industrial exploitation would come back to source nations (Articles 15 and 16) and source communities (Article 8j) in the South, in the form of equitable returns (e.g., royalty sharing, technology transfer, scientific capacity-building). This novel benefit sharing provision has been framed in different ways, with invocations of its importance for sustainable development and global biodiversity conservation sitting, sometimes uneasily, alongside equally strong invocations of the need for social or redistributive justice, across North-South lines. In either case, the idea has not been universally well-received; the U.S. government, most notably, has steadfastly registered its opposition to the benefit sharing provisions on the grounds that they are not in the interest of the U.S. biotechnology and pharmaceutical industries.

U.S. trade representatives' objections notwithstanding, the processes set in motion under the rubric of the CBD continue to generate discussions on benefit sharing as a central feature of new definitions of good practice in pharmaceutical- and biotech-related research and development. Questions of what constitutes a benefit, who might be defined as a benefit recipient, and on what basis, reverberate powerfully in research practice, international law, and community development initiatives. Following ten years of practical experiments in bioprospecting worldwide, the 2001 Bonn Guidelines (drafted in conjunction with the CBD Conference of Parties of that year) elaborated in unprecedented detail a series of recommended principles and practices for benefit sharing. The guidelines highlight, among other things, the importance of indigenous claims, whether in a context of existing legal rights or through a strong commitment to prior informed consent. They also encourage novel uses of Intellectual Property (IP), such as joint ownership, or the use of IP-related instruments such as certificates of origin, documenting the source of biological material and traditional knowledge in any derivative patent applications (the United States, Canada, and Australia remain opposed to this move).

The benefit sharing principles instantiated in the CBD and the Bonn Guidelines rest, formatively, on a nationalization of wild genetic resources and cultural knowledge; that is, the CBD took these things out of the global commons and renamed them as national sovereignty. Signatory nations are thus entitled to set the terms for corporate access to their resources through national legislation, provided that they ensure that access not be unreasonably restricted. (That hedging indeed works as a textbook definition of sovereignty, which, the *Oxford Dictionary of Politics* reminds us, should not be confused with total freedom of action; sovereignty is, rather, "freedom of decision-making within often highly constrained circumstances"). And certainly, as legal scholar Keith Aoki reminds us, invocations of nations' sovereignty vis-à-vis an international order are always, foundationally, wrapped up in the question of nations' sovereignty over the subjects/citizens contained within their jurisdiction (Aoki 1996). The CBD has unleashed some consequential negotiations on both fronts, sparking conflicts over the relationship between national rights and the trade and IP obligations required by the World Trade Organization and the Trade-Related Aspects of Intellectual Property Rights (TRIPS) agreement, and the relationship between national claims and those of indigenous and other communities living within their borders. These axes of conflict are intertwined, but let me discuss them in turn for the moment.

First, international IP and trade. The U.S. government and various industry representatives have argued relentlessly that the CBD, and subsequent elaborations of its benefit-sharing mandate, contravenes trade liberalization policies required by the WTO and the TRIPS Agreement. Certainly, it is not hard to identify differences between the CBD and TRIPS, as Susan Sell among others has noted (Sell 2003). Stated bluntly, TRIPS promotes private intellectual property ownership—here, corporate drug patents—as the form of rights that shall, except in public health emergencies, trump all other claims; the CBD provides a very different model that places emphasis on the interests of parties that might be understood as both resource providers *and* potential consumers or importers of resulting patented products.[1] Policymakers in many signatory nations to the CBD (including Mexico) have lamented the fact that they are being asked to choose, by the United States and others, between the CBD and TRIPS, and that the costs of contravening a trade agreement backed by the United States are quite high; the CBD does not carry the same enforcement power. The developing country argument, advanced by India, a coalition of African nations, and some Latin American countries, among others, has been that the CBD should take precedence.

Second, community rights. Article 8j of the CBD states that, when genetic resources are collected in lands pertaining to indigenous peoples, community consent must be sought, and benefit-sharing requirements negotiated. Again, this conceivably sets the CBD at odds with TRIPS (in part because it opens the door to recognizing collective claims, where TRIPS favors individual property rights). But it also threatens to set the CBD at odds with itself, insofar as it effectively sets up two unequal yet competing sets of claimants: nations, which have sovereignty, and communities, whose knowledge (more particularly, that which is deemed relevant to the conservation of biodiversity) must be respected and maintained. Those are of course very different idioms of entitlement. In this sense, the CBD has refueled longstanding struggles between indigenous groups and nation-states—these are relations that anthropologist and lawyer Rosemary Coombe aptly characterizes as often marked by distrust, betrayal, and violence (Coombe 2003, 286). This is certainly the case in Latin America, where nation-state and indigenous groups have long clashed over territorial and political sovereignty (see Urban and Sherzer 1991; Warren and Jackson 2002).

Yet the advent of benefit sharing as a multilateral principle has also opened the door for some significant indigenous rights mobilizations, in which intellectual property and control over biological resources have become central to wider movements for self-determination (see Posey 1996; Coombe 2003; Greene 2004). Consider, just for a start, the movement in international law on the question of protecting traditional knowledge. The World Intellectual Property Organization (WIPO), a group that falls under the UN's auspices and has as its mandate, in large part, the promotion of intellectual property as much as humanly/institutionally possible, has become an interesting forum for indigenous mobilization on these fronts: the WIPO special working group on 8j has become a site of unprecedented indigenous access to broader UN discussions on intellectual property and trade. At the same time, WIPO has engaged in a "new mission to 'reach out to new beneficiaries'—sending fact-finding missions around the world to ascertain how the intellectual property system could be used, amended, or altered, to better protect traditional or indigenous knowledge" (Coombe 2003, 1177).

Indeed, more broadly, the assumption of a fundamental conflict between benefit sharing and intellectual property can be countered, certainly in the terms of international law itself. A case in point is the hotly contested proposal in the Bonn Guidelines to require patent applicants to document the source of any biological material and traditional knowledge used therein; Coombe suggests that, objections by the United States, Canada, and Australia notwithstanding, TRIPS allows national governments the final word on the novelty of any potential patent application—and thus it would be entirely within their remit to request as much information as possible, including documentation of the origin of source material and related knowledge, in order to make that assessment (Coombe 2001, 282). This indeed has been one important tactic in ongoing negotiations over benefit sharing as an ascendant idiom for regulating trade, research, and intellectual property rights—working towards interpretations of agreements such as TRIPS to argue that their national, public interest provisions (for example) are in fact very much in line with the Convention on Biological Diversity and the Bonn Guidelines.

From Field to Clinic

The international traffic in biological diversity and cultural knowledge is not the only domain being transformed by appeals to the quasi-redistributive language of benefit sharing. Since the late 1990s, bioethicists and policymakers working on guidelines for clinical research—clinical trials, research on human genetic disease, the management of blood and tissue banks—have become subscribers to this language as well. Here the task has been to grapple with the ethics and politics of an increasingly (visibly) commercialized clinical research: in view of the enormous fortunes on the speculative horizon that may be derived from human biologicals, legal scholars and ethicists are making a case that pharmaceutical companies may well have an obligation—of some sort—to distribute some slice of their profits to relevant/appropriate beneficiaries or stakeholders.

As ever, the questions of who counts as a benefit recipient, what a benefit is, and what principles and mechanisms shall guarantee such redistributions loom provocatively. If the key document in the biodiversity world is the CBD, the obligatory citation in this emergent discussion is the Human Genome Organziation (HUGO) Ethics Committee's 2000 Statement on Benefit Sharing, which laid out six rather wide-ranging principles meant to stimulate discussion and to elicit further elaboration. These principles range from the rather diffuse insistence "that all humanity share in, and have access to, the benefits of genetic research" (principle 1), to the slightly more concrete notion, exactly mirroring the entrenched figures tossed about in the world of bioprospecting, "that profit-making entities dedicate a percentage (e.g., 1%–3%) of their annual net profit to healthcare infrastructure and/or to humanitarian efforts" (point 6) (HUGO Ethics Committee 2000).

Given HUGO's broader commitment to the idea of the human genome as "common heritage," it is thinkable, though dauntingly so, to designate "humanity at large" as one potential benefit recipient. But so, too, are potential benefit recipients framed as nations (national health-care infrastructures) and/or communities or groups—understood variably as ethnic or other epidemiologically construed populations, patient advocacy groups, or perhaps people with such conditions as Tay–Sachs disease or breast cancer. The Committee recognizes that this might require some thinking about how we define community (see also Weijer 2000). The range of potential benefits is also understood widely, again mirroring for us the terms set forth in bioprospecting discussions: from infrastructure building, to community health and development projects, to a royalty-sharing scheme that would send a small percentage of corporate profits into some kind of charitable circulation.

While the idea of benefit sharing in clinical research bounces around an ever-expanding set of institutional conversations (e.g., in establishing rules of engagement for national Biobanks, in U.S. Presidential Bioethics Task Force discussions on organ donation, in UNESCO reports on genetic data), very few explicit benefit-sharing arrangements have thus far been put into motion in clinical and genetic research. Patient activist and advocacy groups (especially in the United States but also in France, the United Kingdom, and elsewhere) have been the most active on this front, funding research on specific diseases and demanding, for example, jointly owned patents and control over licensing agreements with researchers and companies (see Merz, Magnus, Cho, and Caplan 2002, 966).

Practices and Idioms of Inclusion

Indeed, beyond international agreements and statements of principle, some of the most important negotiations of benefit sharing as an idiom of inclusion have taken place through individual research agreements themselves. A growing body of ethnographic work on bioprospecting, and a small but vivid set of discussions on clinical ethics and benefit sharing, together provide some useful perspectives here. Drawing on some of that literature, let me highlight a few ways of understanding benefit sharing through the prism of its relationship to property rights (especially but not exclusively intellectual property rights).

The first, and perhaps the most straightforward, point here is that intellectual property serves, and is invoked, as an *enabling device* for benefit sharing. In most bioprospecting agreements, patents, in particular, play a much-touted role as revenue-generating engines. As I mentioned before, the standard royalty-sharing rate hovers between 1–3% of net profit, with some institutions negotiating differential rates according to the distance or proximity between a provided lead and a patented compound. The reliance on patents as a primary source of benefits has drawn criticism from auditors of major prospecting initiatives such as the U.S. government's International Cooperative Biodiversity Groups (ICBG) program, on the grounds that pharmaceutical patents are by no means guaranteed outcomes of plant-based drug discovery, and that the ten to twenty years it may take to generate a royalty-producing product significantly undercuts any commitment to providing short to medium-term benefits (see Greene 2002; Hayden 2003a). And certainly, given the fact that no patented drugs have yet emerged from any of the high-profile prospecting arrangements that took off in the early to mid-1990s, we might argue that the ICBG auditors had a decent point.

The second is that intellectual property serves as an idiom (i.e., a metaphor, or a language) for defining who is entitled to benefits. Lockean notions of property revolve around the idea of innovation, figured through the idea of mixing one's labor (physical or mental) with nature. These formulations figure routinely in assessments of who shall be included in benefit-sharing arrangements (or not) and why. Thus, a Mexican ethnobotanist may note that urban plant vendors do not figure as benefit recipients because they are merely "vectors of transmission" of information and not sources of knowledge (see Hayden 2003a, 2003b); thus, too, Costa Rican bioprospecting pioneer Rodrigo Gámez suggests that the classifying labors of his institute's newly trained parataxonomists add value to the samples sent out to the drug company Merck and thus the institute, INBio, merits a higher royalty payment than if they were just sending raw samples abroad (Sittenfeld and Gámez 1993).

Certainly, the political importance of such Lockean logics to indigenous rights mobilizations should not be underestimated; researchers and indigenous rights activists set the stage for the current moment precisely by arguing, starting in the mid- to late-1980s, that much biodiversity was already infused with innovative labor and thus merited compensation or property rights. As rural sociologist Jack Kloppenburg (1991, 16) stated the case, "Genetic and cultural information has been produced and reproduced over the millenia by peasants and indigenous people." Since "value already exists in the collected materials," Kloppenburg argued, then people who have put labor (intellectual and otherwise) into them should be granted rights of ownership and compensation. At the same time, as literature on this topic and on struggles over cultural property more widely have shown, the requirements for traceability—for identifying who exactly has added labor to what—generates its own complexities. Benefit-sharing relations often require a bounded community to take shape in order to step in as a collective author; efforts to designate just such an entity for these purposes can create new exclusions as well as enable new inclusions.[2] (On a related but slightly distinct front, the questions of traceability are also running up against the increasing digitization of bioinformation (see Parry 2004).[3]

Their complexities notwithstanding, conceptual investments in Lockean languages of labor, innovation, and identifiable contributions to value-production also animate some U.S. bioethicists' articulations of the need for a new ethic of benefit sharing in clinical research. Where many indigenous rights activists and allies have argued that much biodiversity on the ground is, by definition, already suffused with innovative labor that should be recognized and rewarded, Jon Merz and colleagues from the University of Pennsylvania and Stanford suggest that the presumption of altruism as the motivating force for participation in clinical research (i.e., participation as an unremunerated gift) similarly has given rise to an injustice. The participation of research subjects or patient groups in the development of new therapies is indispensable, they note—the fact that current ethical standards prohibit direct returns of benefits to those participants is, in effect, a market failure. Stakeholders' interests have not been aptly represented, and new ways, they argue, must be found to "recognize and reward their contributions" (Merz et al. 2002).

This appeal for redistributive justice in the language of (failed) markets and stakeholder contributions leads me to my third point about the relationship between intellectual property and benefit sharing. For all of its prominence as an idiom, intellectual property itself is rarely, if ever, considered part of the package of goods to be redistributed to benefit recipients. Benefits are, in other words, posed as *not-rights*. The most notable exception in the realm of bioprospecting, as ever, proves the rule: anthropologist Shane Greene has documented how Aguaruna organizations in Peru managed to negotiate a Know-How license directly with Monsanto-Searle, as part of an ICBG-sponsored collaboration. Among the legions of prospecting collaborations that have taken worldwide, this is one of the only documented arrangements of its kind. (It is perhaps worth noting that when the original license ran out, Searle opted not to renew, and thus this particular form of indigenous intellectual property ran its course quite quickly; Greene 2004).

The larger point is that, as we have seen, many actors frame the problem that benefits can address as an asymmetry in the ways that property works. Yet the actors and institutions charged with the giving-back part of the benefit-sharing relationship are often quite insistent that a solution not be framed in the same language. Consider the host of competing terms preferred by many of those on the northern side of prospecting collaborations: technology transfer, incentive, and donation. These terms pointedly steer entitlements away from anything that intimates rights or even reward (see Hayden 2003a). The aversion to granting rights as a form of benefit is perhaps made most explicit in recent proposals by U.S. bioethicists to establish benefit sharing in human genetic research. The previously quoted appeal to find ways of recognizing and rewarding research participants' contributions to the bio-science enterprise draws up short when it comes time to elucidate the conceptual underpinnings of this incitement to share. The authors are clear to note that the arguments they make in favor of benefit sharing are based "not on property or any other kind of rights." They are, instead, based on something rather different—equity: "simply because it is the right thing to do" (Merz et al. 2002). We might note that the patient advocacy groups with whom they work seem to have a different view, militating in courtrooms and in laboratories for shared patent rights, downstream control over licensing agreements, and other forms of benefit that hover noticeably in the domain of rights, plural.

Benefit-Sharing Futures

As with a consideration of these matters at the level of international law and trade policy, there are then (at least) two stories to be told, simultaneously, about the status of benefit sharing and its place at the edges of intellectual property. On the one hand, we could certainly argue that benefit sharing, as framed by some of its proponents, serves as a hedge against a redistribution of property rights in any radical sense (see Brush 1999);—whether the rights in question are those of indigenous peoples over their plants and knowledge, or of patient groups in the United States over tissue, gene sequences, or other contributions to the bioscience enterprise. Benefit-sharing proposals often reaffirm the rights of firms to profit from patents on biologicals while offering some kind of downstream redistribution framed precariously, nervously, in the space between (not-) rights and "what is right."[4]

At the same time, more energetic visions of what benefit sharing can and must do are also prying open the lockbox of intellectual property as it has been practiced and allocated, both nationally and internationally. In arguing, whether strategically or unreservedly, that patient groups or indigenous peoples have indeed "contributed to processes of value-production," activists and researchers are also deliberately drawing attention to the arbitrariness of patent regimes as they stand. Rosemary Coombe notes what is at stake in developments such as the WIPO initiatives on the protection of traditional knowledge: "This is a fascinating process of international lawmaking and an increasingly important field of global politics, which may or may not result in the establishment of new intellectual property rights [for indigenous peoples]. Perhaps more significantly, these efforts have served to expose the shortcomings and inadequacies of existing regimes of intellectual property" (Coombe 2001, 275). The effects of this exposure are not inconsequential: Coombe suggests that these efforts are indeed "contributing to a crisis of legitimacy in the world intellectual property system" (Coombe 2001, 275).

Many others are making similar points, with an eye not just on the status of traditional knowledge within WIPO, but also on the ways in which the pharmaceutical industry's use of patents and differential pricing is coming under fire on many fronts: U.S. citizens are streaming across the Mexican and Canadian borders in search of cheaper pharmaceuticals; Brazil and India are churning out generic versions of patented medicines essential to public health in developing nations; and (on precisely that front), the South Africa AIDS drugs/patent dispute has served as a visible example of the WTO's (grudging) willingness to allow nations to override corporate patents in the name of a public health emergency. Such developments have led a number of commentators in international law, political economy, and elsewhere, to argue that, just as copyright regimes (and those who rely on strong interpretations thereof) are being challenged quite effectively by open source, so, too, are patent regimes, in their current form, becoming increasingly unviable—politically—for big pharma (see Hubbard and Love 2003; Weber 2003). Despite itself, the ascendance of an ethic and politics of benefit sharing may well be symptomatic of this increasingly discussed fissure in the political legitimacy of the patent regimes on which the pharmaceutical industry relies. As ever, it remains to be seen what kinds of relations benefit sharing itself will generate as an idiom of inclusion and exclusion.

Notes

This is a revised version of a paper initially prepared for the SSRC (Social Science Research Council) Workshop, "Intellectual Property, Markets, and Cultural Flows," New York, October 24–25, 2003.

1. But it is not just benefit sharing that is at stake here. TRIPS also requires signatory nations to devise some form of patent or patent-like protection for crop varieties, while the CBD's emphasis on technology transfer, sustainability, and conservation provides a framework for developing nations to assert biosafety and biodiversity concerns over and above property rights of first-world seed companies.

2. As Stephen Brush, myself, and many others have argued, forms of entitlement based on collective authorship of both biological and intellectual resources can quickly turn into forms of exclusion, given the degree to which, in many contexts, plants, knowledge, and people are all quite cosmopolitan and do not always cohere in one bounded package (see Brush 1999; see also Greaves 1994; Posey 1996; Coombe 1998; Greene 2002; Hayden 2003a).

3. Here, the fight, as is evident in the Bonn Guidelines provisos on declarations of origin for derivative patents, is to retain political and legal commitments to traceability in a technological/industrial realm in which biological samples, rendered as information, travel far and rapidly. What are the infrastructures of monitoring that must be put in place for equitable returns to have a minimal chance of materializing?

4. Long-running and anxious debates over the commodification of blood, tissue samples, and organs play these arguments out in extraordinary detail.

References

Aoki, Keith. 1996. Notes toward a cultural geography of authorship. *Stanford Law Review* 48(5): 1293–1355.

Brush, Stephen B. 1999. Bioprospecting the Public Domain. *Cultural Anthropology* 14(4): 535–555.

Coombe, Rosemary. 1998. *The cultural life of intellectual properties: Authorship, appropriation and the law*. Durham, NC: Duke University Press.

———. 2001. The recognition of indigenous peoples' and community knowledge in international law, *St. Thomas Law Review* 14(2): 275–285.

———. 2003. Fear, hope, and longing for the future of authorship and a revitalized public domain in global regimes of intellectual property. *DePaul Law Review* 52(4): 1171–1192.

Greaves, Tom, ed. 1994. *Intellectual property rights for indigenous peoples, A sourcebook*. Oklahoma City, OK: Society for Applied Anthropology.

Greene, Shane. 2002. Intellectual property, resources, or territory? Reframing the debate over indigenous rights, traditional knowledge, and pharmaceutical bioprospection. In Mark P. Bradley and Patrice Petro (eds.), *Truth claims: Representation and human rights*. New Brunswick, NJ and London: Rutgers University Press.

―――. 2004. Indigenous peoples, incorporated? Culture as politics, culture as property in contemporary bioprospecting deals. *Current Anthropology* 45(2): 211–237.

Hayden, Cori. 2003a. From market to market: Bioprospecting's idioms of inclusion. *American Ethnologist* 30(3): 1–13.

―――. 2003b. *When nature goes public: The making and unmaking of bioprospecting in Mexico*. Princeton: Princeton University Press.

Hubbard, Tim, and Jamie Love. 2003. Medicines without barriers. *New Scientist* (14 June): 29. Comment and analysis.

Human Genome Organization (HUGO) Ethics Committee: 2000. Statement on Benefit Sharing. *Clinical Genetics* 58(5): 364–366.

Kloppenburg, Jack. 1991. No hunting! Biodiversity, indigenous rights, and scientific poaching. *Cultural Survival Quarterly* 13(3): 14–18.

Merz, Jon F., David Magnus, Mildred K. Cho, and Arthur Caplan. 2002. Protecting subjects' interests in genetics research. *American Journal of Human Genetics* 70: 965–971.

Parry, Bronwyn, 2004. *Trading the genome: Investigating the commodification of bio-information*. New York: Columbia University Press.

Posey, Darrell A. 1996. *Traditional resource rights: International instruments for protection and compensation for indigenous peoples and local communities*. Gland, Switzerland: IUCN and the World Conservation Union.

Sell, Susan. 2003. Competing knowledge networks: The quest for global governance in intellectual property. From Intellectual Property, Markets, and Cultural flow workshop. Social Science Research Council, New York, October 2003.

Sittenfeld, Ana and Rodrigo Gámez. 1993. Biodiversity prospecting by INBio. In: Walter V. Reid, Sarah A. Laird, Rodrigo Gamez, Ana Sittenfeld, Daniel H. Jantzen, Michael Gollin, and Calestous Juma (eds.), *Biodiversity prospecting: Using genetic resources for sustainable development.* Washington, DC.: World Resources Institute; Instituto Nacional de Biodiversidad; Rainforest Alliance; African Center for Technology Studies.

Urban, Greg, and Joel Sherzer, eds. 1991. *Nation states and Indians in Latin America.* Austin: University of Texas Press.

Warren, Kay, and Jean Jackson, eds. 2002. *Indigenous movements, self-representation, and the state in Latin American.* Austin: University of Texas Press.

Weber, Steven. 2003. Untitled issue paper. From Intellectual Property, Markets, and Cultural Flow workshop. Social Science Research Council, New York, October 2003.

Weijer, Charles. 2000. Benefit-sharing and other protections for communities in genetic research. *Clinical Genetics* 58: 367–368.

9

Trust among the Algorithms: Ownership, Identity, and the Collaborative Stewardship of Information

Christopher Kelty

This precisely is the long story of how responsibility originated. The task of breeding an animal with the right to make promises evidently embraces and presupposes as a preparatory task that one first makes men to a certain degree necessary, uniform, like among like, regular, and consequently calculable.

—NIETZSCHE[1]

Introduction

Nonproprietary ownership might seem an oxymoron were it not for the detailed elaboration of the circulation of payments among New Irelanders that Marilyn Strathern (in this volume) uses to show how "[b]orrowing, sharing, exchanging are all effected *through* payments." In other words, here is a strange culture in which "sharing" means *paying* for something but not *owning* it. What it is to own something, or to be an owner is analyzed by Strathern as complicated formal relationships of transaction, exchange, authentication, or trust that help ensure a "right to make promises."

It may be strange, but it should also be familiar: "sharing" without payment has also been rendered criminal in the modern global digital economy—an economy absolutely saturated with proprietary forms of ownership. To understand what it is to own, or to be an owner in, among this contradictory set of technical and legal forms must similarly be understood through the ways in which transactions, payments, rights, and ownership are formatted in a social network. Whether New Irelanders or Napster users, owning and sharing do not come with innate or even determined meanings, but are actions that are continuously produced within social and technical structures.

In this chapter I focus on the productive power of the legal and technical regimes formatting identity and ownership on the Internet today. Just as technical and legal rearrangements of property change the meaning of what can be owned, technical and legal rearrangements of "identity" change the meaning of who owns—and open the door to new modes of collaborative ownership and stewardship of digital information.[2]

The last few years have witnessed increasing concern about "identity theft," even though personal information is one of the few kinds of information that is neither owned nor quite unowned under modern U.S. and EU legal regimes. There are endless debates about privacy (civil liberty) and even more endless debates about security (whether of persons or information). Both share a strong commitment to an inalienable and authentic core of identity (individual selfhood or autonomy) that must be protected either by more laws, technology, and police power, or by less.

What this debate misses, however, is the productive power of the legal and technical regimes intended to offer such protection. Instead of securing the individual, they create new forms of collective interaction and new possibilities for collaboration or creativity (of both good and foul intent). In a world of cryptographic pseudonyms, identity thieves, face recognition, spam laws, rights management markup languages and proliferating schemes of credit measurement and protection, the idylls of possessive individualism seem to be less sacred principles than dusty curios from another time. Instead we are confronted, everyday and everywhere, with new kinds of personal and public information, new modes of circulation and expanded networks of "trust," reputation, credit, and security that are, as Strathern puts it "minutely differentiated in the way entitlements between persons are worked out."

In this chapter, I focus on the very particular technical and political ways in which modern identity and especially, "trust" are formatted and circulated within collective social networks. Rather than argue for or against certain technologies, I prefer to explore the ways in which anonymity and authentication (or identity and its verification) are combined in novel and interesting ways in a variety of emergent technical and legal rearrangements such as the use of cryptographic authentication, identity theft policing, digital rights management systems, or open content licensing commons.

To explain the productive power these new tools bring about, I first introduce work in science and technology studies (STS) and economic sociology, particularly Michel Callon's, notion of "calculative agencies" and the role of money in the management of trust. The following two sections explore the issues of trust, authentication, and identity in the context of cryptography and the management of network security (in particular focusing on two companies: VeriSign and Vontu). The final section compares the technical formatting of networks of "unowned" information with that of "owned" information in the cases of digital rights management and its responses in the Free Software and open content movements.

A Peculiar Anthropology

In *The Laws of the Market*, Michel Callon (1998) offers a complicated review of some debates in sociology, economics, science studies, anthropology, accounting, and philosophy on how to combine studies of actual exchange behavior with theoretical descriptions of markets in economics. Perhaps the most famous of these debates was that between anthropologists and economists (the so-called substantive vs. formalist controversy, which ended in a more or less mutual agreement between the disciplines to ignore each other).[3] Callon seeks not to revive this debate, however, but to make a claim at once more mundane and more extraordinary: "economics, in the broad sense of the term, performs, shapes and formats the economy, rather than observing how it functions."[4] Rather than reconcile opposing views, Callon simply takes a step back, and lets the work of economists (and for that matter anthropologists) rest on the same plane as the phenomena they claim to observe. It is a version of Ian Hacking's (1983) argument about the imbrication of "representing and intervening" in scientific work applied instead to technical practices.[5] Economic theories are implemented through the creation of specific accounting and management tools and they change the way in which markets and actors relate to each other, and hence the behavior of markets. But since humans do not naturally possess at birth fully worked out econometric models, or fancy double-entry bookkeeping software, it is necessary for Callon to introduce a more complicated creature that he calls "calculative agencies" and to propose a "peculiar anthropology" necessary to track and understand them.

Calculative agencies are assemblages of humans in networks, tools in use, and theories applied case-by-case. For Callon, the human agent can be neither the a rational calculating person with perfect information making frictionless transactions (i.e., *homo economicus* as Sasquatch—the untraceable but evolutionarily necessary beast of theoretical economics) nor simply the culturally or socially embedded human agent whose actions are either determined by a network of relations, or actively focused on manipulating such a network by acquiring "social capital" (i.e., *homo economicus* as Santa Claus, the fictional gift-giver who knows who's been naughty and who's been nice). Rather it is the anthropology of an agency who is not simply a natural being with natural desires, nor a brain in a jar, but a deliberately formatted, trained, and pro-grammed agent-network who can either calculate or not, depending on the configuration of humans, tools for accounting and the history that has pro-duced it (i.e., *homo economicus* as Borg—the empirically abundant, but mani-festly unnatural human-machine collage that, when turned on, actually *can* calculate in the complex ways economics describes).

Calculative agencies are not the cyborgs of science fiction, however. Instead, Callon suggests that we imagine strawberry farmers.[6] Callon cites an article by M. F. Garcia 1986, that details how, strawberry farmers in a rural region of France emerged from a situation of isolation where price was an imperfect measure of demand and middlemen controlled sale and distribution to one where farmers met together in a warehouse, their strawberries were counted, graded, and the results displayed on a board that everyone could see, and whereby auction prices could be determined. What this transformation is meant to demonstrate, is that price is not just an equilibrium measure of demand or of quality, but is inextricably linked to a set of other things: loca-tion, tools for counting and grading, information and accounting technolo-gies, auction procedure, the relation between producers, middlemen, and buyers, and so forth. Far from being strictly rational, humans are rational only by entangling and disentangling themselves within a web of things and pro-cedures; "No calculation is possible without this framing which allows one to provide a clear list of entities, states of the world, possible actions and expected outcomes of these actions."[7] Callon points out in particular that this entan-gling and disentangling, which he calls a "formatting" of the network, is actu-ally carried out not only by actors, tools, and relationships, but by the crucial presence of economic *theories* as well. Garcia's strawberry market was largely designed and implemented by an economist from the Regional Chamber of

Agriculture, whose understanding of the minimal requirements of a functioning market guided the redesign of the local strawberry farmers' world. The format of the market emerged from a confluence of factors—location, standards, strawberries, warehouses, information technologies, and chief among all these, a theory of what the market should look like.

Calculative agencies, therefore, are not autonomous human actors who know their own preferences, but humans connected in webs of technologies, laws, judgments, and theories whose preferences are warped and woven by the outlines of the networks that they can visualize and/or traverse. These complex acts of calculation are difficult to describe, but not to perform. For people enmeshed in them, they are naturalized mnemotechnical systems—more than just an organic human body with a taste for shortcake. Where exactly the borders of any given agency are drawn (e.g., including shortcake, or deeming it irrelevant) is the purpose of empirical research and analysis according to Callon.

Some components of a calculative agency are clearly more essential than others—especially money. Callon's observations extend those made years ago by the German sociologist Georg Simmel (1978/1907) on the character of money. In Simmel's version, money is a tool present within a network of exchanges whose purest function is not to measure value, but to represent the network:

The dual nature of money, as a concrete and valued substance and, at the same time, as something that owes its significance to the complete dissolution of substance into motion and function, derives from the fact that money is the reification of exchange among people, the embodiment of pure function.[8]

Money is the symbolic and concrete indication of trust—its fungibility allows for strangers to be trusted, for goods to be universally compared, and when stable, stands for the guarantee of a sovereign. Money is a tool for reformatting a network of relations, through the particular forms it takes—as gold, as paper, as backed by institutions, governments, treaties, wars—and through the particular ways in which it is manipulated—usury, credit, risk-management, and insurance. For Simmel, money was a powerful tool whose principle function was to manage trust among strangers: it stood between any two arbitrary objects, just as the merchant or trader—whose principle role was the manipulation of these networks through money—stood between organic communities, or among other strangers, i.e., in markets.

In a passage devoted to exploring the many historical cases of strangers who are also traders,[9] Simmel suggests that in the most recent period of international trade, the distinction is disappearing, producing a peculiar problem for moderns:

The contrast that existed between the native and the stranger has been eliminated, because the money form of transactions has now been taken up by the whole economic community. The significance of the stranger for the nature of money seems to me to be epitomized in miniature by the advice I once overheard: never have any financial dealings with two kinds of peoples—friends and enemies.[10]

For Simmel, writing in the late nineteenth century, the stranger is both a fantasy abstraction that makes sense of money and markets, and a very real feature of the urban landscape. It is not the stranger, as he says "who comes today and goes tomorrow, but rather the person who comes today and stays tomorrow." Simmel's stranger is a recombinant stranger—the stranger who imports one world and background into another, and breaks the unity (imagined or otherwise) of a group that sees itself as having always been whole. To never deal with friends or enemies would seem paradoxical, if one lived in George W. Bush's world where "you are either with us or against us"—but to Simmel it is an indication that the generalization of a money economy brings with it a corresponding generalization of strangeness. We are all strange to someone; in fact, we are even willing to make ourselves strange in order to transact with someone, and, against our better judgment, occasionally do so with friends and enemies. We therefore all use money as a way to manage these instances of trust. It is a tool that is possessed but not owned, and by circulating it, it gives its temporary bearer a way to work in concert with others to achieve ends that may differ drastically from each other without being in conflict.

Identity, Authentication, and Anonymity

Recently there has been much hysteria concerning the issue of "identity theft." The words have a bizarre ring, coming as they do after a decade of some of the most intense cultural battles for identity—ideologically speaking in the United States and Europe, violently so in terms of ethnicity in many other places. Isn't identity precisely what can't be stolen—that core we fight for when all else is lost? What would it mean to own one's identity such that it could therefore be stolen? Even if the anecdotal stories are true that people who suffer this crime spend "years putting their lives back together," this can only be a tribute to the triumph of American-style consumerism, where life is confused with credit rating, and the power to buy is the power to remake oneself. Surely no one's identity—in the sense of an elaborately constructed and performed sense of self, rooted in time and space and directed by desire, belief, and know-how—is literally being stolen. Surely it is only *numbers* that are being stolen: credit card numbers, addresses, passwords, social security numbers, and so forth. And since the (U.S. and EU) courts have generally decided that even if we have a right to privacy, we cannot *own* these numbers, is "theft" really the right word?

A recent widely seen Citicards advertisement made this issue particularly clear. The advertisements showed, for example, upstanding, middle-American looking women with captions that said "There are three warrants for my arrest. One of them involves smuggling," or "I spent $2,342 on violent and suggestive video games," or a middle-aged man with the caption "I had $23,000 worth of liposuction."[11] These ads succinctly captured the idea that identity theft consists of the ability to entangle more than one human body in a web of numbers, transactions, and desires. It is the ability to reformat the networks of signs and promises that connect us in such a way that what once was proper to one unassuming human body, is now connected to a different but putatively real human body with quite other desires. Rendering this skillful reweaving *criminal* and distinct from the normal ability to do so turns out to be quite difficult. The curious thing about such "identity theft" is the fact that there is, in the absence of an avalanche of biometric sensors or final cyborg solution, no way to distinguish the identity thief from the secret identity of these human bodies—a fact this ad makes curiously clear. An individual might well commit such fraud in his or her own name only to criminally disavow it later (is it really so hard to imagine an older man getting liposuction, or a middle-aged woman smuggling drugs?). If you can't trust yourself, who can you trust?

But, why is identity theft a *financial* crime? Why, when we have money— a standardized and widely used tool for maintaining anonymity but expressing trust—do we today demand such elaborate systems of authentication *in order to transact*: passwords and phrases, smart cards, cryptography, shredders, certificates, signatures, picture IDs, mother's maiden name, and social security numbers? The very possession of money is the ultimate authentication—it is precisely the indifference to the reputation or trustworthiness of the individual that makes possible so-called free markets, not to mention constituting its famed power to corrupt. What has appeared in its stead?

Consider what VeriSign, one of the largest and most established Internet security and authentication corporations, says about strangers. Their white paper (2000) called "VeriSign Authentication Services" begins:

People and institutions need to get to know one another before conducting business . . . Regardless of whether commerce takes place online or in the physical world, the parties involved must be able to answer these questions:

- Who are you?
- To what community do you belong? Are you still a trusted member?
- How can you prove your identity?[12]

VeriSign's questions are precisely the opposite of Simmel's overheard advice: they suggest you deal only with known friends (or perhaps with known enemies), but never with strangers. Naturally, VeriSign offers to take care of this—they offer to ensure for their customers that the customers of their customers are who they say they are by authenticating not only these particular buyers and sellers, but the very *systems* they use to authenticate each other. They ensure that the cryptographic keys used to authenticate transactions are valid and uncompromised, through the use of certificates (this is explained in more detail in the following section).

Consider for a moment what makes money authentic and what makes an identity so; consider both from the perspective not of theft, but of counterfeiting. Fool's gold and counterfeit paper money rely only on the gullibility— a network of two people (three, when you include the sovereign whose good name is impugned by the act). But in between gold-backed monetary systems and the notion of pure credit lies a whole world of information technologies that extend this network in multiple directions: from double-entry books to promissory notes to greenbacks to stocks and bonds to credit histories to the new technical infrastructures of payment and marketing. To counterfeit credit means to reliably produce the belief among a small but relatively complex network of actors and machines in the future existence of money. It means making believable promises.

To clarify this, Callon cites the example of gift-giving as theorized by Marcel Mauss and later extended by Pierre Bourdieu.[13] In a gift-economy, to give a gift sets up an obligation to return it, but without setting a frame on the time, place, or manner within which such an obligation is fulfilled. In Bourdieu's discussion, setting a time and place renders gift-giving identical to offering credit. The difference between real credit and counterfeit credit, therefore, is impossible to pinpoint—both trade on the promise of future money—because both are mere promises in the near term. The assertion that there is "no such thing as a pure gift" depends therefore on how the social network of actors is framed in time and space. Whether a gift is calculated (or calculable) depends on the tools with which agencies keep track of them. Similarly the management of credit depends on a whole range of tools (e.g., smart and dumb cards, software, databases, credit history, algorithms, etc.), laws and regulations (e.g., the Fair Credit Reporting Act, HIPAA, Gramm-Leach-Blaily Act)[14] and corporations (Equifax, Experian, and TransUnion) that are involved in securing the function of credit-money. It is for this reason that Mauss and other anthropologists refer to the gift as a "total social fact": one that reveals not just economic concerns, but the whole structure of a society.

Gifts and credit-money differ only to the extent that calculative agencies work to reduce the uncertainty of the promises they make by rendering trust, reputation, or identity more similar, like among like—that is, they extend the story of responsibility to include not just the moral human but the suprahuman network, the calculative agencies that make promises. The productive effects of the complex systems to ensure credit-money's function are the creation of new networks of people, tools, and corporations formatted and framed in ways that determine whether an activity is considered productive economic activity or criminal behavior. It is this formatting that produces an inside and an outside, that distinguishes between petty thievery and systematic corruption, or between white-collar crime and financial innovation. Trust, therefore, is not what morally upright humans possess—it is something produced and circulated. What VeriSign claims to do, put bluntly, is to replace money with a particular kind of standardized and authenticated trust. VeriSign offers to make trust fungible. The irony of course, is that VeriSign expects its customers to pay them (in money) to do so. To understand better what this trust is, and how it is constructed, consider the way in which public-key cryptography is used, and how "trust" is said to be achieved by it.

Crypto

The turn of the century has been a tumultuous time in the crypto world. Approximately one year before the September 11, 2001, attacks in the United States and the renewed calls for government control of all communications (not only encrypted ones), the patent on one of the most effective, profitable, and widely licensed crypto algorithms expired. The RSA algorithm, named for Ronald Rivest, Adi Shamir, and Leonard Adelman, was a cryptographic breakthrough, mixing mathematical virtuosity with a surprisingly simple concept.[15] One year before that, the U.S. Government had announced that it would loosen export restrictions on cryptography, essentially removing it from the export-controlled munitions list where it languished next to tanks and rocket launchers.[16] Terrorist nations were exempted.[17]

Long before these last few Septembers, however, cryptography, particularly a form known as asymmetric or "public key" cryptography was wending its way into just about every financial infrastructure in existence.[18] Public Key Infrastructures (PKIs) are what make the RSA algorithm clever, even if it is the mathematical sophistication that "crypto-geeks" and math professors admire. A PKI allows two parties to send encrypted messages to each other without needing to exchange the key. Rather, two complementary keys exist, a private and a public one. Sender A uses the recipient B's public key to encode the message, while recipient B uses her own private key to decrypt it. Clever, but why should humans care? It's true that crypto has a bad reputation: most people—especially in these days of the so-called war on terrorism—seem to assume that simply using crypto is an admission that you're saying something the U.S. government should know about. And while it's true that crypto is used to hide potentially momentous messages from prying eyes, it is also a mainstay of crypto users and defenders to take a line much like that of the American National Rifle Association, i.e., crypto doesn't kill, people kill.

Regardless, the vast majority of crypto uses today are not for encryption of nefarious messages. Rather, public key cryptography is used overwhelmingly today for authentication: a cryptographic method for verifying that the message I got was the same one—and the exact same one to the bit—that you sent. It is a signature in a sense stronger than that concept has previously been able to bear.[19] Using PKIs for authentication allows a message that is not encrypted to be authenticated to a degree of mathematical certainty that is impossible for humans to calculate, and allows the recipient to be certain that the message is both unchanged, and was signed only by the person in possession of the key with which it was signed.

While it may sound complicated, such an exchange can—and most often does—happen automatically. Billions of transactions a day are negotiated automatically when computers connect through a "Secure Sockets Layer" and conduct a "handshake" with the gregarious browsers of American consumers, so that human agency can be safely restricted to the domain of choosing what to buy, not how to do so. More frequently more this infrastructure is invisible to most users, and more people are unaware that they use a PKI on a daily basis. To the average cypherpunk, however, this is somewhat bizarre: the point of authentication is to ensure the knowledge that who you are dealing with is who they say they are. Embedded PKI infrastructures that bypass human agency effectively decide not which humans to trust, but which machines to trust. But these days, your average cypherpunk looks a lot like your average clean freak—someone who would never dare use a publicly accessible and untrusted machine or who brings his own virus software with him to LAN-parties. The rest of us promiscuously and cavalierly connect and rather than trust no one, trust whatever seems to work best.

The notion of who, or what should be trusted is the most interesting—and deeply troubling—aspect of how cryptography is related to human bodies and the classical ways in which they establish trust between each other (by group membership, by repeated interaction, by eye contact or in the case of economic transactions, through the use of money). In fact, the very use of the word "trust" in cryptography circles has less to do with the kind of people assumed to be untrustable—criminals, pirates, hackers or any other ostensible reasons for the existence of so-called computer security—and much more to do with the way in which asymmetric cryptography itself is authenticated. Trust, in this instance, does not mean whether I trust either the person, the software, or his/her authenticated message—it refers to whether I trust the authenticator. The existence of cryptography does not ensure trust, it produces a situation in which trust is made into a more "necessary, uniform, like among like, regular, and consequently calculable" entity—another chapter in the long story of responsibility.

When one considers more carefully how PKI authentication works, it is quickly complicated by what Bruce Schneier (1996) refers to as a noncryptographic issue—a telling admission of the beyond that cryptographers rarely acknowledge—the social network of individuals.[20] The basic two-party version of PKI is simple enough to understand. You give me (in person perhaps) your public key, and I use it to decrypt the messages you encrypt with your private key, which you guard with your life. However, there are limited ways to imagine it working for a large and arbitrary number of people. For instance where does one find an arbitrary recipient's "public key"—how does one establish contact reliably with an anonymous person (a consumer, say) without already being able to authenticate communication with them? Well, the recipient could give or send you their public key either in an unencrypted form or encrypted under a different system. But this begs the question: Either I need to take it on faith that the person I am communicating with is the same person whose key I receive (because, as the reader will no doubt remember, "on the Internet, no one knows you are a dog"), or I need yet another trusted party to authenticate that the key I am sent is the same one as the key they trust.

It is at this point, the point where a third party becomes necessary, that the political nature of cryptography becomes apparent. In a kind of Hobbesian or Rousseauian moment of social contract negotiation, two alternatives present themselves. The first (the one crypto-geeks prefer) is a decentralized model in which individuals place their keys on one of many interlinked keyservers, accessible to anyone on the Internet, which allows one to find an arbitrary key by looking up a name or e-mail address. However, while I can trust absolutely that the document I decrypted with this public key is the one signed with its corresponding private key, I cannot be sure that you, the physical blob of protoplasm, are the same blob using the key with your name on it. This can only be verified when that key is trusted, i.e., when it is signed by others who verify that you, qua physical-blob-of-protoplasm, carry the key you use to sign things—the string of numbers on a piece of paper or diskette. The more such signatures you collect, the more trusted your key is, and, in turn, the more trusted the keys you sign. This is called—an uncharacteristically straightforward term for cryptographers—a "web-of-trust."

The web-of-trust links people in strong and weak ways—but like most network phenomena, it tends to create a "small world" structure. That is, a structure of trust that creates small communities of strong bonds connected to similar small communities by a much smaller number of people who straddle them. In the world of cypherpunks and crypto-geeks, connecting communities of trust is the principal role of what are called "key-signing parties"—get-togethers in which people, diskette in hand, meet, talk to each other and then sign each other's public keys.

What makes this decentralized model fascinating, is that, ideally, no one is outside of the network, the frame is putatively totalizing. There are no strangers in this ideal world of cryptography, only those who are trusted and those who are not. The stranger (or the middleman, the wanderer, or the Jew) by definition cannot exist in this web-of-trust. People who do not use cryptography are as untrustable as people who sign with untrusted keys. Often there are people who straddle two communities—as the trader did in the past—but they are called "central signers" and are in fact precisely the opposite of a stranger: they are someone who knows everyone, an envoy, a diplomat, a mensch. In the fantasy world of perfect authentication, money itself disappears and is replaced with something such as trust, or reputation. Whatever function money served by being fungible can equally be served by using cryptographically signed and unique tokens that are not only infinitely difficult to counterfeit, but can be perfectly but pseudonymously tied (through authentication) to the parties exchanging them. Even if real human bodies have hundreds of pseudonymous identities, the crypto-geeks' perfect web-of-trust makes them perfectly responsible.

In reality of course no such total web-of-trust exists. Existing PKIs are not signed in this way and crypto-geeks who sign each other's keys are a tiny and isolated (though widely distributed geographically) web-of-trust. Few businesses, online retailers, lawyers, or doctors, and so forth are part of this web, and so crypto-geeks and cypherpunks are reduced to trusting them in the old-fashioned ways and to encrypting and authenticating only the most mundane messages. What does not figure in this fantasy is the manner in which existing forms of trust—money in particular—combine with cryptography in new ways, and this is where the second alternative form (the one crypto-geeks despise) of key authentication emerges: centralized authorities. The irony is that the easiest way to ensure the authenticity of cryptographic keys in our fallen world of imperfect money is simply to pay someone to do so. Simmel's "stranger" in this new world of authentication and trust is the "certificate authority" (CA), such as VeriSign. Just as the small world of "key-signing parties" creates a mythical Gemeinschaft of trusted individuals, the introduction of a corporation that will, for a price, sign your certificate, returns cryptographic authentication to that pesky problem of determining trusted entities—the gesellschaft of anonymous actors whose preferred mechanism of trust is money. For cypherpunk purists, a completely distributed web-of-trust with mutually signed keys extending throughout the network is the only way to bypass the sovereignty of some "certificate authority"; that is, it is the only way around the necessity of trusting a stranger (CA) to guarantee an exchange. To the cypherpunk, the CA is untrusted, but to the rest of us, it is neither friend nor enemy.

The various businesses who pay VeriSign for their authentication services might be compared to the strawberry farmers mentioned before. Online electronic transaction in the absence of VeriSign is an isolated and imperfect system, not least because no real money changes hands, and there is no equivalent stable enough to produce that trust. While VeriSign imagines itself to be the entity that does so (its slogan is nothing less than "The Sign of Trust on the Net"), what they actually do is more akin to the production of a local strawberry market; VeriSign formats the network—and in this case, in a sense starkly more literal than what Callon or Garcia might have meant—by literally programming the Web sites and servers of VeriSign-authenticated sites. In VeriSign's strawberry market, the network is rigidly demarcated into those who are trusted (because they have paid VeriSign) and those who are not. Just as it would be absurd to assume that there were no fairly priced quality strawberries outside of rural France, so it would be absurd to suggest that VeriSign is the only sign of trust on the Net. But just as Garcia's strawberry farmers get good prices for their strawberries, if you trust VeriSign, you can safely trust the sites VeriSign authenticates. Markets are formatted, they do not just happen (even if the theories used to create them insist that they do). In VeriSign's case, they have formatted a network that allows calculative agencies (made up here of humans, consumer desires, SSL-enabled browsers, credit card numbers, passwords, and addresses) to buy what they want. Through authentication they enable markets—they produce and format a particular kind of network within which it can be said that people (or at least, calculative agencies) trust each other. The trust (the information, the cryptographic keys, and certificates) that circulates here, like money, is not owned by anyone, yet is made to circulate in very particular and restricted ways.

Insider Threats and Collaborative Stewardship

Needless to say, not everyone trusts VeriSign. Consider the San Francisco start-up company Vontu whose motto is "Protect. Detect. Correct." Vontu is a corporation devoted to dealing with the "Insider Security Threat." For Vontu, untrusted outsiders, hackers or meth-addicted, dumpster-diving identity thieves are not the biggest threat—your employees are. It is not the unknown criminal who is dangerous, but the *known* one, the employee who, like Philip Cummings, steals 30,000 credit reports from his place of work and sells them for around $60 each.[21] These insider threats are what Vontu seeks to stem with their patent-pending "Secure Data Profiles" that will allow a company to monitor all electronic communications of employees for potential violations of federal regulations, or for that matter, of company policy. Vontu also uses encryption, not to authenticate data, but to define it. Vontu's system works like this: You, the employee-suspecting business owner, hand over to Vontu (along with a sizable amount of money) a copy of all of your "sensitive" data. Vontu encrypts it (primarily in order to reassure you), and uses it as the database from which to monitor all electronic communications going out of the enterprise for any similarities to the information you want to protect. Violations are reported to you, or stopped at the door, depending on your paranoia level. For Vontu, the biggest threat is not from people outside the network (those from whom VeriSign protects your credit-card number) but those on the inside (those whom VeriSign has no way to monitor—employees who must have access to "sensitive data" in order to fulfill customers' or clients' desires). While VeriSign formats networks to allow for particular kinds of transactions to occur safely with respect to one feared set of people (outsiders), they also *produce* a situation in which new forms of abuse are rendered possible by another (insiders).

Like VeriSign, Vontu is trusted only by virtue of being paid money. Practically speaking there is no less "insider threat" with Vontu guarding your data, than there is in guarding it yourself or trusting VeriSign to authenticate it. However, Vontu creates a system in which it becomes possible for an employer to differentiate information that can be stolen, from that which needs to be given away or circulated for particular reasons. Existing legal regimes are schizophrenic about the proprietary status of information—some information is owned (patented, copyrighted, and trademarked, giving private citizens sovereignty over its movement) some information is deemed unownable (public domain or government documents, over which the government and occasionally citizens have control), and some exists in a netherworld between the two (secret, private, personal, classified, etc.). Yet for complicated historical and moral reasons involving the notions of privacy, publicity, human

rights, informed consent laws and lingering notions of communal responsibility, there is no simple market in personal information—I cannot sell my
name, address, social security number, or other vitals. Others can, however,
and often do: especially to telemarketing, advertising, and spam companies.
The best I can do is to *give away* such information, and am increasingly
required to in order to conduct any kind of transaction—putatively because
it ties my assertions to a responsible body, the same one that is prevented from
profiting by the sale of such information.

This distinction between *information-as* and *information-for* cannot be captured by legal definition, but must be actively instantiated—formatted—
through the use of tools of calculation and management. Vontu, among others
tries to achieve just this, by providing a technical manner in which to differentiate between the same information as stolen and as legitimately circulated
or shared, where legitimacy is defined by the corporations (their security managers, legal staff, ethicists, and/or CIOs) who pay Vontu to provide them with
a system for technically instantiating the distinction. At a greater scale, governments have attempted to achieve similar results through legislation concerning the circulation of private information.[22] However, it should be clear
that such legislation does not do the work of protecting customer information, it only sets up demands and incentives for corporations who pay Vontu
to protect them from themselves. Such corporations may pay Vontu only to
comply with regulations or they may do so to proactively manage other unregulated forms of information as well. There is always room for old-fashioned
moral responsibility to assert itself, perhaps especially when it is unnecessary.

Vontu's solution shimmers between an image of total surveillance and one
of elegant design. On the one hand, it is true that they treat every employee—
indeed every keystroke of every employee—as guilty until proven innocent;
on the other hand, they also produce a very exact form of responsibility—one
in which their customers (the employers) designate what they will promise to
protect, either as a guarantee to individuals, or as a response to federal regulation.[23] As in the case of the relation between the gift-economy and credit-
money, Vontu offers to explicitly frame the use of information, in time and
space and in terms of who will see it and who will communicate it. Just as
there is no pure gift, there is no such thing as pure information. Vontu creates
a situation of mutual stewardship of information that navigates somewhere
between irresponsibility and state-based autocratic definitions of privacy,
safety, or security.

In some ways, perhaps counterintuitively, what Vontu provides is a way to define the conditions of collaborative stewardship of "unownable" private information. Insofar as the corporations they provide service to are encouraged to consider their own data and information resources, and the ways in which they care for it, Vontu frames and formats a system within which they can make those promises to the people who give them that information in expectation of some other return. It creates a market for implementing variable ethical concerns—ways of "caring for the data." It leverages one form of trust—money—to implement a different kind of trust in the management of information that needs to be held private and yet circulated at the same time.[24]

Digital Rights Management and Its Discontents

If Vontu's services, read so charitably, are seen as a way of caring for and collaboratively managing information of an uncertain kind, it is in rather stark contrast to the recent history of intellectual property. Quite a different concern with sharing information is represented by the entertainment industries, who seek to control the circulation of other kinds of information: principally music, text, and movies. For these industries, the concern is not with particular networks of people, but with any arbitrary listener or viewer, and the ability to control their use of the kind of information they circulate. Like cypherpunks, the entertainment industry's fantasy world of consumption has no outside, not only is every human a potential consumer, but so is every act of listening, viewing, or reading. Digital Rights Management is one manner in which the fantasy has been partially implemented.

Digital Rights Management (DRM) seeks to address a different kind of "insider threat": that posed by the supposedly illegitimate actions of legitimate customers, i.e., the "sharing" of music and movies—those uses that come after the purchase, but have hitherto been impossible to control: home recording, gifting, circulating, borrowing, sharing, and so forth. DRM, inasmuch as the moniker designates a single thing, includes a number of different schemes to manage intellectual property rights of a given work using everything from secrecy and obscurity, to cryptographic authentication, to watermarking to elaborate "rights markup languages" that attempt to specify all possible uses, destinations, or durations of some object. DRM, so conceived is much more general than copy-protection technology, because in addition to preventing copying, it literally programs (existing) law concerning intellectual property rights into devices and products. It represents the possibility of combining legislation and enforcement in the same gesture.[25]

To give just one example, consider the Adobe e-Book reader, a piece of software intended for reading a book online, or perhaps on a book-shaped device. When you "buy" an e-Book, Adobe delivers to you the text, encrypted and with a signed contract that tells you what exactly you can do with this book. The terms of this contract can be set and controlled through the DRM software, creating the possibility of price discrimination. For instance, one might set prices to copy the book, modify the book, transfer the book to a different machine or device, lend the book, read the book more than once, or even read the book out loud. To show off these Draconian possibilities, Adobe famously demonstrated its software using *Alice in Wonderland*—a book which has been in the public domain for over thirty years—conveniently showcasing the manner in which technology can be used to bend the legal definitions of public rights in unowned works.[26] Some have suggested that this represents an assault on the right to read anonymously.[27] Indeed, in the perfect dream world of DRM imagined by corporations and entertainment lawyers, DRM makes not just every book, but every act of reading, listening, and watching calculable. It would be a way to extract the maximum form of profit from each imaginable action conceived as consumption of information—the more finely defined, more exact the extraction of value from information can become.

However, as with personal information's need to be circulated, there are also rights and requirements for the circulation of owned information—from fair use to advertising to marketing to forms of licensing. But at this point the story becomes even more convoluted. In June 2001, a young Russian computer researcher attended a well-known hacker conference (DefCon) where he demonstrated before an assembled crowd that, even if such licensing terms were legal and acceptable, the encryption on the device was trivially easy to break, and he proceeded to demonstrate how it could be done.

The FBI arrested Dmitri Sklyarov, not for violating the intellectual property rights of Adobe or Lewis Carroll, but for violation of the Digital Millennium Copyright Act's (DMCA) "anticircumvention" provisions, which declare illegal the attempt to circumvent any device intended to prevent illegal copying. Sklyarov's crime is, moreover, for almost the first time in the history of intellectual property law a felony—and one the United States seeks to enforce on foreign nationals as well as its citizens, all under the general rubric of "security."

The DMCA represents one of the most sophisticated attempts to articulate law and technology together. In the case of the e-Book Reader, it shores up some of the excessive uses that might otherwise be considered by users as legitimate: namely taking apart the device they have purchased, or making use of information in ways that hitherto have seemed noncontroversial and noncommercial. But as with cryptography and authentication, it is not simply a question of whether civil, human, or economic rights are violated by such devices, or whether humans should (or will) pay for every definable act of reading, but whether such devices transform the meaning of reading, as peer-to-peer systems have transformed the meaning of "sharing." Even if an only partial version of DRM comes to be the standard mode of distributing information, it will have changed what it means to read, view, or listen by training people to understand the value of something so simple as, for example, rereading, to be an excessive, potentially expensive use. The combination of a technical system for managing such rights, and a legal regime that prevents people from tampering with it (even where trivial) de-authorizes some kinds of reading, viewing, or listening.[28] If successful, these acts might indeed become more calculable—but what then will become of the acts of writing, producing, or performing?

While the felonious tinkering of people like Sklyarov will no doubt continue, either as crime or as civil disobedience, the more unusual and interesting response to this configuration of legal and technical regimes is the emergence of a wide variety of attempts to manage a "commons" in intellectual property. The forms of collaboration and collaborative ownership examined in this volume, and especially the emerging attempts outside of software, such as Creative Commons, Rice University's Connexions project, MIT's Open CourseWare, and The Public Library of Science, represent an agreement to play by the some of the rules set out by DRM proponents in a world of strong intellectual property—but at minimum insist that there be just as many ways to format a network to allow for the free flow of information as there are ways to format a network to allow for the restriction of that information. Such projects recognize that there is no such thing as information-as-such, and that no law or technology will therefore govern all possible uses. Like Vontu, such attempts to create a commons recognize the need for collaborative stewardship and protection of some kinds of information, and navigate a pragmatic path between totalitarian monopoly rights in information, and the equally problematic ideology of completely unrestricted (irresponsible) information.

Such initiatives generally tend to occupy a moral high-ground based on the belief that freely circulating information contributes to scientific or cultural progress, rather than (as in case of Vontu) becoming profitable by exploiting either regulatory opportunities, or generalized fears about insider identity theft. Nonetheless, both are ways of formatting networks that allow for some kinds of collaborative stewardship to be achieved through the creation of legal and technical tools for rendering trust, openness, or reputation more calculable.

Conclusion

The notion of "collaborative ownership" seems to suggest both agreement among the collaborators and the existence of ownable things. But as the Free Software Movement demonstrated, there are ways to have collaboration with a minimum of agreement or coordination and to have ownership without restricting circulation or innovation. But what should we make of things like money or personal data: information that is not "ownable" and yet must be circulated in highly specific and restricted ways in order to be valuable?

Even in the totalitarian fantasy world of Digital Rights Management, the ownership of information is preparatory to its circulation—which is imagined to be just as swift and massive as that of all things in the digital economy— but not without a promise. It is the promise, and the right to make it, which requires making men (and networks as well) more "necessary, uniform, like among like, regular, and consequently calculable." But these formatted networks are never simply solutions to existing problems—they produce new arrangements and possibilities, new promises, and new forms of responsibility.

As I've shown here, the emergence of the Public Key Infrastructure (PKI), for instance, is not simply a solution to the problem of insecure transactions, but an occasion for new concerns about the "web-of-trust" and new ways of formatting markets in "secure transactions" in which "trust" can mean many different things. In turn, the creation of such formatted networks of insiders and outsiders is an occasion for Vontu's concerns about insider threats and the need for alternative forms of information definition and management. At the same time, the attempts by the entertainment and software industries to implement Digital Rights Management creates new conflicts in the use and reuse of information, rather than simply solving the problem of file-sharing. In turn, alternative modes of sharing and licensing material, such as Creative Commons, produce new questions about the definitions of authorship, ownership, liability, and collaboration even as they agree to basic definitions set out in intellectual property law.

These productive rearrangements and formattings are all, in their own ways, fundamentally creative. They are not simply unintended consequences of the inevitable march of technology or the overly enthusiastic passing of legislation, not simply reactive but spontaneous, aggressive, expansive, and form-giving. The question remains open, however, as to whether Nietzsche's ultimate diagnosis of man—the transformation of responsibility into guilt and bad conscience—yet has a role to play among the networks and algorithms.

Notes

1. See Nietzsche (2000), p. 495.

2. Theorizations of the relation between the "possessive individual" and the rise of modern property regimes are too numerous to note. The philosophical locus classicus is almost always John Locke (1967). More proximately, the widely cited C. B. Macpherson (1962).

3. In anthropology, see Karl Polanyi (1957) and Marshall Sahlins (1972). In economics see Harold Demsetz (1967) and Richard A. Posner (1980).

4. See Callon (1998, 2).

5. See Hacking (1983).

6. See Callon (1998, 19 ff). Callon cites M. F. Garcia 1986.

7. See Callon (1998, 19).

8. See Simmel (1978 [1907], 176).

9. See Simmel (1978 [1907], 224 ff).

10. See Simmel (1978 [1907], 227).

11. Similar ads were run on television. The ads referred to here ran in the Dec. 1, 2003 issue of the *New Yorker* magazine.

12. See VeriSign Corporation (2000, 1).

13. See Callon (1998, 12ff).

14. At the U.S. federal level, for instance, there have been a flurry of laws and amendments since about 1995: the Fair Credit Reporting Act (FCRA), 15 U.S.C. § 1681 et seq., The Health Insurance Portability and Accountability Act of 1996 (HIPAA) Public Law 104–191, Federal Register: December 28, 2000 (Volume 65, Number 250) Gramm-Leach-Bliley Act of 1999, Public Law 106–102 15 U.S.C. § 6801 et seq.

15. The RSA algorithm (Patent no. 4,405,829) was the first patented implementation of a public key cryptography system. Public key systems are commonly attributed to Diffie and Hellman (1976).

16. An announcement is archived at the Electronic Privacy Information Center (EPIC) (2000).

17. Terrorist nations at the time included Cuba, Iran, Iraq, Libya, North Korea, Sudan, or Syria. Just for the record, Afghanistan was not considered a terrorist nation—though in all fairness, no one considered it a market either.

18. Most notably, the Secure Electronic Transaction (SET) system developed by Visa and MasterCard and the Secure Sockets Layer (SSL) system designed for transactions conducted in Web browsers such as Netscape and Internet Explorer.

19. The Electronic Signatures in Global and National Commerce Act 15 U.S.C. § 7001 was signed into law on June 30, 2000 to allow such forms of authentication to be considered legally binding.

20. See Schneier (1996).

21. See Weiser (2002).

22. See VeriSign Corporation (2000, 1).

23. Whether a corporation does this autocratically or in consultation with its own employees no doubt varies drastically from company to company. Vontu offers to help

corporations respond to federal regulations and assess their own security threats as well as providing software. It is no doubt in the action of deciding what to protect and from whom that will determine whether employees are treated as—or come to see themselves as—criminals.

24. See Fortun (2003).

25. The original proposal by Mark Stefik was explained in Stefik (1997). Some current standardization attempts have included the World Wide Web Consortium (W3C), The Motion Picture Experts Group's MPEG-21 standard, Oasis' XrML Rights Language, and the Open e-Book Forum's (OeBF) Rights and Rules Working Group.

26. Adobe does not remove *Alice in Wonderland* from the public domain by so managing it, yet this represents a limit case in which it is unclear whether the contract one signs with Adobe could supercede the rights to use or reuse material in the Public Domain. The DMCA makes it illegal to tamper with the e-Book, even if the material is not copyrighted.

27. See Cohen (1996).

28. This is most visible in the challenges brought against the DMCA to date—academic freedom in computer security research, the question of whether software code is considered speech—as well as the variety of court cases involving fair use such as sampling, appropriation, and parody. The term de-authorize is deliberate, insofar as the existing contract between an author and his/her imagined audience depends a great deal on the forms a work can take, and the limits of the media. The libratory claims made in the name of "hypertext" novels over the last fifteen years largely depended on an enthusiastically expansive notion of reading freely, while DRM, rather than stressing the total liberation of the reader, imagines the opposite.

References

Callon, Michel. 1998. *The laws of the market.* Oxford: Blackwell Publishers.

Cohen, Julie. 1996. A right to read anonymously: A closer look at "copyright management" in cyberspace. *Connecticut Law Review* 28: 981.

Demsetz, Harold. 1967. Toward a theory of property rights. *American Economic Review* 57(2): 347–359.

Diffie, Whitfield, and Martin E. Hellman. (1976). New directions in cryptography. *IEEE Transactions on Information Theory*, IT-22(6): 644–654.

Electronic Privacy Information Center (EPIC). 2000. Revised U.S. encryption export control regulations, January 2000. Available at: <http://www.epic.org/crypto/export_controls/regs_1_00.html> (Last Visited Dec. 15, 2003).

Fortun, Michael. 2003. Populations, addiction and the "care of the data." Paper presented at the Annual Meeting of the Society for the Social Studies of Science, Atlanta, GA, November 2003.

Garcia, M. F. 1986. La construction sociale d'un marché parfait: Le marché au cadran de Fontaines-en-Sologne. *Actes de la Recherche en Science Sociales* 65: 2–13.

Hacking, Ian. 1983. *Representing and intervening: Introductory topics in the philosophy of natural science.* Cambridge: Cambridge University Press.

Locke, John. 1967. *Two treatises of government: A critical edition with an introduction and apparatus criticus by Peter Laslett.* 2nd ed. London: Cambridge University Press.

Macpherson, Crawford B. 1962. *The political theory of possessive individualism: Hobbes to Locke.* Oxford: Clarendon Press.

Nietzsche, Friedrich. 2000. The genealogy of morals, second essay. In *Basic writings of Nietzsche.* New York: Modern Library.

Polanyi, Karl. 1957. *The great transformation.* Boston: Beacon Press.

Posner, Richard A. 1980. A theory of primitive society, with special reference to law. *Journal of Law and Economics* 23(1): 1–53.

Sahlins, Marshall. 1972. *Stone age economics.* Chicago: Aldine-Atherton.

Schneier, Bruce. 1996. *Applied cryptography: Protocols, algorithms, and source code in C.* 2nd ed. New York: Wiley.

Simmel, Georg. 1978 [1907]. *Philosophy of money*, translated by Tom Bottomore and David Frisby. London: Routledge.

Stefik, Mark. 1997. "Trusted systems." *Scientific American* 276(3): 78–80.

VeriSign Corporation. 2000. VeriSign authentication services. Available at <http://www.verisign.com/rsc/wp/auth_srv/index.html> (last visited Dec 15, 2003).

Weiser, Benjamin. 2002. Identity ring said to victimize 30,000. *New York Times*, Nov. 26, 2002, A-1.

10

Cooking-Pot Markets and Balanced Value Flows

Rishab Aiyer Ghosh

On the face of it, the way many people behave on the Internet is quite different from how they behave offline. They work without pay. They follow rules without the threat of enforcement from policing authorities. They form strong communities without the bonds of geography or physical interaction.

On the face of it many people seem to take leave of their senses when online, turning into altruists driven by fuzzy feelings of goodwill and happiness that replaces their more-or-less rational behavior offline, resulting in a burst of collaborative, productive activity that appears to bear no relationship with economics, let alone money. But that's only on the face of it. In fact, people's behavior online is probably just as rational as offline. After all, why would it be any different, when the people are the same?

And although the same rationality may lead to apparently different results, this is due to special features of the cyberspace environment, which can be studied, understood, and modelled. That such modelling is necessary is most apparent with the phenomenon of free software/open source development. This aspect of the "intangible" part of the Net has had a very significant—and certainly *tangible*—impact on the offline world of brick-space, not least in the business community, but is hard to measure or analyze in detail.

In 1996 I wrote an explanation of forms of nonmonetary economic activity on the Internet—of which free software is only one part, albeit the most publicized one. I eventually published this two years later, in a paper describing "cooking-pot markets" (Ghosh 1998). I summarized it as describing a model for the nonmonetary economics of implicit transactions on the Internet.

Although the term nonmonetary economics might sound to many readers as peculiar today as it did then, mainstream economists have, in the past couple of years, rushed to produce studies of free software, so clearly *nonmonetary* and *economics* are not contradictory. But perhaps the nonmonetary aspect of this "cooking-pot market" model is less significant than the fact that transactions are implicit to the point of practical nonexistence.

The basic principle of this model is that access to a vast collection of diverse resources—people, goods, or information—is more valuable to people participating in this system than the cost of their own work. They are implicitly aware of, and willing to participate in networks of value-flow unassisted (and unhampered) by explicit measures such as prices, or even barter exchange rates.

Without one-to-one transactions, there cannot be any barter exchange. Rather, these networks work in a way analogous to a hypothetical tribal cooking-pot, where tribe members contribute their products to a common pool in implicit exchange for a higher-value end-product. The analogy to free software would be the contributions of individual patches of code to a common pool, in implicit exchange for access to the combined software that results from several contributions, a whole that is far more valuable than the sum of its parts. On the Internet, thanks to the nature of networked information products, this end-product is infinitely reproduced. In the offline world of physically reproduced goods, where participants might be inclined to argue over their relative shares of the end-product, a "cooking-pot" system would be unlikely to work on a large scale, without very strong adherence to communal values. This is why potlatch and gift-giving is typically associated with small communities. But with information products, no sharing out of the end-product is necessary—each contributor can have (or freely access) her own personal copy of the entire pool.

Modeling communities and economic activity usually depends on measurement, which is why it seems very hard to model cooking-pot networks—such as the community of open source software developers. I propose various methods of getting around the problems of cooking-pot networks, of modelling and understanding them so that their benefits can be truly appreciated and worked with.

A comparison of some key aspects of cooking pot networks, priced markets and barter exchanges (table 10.1) shows that the major defining attribute of cooking-pot markets is the implicit nature of "transactions" and their non-

Table 10.1 Priced markets, barter exchanges, and cooking-pot networks compared

Priced markets	Barter exchanges	Cooking-pot networks
Price tags	No price tags, but exchange rates for types of barter goods—i.e., relative price tags—are available	No price tags
Priced transactions—buying/selling—at every step	Identifiable barter transactions—trades—at every step	Few identifiable transactions—production is gratis, and value is received from the whole network with no explicit linkage; only a *value flow*
Quantifiable by price and volume (number of transactions)	Partly quantifiable by relative size and number of transactions	Not directly quantifiable—no price tags to add up; no transactions to count
Tangible benefits partially indirect (money to buy other things); quantifiable	Tangible benefits completely direct (end-products exchanged); partly quantifiable	Tangible benefits indirect and hard to quantify
Intangible benefits less important, less direct?	Intangible benefits less important, less direct?	Intangible benefits direct and apparent (reputation; sense of satisfaction, etc.)

quantifiable nature. On the other hand, "intangible" benefits such as reputation are by no means limited to cooking-pot networks, though they may be perceived as more important here for want of anything easier to measure.

Like Barter, but Where Are the Transactions?

To measure something, it is useful to know what one is measuring. And with cooking-pot markets, more so than barter, this is not easy. A barter economy is nonmonetary but not transaction-less; indeed it involves transactions that are quite explicit. I give you a fish, you give me two potatoes. If we stop and look at what happens here, we can get a lot of information: I transact with you; fish and potatoes are related; we both agree that a fish is equivalent in value to two potatoes. Even though no money was involved, the information that the involvement of money would represent—the relative value of whatever goods or services we exchanged—is still available in a barter transaction.[1]

Now to make things a bit more interesting, let's suppose that we both realize that this barter transaction leaves us pretty much where we began, except that the fish and potatoes have changed hands. We see that combining our inputs by tossing the fish and potatoes into a shared cooking-pot would lead to a fish-potato stew that would be more valuable to each of us than just the fish, or just the potatoes. In the physical world we might squabble over the stew that would have to be shared out based on how much we each thought our contributions were worth. On the Internet, we can each eat the whole stew—entire personal copies of the whole cooking-pot, so we're saved a fight.

But what have we done here? While contributing one thing—on the cooking-pots of the Internet this would be an article, say, or a piece of code—we are receiving, or able to access, our own personal copy of a million different creations of a million different people, often combined into larger, more valuable collaborative creations. There are many ways in which this is interesting but one I want to focus on here is that we haven't actually had a single explicit transaction, no identifiable exchange. I'm not transacting with you; I'm not giving you anything or getting anything from you, as an individual; and a cooking-pot is an abstraction, I can't be transacting with it. I'm contributing, certainly—and just as certainly I'm receiving back. Whom to and whom from is what is not quite clear. And I argue that it doesn't matter, not really.

If you can't identify transactions, you apparently have nothing to measure. Without measurement, it's difficult to develop any economic tools, without which talking of an "economic model" is sort of hollow. But you can abstract out from the explicit transaction, the exchange, into what I call balanced value-flow.

When I give you a fish in exchange for two potatoes, (and it's the same if I give you a dollar for two potatoes) it's clear who is doing how much of what with whom. But instead of looking at what happens from some point in between the two of us, we could look at it simultaneously from our two individual perspectives. I value the fish I give (to you) less than I value the potatoes I get (from you). You value the fish you get (from me) more than the potatoes you give (to me). We both profit, in that we each believe the transaction is beneficial to us. That is why we engage in this transaction.

An abstraction of this exchange to balanced value-flow is to erase the parenthetical phrases: I value the fish I give less than the potatoes I get—and it doesn't really matter who gets that fish and where those potatoes come from. If what I give costs me less than what I get, if my outward value-flow is less than my inward value-flow, in my subjective perception I have profited. (And we should keep in mind that economic objectivity is merely the aggregation of several individual subjective perceptions.)

If it doesn't matter to me as a fish-distributor who gets the fish, it doesn't matter to me as an economist if it's possible to identify or trace where that fish eventually goes, and where the potatoes originally come from. The value I create could just as well go into this common pool, these cooking pots—this "Internet" thing which, happily enough, is also a source of the value I receive.

Thus: the economic activity in a market based on monetary transactions is measured and modelled by aggregating the value *exchanged* in transactions between individuals. Similarly, the economic activity in a market based on nonmonetary nontransactions (or pseudo-?) could be measured and modelled by aggregating the value flowing from and toward individuals.

Measurement, but of What?

Let us look more closely at how we identify and measure an economic transaction. In any given economic transaction, whether it is monetary or barter, there is usually an exchange. A commodity or service is provided by *Bob* to *Alice* (a potato, say, see figure 10.1). *Alice* meanwhile provides in return to *Bob* some commodity or service, in the case of barter, or money, in a commercial transaction. In the figure, *Alice* returns fish, or dollars.

There is no absolute rule governing this exchange, no absolute value of what *Alice* or *Bob* provide each other. *Alice* believes her own produce to be of some value. Let's write this as $V_A(A)$: *A's* valuation of *A's* produce. *Alice* also values what *Bob* offers in exchange, at $V_A(B)$. When *Alice* believes she is getting equivalent or greater value from *Bob* in return for what she gives, i.e., $V_A(B) \geq V_A(A)$, she is satisfied with the terms of exchange. The difference between what she gets from *Bob* and what she gives to *Bob*: $V_A(B) - V_A(A)$, is *Alice's* subjective profit value.

In a similar way, *Bob* values what is being offered by *Alice* at $V_B(A)$ and what *Bob* is offering *Alice* in return (which could be money) at $V_B(B)$. It is a

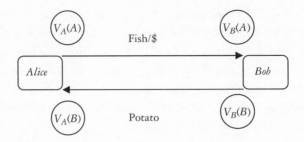

Figure 10.1 Subjective value perceptions in a barter or monetary exchange.

satisfactory exchange for *Bob* when, from *Bob*'s point of view, *Bob* is receiving at least as much as *Bob* is providing: $V_B(A) \geq V_B(B)$. Naturally, *Alice* and *Bob* may have different contexts and points of view, so they may well value each other's produce differently: $V_A(A)$ need not equal or even be comparable in any meaningful sense to $V_B(A)$.

Note that the function V here does not in any way reflect the *price* of a service or commodity, although in a monetary market system it is price that invariably becomes the measure of any transaction. Rather, V reflects the perceived value from the point of view of the individual participant, which—as common phrases such as "value for money" make clear—is not the same thing as a price, although a price does provide a good abstraction.

The purpose of this simplistic description of economic exchanges in terms of perceived value is this: it is possible to view an exchange as two independent decisions by *Alice* and *Bob*, two economic actions that can be treated distinctly, rather than blurred together as one "exchange." In the above exchange, there is a flow of value from *Alice* to *Bob*, and a corresponding flow of value from *Bob* to *Alice*. Normally, exchanges are examined at the point at which these two flows of value meet. In fact, they could be examined from the independent points of view of the participants in the exchange, *Alice* and *Bob*.

From A's point of view, there is an outflow of value, and an inflow of value. Value happens to be flowing out to *Bob*: $V_A(A)$ in the previous example. But from *Alice*'s point of view, this could just as well be treated independently of *Bob* (see figure 10.2); the "value of what goes out from *Alice*": $V_A(O)$. Similarly, the value for *Alice* of what comes *in* from *Bob*, $V_A(B)$ in the example, could just as well be treated as the "value of what comes in to *Alice*": $V_A(I)$.

Similarly from *Bob*'s point of view, for this specific transaction, there is an inflow of value, $V_B(A) \equiv V_B(I)$, and an outflow of value $V_B(B) \equiv V_B(O)$.

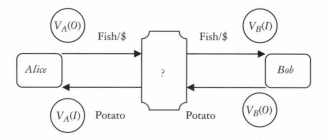

Figure 10.2 Perceived value-flow independent of the source or destination.

Both *Alice* and *Bob*, therefore, can make a decision to produce something based on what they receive or will receive. For example, *Alice* can decide it is worth creating an outflow of value $V_A(O)$ in response to an expected inflow $V_A(I)$ when the inflow is at least as much as the outflow: $V_A(I) \geq V_A(O)$. Again, the difference between the value of the inflow and the outflow: $V_A(I) - V_A(O)$ is *A*'s subjective "profit" value.

It is possible for *Alice* to make this decision regardless of the source of value inflow or the target of value outflow, i.e., *Alice* can make this decision to produce and consume in complete ignorance of *Bob*—providing this is practically possible.

In barter or monetary markets, where a binary exchange is the main form of economic transaction, this is usually not possible in practice, by definition—*Alice* has to give to and receive from only *Bob*, in order to complete an exchange with *Bob*. *Alice* cannot simply produce and consume without *Bob*, because *Alice* can only produce and consume via explicit exchanges.

However, in the cooking-pot market of the Internet, every entity *Alice* can and *does* produce and consume value without any knowledge of any specific counterpart *Bob*. It is feasible to provide a service without necessarily placing a restriction or limit on the service's beneficiaries—i.e., it is feasible in the cooking-pot model to simply provide value to all takers without necessarily excluding those who don't pay, for example. It follows that it is possible, indeed natural, for *Alice* to make rational choices concerning her production of value, based on the value available to her.

It is possible for *Alice* to balance inward and outward flows of value *in the aggregate*. As long as $V_A(I) \geq V_A(O)$ there is an incentive for *Alice* to produce, regardless of where inward value flows *from*. Indeed, it is often hard for *Alice* to identify who is providing her value, and who benefits from what she does (let alone how much—a measurement problem usually well beyond the means of individuals in the priceless cooking-pot market). *Alice* is thus encouraged to continue to produce an outward value-flow as long as *total* inward value flow is balanced with *total* outward value-flow: $V_A(I_{total}) \geq V_A(O_{total})$.

Value-Flow and the Point of Measurement

In a commercial market, measurement of economic activity is focused on the transactions more than on the buyer and seller. That is, the intersecting point of value-flows is paid more attention than the points of origin and destination. Indeed although it may be unclear what or who the transacting parties are, it is generally clear where the transaction itself is, because that point is marked by a price tag.

In a cooking-pot market, measurement is not through prices at the point of transaction—because it is the individual transactions that are hard to identify. Instead, measurement where possible must be at the points of origin of value-flow—i.e., the producers and consumers of value. At these points, what can be measured is not the price of a single transaction, but the balance between inflow and outflow of value.

These flows are not easily quantifiable. But they are no less a useful measure of economic activity than price. The crucial difference between these two methods of measurement is the focal point of view—transaction (which can be tracked by price) versus transacting entity (tracked by value-flow balance).[2]

Value-flow measurement requires the development of a whole range of tools and indicators capable of representing the subjective perceptions of value by economic actors in a reasonably accurate manner. The value perceptions are subjective by definition, as they are from the points of view of individual participants in the cooking-pot economy. In price markets too, perceptions of value are subjective. However the perceptions of value themselves—the basis of what motivates people to produce and consume—are less frequently the target of measurement than the amount of transaction that results from such subjective perceptions and motivations. The why of economic activity is usually subsumed by the how much—which in a price market is, for practical purposes, objectively encapsulated in the single measure of price.

Measuring at the source of a transaction, the root of production as it were, requires addressing the why of economic activity directly, at every step. Because we can't blindly assume that, for practical purposes, money is what completely motivates every economic act, we must look more closely at what motivates production, and this is naturally a fairly subjective question, differing from individual producer to producer. (In truth, even in a priced market, individuals' perceptions of value vary considerably, and the result is termed work preference or consumer choice, while it is, of course, a matter of differences in value perceptions that are not captured in a uniform price measure.)

Economics is often about measuring objectively quantifiable interaction between people; subjective measures are usually left to sociologists. This approach works in priced markets where the primary economic measures are not directly, or even apparently affected by subjective differences in value perception. But in a market without price measures, acknowledging subjective differences in value perception can drastically change our understanding of the economic rationale of initially perplexing behavior.

Take, for example, an author of an essay on the instrumental music of the baroque period. Such an author might, in a priced market, charge money from readers. Such an author may also indirectly—after a series of transactions—transfer most of the money to those very readers for other services. Those readers in turn would charge for the services they provide. In such a situation, economic activity is being measured via priced transactions without any need for—or relevance of—a better understanding of what motivates the author to write.

In the cooking-pot markets of the Internet, this author does not charge his readers. And if he benefits from anything those readers produce, directly or indirectly, he does not pay them either. Now that the veil of price has been lifted from the gritty reality of apparently irrational economic activity, subjective differences in value perception are crucial for any useful understanding. Looking through the lens of balanced value-flow, the author must place a value on his readership that is equal or greater than the value he places on his essay. The greater this difference in perceived value, naturally, the greater his level of satisfaction, (i.e., if he values his readership of five hundred people twice as much as he values his essay, he is making, in balanced value-flow terms, a 200% "profit").

On the other hand, an individual reader probably values the essay far more than she values her own contribution to the author's growing readership. She certainly values the essay at least as much as she values her time spent reading it. Her access to the author's essay is satisfactory and profitable, too. Thus the "transaction" between author and reader is mutually satisfactory, as it should be.

Without the notion of value-flow and subjective value perceptions to explain this interaction, motivating factors for reader and author are ignored, and so the entire activity appears noneconomic in the extreme. Altruism, sentimental enthusiasm, and similar terms come to mind as explanations, but they are certainly not the economic cornerstone of rational self-interest.

Looking through the filter of balanced value-flow, however, makes the entire transaction more reasonable, albeit quite hypothetical. The need to examine—or at least acknowledge—the differing, subjective motivation that is a key to value-flow modelling certainly makes it easier to explain why anyone would publish an essay without payment. To put it bluntly, value-flow analysis shows that an author who writes because she wants to be read, could in sound mind and with all rationality publish without payment—she may not get money, but she will be read, which is her primary goal. On the other hand, an author who writes largely to pay the rent will think twice before doing this.

Perhaps the most useful demonstration of the value-flow model is in perceptions of costs of various forms of "intellectual property." The cost of creating an original information product—whether an idea, a song, or a software application—is much higher for the creator than its replication, broadcast, or distribution. This is the essential problem referred to in the introduction to this volume—each copy of an information product is essentially of zero value, in terms of the marginal cost of reproduction; but it can cost a lot to create the original work in the first place, and its existence—as a unique information product—can clearly be of considerable value. Trying to extract the high value of the original work by creating a property-rights framework around the low-value copies is what leads to such unsurprising practices such as "software piracy" or unlicensed music downloads. But the high value of the original creation cannot be ignored altogether. In the cooking-pot market, it seems to get compensated through other ways, the value-flow is balanced.

The act of creating a product, or originating a service, is an outflow of value. Duplication of that product is not necessarily a significant value outflow at all, and can even be a value inflow, as for the author in the preceding example (where duplication results in a wide readership).

For anyone receiving such an information product or service, however, receiving a copy is usually an inflow of value. Very rarely does receiving the original, rather than a copy, have any special value, and the distinction between original and copy is not significant with pure information products, such as on the Internet. This results in an implicit exchange, or balance of value-flow for creators of original works and their consumers alike, between the value of creating a single work and the value of being able to access a diversity of works by others.[3]

Identifying, Tracking, and Measuring Cooking-Pot Networks

Accepting a model of transaction-less value-flow for the nonmonetary economic activity of the Internet does not solve the problem of measurement, which is necessary to analyze in detail what's going on and predict further developments. Indeed, measurement is more complicated once a whole range of subjective value-flow perceptions must be taken into account.

To measure price-based economic activity is straightforward— individual transactions are clearly identified, transactions can be tracked and collated into defined and segmented markets, and the activity on price-based markets can be measured (by definition, there is always a price on everything).

With cooking-pot markets, however, the nonmonetary aspect comes back to bite again. Money is really nice for economists; maybe even more so than it is for those who have money, rather than only to measure it. Money is quantified, which means you can do all sorts of wonderful mathematical magic with it; it is a generalized proxy for all value, which means you don't really have to bother about what money means or represents; and it has a sort of false objectivity that allows you to leave any real (and therefore inconveniently complicated) discussion of the subjective perceptions of value behind monetary indicators to specialists in niche studies of socioeconomics, such as theories of preference and consumer behavior.

Without money as a tool of measurement, you have all these issues to consider. You must find other ways of quantifying value; you must examine the different sorts of things people value and the different expressions they have for value; and you really can't avoid the fact that very different people value the same thing very differently.

Add to all this the fact that without identifiable explicit transactions you don't have explicitly identifiable transactors—i.e., you don't know who's doing the valuing, the production, the consumption. So translating the cooking-pot model of nonmonetary, implicit transaction economics from a metaphorical explanatory model of reality, into a functional way of measuring and working with unusual changes in how large parts of society seem to be developing, is quite a complex task.

The broad question of identifying who is doing how much of what with whom is something that gets concisely focused in a price market, by examining a transaction, a price, or a collection of transactions in a market.

On a cooking-pot network, without a transaction, the *who* is a nontrivial question, as there are no clearly identified transacting parties. The closest equivalent to transacting parties is contributor groups, e.g., the "Linux developer community."

Such amorphously defined groups change shape, and often have a radiating identity—with a central core of group members where contribution peaks, surrounded by members of reducing contribution and group identity. The sharpness of the contrast between center and surroundings, peak and valley, is what defines the cohesiveness of the group, and determines its suitability for treatment as a single economic entity.

Identifying these groups involves measuring contribution levels and monitoring perception of both group identity and value-flow among members. Understanding the interaction between economic entities—who is doing *what* with whom—involves studying shifts in patterns of membership and cross-membership between different groups. In the case of free software, for instance, the economic dependence and value-flow across free software/open source projects such as Linux, Perl, and various parts of GNU/Free Software Foundation (FSF) can be mapped across time by tracking the authorship of program source code and identifying author group membership. Tracking authorship is quite easy in theory, though it isn't very easy in practice since authors aren't always easy to identify. Once authors are identified, their group membership can be determined by following them and their source code components across projects.

Tracking value-flow could make it possible to model and predict group membership, flux in exchange and membership between groups. It could even help identify the value exchange rate across groups—there is a measurable value given to GNU/FSF software within Linux groups, which translates to value placed on authors of such software; but probably much less value is given by Linux programmers to members of and content from <rec.music.early>, a newsgroup on early music.

Measures of contribution, its concentration and distribution within groups can help model shape changes within groups—enabling one to predict their disintegration, for instance, or pressures toward commercialization or guild-type segmentation (by shutting out nonmembers).

Determining who is doing *how much* is partly a problem of quantification. Although no simple measure such as number of transactions or price levels is possible, other indicators of value-flow and proxies for value can be used.

For example, it is possible to monitor producer/consumer activity and concentration by area—such as population, frequency, distribution, and overlap among participants in Linux and Perl developer communities, or readers of newsgroups such as <rec.pets.cats> and <rec.music.classical>.

More practically useful measures are possible. The health of a cooking-pot market economy can be measured through macroeconomic means. These could include: the lurker coefficient, indicating the concentration of active participants within a group (and share of inactive ones, or "lurkers"), arrived at by calculating the ratios of contributions to contributors.

A high lurker coefficient may reduce the motivation of the relatively small number of active participants to contribute free of charge and hence encourage barriers, analogous to the formation of guilds—or a shift to price-based model, as in the case of the Internet Movies Database (IMDb), once all free, now advertising-based.[4]

Easier measures could be possible with the widespread use of reputation networks: measures indicating the level of trust in the economy are indicative of economic activity. The distribution or concentration of high reputations is similar to concentrations in the level of (monetary) wealth, and could be analogous to the Gini coefficient, a common statistical measure of concentration.

Equivalence measures, quantifying links between information exchanges and price-based markets outside, are possible too. These could be based on time spent in "free" production or by comparing equivalent priced products, where applicable.

Conclusion, and a Starting Point for Measurement

The nonmonetary-with-implicit-transaction characteristics of cooking-pot markets are ever present on the Internet. In order to examine them through the perspective of balanced value-flow, we need to find ways to measure this activity, and to measure and find possible value-flows. Where to start trying out new forms of measurement of such economic activity? Free software seems an obvious choice.

Unlike many aspects of the Internet's nonmonetary economy, such as USENET discusson groups, free software has clearly recognizable brick-space equivalents—such as commercial software, against which it can be measured. Free software leaves its traces everywhere—access to source code has the most amazing and possibly unintended effect of making the functioning of software development open to scrutiny, as it is possible to analyze credits, comments, dependencies, and lots of other things. Finally, and this is not the least important when the impact of research results could depend on something interesting and dramatic, free software is the part of cyberspace's cooking-pot economy that grabs the most headlines.

So, how do you measure value in the free software community? Initial approaches in this area have been divided into two areas—studies of the categories of motivation that are exist (possible sources of value *inflow*),[5] and studies aiming to quantify the output of developers and the extent of collaboration (mainly, but not only, measures of value outflow). Several studies[6] have shown that it is possible to identify, in addition to concentrations of individual contribution: change over time; group identification by project; dependencies between projects; exchange rate between value attached to groups of authors; assorted demographics; free-rider and guild pressures; lurker coefficients, and more.

Of course writing code is not the only contribution in the free software community; reading it, commenting on it, and using it are important too—just even harder to measure. Some attempts have been made at organizing and making sense of online discussion groups including USENET,[7] but there's clearly a long way to go.

Acknowledging only monetary exchange as the basis for economic activity left a vast area of collaborative production on the Internet inexplicable and unaccounted for. Seeing this area through the lens of value-flow, seeing it for what it is—nonmonetary but usually clearly economic activity—makes it explicable. But we still have to measure and account for it as value-flow.

Notes

1. In this case, we agree that one fish is worth two potatoes; this lets us, or our observers, make generalizations about the relative worth of fish, potatoes, and other products involved in a series of barter exchanges.

2. This leads one to wonder whether a reason for the open source software community's comfort with this economics is its similarity to the programming concept of object-oriented design—where programs are considered from the point of view of objects rather than the point of view of transactions between objects.

3. See Ghosh (1995a, 1995b, 1995c, and 1995d); Ghosh (1998).

4. See Ghosh (1998).

5. Such studies include the Robles-Martinez et al. (2001), the European Union-funded FLOSS study (Ghosh, Glott, Krieger, and Robles 2002) and its successors—FLOSS-US at Stanford and FLOSS-JP by Mitsubishi Research, and BCG 2002.

6. See Ghosh and Ved Prakash (2000); Dempsey, Weiss, Jones, and Greenberg (2002); Ghosh et al. (2002); Tuomi (2002); Ghosh and David (2003), Robles et al. (2003).

7. Microsoft Research's experimental service, <netscan.research.microsoft.com>, led by Marc Smith, is a fascinating exploration of USENET by group affinities based on common content and the degree of collaboration between groups.

References

BCG. 2002. Survey of free software/open source developers conducted by the Boston Consulting Group. <www.osdn.com/bcg>.

Dempsey, Bert J., Debra Weiss, Paul Jones, and Jane Greenberg. 2002. Who is an open source software developer? *Communications of the ACM* <http://www.ibiblio.org/osrt/develpro.html>.

Ghosh, Rishab Aiyer. 1995a. Traders and originators. (Electric Dreams, July 3). *The Asian Age 64.* Available at <http://dxm.org.dreams/>.

———. 1995b. Trade reborn through diversity. (Electric Dreams, July 10). *The Asian Age 65.* Available at <http://dxm.org.dreams/>.

———. 1995c. Trading in people. (Electric Dreams, July 24). *The Asian Age 66.* Available at <http://dxm.org.dreams/>.

———. 1995d. Paying your readers. (Electric Dreams, July 31). *The Asian Age 67.* Available at <http://dxm.org.dreams/>.

————. 1998. Cooking pot markets: An economic model for the trade in free goods and services on the Internet. *First Monday* 3(3). <http://www.firstmonday.org/issues/issue3_3/ghosh/index.html>.

Ghosh, Rishab Aiyer, and Paul A. David. 2003. The nature and composition of the Linux kernel developer community: A dynamic analysis. SIEPR-Project NOSTRA Working Paper, draft available at <http://dxm.org/papers/licks1/>.

Ghosh, Rishab Aiyer, Ruediger Glott, Bemhard Krieger, and Gregorio Robles-Martinez. 2002. FLOSS: Free/Libre/Open Source Software Study: Final report" Part IV & V; International Institute of Infonomics/MERIT <http://www.flossproject.org/report/>.

Ghosh, Rishab Aiyer, and Vipul Ved Prakash. 2000. The Orbiten free software survey. In *First Monday* 5(7). <http://www.firstmonday.org/issues/issue5_7/ghosh/>.

Raymond, Eric S. 1998. The cathedral and the bazaar. *First Monday* 3(3). <http://www.firstmonday.org/issues/issue3_3/raymond/>.

Robles-Martínez, Gregorio, Hendrik Scheider, Ingo Tretkowski and Niels Weber 2001. WIDI: Who is doing it? Technical University of Berlin. <http://widi.berlios.de/paper/study.html>.

Robles-Martínez, Gregorio, Jesús M. González-Barahona, José Centeno González, Vicente Matellán Olivera, and Luis Rodero Merino. 2003. Studying the evolution of libre software projects using publicly available data. 25th International Conference on Software Engineering. Portland, Oregon, <http://opensource.ucc.ie/icse2003/>.

Tuomi, Ilkka. 2002. Evolution of the Linux Credits File: Methodological Challenges and Reference Data for Open Source Research—working paper. Available at <http://www.jrc.es/~tuomiil/moreinfo.html>.

11

Coase's Penguin, or, Linux and the Nature of the Firm

Yochai Benkler

Introduction

For decades our common understanding of the organization of economic production has been that individuals order their productive activities in one of two ways: either as employees in firms, following the directions of managers, or as individuals in markets, following price signals. This dichotomy was first identified in the early work of Ronald Coase and was developed most explicitly in the work of institutional economist Oliver Williamson. In this chapter I explain why we are beginning to see the emergence of a new, third mode of production, in the digitally networked environment, a mode I call "commons-based peer production."

At the heart of the economic engine of the world's most advanced economies, and in particular that of the United States, we are beginning to take notice of a hardy, persistent, and quite amazing phenomenon—a new model of production has taken root. It should not, the intuitions of the late twentieth-century American would say, be the case that thousands of volunteers will come together to collaborate on a complex economic project. It certainly should not be that these volunteers will beat the largest and best-financed business enterprises in the world at their own game. And yet, this is precisely what is happening in the software world.

The emergence of free software,[1] and the phenomenal success of its flagships—the GNU/Linux operating system, the Apache Web server, Perl, sendmail, BIND—and many others,[2] should force us to take a second look at the dominant paradigm we hold about productivity. In the late 1930s, Ronald Coase wrote his article, *The Nature of the Firm*,[3] in which he explained why firms—clusters of resources and agents that interact through managerial command systems rather than markets—emerge. In that paper Coase introduced the concept of transaction costs—that is, that there are costs associated with defining and enforcing property and contract rights—which are a necessary incident of organizing any activity on a market model. Coase explained the emergence and limits of firms based on the differences in the transaction costs associated with organizing production through markets or through firms. People would use the markets when the gains from doing so, net of transaction costs, exceed the gains from doing the same thing in a managed firm, net of the organization costs. Firms would emerge when the opposite was true. Any individual firm would stop growing when its organization costs exceeded the organization costs of a newly formed, smaller firm. This basic insight was then extended and developed in the work of Oliver Williamson and other institutional economists who studied the relationship between markets and managerial hierarchies as models of organizing production.[4]

The emergence of free software as a substantial force in the software development world poses a puzzle for this conception of organization theory. Free software projects do not rely either on markets or on managerial hierarchies to organize production. Programmers do not generally participate in a project because someone who is their boss told them to. They do not generally participate in a project because someone offers them a price to do so, though some participants do focus on long-term appropriation through money-oriented activities, such as consulting or service contracts. But the critical mass of participation in projects cannot be explained by the direct presence of a price or even a future monetary return, particularly in the all-important microlevel decisions regarding selection of projects to which participants contribute. In other words, programmers participate in free software projects without following the normal signals generated by market-based, firm-based, or hybrid models.

This puzzle has attracted increasing attention from economists[5] and participants in the practice[6] trying to understand their own success and its sustainability given widespread contrary intuitions. Lerner and Tirole (2002) present an overarching view from an economics perspective of the range of diverse micromotivations that drive free software developers.[7] This diversity of motivations, somewhat more formalized and generalized, plays an important role in my own analysis. Some writing by both practitioners and observers, supporters and critics, has focused on the "hacker ethic," and analogized the sociological phenomenon to gift exchange systems.[8] Other writing has focused on the special characteristics of software as an object of production.[9] In this chapter I approach this puzzle by departing from free software. Rather than trying to explain what is special about software or hackers, I generalize from the phenomenon of free software to suggest what makes large-scale collaborations in many information production fields sustainable and productive in the digitally networked environment without reliance either on markets or on managerial hierarchy. Hence the title of the article, to invoke the challenge that the paunchy penguin that is the mascot of the Linux kernel development community poses for the view of organization rooted in Coase's work.

One important caveat is necessary. I am not suggesting that peer production will supplant markets or firms. I am not suggesting that it is always the more efficient model of production for information and culture. What I am saying is that this emerging third model is distinct from the other two, and has certain systematic advantages over the other two in identifying and allocating human capital/creativity. When these advantages will outweigh the advantages that the other two models may have in directing human behavior is a matter for more detailed study.

Peer Production All Around

While open source software development has captured the attention and devotion of many, it is by no stretch of the imagination the first or most important instance of production by peers who interact and collaborate without being organized on either a market-based or a managerial/hierarchical model. Most important in this regard is the academic enterprise, and in particular scientific research. Thousands of individuals make individual contributions to a body of knowledge, set up internal systems of quality control, and produce the core of our information and knowledge environment. These individuals do not expect to exclude from their product anyone who does not pay for it, and for many of them the opportunity cost of participating in academic research, rather than applying themselves to commercial enterprise, carries a high economic price tag. In other words, individuals produce on a nonproprietary basis, and contribute their product to a knowledge "commons" that no one is understood as "owning," and that anyone can, indeed is required by professional norms to, take and extend. It is easy, though unjustifiable, in the excitement of moment that feels like one of great transformation to forget that information production is one area where we have always had a mixed system of commercial/proprietary and nonproprietary peer production—not as a second best or a contingent remainder from the middle ages, but because at some things the nonproprietary peer production system of the academic world is simply better.[10]

The differences between academic peer production and commercial production reside in the modes of appropriation and in the modes of organization—in particular how projects are identified and how individual effort is allocated to projects. Academics select their own projects, and contribute their work to a common pool that eventually comprises our knowledge of a subject matter, while nonacademic producers will often be given their marching orders by managers, who themselves take their focus from market studies, and the product is then sold into the market for which it was produced.[11]

Alongside the professional model, it is also important to recognize that we have always had nonprofessional information and cultural production on a nonproprietary model. Individuals talking to each other are creating information goods, sometimes in the form of what we might call entertainment, and sometimes as a means for news distribution or commentary. Nonprofessional production has been immensely important in terms of each individual's information environment. If one considers how much of the universe of communications one receives in a day comes from other individuals in one-to-one or small-scale interactions—such as e-mail, lunch, or hallway conversations—the effect becomes tangible.

Nonetheless, ubiquitous computer communications networks are bringing about a dramatic change in the scope, scale, and efficacy of peer production. As computers become cheaper and as network connections become faster, cheaper, and more ubiquitous, we are seeing the phenomenon of nonprofessional peer production of information scale to much larger sizes, performing more complex tasks than were in the past possible for, at least, nonprofessional production.

There are many examples of peer production on the Net.[12] A good illustration of content creation is the tens of thousands of NASA clickworkers[13] collaborating in five-minute increments to map Mars's craters, fulfilling tasks that would normally require full-time PhDs. Further, the World Wide Web itself is a global library produced by millions of people, and Wikipedia[14] involves some 2,000 volunteers who are collaborating to write an encyclopedia. Examples of peer-production producing "accreditation and relevance" are Amazon, Google, Open Directory Project,[15] and Slashdot.[16] Finally, the value-added distribution remains. The most notorious example is Napster,[17] and a less well-known one is Project Gutenberg.[18] The point is simple. The phenomenon of large- and medium-scale collaborations among individuals, organized without markets or managerial hierarchies, is emerging everywhere in the information and cultural production system. The question is how we should understand these instances of socially productive behavior—how we should think about their economic value, how we should understand the dynamics that make them possible and make them tick.

These examples demonstrate the feasibility of this approach throughout the information production and exchange chain. While it is possible to break an act of communication into finer-grained subcomponents,[19] largely we see three distinct functions involved in the process. First, there is an initial utterance of a humanly meaningful statement. Second there is a separate function of mapping the initial utterances on a knowledge map. In particular, an utterance must be understood as "relevant" in some sense and "credible." Finally, there is the function of distribution, or how one takes an utterance produced by one person and distributes it to other people who find it credible and relevant. What the Net is permitting is much greater disaggregation of these functions.

In the remainder of the chapter I focus on general observations about peer production, what makes it work, and what makes it better under certain circumstances than market- or hierarchy-based production. Peer production is a phenomenon of much wider application than free software, and it is something that actually exists. What remains is the interesting and difficult task of explaining it in terms comprehensible to those who make economic policy, to begin to think about the policy implications of the emergence of this strange breed in the middle of our information economy. I will by no stretch of the imagination claim to have completed this task in the following pages. But I hope to identify some basic regularities and organizing conceptions that will be useful to anyone interested in pursuing the answer. Even if you do not buy a single word of my initial efforts to theorize the phenomenon, however, seeing these disparate phenomena as instances of a general emerging phenomenon in the organization of information production should present a rich topic of study for organization theorists, anthropologists, institutional economists, and business people interested in understanding new production models in a ubiquitously networked environment.

Why Would Peer Production Emerge in a Networked Environment?

Locating the Theoretical Space for Peer Production

In this early study of the phenomenon of peer production it seems important to establish its baseline plausibility as a sustainable and valuable mode of production within the most widely used relevant analytic framework than to offer a detailed explanation of its workings. Doing so should provide wider recognition of the policy implications, and create a space for more methodologically diverse inquiries.

My effort here will be directed towards offering an explanation within the framework that has largely become the mainstream economic theory of organizations, namely, the approach that followed Ronald Coase's (1937) *The Nature of the Firm* in focusing on the comparative costs of institutional alternatives as an explanation for their emergence and relative prevalence. At the most general intuitive level, we can begin by looking at Coase's explanation of the firm and Harold Demsetz's explanation of property rights.[20] Coase's basic explanation of why firms emerge is that using the price system is costly. Where the cost of achieving a given outcome in the world through the price system will be higher than the cost of using a firm to achieve the same result, firms will emerge to organize the behavior that would attain that result. Assuming that the cost of organization increases with size, Coase posited that we have a "natural" limit on the size and number of organizations.

Demsetz's basic explanation of why property emerges with regard to resources that previously were managed without property rights—as commons—can be resolved to a very similar rationale. Property in a resource emerges if the social cost of having no property in that resource exceeds the social cost of implementing a property system in it. This can include within it common property regimes, managed commons, and other nonproperty approaches to managing sustainable commons.

It is important to recognize that if we posit the existence of a third option, it is relatively easy to adapt the transactions cost theory of the firm and the comparative institutional cost theory of property to include it (see table 11.1). We would say that when the cost of organizing an activity on a peered basis

Table 11.1 Organizational forms as a function of relative social cost of property vs. no-property and firm-based management vs. market vs. peering

	Property more valuable than implementation costs	Cost of implementing property higher than opportunity cost of property
Market exchange of x more efficient than organizing/peering x	Pure market (farmers markets)	Pure commons (ideas and facts; highways?)
Organizing x more efficient than market exchange or peering of x	market with firms	Common property regimes (Swiss pastures)
Peering more efficient than market exchange or organization of x	Proprietary "open source" efforts (Xerox's Eureka)	Peer production processes* (free software; academic science; NASA clickworkers)

Note: *"Cost" here would include the negative effects of intellectual property on dissemination and downstream productive use.

is lower than the cost of using the market, and the cost of peering is lower than the cost of hierarchical organization, then peer production will emerge.

Understanding that in principle the same framework that explains the emergence of property and firms could explain the emergence of peer production focuses our effort on trying to understand why it is that peering could, under certain circumstances, be a more cost-effective institutional form than either markets or hierarchical organizations. Because the emergence of peer production seems to be tied to the emergence of a pervasively networked information economy, my explanation seeks to be in some sense sensitive to changes in the nature of the human and material resources used in information production relative to other productive enterprises, and affected by the cost and efficiency of communication among human participants in the productive enterprise.

Peer Production of Information in a Pervasively Networked Environment

Peer production is emerging as an important mode of information production because of four attributes of the pervasively networked information economy. First, the object of production—information—is quirky as an object of economic analysis, in that it is purely nonrival and its primary nonhuman input is the same public good as its output—information. Second, the physical capital costs of information production have declined dramatically with the introduction of cheap processor-based computer networks. Third, the primary human input—creative talent—is highly variable, more so than traditional labor, and certainly more so than many material resources usually central to production. Moreover, the individuals who are the "input" possess better information than anyone else about the variability and suitability of their talents and level of motivation and focus at a given moment to given production tasks. Fourth and finally, communication and information exchange across space and time are much cheaper and more efficient than ever before, which permits the coordination of widely distributed potential sources of creative effort and the aggregation of actual distributed effort into usable end products.

The first attribute—the public goods nature of information—affects the cost of one major input into production—existing information. It means that the social cost of using existing information as input into new information production is zero. This has two effects on the relative cost of peer production of information.[21] First, it lowers the expected social cost of peer production of information because in principle it means that a central input—preexisting information—could be available to human productive agents without limit. Second, it underlies a pervasive social cost of market and hierarchy in this field of production, because of the losses in both static and dynamic efficiency entailed by the implementation of property rights in a nonrival public good usually thought necessary to sustain market and hierarchy-based production of information.[22]

The second attribute—the decline in the capital cost of information production—similarly lowers the cost of another major capital cost of information production. The declining cost of computer processors coupled with the digitization of the fixation and transmission of all forms of information and culture, have made the physical capital necessary to embody and disseminate such goods cheaper by orders of magnitude than in the past.

Together, these first two attributes make information production a potentially sustainable low-cost, low-return endeavor for many individuals relying on indirect appropriation.[23] It is important to note, however, that the public goods attribute limits the applicability of my observations about peer production, so that I make no claim about the applicability of these observations to traditional economic goods.

The third characteristic—the centrality of human capital to information production and its variability—is the primary source of efficiency gains from moving from markets or hierarchical organization to peering. Peer production better produces information about available human capital, and increases the size of the sets of agents and resources capable of being combined in projects—where there are increasing returns to scale, in terms of allocation efficiency, for these sets.

The fourth attribute—the dramatic decline in communications costs—radically reduces the cost of peering relative to what was possible in the material world. This allows substantially cheaper movement of information inputs to human beings and of human talent to resources, and movement of modular contributions to projects, so that widely dispersed contributions can be integrated into finished information goods. It also allows communication among participants in peer production enterprises about who is doing what, and what needs to be done.

Markets, Hierarchies, and Peer Production as Information Processing Systems

Peer production has a relative advantage over firm- or market-based production along two dimensions, both a function of the highly variable nature of human capital. The first emerges when one treats all approaches to organizing production as mechanisms by which individual agents reduce uncertainty as to the likely value of various courses of productive action.[24] Differences among these modes in terms of their information-processing characteristics could then account for differences in their relative value as mechanisms for organizing production. The second dimension is that a particular strategy that firms, and to a lesser extent markets, use to reduce uncertainty—securing access to limited sets of agents and resources through contract and property—entails a systematic loss of productivity relative to peer production. This is so because there are increasing returns to scale to the size of the sets of agents and resources capable of being applied to sets of projects in terms of allocation efficiency, and peer production relies on unbounded access of agents to resources and projects.

Information Gains and Allocation Gains

Commons-based peer production relies on decentralized information gathering and exchange to reduce the uncertainty of participants, and has particular advantages as an information process for identifying human creativity available to work on information and cultural resources in the pursuit of projects, and as an allocation process for allocating that creative effort. It depends on very large aggregations of individuals independently scouring their information environment in search of opportunities to be creative in small or large increments. These individuals then self-identify for tasks and perform them for complex motivational reasons. If the problems of motivation and organization can be solved, however, then such a system has two major advantages over firms and markets. First, it places the point of decision about assigning any given person to any given set of resources with the individual. Given the high variability among individuals in terms of creativity, motivation, focus at any given point, availability, and so forth, human creativity is an especially difficult resource to specify for efficient contracting or management. Firms recognize this and attempt to solve this problem by creating various incentive compensation schemes and intangible reward schemes, such as employee-of-the-month awards. These schemes work to some extent to alleviate the information loss associated with managerial production, but only insofar as a firm's agents and resources are indeed the best, and only insofar as these schemes capture all the motivations and contributions accurately. What peer production does is provide a framework, within which individuals who have the best information available about their own fit for a task can self-identify for the task. This provides an information gain over firms and markets, but only if the system develops some mechanism to filter out mistaken judgments agents make about themselves. This is why practically all successful peer production systems have a robust mechanism for peer review or statistical weeding out of contributions from agents who misjudge themselves.

As important as the information gains of peer production are its allocation gains, assuming that the variability in talent, wisdom, focus, and creativity among human agents makes individuals highly diverse in their fit for the job of converting various existing information and cultural resources into new projects. Human creativity cannot be assumed to be an on-off switch of suitability to a job, as simple industrial treatments of labor might have. It is more likely that different people will be more or less productive with any given set of resources and collaborators for any given set of projects, and that this variability is large. This diversity can be viewed as a probability that any agent has of being a good fit with a set of resources and agents to produce highly valuable new information or cultural goods. Peer production has an advantage over firms and markets because it allows larger groups of individuals to scour larger groups of resources in search of materials, projects, collaborations, and combinations than do firms or individuals who function in markets. This is because when production is organized on a market or firm model, transaction costs associated with property and contract limit the access of people to each other, to resources and to projects, but do not do so when it is organized on a peer production model.[25] Because fit of people to projects and to each other is variable, there are increasing returns to the scale of the number of people, resources, and projects capable of being combined. These increasing returns reflect the increased probability that the best combination will emerge from larger clusters than from smaller clusters and result in a substantially higher probability that the right resource and human creative effort will be allocated to the project at which they would best be combined.

Of Motivation and Organization: The Commons Problem

The "Incentives" Problem of Diverse Motivations and Small Contributions

What makes contributors to peer production enterprises tick? Why do they contribute? There are two versions of this question. The first is the question of the economic skeptic. It questions the long-term sustainability of this phenomenon, given that people will not, after the novelty wears off, continue to work on projects in which they can claim no proprietary rights.[26] It is to this question that my discussion here responds, in an effort to show that the network as a whole can be a sustainable system for the production of information and culture. There is a second, narrower version of the question, which arises once one overcomes the skepticism and begins to consider how peer production can be steered or predicted. It would seek to understand the motivations and patterns of clustering around projects in the absence of property rights and contracts, and the emergence of the effective networks of peers necessary to make a *particular* project succeed. These are questions that present rich grounds both for theoretical and empirical study. My hunch is that these would best be done in the domains of social psychology and anthropology, or, if done formally, through artificial life-type (e.g., agent-based) modeling. They are, in any event, beyond the scope of this initial study, which is intended solely to define the phenomenon and assess its sustainability and welfare effects in general terms.

The incentive problem as an objection to the general sustainability of peer production is in large part, as a practical matter, resolved by the existence of a series of mechanisms for indirect appropriation of the benefits of participation catalogued quite comprehensively by Lerner and Tirole.[27] At the broadest level, there is the pleasure of creation. Call it dispassionately "hedonic gain" or romantically "an urge to create," the mechanism is simple. People are creative beings. They will play at creation if given an opportunity, and the network and free access to information resources provide this opportunity.[28] More closely related to the project of keeping body and soul together, there are a variety of indirect appropriation mechanisms for those who engage in free software development. These range from the amorphous category of reputation gains, through much more mundane benefits such as consulting contracts, customization services, and increases in human capital that are paid for by employers who can use the skills gained from participation in free software development in proprietary projects. In this regard, it is important to note that about two-thirds of the revenues in the software industry are not tied to software publishing, but to service-type relationships.[29] Given that the software industry is more than three times the size of, for example, movie, video, and sound recording put together,[30] two-thirds of this industry still provides a field from which to extract value for software developers who participate in free software projects that is more than twice the size of those smaller, albeit more flamboyant industries.

The reality of phenomena like academic research, free software, the World Wide Web, NASA's clickworkers or Slashdot supports these explanations with robust, if not quantified here, empirical grounding. All one need do is look at the Red Hat founders and IBM's billion-dollar commitments to supporting Linux and Apache on the one hand, and the tens of thousands of volunteer clickworkers, thousands of Linux developers, and hundreds of distributed proofreaders, on the other hand, to accept intuitively that some combination of hedonic gain and indirect appropriation can resolve the incentives problem. In this part I abstract from this intuitive observation to offer an answer that is more analytically tractable and usable to understand the microanalytical questions of peer production and the potential range in which peer production will be more productive than firms or markets.

Abstracting the Effect of Diverse Motivations   Saying that people participate for all sorts of reasons is obviously true at an intuitive level. It does not, however, go very far toward providing a basis for understanding why some projects draw many people, while others fail, or how the presence or absence of money affects the dynamic. Now I propose a framework to generalize the conditions under which peer production processes will better motivate human effort than market-based enterprises. Given the discussion of the information and allocation gains offered by peer production, this section outlines a range in which peer production should be more productive than market-based or firm-based production. At the broadest level, wherever peer production can motivate behavior better than markets or firms, then certainly it will be superior. It will also be potentially better over a range where it may motivate behavior less effectively than markets or firms, but the contribution of the lower overall effort level will be less than the contribution of the added value in terms of information about and allocation of human creativity.

Let any agent have a set of preferences for rewards of three types:

M $\Rightarrow$ Monetary rewards, which decrease in value because of the decreasing marginal utility of money. Call the rate at which M decreases s (satiation).

H $\Rightarrow$ *Intrinsic hedonic rewards* experienced from taking the actions

SP $\Rightarrow$ *Sociopsychological rewards*, which are a function of the cultural meaning associated with the act, and may take the form of actual effect on social associations and status perception by others, or on internal satisfaction from one's social relations or the culturally determined meaning of one's action, etc.

At an intuitive level, three common examples help to clarify this diversity of motivation. Simplest to see is how these motivations play out with regard to sex: the prostitution fee (M), the orgasm (H), and love (SP). One can also make and serve dinner to others for any combination of a fee, the pleasure of cooking, and companionship, and which combination of these is involved in an interaction will shape our understanding of whether we are observing a short-order cook, a restaurant chef, or a dinner party host. Similarly, one can write about law for a legal fee, the pleasure of creating a well-crafted argument, or the respect of the legal community or one's colleagues. To some extent, all three exist for anyone writing, but in different measures depending on social role, such as whether the author is a practitioner, a judge, or an academic, or on other factors, such as how time-constrained they are.

The value of the three types of rewards for any given action might be independent of the value of the others, or it might not.[31] For purposes of this analysis I assume that H is a personal preference that is independent of the other two,[32] but that M and SP can be positively or negatively correlated depending on the social construction of having money associated with the activity. I will call this factor p, which can be negative (as in $p$rostitution) or positive (as in $p$rofessional sports). The p factor is most interesting when it is negative, and is intended to allow for the possibility of a "crowding-out" phenomenon,[33] which has mostly been studied in the context of the relatively rare instances where altruistic provisioning has been the major, if not exclusive, mode of provisioning of socially important material goods, at least in some societies, such as blood.[34] While analysis leaves serious questions as to whether altruistic provisioning of these types of goods is indeed superior to market-based provisioning as a general social policy,[35] the primary disagreement concerns which is more efficient in the aggregate, not whether market provisioning displaces altruistic provisioning and whether each mode draws different contributors.[36] Using our three intuitive examples, an act of love drastically changes meaning when one person offers the other money at its end, and a dinner party guest who will take out a checkbook at the end of dinner instead of bringing flowers or a bottle of wine at the beginning will likely never be invited again. The question of money in legal writing will depend on role. It will have a different effect based on the social construction of the role of the author. For a practicing advocate, p usually is positive, and higher monetary rewards represent the respect the author receives for her craft. For a judge, p with regard to payment for any particular piece of writing is strongly negative, representing the prohibition on bribes. For academics, p for a particular piece of writing may be positive or negative, depending on whether its source is considered to be an interested party paying for something that is more akin to a brief than an academic analysis, or, for example, a foundation or a peer-reviewed grant, in which case "winning" the support is considered as adding prestige.

A distinct motivational effect arises when SP is associated with participation in collective action, and concerns the presence or absence of rewards to the other participants and the pattern of the reward function—that is, whether some people get paid and others do not, or if people get paid differentially for participating. This relationship could be positive where altruism or a robust theory of desert culturally structures the sociopsychological component of the reward to support monetary appropriation by others, or, more commonly perhaps, negative, where one agent is jealous of the rewards of another. I denote this factor "jalt" (jealousy/altruism).

Agents will then face different courses of action that they will perceive as having different expected rewards, R, described by the following equation:

$$R = M_s + H + SP_{p,jalt}$$

At any given time, an agent will face a set of possible courses of action, and will have a set of beliefs about the rewards to each course of action, each with this form. A rational agent will choose based on the value of R, not of M. Irrespective of one's view of whether the agent is a maximizer or a "satisficer"—aiming at a satisfactory rather than maximum level of rewards—the agent will have some total valuation of the rewards to differing courses of action, and hence of the opportunity cost of following courses of action that exclude other courses of action.

It is quite intuitive to see then that there will be some courses of action whose reward will be heavily based on hedonic or sociopsychological parameters, a combination of all three factors, or primarily monetary rewards. At the broadest level one can simply say that agents will take actions that have a positive value and low opportunity cost because they do not displace more rewarding activities. Similarly, where opportunities for action do compete with each other, an agent will pursue an activity that has low, no, or even negative monetary rewards when the total reward, given the hedonic and sociopsychological rewards, is higher than alternative courses of action that do have positive monetary rewards attached to them. Hence the phenomena of starving artists who believe they are remaining true to their art rather than commercializing, or of law professors who forego large law-firm partner draws when they choose teaching and writing over the practice of law.

What more can we say about the likely actions of agents whose preferences for rewards have the form I describe? First, there is a category of courses of action that will only be followed, if at all, by people who seek sociopsychological and hedonic rewards. Assume that there are transaction costs for defining and making M and SP available to the agent, C_m and C_{sp}, respectively. I assume that these costs are different, because the former require definition and enforcement of property rights, contracts, and pricing mechanisms, while the latter require social mechanisms for the association of sociopsychological meaning with the act generically and with the individual agent's act in particular.

There is potentially a category of cases where the marginal value (V) of an agent's action will be less than the transaction costs of providing monetary rewards for it, in which case the expected monetary reward will be zero. If the social value of the contribution is greater than zero, however, and if the hedonic and sociopsychological rewards are greater than zero and greater than the cost of making the sociopsychological rewards available, then it will be socially efficient for agents to act in this way when opportunities to act arise. Agents will in fact do so if someone has incurred the costs of providing the opportunities for action and the sociopsychological or hedonic rewards.

Behaviors in the following range will therefore occur only if they can be organized in a form that does not require monetary incentives and captures behaviors motivated by sociopsychological and hedonic rewards:

$$C_m > V > C_{sp}, \text{ and } SP - C_{sp} + H > 0$$

Whether this range of activities is important depends on the granularity of useful actions. The more fine-grained the actions, and the more of these small-scale actions need to be combined into a usable product, the higher the transaction costs of monetizing them relative to the marginal contribution of each action.[37]

Second, approaches that rely on sociopsychological rewards will be particularly valuable to motivate actions that are systematically undervalued in the market, because they generate high positive externalities. A fairly intuitive example is basic science, which is particularly ill-suited for proprietary information production because of its high positive externalities,[38] and where our sociocultural framework has developed an elaborate honor-based rewards system rather than one focused on monetary rewards. We see similar sociopsychological reward structures to reward and motivate participation in other practices that produce high-positive externalities that would be difficult fully to compensate in monetary terms, like teaching, military service, or uncorrupt political, cultural, or spiritual leadership. Similarly, to the extent that peer production can harness motivations that do not require monetization of the contribution, the information produced using this model can be released freely, avoiding the inefficiencies associated with the public goods problem of information.

It is important to recognize that actions involved in creating the opportunities for others to act are themselves acts with similar reward structures. The crucial point is that the presence of M-type rewards for the agent generating the opportunities does not negatively affect the sociopsychological returns to agents who act on these opportunities. In other words, that there be some reason why the different reward structure will not give the *jalt* factor for the contributors a strong negative value based on the monetary rewards captured by the person providing the opportunity for collaboration.

We need, then, to state the relationship between the presence of M-type rewards for an action and the SP-type rewards associated with it. For simplicity I treat the total effect of both modifiers of SP as p, and will separate out *jalt* only where there is a reason to differentiate between effect of monetary returns to the agent and effects of differential reward functions for different agents in a collaborative group—as in the case where the person offering the opportunity to collaborate has different rewards from the participants in the collaboration.

Keeping hedonic gains to one side, the reward function looks like this:

$$R = M_s + SP_p$$

We can confidently say that whenever M and SP are independent of each other or are positively correlated (that is, when $p \geq 0$), approaches that provide monetary rewards for an activity will dominate nonmonetizable approaches towards the exact same activity. A rational agent will prefer a project that provides both sociopsychological and monetary rewards than one that offers only one of these rewards. Someone who loves to play basketball will, all other things being equal, prefer to be paid for playing at Madison Square Garden over playing at West Third and Sixth Avenue without being paid.

We can say that when M and SP are negatively correlated ($p < 0$), an activity will be more or less attractive to agents depending on the values of s and p, that is, on the rate at which the value of marginal monetary rewards for a new action is discounted by the agent and the rate at which the presence of money in the transaction devalues the sociopsychological reward for that action. Table 11.2 maps the likely effects of monetary rewards on the value of

Table 11.2 Effects of monetary rewards on the total rewards seen to an activity as a function of s and p

$p < 0$ s	High	Low
High	Monetary rewards lower R substantially	Monetary rewards decrease R through SP, but increase R through M, total R may be improved
Low	Monetary rewards affect R only slightly in either direction	Monetary rewards likely increase R

R as a function of the values of s and p. We can say generally that individuals with a high discount rate on money (high s) will be likely to pursue activities with a high absolute value negative p rate *only* if these are organized in a nonproprietary model, because the value of M_s for them is low, while the presence of any M-type reward substantially lowers the value of SP_p. At the most simple level, this could describe relatively wealthy people—for example, a wealthy person is unlikely to take a paying job serving lunch at a soup kitchen, but may volunteer for the same job. More generally, most people who have finished their day job and are in a part of the day that they have chosen to treat as leisure, even though a second job is available, can be treated as having a higher s value for that part of the day. There, it will likely be easier to attract people to a project with sociopsychological benefits, and if p is large and negative, adding monetary rewards will lower, rather than increase, participation. As we move toward a situation where the value of s for an individual is low, and the p rate, though negative, is low, we will tend to see a preference for combining M and SP, as one would where p is neutral or positive.

Finally, there may be ways in which p can be changed from negative to positive, or its negative value can be reduced, by changing the way M is correlated to the action. To stay with the sex example, while there is some social discomfort associated with marriage "for money," it does not approach the level of social approbation associated with prostitution. The p value is negative, but smaller. In other societies, perhaps in times holding less egalitarian ideals about marriage, there might have actually been a positive p value—as in "a good catch." Similarly, professional performers or athletes may have been treated with less respect than amateurs a hundred years ago, but this has obviously changed quite dramatically. The same can be said for the *jalt* factor. One can imagine that free software development communities would attach a negative social value to contributions of those who demand to be paid for their contributions. The same communities may have different feelings toward programmers who contributed for free, but who later get large consulting contracts as a result of the experience and reputation they gained from their freely shared contributions.

This analysis suggests a series of likely conditions under which nonproprietary organizational approaches will be sustainable. First, there is the case of projects that are broken down into fine-grained modules, where market remuneration would likely be too costly to sustain, but where hedonic and sociopsychological rewards can provide contributors with positive rewards. As I explain in the following section, fine-grained modularity is an important characteristic of the large-scale collaborations that form the basis of peer production. The analysis of motivations suggests that peer production will not likely be harnessed effectively using direct monetary incentives. Second, there are instances where the value of monetary return is small relative to the value of the hedonic and sociopsychological rewards, particularly where the cultural construction of the sociopsychological rewards places a high negative value on the direct association of monetary rewards with the activities.

Teenagers and young adults with few economic commitments and a long time-horizon for earning and saving, on the one hand, and high social recognition needs, on the other hand, are an obvious group fitting these characteristics. Another group comprises individuals who have earnings sufficient to serve their present and expected tastes, but who have a strong taste for additional hedonic and sociopsychological benefits that they could not obtain by extending their monetarily remunerated actions. Academics in general, and professional school academics in particular, are obvious instances of this group. Many of the volunteers to Internet-based projects who volunteer instead of watching television or reading a book likely fall into this category. Individuals whose present needs are met but whose future expected needs require increased monetary returns might participate if the sociopsychological returns were not negatively correlated with future, indirect appropriation, such as through reputation gains. This would effectively mean that they do add an M factor into their valuation of the rewards, but they do so in a way that does not negatively affect the value of SP for themselves or for other contributors to collaborative projects.

Diverse Motivations and Large-Scale Collaborations   The diversity of motivations allows large-scale collaborations to convert the motivation problem into a collaboration problem. In other words, the motivation problem is simple to resolve if the efforts of enough people can be pooled.

In a corollary to "Linus's Law,"[39] one might say

Given a sufficiently large number of contributions, direct monetary incentives necessary to bring about contributions are trivial.

The "sufficiently large" aspect of this observation requires some elaboration. "Sufficiently" refers to the fact that the number of people who need to collaborate to render the incentives problem trivial depends on the total cost or complexity of a project. The sustainability of any given project depends, however, not on the total cost but on how many individuals can contribute to it relative to the overall cost. If a project that requires thousands of person-hours can draw on the talents of 30,000 or 15,000 individuals instead of a few dozen or a few hundred, then the contribution of each, and hence the personal cost of participation that needs to be covered by diverse motivations, is quite low. Similarly, a project that requires ten or twenty person-hours can be provided with little heed to incentives if it can harness the distributed efforts of dozens of participants.

More generally, one can state:

Peer production is limited not by the total cost or complexity of a project, but by its modularity, granularity, and the cost of integration.

Modularity is a property of a project referring to the extent to which it can be broken down into smaller components, or modules, that can be independently and asynchronously produced before they are assembled into a whole. If modules are independent, individual contributors can choose what and when to contribute independently of each other, thereby maximizing their autonomy and flexibility to define the nature, extent, and timing of their participation in the project. Given the centrality of self-direction of human creative effort to the efficiencies of peer production, this characteristic is salient.

Granularity refers to the size of the modules, in terms of the time and effort that an agent must invest in producing them. The number of people who will likely participate in a project is inversely related to the size of the smallest-scale contribution necessary to produce a usable module. Usability may place a lower boundary on granularity either for technical or economic reasons, where at a minimum the cost of integrating a component into a larger modular project must be lower than the value that adding that component adds to the project. But above that boundary, the granularity of the modules sets the smallest possible individual investment necessary to participate in a project. If this investment is sufficiently low, then incentives for producing that component of a modular project can be of trivial magnitude and many people can contribute. If the finest-grained contributions are relatively large and would require large investment of time and effort, the universe of potential contributors decreases. A successful large-scale peer production project must therefore have a predominate portion of its modules be relatively fine-grained. The discussion in the preceding section suggests that, given the relatively small independent value such fine-grained contributions will have and the transaction costs associated with remunerating each contribution monetarily, nonmonetary reward structures are likely to be more effective to motivate peer production efforts.

Independent of the minimal granularity of a project, heterogeneity in the size of the modules may add to its efficiency. Heterogeneity allows contributors with diverse levels of motivation to collaborate by contributing modules of different sizes, whose production therefore requires different levels of motivation. Contributors may vary widely in their hedonic taste for creation, their sociopsychological attitude toward participation, or in opportunities for indirect monetary appropriation. A project that allows highly motivated contributors to carry a heavier load will be able to harness a diversely motivated human capital force more effectively than a project that can receive only standard-sized contributions.

Integration: Problem and Opportunity

The remaining obstacle to effective peer production is the problem of integration of the modules into a finished product. Integration includes two distinct components—first, a mechanism for providing quality control or integrity assurance, to defend the project against incompetent or malicious contributions, and second, a mechanism for combining the contributed modules into a whole. It is here that the term "commons" that I use in describing the phenomenon as "commons-based peer production" gets its bite, denoting the centrality of the *absence of exclusion* as the organizing feature of this new mode of production, and highlighting the potential pitfalls of such an absence for decentralized production. Observing commons-based peer production on the background of the commons literature, we see integration and the commons problem it represents solved in peer production efforts by a combination of four mechanisms: iterative peer production of the integration function itself, technical solutions embedded in the collaboration platform, norm-based social organization, and limited reintroduction of hierarchy or market to provide the integration function alone. In all events the integration function must be either low-cost or itself sufficiently modular to be peer-produced in an iterative process, in order for a project to be susceptible to sustainable peer production.

What kind of commons is it, then, that peer production of information relies upon? Commons are most importantly defined by two parameters. The first parameter is whether use of the resource is common to everyone in the world or to a well-defined subset. The term "commons" is better reserved for the former, while the latter is better identified as a common property regime (CPR)[40] or limited common property regime.[41] The second parameter is whether use of the resource by whoever the set of people whose use is privileged is regulated or not. Here one can more generally state, following Rose,[42] that resources in general can be subject to regimes ranging from total (and inefficiently delineated) exclusion—the phenomenon Heller has called the anticommons[43]—through efficiently delineated property and otherwise regulated access, to completely open, unregulated access. The infamous "tragedy of the commons" is best reserved to refer only to the case of unregulated access commons, whether true commons or CPRs. Regulated commons need not be tragic at all, and indeed have been sustained and shown to be efficient in many cases.[44] The main difference is that CPRs are usually easier to monitor and regulate—using both formal law and social norms—than true commons, hence the latter may more often slip into the open access category even when they are formally regulated.

Ostrom also identified that one or both of two economic functions will be central to the potential failure or success of any given commons-based production system. The first is the question of provisioning, the second of allocation. This may seem trivial, but it is important to keep the two problems separate, because if a particular resource is self-renewing if allocated properly, then institutions designed to assure provisioning would be irrelevant. Fishing and whaling are examples. In some cases, provisioning may be the primary issue. Ostrom describes various water districts that operate as common property regimes that illustrate well the differences between situations where allocation of a relatively stable (but scarce) water flow exists, on one hand, and where provisioning of a dam is the difficult task, after which water is abundant relative to demand.[45] Obviously, some commons will require both.

Information production entails purely a provisioning problem. Because information is nonrival, once it is produced no allocation problem exists. Moreover, commons-based provisioning of information in a ubiquitously networked environment may present a more tractable problem than provisioning of physical matter, and shirking or free riding may not lead quite as directly to nonproduction. This is so for three reasons. First, the modularity of the projects allows redundant provisioning of "dropped" components to overcome occasional defections without threatening the whole. Second, a ubiquitously networked environment substantially increases the size of the pool of contributors.

At first glance this should undermine peer production, because, generally speaking, the likelihood of free riding increases as the size of the pool increases and the probability of social-norms-based prevention of free riding declines. But as the size of the pool increases, the project can tolerate increasing levels of free riding, as long as the absolute number of contributors responding to some mix of motivations remains sufficiently large so that the aggregation of the efforts of those who do contribute, each at a level no higher than his or her level of motivation dictates, will be adequate to produce the good. As long as free riders do not affirmatively undermine production, but simply do not contribute, the willingness of contributors to contribute should depend on their perception of the likelihood of success given the number of contributors, not on the total number of users. Indeed, for contributors who seek indirect appropriation through means enhanced by widespread use of the joint product—such as reputation or service contracts—a high degree of use of the end product, even by "free riders" who did not contribute to providing it, increases the expected payoff. Third, the public goods nature of the product means that free riding does not affect the capacity of contributors to gain full use of their joint product, and does not degrade their utility from it. This permits contributors who contribute in expectation of the use value of the good to contribute without concern for free riding.

There are, however, types of defection that are likely to undermine provisioning by adversely affecting either (a) motivation to participate or (b) the efficacy of participation. The first type covers actions that reduce the value of participation, be it the intrinsic hedonic or sociopsychological components, or the expected longer-term extrinsic values, that is, the monetary rewards to reputation, human capital, and so forth. The second type relates mostly to potential failures of integration, due to an absence of an integration process, or due to poor quality contributions, for example.

Threats to Motivation

There are two kinds of actions that could reduce the intrinsic benefits of participation. First is the possibility that a behavior will affect the contributors' valuation of the intrinsic value of participation. Two primary sources of negative effect seem likely. The first is a failure of integration, so that the act of individual provisioning is seen as being wasted, rather than adding some value to the world. This assumes that contributors have a taste for contributing to a successful joint project. Where this is not the case—if integration is not a component of the intrinsic value of participation—then failure to integrate would not be significant. The World Wide Web is an example where it is quite possible that putting up a Web site on a topic one cares about is sufficiently intrinsically valuable to the author, even without the sense of adding to the great library of the Web, that integration is irrelevant to the considerations of many contributors.

The more important potential "defection" from commons-based peer production, is unilateral appropriation. Unilateral appropriation could, but need not, take the form of commercialization of the common efforts for private benefit. More generally, appropriation could be any act where an individual contributor tries to make the common project reflect his or her values too much, thereby alienating other participants from the product of their joint effort.

Another form of appropriation that could affect valuation of participation is simple commercialization for private gain. The primary concern is that commercialization by some participants or even by nonparticipants will create a sucker's reward aspect to participation. This is the effect I introduced into the abstract statement of diverse motivations as the *jalt* factor—the effect of monetary rewards for others on the perceived value of participation. It is not implausible to imagine that individuals would be more willing to contribute their time and effort a nonprofit enterprise than to a debugging site set up by Microsoft. Whether this effect exists, how strong it is, and what are the characteristics of instances where it is or is not important is a valuable area for empirical research.

In addition to intrinsic value of participation, there is also an important component of motivation that relies on the use value of the joint project and on indirect appropriation based on continued access to the joint product— service contracts, human capital, and so forth. For such projects, defection again may take the form of appropriation, in this case by exclusion of contributors from the use value of the end product. In free software, the risk of defection through this kind of appropriation is deemed a central threat to the viability of the enterprise, and the GNU General Public License (GPL) is designed precisely to prevent one person from taking from the commons, appropriating the software, and excluding others from it.[46] This type of defection, on its face, looks like an allocation problem—one person is taking more than their fair share. But again, this is true only in a metaphoric sense. The good is still intrinsically a public good, and is physically available to be used by everyone. Law (intellectual property) may create this allocation problem in a misguided attempt to solve a perceived provisioning problem, but the real problem is effect on motivation to provision, not an actual scarcity that requires better allocation. The risk of this kind of unilateral appropriation lowers the expected value contributors can capture from their contribution, and hence lowers motivation to participate and provide the good.

Provisioning Integration

Another potential problem that commons-based peer production faces is provisioning of the integration function itself. It is important to understand from the discussion here that integration requires some process for assuring the quality of individual contributions. This could take the form of (a) hierarchically managed review, (b) peer review, (c) norm-based social organization, or (d) aggregation and averaging of redundant contributions. Academic peer production of science is traditionally some combination of the first three, although the Los Alamos Archive[47] and the Varmus proposal for changing the model of publication in the health and biomedical sciences[48] toward free online publication coupled with postpublication peer commentary as a check on quality would tend to push the process further toward pure peer review and norms-based enforcement of the core values of completeness and accuracy, as well as attribution and respect for priority.

The first thing to see from the discussion of threats to motivation is that provisioning integration by permitting the integrator to be the residual owner (in effect, to "hire" the contributors and act as the entrepreneur) presents substantial problems for the motivation to provision in a peer-based production model. Appropriation may so affect motivation to participate that the residual owner will have to resort to market- and hierarchy-based organization of the whole production effort. Second, property rights in information are always in some measure inefficient.[49] Creating full property rights in any single agent whose contribution is only a fraction of the overall investment in the product is even less justifiable than doing so for a person who pays all of the production costs. Third, and related, integration is quite possibly, particularly with the introduction of software-based management of the communications and to some extent the integration of effort, a low-cost activity. To the extent that this is so, even though integration may require some hierarchy, or some market-based provisioning, it is a function that can nonetheless be sustained on low returns—be it by volunteers, or by firms that appropriate the integration value they add by means less protected from competition than intellectual property rights-based business models.

The cost of integration—and hence the extent to which it is a limit on the prevalence of peer production—can be substantially reduced by both automation and the introduction of an iterative process of peer production of integration itself. First, integration could be a relatively automated process for some products. Second, the integration function itself can be peer produced. As peer production is iteratively introduced to solve a greater portion of the integration function, the residual investment in integration that might require some other centralized provisioning becomes a progressively smaller investment, one capable of being carried on by volunteers or by firms that need not appropriate anything approaching the full value of the product.

Moreover, integration, not only or even primarily integration into a general product but integration as a specific customization for specific users could provide an opportunity for cooperative monetary appropriation.[50] There are no models for such cooperative appropriation on a large scale yet, but the idea is that many peers will be admitted to something that is more akin to a common property regime or partnership than a commons, probably on the basis of reputation in contributing to the commons, and these groups would develop a system for receiving and disseminating service/customization projects (if it is a software project) or other information-production processes. This would not necessarily work for all information production, but it could work in some. The idea is that the indirect appropriation itself would be organized on a peer model, so that reputation would lead not to being hired as an employee by a hierarchical firm, but would instead be an initiation into a cooperative, managed and owned by its participants. Some mechanism for assuring quality of work in the products would be necessary, but it would be achievable on a distributed, rather than a hierarchical model, with some tracking of individual contribution to any given project (or some other mechanism for distribution of revenues). The idea here would be to provide a peer-based model for allowing contributors to share the benefits of large-scale service projects, rather than relegating them to appropriation based on whatever they can individually and personally do as a result of participating in the common project.

To conclude, whether or not a peer production project will be able to resolve the integration problem is a central limiting factor on the viability of peer production to provision of any given information goods. Approaches to integration include technology, iterative peer production, social norms, and market or hierarchical mechanisms that integrate the project without appropriating the joint product.

Conclusion

In this chapter I suggest that peer production of information is a phenomenon with much broader economic implications for information production than thinking of free software alone would suggest. Commons-based peer production enterprises occur throughout the value chain of information production on the Net, from content production, through relevance and accreditation, and to distribution. I then explain that peer production has a systematic advantage over markets and firms in matching the best available human capital to the best available information inputs to create information products.

Peer production of information is emerging because the declining price of physical capital involved in information production and the declining price of communications lower the cost of peer production and make human capital the primary economic good involved. This both lowers the cost of coordination and increases the importance of the factor at which peer production has a relative advantage—identifying the best available human capital in highly refined increments and allocating it to projects. If true, this would have a number of implications both for firms seeking to structure a business model for the Net, and for governments seeking to capitalize on the Net to become more innovative and productive.

For academics, peer production provides a rich area for new research. Peer production, like the Net, is just emerging. While there are some studies of peer-produced software, there is little by way of systematic research into peer production processes more generally. There is much room for theoretical work on why they work, what are potential pitfalls, and what are solutions that in principle and in practice can be adopted. The role of norms, the role of technology, and the interaction between volunteerism and economic gain in shaping the motivation and organization of peer production are also important areas of research, in particular in the study of how peer groups cluster around projects. Qualitative and quantitative studies of the importance of peer production in the overall information economy, and in particular the Internet-based information economy would provide a better picture of just how central or peripheral a phenomenon this is.

For firms, the emergence of peer production may require a more aggressive move from information product-based business models to information-embedding material products and service-based business models. Businesses could, following IBM or Red Hat in open source software, focus their "production" investment in providing opportunities for peer production, aiding in that production, and performing some of the integration functions if necessary. Firms that adopt this model, however, will not be able to count on appropriating the end-product directly, because the threat of appropriation will largely dissipate motivations for participation. Indeed, the capacity of a firm to commit credibly not to appropriate the joint project will be crucial to its success in building a successful business model alongside a peer production process. This would require specific licenses that secure access to the work over time to contributors and all. It would also require a business model that depends on indirect appropriation of the benefits of the product. Selling products or services, for which availability of the peer-produced product increases demand could do this. Conversely, firms that benefit on the supply side from access to certain types of information can capitalize on peer-production processes to provide that input cheaply and efficiently, while gaining the firm-specific human capital to optimize their product to fit the information. Another option is sale of the tools of peer production itself.

For regulators, the implications are quite significant. In particular, the current heavy focus on strengthening intellectual property rights is exactly the wrong approach to increasing growth through innovation and information production if having a robust peer-production sector is important to an economy's capacity to tap its human capital efficiently. Strong intellectual property rights, in particular rights to control creative utilization of existing information, harm peer production by raising the cost of access to existing information resources as input. This limits the capacity of the hundreds of thousands of potential contributors to consider what could be done with a given input, and applying themselves to it without violating the rights of the owner of the information input. This does not mean that intellectual property rights are all bad. But we have known for decades that intellectual property entails systematic inefficiencies as a solution to the problem of private provisioning of the public good called "information." The emergence of commons-based peer production adds a new source of inefficiency.

The strength of peer production is in matching human capital to information inputs to produce new information goods. Strong intellectual property rights inefficiently shrink the universe of existing information inputs that could be subjected to this process. Instead, owned inputs will be limited to human capital with which the owner of the input has a contractual—usually employment—relationship. Moreover, the entire universe of peer-produced information gains no benefit from strong intellectual property rights. Since the core of commons-based peer production entails provisioning without direct appropriation, and since indirect appropriation—intrinsic or extrinsic—does not rely on control of the information, but on its widest possible availability, intellectual property offers no gain, and only loss, to peer production. While it is true that free software currently uses copyright-based licensing to prevent certain kinds of defection from peer-production processes, that strategy is needed only as a form of institutional jiujitsu to defend from intellectual property. A complete absence of property from the software domain would be at least as congenial to free software development as the condition where property exists, but copyright permits free software projects to use licensing to defend themselves from defection. The same protection from defection might be provided by other means as well, such as creating simple public mechanisms for contributing one's work in a way that makes it unsusceptible to downstream appropriation—a conservancy of sorts.

Regulators concerned with fostering innovation may better direct their efforts to provide the institutional tools that would help thousands of people to collaborate without appropriating their joint product and to make the information they produce freely available, rather than spending their efforts as they now do, to increase the scope and sophistication of the mechanisms for private appropriation of this public good.

That we cannot fully understand a phenomenon does not mean that it does not exist. That a seemingly growing phenomenon refuses to fit our settled perceptions of how people behave and how economic growth occurs counsels closer attention, not studied indifference and ignorance. Peer production presents a fascinating phenomenon that could allow us to tap substantially underutilized reserves of human creative effort. It is of central importance to policy debates today that we not squelch it, or, more likely, move its benefits to economies that do appreciate it and create the institutional conditions needed for it to flourish.

Acknowledgments

This chapter is a substantially compressed version of the full paper, published in the *Yale Law Journal* 369 (2002). Research for this paper was partly supported by a grant from the Filomen D'Agostino and Max Greenberg Fund at NYU School of Law. I owe thanks to many for comments on this and earlier drafts, including: Bruce Ackerman, Ed Baker, Elazar Barkan, Dan Burk, Jamie Boyle, Niva Elkin Koren, Terry Fisher, Natalie Jeremijenko, Dan Kahan, Doug Lichtman, Tara Lemmy, Mark Nadel, Carol Rose, Bob Ellickson, Peggy Radin, Clay Shirky, Helen Nissenbaum, Jerry Mashaw, Eben Moglen, Larry Lessig, Chuck Sabel, Alan Schwartz, Richard Stallman, and Kenji Yoshino. I owe special thanks to Steve Snyder for his invaluable research assistance on the peer-production enterprises described here.

Notes

1. I use the terms "free software" and "open source software" interchangeably in this chapter.

2. For an excellent history of the free software movement and of the open source development methodology see Moody (2001).

3. See Coase (1937).

4. See Williamson (1975, 1985) and Klein, Crawford, and Alchian (1978).

5. An excellent overview of is a working paper by Steven Weber (2000).

6. The canonical references here are two works by Eric Raymond, "The Cathedral and the Bazaar" (1998a) and "Homesteading the Noosphere" (1998b).

7. See Lerner and Tirole (2002).

8. In addition to Raymond (1998a, 1998b), supporters of the sustainability of free software development who have used this framework include Rishab A. Ghosh (1998) and Peter Kollock (1999). Less sanguine views of this development model include R. L. Glass (2000) and David Lancashire (2001). See also Pekka Himanen, Torvalds, and Castells (2001).

9. See Bessen (2001).

10. An early version of this position is Richard R. Nelson (1959); more recently one sees the work, for example, of Rebecca S. Eisenberg (1996, 1663, 1715–1724).

11. For a historical description of the role of market and nonmarket institutions in science, see David (1997).

12. For a more detailed description and discussion of the different (and more) examples see the full version of this paper, Yochai Benkler (2002–2003).

13. <http://clickworkers.arc.nasa.gov/top>.

14. <http://wikipedia.com>.

15. <http://www.dmoz.org>.

16. <http://slashdot.org>.

17. See generally <http://dir.salon.com/topics/napster/index.html>.

18. <http://promo.net/pg/>.

19. See Yochai Benkler (1998).

20. Harold Demsetz (1967).

21. The public goods problem of information production is usually described as comprised of two distinct characteristics, its nonrivalry and its nonexcludability. See Romer (1990, S73–S74.) A good is excludable to the extent that its producer can exclude others from its use, unless they pay. If a good is not excludable, it also presents a problem for market provisioning, but not because it is inefficient to price it positively, but because it is difficult to do so, and hence firms will provide too little of it. Nonexcludability of information is less important to the analysis here, because it does not relate to the characteristics of information that are important to making peer production both feasible and efficient: that is, that its most efficient price is zero, and that it can be used by any number of people without diminishing its availability for others.

22. See Kenneth J. Arrow (1962, 617), ("precisely to the extent that [property rights in information] are successful, there is an underutilization of the information").

23. "Indirect appropriation" is appropriation of the value of one's effort by means other than reliance on the excludability of the product of the effort. The term is intended to separate out appropriation that is sensitive to excludability of information, which is what intellectual property is aimed to provide. See Benkler (2002, 87).

24. This individual-centric view of organization diverges from the traditional framework for the theory of the firm, in that the firm here is explained in terms solely related to the question of why agents use this form of organization to order their individual productive behavior. I do not differentiate between entrepreneurs, managers, and employees, but rather treat all of them as agents who have a set of possible open courses of action.

25. This is not to say that there are no transaction costs associated with peer production. It is merely to say that the transaction costs are of a different type. They may undermine the successful integration of a project, or may make participation too costly for contributors, but they do not arise as a barrier to prevent many individuals from collaborating in the same resource space, or many resources from populating that space.

26. A well-articulated written example of a skeptic's view is Glass (2000).

27. See Lerner and Tirole (2002).

28. Moglen makes this central to his explanation. See Moglen (1999), Raymond (1998b, 13–14), and Lerner and Tirole (2002) also offer hedonic gains as one component of their respective explanations. There is, of course, something counterintuitive about calling hedonic pleasure "indirect" appropriation. I use the terms "direct" and "indirect" to distinguish between appropriation that relies directly on the economic exclusion made possible by intellectual property law, and all other forms of appropriation. The distinction is made to enable us to map whenever talking about appropriation whether it is a form of appropriation that supports the utility of intellectual property rights or a form of alternative appropriation, which undermines the justification of intellectual property rights.

29. The Economic Census of 1997 breaks up software into several categories: software publishing (32.4%), computer systems design and related services (57.9%), systems consultants, (8.5%), and computer training (1.2%). Software publishing (NAICS 5112) had receipts of over $61 billion dollars; Computer systems design and related services (NAICS 5415) roughly $109 billion dollars; systems consultants (NAICS 5415122) roughly $16 billion dollars, and computer training, roughly $2.5 billion dollars.

30. See 1997 Economic Census. All movie, video, and recording industries (NAICS 512) had total receipts of roughly $56 billion dollars, as compared to roughly $188 billion dollars for the software industry, see previous note.

31. Needless to say, the independent value of each may be positive or negative. One might be willing to pay money to engage in a hedonically pleasing or sociopsychologically satisfying activities, as people do all the time for hobbies, and people often take hedonically unpleasant or socially awkward or even demeaning jobs in order to get the positive monetary rewards.

32. Though separating out purely physical pleasure or pain from the sociopsychological meaning of the cause of the pleasure or pain is artificial in the extreme. In principle, hedonic gain can be treated as part of SP, and indeed I ignore it as an independent factor in the analysis. I have it in the general statement largely to separate out the sociopsychological aspect, which, unlike hedonic gains, is usually submerged in economics.

33. See Frey and Jege (2001), Frey and Oberholzer-Gee (1997); see also Fehr and Gächter (2002). For a broader moral claim about this trade-off see Radin (1996), and a critique in Arrow (1997).

34. The quintessential source of the claim that altruism is superior to markets in providing blood is Richard M. Titmuss (1972).

35. Titmuss's thesis was challenged in a series of papers in the 1970s, see e.g., Arrow (1972), Solow (1971), and Healy (1999).

36. Specifically for an evaluation of Titmuss's argument in light of the HIV crisis see, e.g., Healy (2000). More generally, for a description of empirical surveys in a number of areas, see Frey and Jege (2001), describing empirical research in multiple disciplines supporting the displacement effect money has on voluntaristic motivations.

37. If these transaction costs can be lowered by technology, this would counteract the effect and decrease the size of the group of cases that fall into this category.

38. See Nelson (1959), Arrow (1962, 623–625), Eisenberg (1996), Nelson (1992, 65–67), and Gomory (1992, 388).

39. Coined by Eric Raymond to capture one of the attributes of the approach that developed Linux: "Given enough eyeballs, all bugs are shallow." Raymond (1998a, 9).

40. See Ostrom (1992).

41. See Rose (1998).

42. See Rose (2000).

43. See Heller (1998).

44. Ostrom (1992) is the most comprehensive survey. Another seminal study was Acheson (1988).

45. See Ostrom (1992, 69–88).

46. The General Public License is available at: <http://www.fsf.org/copyleft/gpl.html>.

47. <http://www.ArXiv.org>.

48. Varmus (1999).

49. See above, note 21.

50. I owe the idea of cooperative appropriation to an enormously productive conversation with David Johnson. It was his idea that the peer-production model can be combined with the producers' cooperative model to provide a mechanism of appropriation that would give contributors to peer-production processes a more direct mechanism for keeping body and soul together while contributing, rather than simply awaiting for reputation gains to be translated into a contract with a company.

References

Acheson, James M. 1988. *The lobster gangs of Maine*. Hanover, NH: University Press of New England.

Arrow, Kenneth J. 1962. Economic welfare and the allocation of resources for invention. In Richard R. Nelson (ed.), *The rate and direction of inventive activity: Economic and social factors*. New York: National Bureau of Economic Research.

————. 1972. Gifts and exchanges. *Philosophy and Public Affairs* 1(4): 343–362.

————. 1997. Invaluable goods. *Journal of Economic Literature* 35(2): 757–765.

Benkler, Yochai. 1998. Communications infrastructure regulation and the distribution of control over content. *Telecommunications Policy* 22(3): 183–196.

———— 2002. Intellectual property and the organization of information production. *International Review of Law and Economics*, 22(1): 81–107.

————. 2002–2003. Coase's penguin, or Linux and the nature of the firm. *Yale Law Journal* 112(3): 369–446.

Bessen, James. 2001. Open source software: Free provision of complex public goods. Available at: <http://www.researchoninnovation.org/opensrc.pdf>.

Coase, Ronald H. 1937. The nature of the firm. *Economica* (NS) 4(16): 386–405.

David, Paul A. 1997. From market magic to calypso science policy. Stanford University Center for Economic Policy Research Pub. No. 485.

Demsetz, Harold. 1967. Toward a theory of property rights. 57, *American Economic Review* 5: 347–357.

Eisenberg, Rebecca S. 1996. Public research and private development: Patents and technology transfer in government-sponsored research. *Virginia Law Review* 82: 1663–1727.

Fehr, Ernst, and Simon Gächter. 2002. Do incentive contracts undermine cooperation? Institute for Empirical Research in Economics, Working Paper No. 34 University of Zürich.

Frey, Bruno S., and Reto Jege. 2001. Motivation crowding theory: A survey of empirical evidence. *Journal of Economic Surveys* 15(5): 589–611.

Frey, Bruno S., and Felix Oberholzer-Gee. 1997. The cost of price incentives: An empirical analysis of motivation crowding-out. *American Economic Review* 87(4): 746–755.

Ghosh, Rishab A. 1998. Cooking pot markets: An economic model for the trade in free goods and services on the Internet. *First Monday* 3(3): Available at: <http://www.firstmonday.org/issues/issue3_3/ghosh/index.html>.

Glass, Robert L. 2000. The sociology of open source: Of cults and cultures. *IEEE Software* 17(3): 104–105.

Gomory, Ralph. 1992. The technology-product relationship: Early and late stages. In Nathan Rosenberg, Ralph Landau, and David C. Mowery (eds.), *Technology and the wealth of nations*. Stanford, CA: Stanford University Press.

Healy, Kieran. 1999. The emergence of HIV in the U.S. blood supply: Organizations, obligations, and management of uncertainty. *Theory and Society* 28: 529–558.

———. 2000. Embedded altruism: Blood collection regimes and the European Union's donor population. *American Journal of Sociology* 105: 1633–1657.

Heller, Michael A. 1998, The tragedy of the anticommons: Property in the transition from Marx to Markets. *Harvard Law Review* 111: 621–688.

Himanen, Pekka, Linus Torvalds, and Manuel Castells. 2001. *The hacker ethic*. New York: Random House Trade.

Klein, Benjamin, Robert G. Crawford, and Armen A. Alchian. 1978. Vertical integration, appropriable rents, and the competitive contracting process. *Journal of Law and Economics* 21: 297–326.

Kollock, Peter. 1999. The economies of online cooperation: Gift exchange and public goods in cyberspace. In Marc A. Smith and Peter Kollock (eds.), *Communities in cyberspace*. London: Routledge.

Lancashire, David. 2001. Code, culture and cash: The fading altruism of open source development. *First Monday* 6(12). Available at: <http://www.firstmonday.org/issues/issue6_12/lancashire/index.html>.

Lerner, Josh, and Jean Tirole. 2002. Some simple economics of open source. *Journal of Industrial Economics* 50(2): 197–234.

Moglen, Eben. 1999. "Anarchism triumphant: Free software and the death of copyright. *First Monday* 4(8): Available at: <http://www.firstmonday.org/issues/issue4_8/moglen/>.

Moody, Glyn. 2001. *Rebel code: Inside Linux and the open source revolution*. New York: Perseus Publishing.

Nelson, Richard R. 1959. The simple economics of basic scientific research. *Journal of Political Economy* 67: 297–306.

Nelson, Richard R. 1992. What is "Commercial" and what is "Public" about technology, and what should be? In Nathan Rosenberg, Ralph Landau, and David C. Mowery (eds.), *Technology and the wealth of nations*. Stanford, CA: Stanford University Press.

Ostrom, Elinor. 1992. *Governing the commons*. New York: Cambridge University Press.

Radin, Margaret Jane. 1996. *Contested commodities*. Cambridge, MA: Harvard University Press.

Raymond, Eric. 1998a. The cathedral and the bazaar. Available at: <http://www.tuxedo.org/~esr/writings/cathedral-bazaar/>.

———. 1998b. Homesteading the Noosphere. Available at: <http://www.firstmonday.org/issues/issue3_10/raymond/>.

Romer, Paul. 1990. Endogenous Technological Change. *Journal of Political Economy* 98(5): S73–102.

Rose, Carol M. 1998. The several futures of property: Of cyberspace and folk tales, emission trades and ecosystems. *Minnesota Law Review* 83(1): 129–181.

———. 2000. Left brain, right brain and history in the new law and economics of property. *Oregon Law Review* 79(2): 479–492.

Solow, Robert S. 1971. Blood and thunder. *Yale Law Journal* 80(8): 1696–1711.

Titmuss, Richard M. 1972. *The gift relationship: From human blood to social policy*. New York: Vintage Books.

Varmus, Harold. 1999. E-BIOMED: A proposal for electronic publications in the biomedical sciences. Available at: <http://www.nih.gov/about/director/pubmedcentral/ebiomedarch.htm>.

Weber, Steven. 2000. The political economy of open source. BRIE Working Paper No. 140. Available at: <http://brie.berkeley.edu/~briewww/pubs/wp/wp140.pdf>.

Williamson, Oliver E. 1975. *Markets And hierarchies: Analysis and antitrust implications: A study in the economics of internal organization*. New York: Free Press.

———. 1985. *The economic institutions of capitalism*. New York: Free Press.

12

Paying for Public Goods

James Love and Tim Hubbard

Introduction

Fueled in part by revolutions in information technologies and social concerns over access to medicine, there is a growing awareness that business models and legal and trade frameworks for knowledge goods need to change. In some cases this has occurred, including radical and disruptive innovations. In other cases, older approaches are entrenched, but face growing criticism on a variety of grounds, some focusing on efficiency and efficacy, others on grounds of fairness.

The landscape of these disputes is highly varied. The rise of the Internet as a global system for communication and the World Wide Web as a platform for publishing, the importance of GNU/Linux and other free and open software, the Human Genome Project (HGP), the single nucleotide polymorphisms (SNPs) consortium and other open medical databases, the open journals movement, the open sharing of the Global Positioning Satellite (GPS) data, and the rapid acceptance and much litigated deployment of peer-to-peer file sharing technologies, are just a few areas where social movements, governments, donors, or firms have embraced mechanisms that make information and technologies available to a global public for free.

Among economists, a public good is one that, regardless of its cost to produce, is not rival in consumption. That is to say, the marginal cost of sharing the good is zero, and the use of the good by an additional person does not diminish the availability of the good to others. Another aspect of the economics definition concerns the ability to prevent others from benefiting from the good—sometimes referred to as nonexclusivity of consumption. Few goods meet both criteria perfectly. Some goods are a mixture of private and public benefits. Other goods are nonrival in consumption, but can be managed to exclude access by those who do not pay. For example, television broadcasting, weather reports, databases, music, software, and other goods that are not rival in consumption can be managed so that they are essentially private goods. These are sometimes called quasi-public goods.

Public goods have always attracted the interest of economists, because the price system is, at least theoretically, an inferior way to provide such goods. When the marginal cost of providing a good is zero, the most economically efficient price, on the margin, is also zero. But such goods are often not costless to create. Therein lies the dilemma. How does one allocate resources to create goods that will have a zero price?

Noneconomists use different terms, and sometimes raise different issues. "Information wants to be free" was one popular way of framing the issue, and it implies more than just economically efficient pricing of a good is at stake. Newt Gringrich, as a newly elected Speaker of the House of Representatives, promised "we will change the rules of the House to require that all documents and all conference reports and all committee reports be filed electronically as well as in writing, and that they cannot be filed until they are available to any citizen who wants to pull them up. Thus, information will be available to any citizen in the country at the same moment it is available to the highest-paid Washington lobbyist" (Gillespie and Schellhas 1994). For Gingrich, this was a matter of fairness. By providing the practical means to make Congressional information a public good, he sought to reduce political corruption and empower citizens.

Former President Ronald Reagan and the U.S. National Aeronautics and Space Administration (NASA) embraced the public sector provision of a particular public good as necessary for safe civil aviation. On September 5, 1983, the Soviet Union shot down Korean Airlines Flight 007, when it entered Soviet airspace. President Reagan ordered the military and NASA to freely share the signals from the U.S. Global Positioning Satellite (GPS) system, in order to prevent similar tragedies. Later, NASA was asked to consider charging users for their access to the GPS signal. But NASA concluded that it was more valuable to society as a free good, noting that once the GPS signal was available to the public, a plethora of new nonmilitary and nonaviation uses of the signal were discovered, leading to an estimated $8 to $15 billion in new GPS products and services. NASA saw the free provision of the GPS service as an effective mechanism to encourage technological development and industrial growth.

Richard Stallman has made a career out of promoting the development of free software. Stallman says " 'Free software' is a matter of liberty, not price," and that one should think of "free" as in "free speech," not as in "free beer." (Free Software Foundation 1996).

Among software developers, the benefits of making software code freely available was expressed most famously by the phase: "Given enough eyeballs, all bugs are shallow," which Eric Raymond called "Linus's Law." Raymond was referring to Linus Torvald, the creator and leader of the Linux development effort, who was talking about the benefits of releasing software code early and often, and being "open to the point of promiscuity." In Raymond's account:

Linus demurred that the person who understands and fixes the problem is not necessarily or even usually the person who first characterizes it. "Somebody finds the problem," he says, "and somebody *else* understands it. (Raymond 1999)

Raymond has emphasized the difference between making the code transparent (open) and making it free, but for many the distinction is lost. To a generation that has seen the explosive success of the Internet, which is run on free and open protocols and much free software, and the World Wide Web, which is also based upon free and open standards, and despite Raymond's efforts, the term "open source" is often used as a synonym for free, or more generally as a metaphor for new systems for creating public goods.

The life sciences field is now experimenting with a variety of "open medicine" initiatives, most notably open databases and open academic journals, often justified on the grounds that greater openness leads to better and faster scientific progress. Linus Torvald's claim that "with enough eyeballs, all bugs are shallow" has resonated with researchers who pushed to have the sequencing of the human genome be free of patents and freely available to researchers globally (Sulston and Ferry 2002), as well as a diverse group of stakeholders who have supported a plethora of other new "open medicine" databases (Cukier 2003) and journals. In launching the new Public Library of Science Journal, *PLoS Biology*, Patrick Brown, Michael Eisen, and Harold Varmus explained the rationale for a new publishing model for journals. One consideration was clearly to offer researchers a new strategic model for reducing the costs of journals. But also, they were seeking to expand the usefulness of the information itself (for example see Brown, Eisen, and Varmus 2003):

Freeing the information in the scientific literature from the fixed sequence of pages and the arbitrary boundaries drawn by journals or publishers—the electronic vestiges of paper publication—opens up myriad new possibilities for navigating, integrating, "mining," annotating, and mapping connections in the high-dimensional space of scientific knowledge . . . Consider how the open availability and freedom to use the complete archive of published DNA sequences in the GenBank, EMBL, and DDBJ databases inspired and enabled scientists to transform a collection of individual sequences into something incomparably richer. With great foresight, it was decided in the early 1980s that published DNA sequences should be deposited in a central repository, in a common format, where they could be freely accessed and used by anyone. Simply giving scientists free and unrestricted access to the raw sequences led them to develop the powerful methods, tools, and resources that have made the whole much greater than the sum of the individual sequences. Just one of the resulting software tools—BLAST—performs 500 trillion sequence comparisons annually! Imagine how impoverished biology and medicine would be today if published DNA sequences were treated like virtually every other kind of research publication—with no comprehensive database searches and no ability to freely download, reorganize, and reanalyze sequences. Now imagine the possibilities if the same creative explosion that was fueled by open access to DNA sequences were to occur for the much larger body of published scientific results.

More recently, some has suggested that the role of open medicine can be expanded to address drug development, making it also possible to address ethical concerns over access to medicine (Hubbard and Love 2003, 2004a, 2004b).

For all of these attempts to create or maintain public goods, there are problems of financing the effort. In some cases, work is done by individuals, working in a personal capacity as volunteers (Slashdot.Org editors, many free software developers, or supported in their efforts by employers (i.e., some free software coding, the Internet Engineering Task Force (IETF), and the work of many other standards organizations) (Benkler 2002). In other cases, governments, foundations or corporate benefactors contribute (GPS, Medline, the

Human Genome Project, World Wide Web Consortium [W3C], etc.). These are fairly traditional sources of finance for public goods, even if the social organization for producing the good are novel, as is the case for many of the new collaborative software projects, for example.

There are also efforts to identify new sources or mechanisms for financing public goods, either to protect existing public goods efforts, or to expand or create new projects. As has long been the case (see for example Musgrave 1959), there are important and controversial aspects of expanding the role of governments in funding, managing, or regulating such projects, and these issues are also complicated by the fact that many important public goods projects are truly global. This chapter examines the problem of financing public goods in three settings. Two efforts combine a degree of state coercion in mandating funding, with a decentralized and competitive private sector model for allocating funds. The first is the problem of compensating artists in a world where the most efficient distribution systems are peer-to-peer file-sharing networks. The second concerns the problems of funding the development of new drugs and other medical inventions. Finally, a proposal for new intermediators to facilitate voluntary collective action to finance public goods is considered.

Competitive Intermediators

In simple economic models, markets are made up of producers and consumers. But more realistic assessments include the corporate entities involved in distribution, marketing, and finance. This is particularly important for knowledge goods. Marketing and distribution functions are socially and economically important in their own right. Commercial entities that are positioned between the creators and the users often take the lion's share of the sales, and engage in activities that are fundamentally hostile to the interests of the creators (low compensation, unfair work for hire contracts, disregard for moral rights, etc.) and consumers (high prices, interoperable standards, misleading quality claims, nonmeritorious product differentiation, etc.). Parties that finance the creation of knowledge goods influence profoundly the choices of goods that are available. Products that have high utility to consumers do not necessarily attract the most investment, due to a number of well-known market failures.

The reliance upon commercial organizations to market, distribute, and finance knowledge goods is often the path of least resistance, even when the inefficiencies are overwhelming, such as in the market for client software for personal computers, academic journals, or the wasteful private mechanisms for financing new drug development. There are also important ideological and practical reasons why private commercial markets play such an important role. Historically, many think of government-supplied or controlled goods as the primary alternative to a market dominated by private sellers and consumers. There are nontrivial risks of inappropriate government controls and inefficiency. We don't want the government to have too much say in what artistic works and other knowledge goods are created, and we seek to avoid undue centralization and bureaucracy. With this in mind, we consider models that rely upon new institutions that are private, decentralized, and that compete with each other.

In looking at various models for funding public goods, we considered institutions such as pension funds or stock exchanges that provided a variety of services to the public—pension funds make professional money management accessible to individual investors, and financial exchanges such as the New York Stock Exchange provide private regulation of transparency of investments, making capital markets more efficient. In the Netherlands, the state has historically allocated public funding for competing nonprofit broadcasting organizations on the basis of the number of subscribers they can attract. The BBC in England is an independent organization that is funded by mandatory contributions from everyone who has a television set. In Finland and Germany, the state requires contributions to religious organizations, in part to provide some public services, but allow citizens to choose which congregation will receive their money. There are proposals in the United States to fund private primary schools with government tax-supported "vouchers" to finance competitive choices for primary education. Indeed, there are many such cases utilizing a wide array of strategies, where public goods are provided by nongovernment entities, with sustainable financing.

Compensating Artists in a Word with Peer-to-Peer Filing Sharing

In 1999, Shawn Fanning launched Napster, a peer-to-peer (P2P) software client with a centralized server. Users who downloaded the Napster software and linked to the Napster server could connect with others who were willing to share digital music files. Despite accompanying press coverage that generally described Napster's main activity as illegal infringement under copyright laws, more than 80 million persons registered to use the service. Anyone with an Internet connection could freely download a vast sea of digital MP3 files. The songwriters, performers, producers, and investors who owned and controlled these works were getting nothing.

By December 1999, Napster was embroiled in litigation with the Recording Industry Association of America (RIAA) and a number of owners of copyrighted musical works. The music and film industry had anticipated that digital technologies would be a problem, but they were stunned at the widespread success of Napster. The various legal strategies undertaken against Napster were successful in shutting down that particular service, but not before a number of alternative P2P clients were developed, including clients such as Gnutella or eMule that did not rely upon centralized servers, or offshore networks such as Kaaza, that presented new jurisdictional legal problems. The music and film industry undertook frantic searches for new technological and legal fixes, and braced themselves for an ongoing battle of the wits between the owners of music, clever hackers, and a public that was clearly willing to participate in large-scale anonymous sharing of copyrighted musical works.

For millions of listeners, and even for many musicians and songwriters, the P2P technologies represented something more interesting than a license to steal. The highly oligopolistic music industry was charging hefty prices for music, but it was also not passing on much of the revenue to the songwriters and performers (Henley 2004). The promotion of music was centered on a small number of acts, often packaged and managed by major labels like commodities. The industry frequently allowed beautiful performances to languish or disappear, as distribution efforts were highly selective. For listeners, if one did not hear music in an overly commercialized and concentrated radio market, or on a handful of cable television stations, it was difficult to experiment or learn about new artists or performances.

For millions of P2P users, the experience was far richer than simply stealing music. It was a chance to enjoy music in a different and better way, free from the massive marketing efforts the music industry featured. It was the nature of the searching technology that one typically found multiple performances of a song, often by unfamiliar artists. A search would lead listeners to try out a new artist, collaboration, or genre of music.

The music industry and listeners debated and wondered if the "copyright police" would outsmart the hackers who wrote new file-sharing software programs. And if the P2P technologies were uncontrollable, would musicians be forced to rely upon a new "gift" economy, where listeners would volunteer to compensate artists for works.

Eventually the industry sought to embrace the sale of Internet-downloaded music through such services as Apple's iTunes, but the limitations of the older systems of distribution were still evident. The concentration of the commercial music industry, the unfair contracts between musician and distributors of music, and the limitations of the limited catalogue pay-per-listen model, left many listeners and some artists wondering if there was a missed opportunity to build an entirely new and different way of sustaining artists.

While P2P technologies were embraced first as a triumph of the technology over the law, almost as a deliberate rebellion against the state, there was also a serious discussion of P2P as a candidate for a compulsory license. In the past, a wide range of "new" technologies for disseminating and listening to music had benefited from compulsory licenses, such as player pianos, juke boxes, radio, and for the use of songs on records, compact discs, and other recorded music. The U.S. Congress considered various legislative proposals for a compulsory license on P2P clients, and some countries, most notably Canada, declared that levies on digital storage media and devices would compensate artists for P2P-downloaded music (for an antilevy view see EICTA 2004).

There is an extensive trade framework to regulate the uses of compulsory licenses for copyright or related rights. The WTO TRIPS agreement on the trade related aspects of intellectual property (Uruguay Round Agreement 1994) says: "WTO TRIPS Article 13 *(copyright) Limitations and Exceptions:* Members shall confine limitations or exceptions to exclusive rights to certain special cases which do not conflict with a normal exploitation of the work and do not unreasonably prejudice the legitimate interests of the right holder."

The Berne Convention for the Protection of Literary and Artistic Works, which the United States has signed, says national governments can issue compulsory licenses to use musical works, but only within national boundaries, and in return for equitable remuneration.

Article 11bis:
(2)   It shall be a matter for legislation in the countries of the Union to determine the conditions under which the rights mentioned in the preceding paragraph may be

exercised, but these conditions shall apply only in the countries where they have been prescribed. They shall not in any circumstances be prejudicial to the moral rights of the author, nor to his right to obtain equitable remuneration which, in the absence of agreement, shall be fixed by competent authority.

Article 13:

(1) Each country of the Union may impose for itself reservations and conditions on the exclusive right granted to the author of a musical work and to the author of any words, the recording of which together with the musical work has already been authorized by the latter, to authorize the sound recording of that musical work, together with such words, if any; but all such reservations and conditions shall apply only in the countries which have imposed them and shall not, in any circumstances, be prejudicial to the rights of these authors to obtain equitable remuneration which, in the absence of agreement, shall be fixed by competent authority.

The Rome Convention for the Protection of Performers, Producers of Phonograms, and Broadcasting Organizations, which has been signed by seventy-one countries, but not the United States, also discusses the use of compulsory licenses.

Article 15

[Permitted Exceptions: 1. Specific Limitations; 2. Equivalents with copyright]

1. Any Contracting State may, in its domestic laws and regulations, provide for exceptions to the protection guaranteed by this Convention as regards:

(a) private use;

(b) use of short excerpts in connection with the reporting of current events;

(c) ephemeral fixation by a broadcasting organization by means of its own facilities and for its own broadcasts;

(d) use solely for the purposes of teaching or scientific research.

2. Irrespective of paragraph 1 of this Article, any Contracting State may, in its domestic laws and regulations, provide for the same kinds of limitations with regard to the protection of performers, producers of phonograms and broadcasting organizations, as it provides for, in its domestic laws and regulations, in connection with the protection of copyright in literary and artistic works. However, compulsory licences may be provided for only to the extent to which they are compatible with this Convention. (Rome 1961)

In a series of workshops at New York (Love 2002) and Banff, Canada, a group of artists, lawyers, and economists looked at practical issues of how a compulsory license might work, and like most such inquires, discussed how one might set or collect fees, with alternatives such as levies on purchases of computer equipment or bandwidth, or various systems for subscription services, based either upon a flat rate or the amount of downloaded music. Some thought the fees should be paid directly from general tax revenue. There was no group consensus about these issues, but there was an appreciation that it would be good to structure the fee so that it was in some sense free on the margin (similar to how one now pays for cable television or subscriber-based radio services), and that it would be a positive feature if listeners could freely experiment with unknown artists or music types, thus contributing to discovery, growth, and opportunities for new artists.

But this was only part of the problem. How would the money be distributed to artists? In the traditional approaches, the compensation would be based upon the actual usage of works. The more popular songs and performers would get the most money. This could be based upon very granular measurements of downloaded music, raising privacy concerns, or a method based upon sampling of downloads.

To the artists in the Blur/Banff discussion, the allocation of funds based upon usage was considered flawed. They would mimic the market, but the market was not ideal. There was much discussion of the so-called Britney Spears effect—most of the money now goes to a handful of famous artists, making them fabulously wealthy while other artists barely eke out an existence. Some artists even wanted a portion of revenues allocated in a random, lottery-like fashion. Every artist would have at least some chance of leading the good life. There was considerable interest in allocating at least some of the funds to projects that are not successful in the marketplace, such as experimental music, the recording of folk music, or even to the support of infrastructure, such as performance centers or public recording studios. Some say a role for artists in allocating funds, perhaps by recognizing the contributions of those who had influenced the art in an important way, or ensuring that studio musicians or others that supported the more famous artists were compensated more fairly. Another possibility would be to have some of the funds allocated by governments or elites, who would make sure that opera, avant-garde music, or other types of music were supported. But as indicated before, there were obvious problems in relying on either government or elites to control allocations, as unpopular or controversial views would be vulnerable to repression or censorship.

Listeners Would Have to Pay, But Could Choose Who They Paid

To counter the dangers of government control over allocations, or the lack of legitimacy of elites to allocate funds, there was a proposal that listeners themselves could directly or indirectly decide who received funds. Listeners would not have the discretion to avoid the compulsory licensing fee, but they would decide who would receive the money. There were several variations on this theme, including proposals that listeners would choose artists directly, or they would choose projects or intermediators that supported musicians.

The role of the intermediaries was discussed at length. There were after all, lots of areas where buyer or sellers now choose intermediators for various tasks. For example, as noted before, companies who sell stocks choose exchanges to list shares, and the various exchanges compete against each other for the public's trust. The more trusted is the exchange, the more access to investor support. But even closer to home are the various institutions created to collectively manage the rights of copyrighted musical works. These vary considerably from country-to-country depending upon domestic legal traditions. Some are for-profit while others are nonprofit. Some institutions are purely voluntary, while in other cases the state mandates participation in the collective management organization. Contributions to the collective rights organizations may come from governments, or directly or indirectly from listeners (or performers) of works. And quite relevant to the Blur/Banff discussions, some of the collection societies seek to mimic a market allocation, while others set aside portions of funds for a variety of nonmarket allocations, including cultural affairs, special pensions of artists, or political activity (Ficsor and World Intellectual Property Organization 2002).

It was proposed that for at least part of the compensation to artists, the money would be channelled through intermediators. And moreover, that the intermediators would compete against each other, on the basis of their objectives, competence, and cultural sensitivities, offering listeners very different alternatives for how the money would be distributed. Listeners would decide (and continually reevaluate) where to put their money, effectively choosing the groups that did the best job in supporting artists. Anything would be possible. For example, an intermediator might propose to:

1. give all the money to performances of specific genre of music, such as African music, American jazz, or performances of classical music,
2. ensure that 15% of the revenue supported retired blues artists that are down on their luck,
3. allocate all money on the basis of the volume of downloads, or
4. allow the listeners to directly allocate fees to specific artists, to mention only a few possibilities.

Governments could possibly regulate the intermediators, on such issues as transparency and accountability, not unlike government oversight over securities exchanges.

Governments could also have the money allocated in a mixed system, with some fixed allocations, and some user determined allocations. For example, governments might require that:

1. At least 30% of fees be allocated on the basis of traditional, usage based, distributions,
2. At least 10% support noncommercial music productions,
3. At least 5% be contributed to a retirement fund for burned-out musicians, or
4. There be a minimum contribution to session musicians.

Experiment, Evaluate, and Learn

In the beginning, it would be important to experiment with different approaches, and also to evaluate and consider changes. There was a proposal to create a role for musicians and songwriters to bargain with listeners over key features of the allocation system, including

1. the price of the compulsory license,
2. the minimum allocations to various systems, or
3. to suggest systems of compensation that are more fair that current market outcomes.

The Blur/Banff discussions were seeking to find a way that the listeners and artists could build a new social contract that would compete with and possibly replace the current system of distributing and marketing music. It would seek to liberate the art from the consequences of marketing the art as a commodity. If the P2P model was successful, the expenditures on marketing would fall, and the greater share of resources would be available to artists themselves.

Supporting Health Care R&D

The inability of music, drugs, and other industries (such as scientific publishing) to modify their monopoly-based business models to address substantial unmet needs have in all cases led to conflict. The discussion of new business models for the music industry has been driven by its struggle with consumers and their adoption of P2P. In the pharmaceutical industry the equivalent struggle is more complex but has initially been with countries rather than consumers.

Although much of the underlying research that leads to new drugs comes out of academic institutions funded by government grants, development work has mostly been carried out by pharmaceutical companies, who have been allowed to obtain patents on the resulting products. Such patents have allowed companies to charge prices for drugs that bear no relation to their cost of manufacture, justified as paying back the cost of the research and development (R&D). However since patents have state-based jurisdiction, companies have not been able to obtain such patent protection in all countries. This has allowed some countries, notably India, to develop genetic copies of drugs and manufacture them at marginal cost prices. The highly competitive generics industry that has developed has provided access to lifesaving drugs at affordable prices to millions of people, however, by its very nature has not contributed to initial R&D costs. The international conflict over this issue led the drug industry to spearhead lobbying for international agreements to extend and standardize patent protection globally (Drahos and Braithwaite 2002). This led directly to the World Trade Organization (WTO) agreement on Trade-Related Aspects of Intellectual Property Rights (TRIPS) (Uruguay Round Agreement 1994) that requires all but the least-developed economies to issue patents on medicines by January 1, 2005.

The period of development of the TRIPS agreement, and increased use of patents in bioscience in general, has paralleled the emergence of the AIDS crisis, which has drawn worldwide attention to the consequence of the drug access problem (Correa 2000). Even consumers in rich countries have found themselves unable to afford or gain access to the newest drugs as prices have risen (Families USA 2003). Whereas TRIPS is certainly one way to address the inequities in contribution to drug R&D, it does so at the price of removing generic competition thereby increasing worldwide drug prices and creating inequities in terms of access to treatments. It also makes the drug development system rely too much on patent-based marketing monopolies at a time when it is being shown that they are a hugely inefficient way of purchasing R&D, with most investment going to "me too" drugs, and as little as 1.5–3% of drug sales being spent on research leading to treatments that are better than existing therapies (Love 2003; Hubbard and Love 2004a, 2004b). Finally, there is growing concern that the increasing number of patents is in itself inhibiting new research (CIPR 2002; Royal Society 2003). These issues have led to debate of alternatives or modifications to TRIPS as a mechanism for support health-care R&D, even by the WTO itself in its 2001 Doha Declaration on TRIPS and Public Health, which stated that the TRIPS "should be interpreted and implemented in a manner supportive of WTO members' right to protect public health and, in particular, to promote access to medicines for all" (Doha WTO Ministerial 2001).

From the success and competitive efficiency of the generics industry it is clear that patents are not required to ensure a sustainable supply of drugs at marginal cost prices. The only real benefit to consumers of marketing monopolies and their worldwide extension via TRIPS is to enforce contributions by all to the cost of R&D. However, data from drug sales reveals a surprising uniformity in the fraction of a country's GDP that is spent on drugs, regardless of its populations per capita income (Love 2003). This suggests a potential modification to the TRIPS agreement to allow countries an alternative way to contribute to global health-care R&D by ensuring that a fixed fraction of their GDP is being spent on supporting health care R&D. Meeting such a GDP-based R&D spending norm could release a country from the current TRIPS obligation of allowing patents that block generic drug manufacture, thus enabling all drugs to be accessible at marginal cost prices. The GDP-based norm could be set under WHO (World Health Organization) auspices and the WHO or the World Trade Organization (WTO) could monitor compliance.

Using trade agreements to guarantee sustained national contributions to global health-care R&D in this simple way would ensure that funding for new R&D continues even if all drugs are sold at marginal cost prices. At the same time it would allow countries flexibility on implementation and encourage local R&D capacity building. The outstanding questions are how to implement systems that efficiently collect the funds required by the GDP norm and how to use it to fund innovation in a way that rewards success in the absence of a marketing monopoly.

One obvious approach for governments to meet their new R&D contribution obligations is for them to collect funds for drug development via taxation and use new or existing R&D funding agencies to manage the new resources. However, in countries with a private health insurance system this may be an anathema, and many everywhere will also worry that centralized national drug development agencies taking decisions on R&D priorities and allocation of funds would be bureaucratic and inefficient. Management of drug development is not only about saying yes to promising R&D proposals, but also saying no. Defenders to the current system say the market may do a poor job of priority setting, but it may do a good job of saying no to projects that have too little likelihood of success.

A possible alternative that does not have such potential weaknesses is a financing scheme that would work through the types of competitive intermediators discussed. In this case the intermediator's role would be to manage R&D assets on behalf of consumers. Individuals (or employers) would be required to make minimum contributions into R&D funds, much as there are mandatory contributions to social security or health insurance, or to pension funds. Government would set the required contribution (in order that the country meet the TRIPS-mandated GDP threshold), but the individual (or employer) would be free to choose the particular intermediator that received their contributions.

In this model, intermediators would control the allocation of resources to companies and academics carrying out R&D, but not carry it out themselves (as this would be a conflict of interest). Instead each intermediator would concentrate on embracing the business model for resource allocation that it believed was the most efficient for drug development. This could be a system based upon cash prizes for R&D outputs,[1] micromanaged small grants, peer-reviewed open research projects, or other innovations in financing R&D. The intermediator would also adopt its own system of priority setting. The employer groups or individuals who were required to contribute to R&D funds would make decisions based upon their assessment of the intermediator's prowess in developing new treatments. Since in all cases the final product would be a public good, not owned by any investor, the incentive would be to develop products that represented therapeutic advances, rather than the profitable "me too" products that consume most of the current R&D resources.

Intermediates could also adopt "open" research agendas, since the ability to raise money would not be linked directly to product sales. If employers or individuals believed open research was more productive than proprietary R&D, more money would flow to open R&D projects. As a result of implementing such a system, consumers would enjoy huge savings from the reduction in wasteful marketing practices, which empirically are far larger than R&D outlays. Moreover, waste within the R&D process would be reduced: there is enormous evidence that current marketing practices have led to a growing corruption of the evidence base, as academic researchers enter into business agreements with private drug developers, and carry out and report questionable research that promotes products rather than advances science.

How well would intermediators manage R&D funds? This depends in large measure on how well the contributors can evaluate the intermediator's performance. Here there are several important policy interventions. First, how much and what type of transparency is needed to ensure that contributors have reliable and useful information in order to evaluate the performance of intermediators? Second, what is the optimal policy on entry? Would a small number of competing intermediators be better than a world with free entry and larger numbers of competitors? Should individuals pick the intermediators directly, or should the decision makers be employee groups aggregated together to have the economies of scale to finance due diligence of R&D intermediators? And would it be better to limit intermediators to nonprofit bodies, or to limit the amount of overhead?

Looking at the success of the public goods projects such as the open source software (OSS) movement and the human genome project (HGP) and the way they have been managed, one of the most important factors appears to be the effect of complete data transparency. In both cases this is mandated. In the OSS case the availability of the code is enforced via licenses such as the GNU public license (Free Software Foundation 1989). In the HGP case the DNA sequence being collected was available to all within 24 hours of collection as a result of an agreement between funding agencies and sequencing centers— the Bermuda agreement (Sulston and Ferry 2002). In R&D, one of the greatest drivers is free exchange of knowledge. In both OSS and HGP the free availability of the different types of data (source code and DNA sequence) has driven progress in development in the respected fields.

However, one of the most interesting side effects of such transparency is the way it keeps both producers and managers honest, which can lead to less distortion in the allocation of resources to different projects. This is exactly what an intermediator model requires to be successful in the absence of other market pressures. Anyone is free to analyze the data, check conclusions, and release their findings to all. In OSS projects anyone is free to evaluate the quality of the source and decide to contribute to a project, branch the code if they think they improve on what is already there, or start from scratch if they think they can do better. In the case of the genome project, continuous release of data allowed output and quality information to be monitored independently by funding agencies, which was a driver for decision making in this directed project (Hubbard 2003). However, the availability of the data upon which these assessments were based allowed others both within and outside the project to extend and challenge that analysis. Exposing your data (complete with errors) to all actually turns out to be a largely positive experience and appears to lead to greater trust (Wellcome Trust 2003). Data secrecy is used frequently as a method of competition between innovators; however, if mechanisms for evaluating R&D outputs are based on the continuous release of project data, greater transparency will be rewarded automatically.

Matching Funds—eBay Meets the Public Domain

The models given above are based in part on nonvoluntary mandates from the state to finance knowledge goods. The next and final model will be entirely voluntary. The proposal was developed in a 2002 Rockefeller Bellagio dialogue on collective management of intellectual property goods (Rockefeller Foundation 2002). The working premise was that there exists significant willingness to pay for a wide range of public goods, but that transaction costs are often too high to organize those who would voluntarily contribute. The commercial market is one mechanism to organize buyers, and it is most commonly organized by the sellers, rather than the purchasers of goods. Sellers nearly always withhold access to the goods to those who do not pay. In those cases where the buyers organize the market, buyers are often motivated to obtain better prices for themselves, often in markets for private goods, such as cooperative grocery stores or credit union.

The market for privately provided public goods exists, but it is too small. There is a significant number of private nonprofit charities that solicit and spend contributions, and individuals and corporate entities often contribute time and in-kind resources to create goods such as public databases, listservers (or listservs), free software, public domain computer software protocols, or other information goods. The new open-journals movement is an attempt to organize authors to financially support publishers that place materials in the public domain. These and countless other efforts have provided great value to society. But in general, because the financing mechanisms are more efficient for private goods, society invests too much in private goods, and too little in public goods.

The Matching Funds proposal is to create a new institutional framework that would make it easier to match willing funders and willing suppliers of public goods. The institutional framework would be an intermediator called Matching Funds (MF). The role of MF would be to provide due diligence on proposals for new public goods, and if the review was positive, to list the projects for subscribers. Each project would have a description of the good, a management team to produce the good, and a budget. Subscribers could offer to contribute any amount toward the final budget, but unless their contributions were matched by other subscribers sufficiently to fund the entire budget, the contribution would be returned.

How It Would Work

For the MF entity to work, it would have to enjoy trust and good will, and also confidence in the ability of its management team. We have proposed MF as a nonprofit entity, which we believe is appropriate for this type of institution. The management of MF should be thin. Proposals for public goods should come from the outside, either on the supply or the demand side. For example, a group seeking to commission the creation of a public database on pharmaceutical company mergers could propose a specific research project, complete with a budget and a team of experts and managers who would volunteer to negotiate contracts with individuals or corporate entities that would actually perform the work. The MF management would review the proposal, and if it passed this initial review, the project would be advertised on the MF page for public comment. Anyone would be free to critique the proposal, and to offer suggestions for modifications.

The MF management would encourage the project managers to revise the proposal in response to the community feedback. When and if the MF management determined that the project was mature, it would be available to subscriptions. Subscriptions would be binding commitments to fund the project if sufficient support for the project was forthcoming from the community of persons who wanted the project done. If the project was fully funded, the work would be commissioned. MF would follow the project, and allow the community to provide feedback, providing a transparent record of the performance of the project managers and the persons or corporate entities that did the work. Over time, competent managers or performers would enjoy greater confidence from the MF management and contributors, and the MF management would exclude less-competent managers from new projects.

MF would initially be supported by third-party contributions, such as from foundations. But if MF was successful, it could charge fees to list the projects, possibly creating a sustainable business model for public goods. How might the MF fund project scale? The range could be very large. Contributions could come from individuals, but also from corporate entities or governments.

Here are some examples of small- or medium-sized projects:

- A database of prices of cancer drugs in different countries.
- A public opinion survey on public attitudes on copyright extension.
- A Free/Libre and Open Source Software (FLOSS) software program to help organizations conduct secure online voting.
- A collection of course syllabi for economics classes (available under a creative commons license).
- Financing an information workshop on FLOSS software at WIPO.
- Hiring professional writers to improve GNU/Linux documentation.

Some larger projects that might be appropriate for a MF model would include:

- Sequencing of new genomes.
- Clinical trials that test drugs head-to-head (financed by governments or insurance companies that insure pharmaceutical purchases).
- Litigation to bust poor quality patents.
- Purchase of a permanent global license for the latest version of the Word-Perfect Suite from Corel.

The last item is not an absurd example. Indeed, what is absurd are the billions of dollars spent by consumers to buy very pricey versions of Microsoft Office, largely to have access to Microsoft's constantly changing proprietary standards for document formats. If only a fraction of the cumulative licensing fees by local, state, and federal governments and large corporations could be diverted to a global license of a high-quality office productivity suite, such as the WordPerfect Office Suite, users would likely switch to the new free version, and standards would change. The MF license would obligate Corel to embrace a default document format that was based on open standards, allowing Corel and its competitors to offer commercial products that offered new features and improved performance, but that were interoperable with each other. This would likely be more effective in a shorter period of time than antitrust litigation or government regulation of Microsoft.

Conclusion

Coase (1937) pointed out in his famous essay on the nature of the firm that we create social institutions to replace a highly individualized market outcome that is fraught with high transactions costs and inefficiencies. However, most existing institutions are organized to sell private goods, often at high prices, and to exclude those who don't pay from receiving the benefits of knowledge or new technologies. If we look toward a future of increasing equality and fairness, and if we value the free flow of information, the benefits of sequential innovation, and the sharing of scientific information, then we have to strive for new mechanisms to finance public goods and new institutions that place social priorities first.

Acknowledgments

These ideas have been developed in collaboration with attendees of a series of workshops hosted by Aventis, the Trans Atlantic Consumer Dialogue, the Rockefeller Foundation, Médicins sans Frontières, Oxfam, Health Action International, and others. The views expressed in this article are those of the authors and not necessarily of their organizations.

Note

1. For discussion of prize models see Wright (1983), Kremer (1998), and Shavell and van Ypersele (2001).

References

Benkler, Yochai. 2002. Coase's penguin, or, Linux and the nature of the firm. *Yale Law Journal* 112(3): 369–446. (A condensed version of this article is included as Chapter 11 of this volume.)

Brown, Patrick O., Michael B. Eisen, and Harold E. Varmus. 2003. Why PLoS became a publisher. *PLoS Biol* 1(1): E36. Available at <http://www.plosbiology.org/plosonline/?request=get-document&doi=10.1371%2Fjournal.pbio.0000036>.

Coase, Ronald. 1937. *The Nature of the Firm* [cited March 1, 2004]. Available at <http://people.bu.edu/vaguirre/courses/bu332/nature_firm.pdf>.

Commission on Intellectual Property Rights (CIPR). 2002. *Commission on Intellectual Property Rights Report*. UK Department for International Development (DFID) 2002 [cited Dec. 15, 2003]. Available at: <http://www.iprcommission.org/>.

Correa, Carlos. 2000. *Integrating public health concerns into patent legislation in developing countries* [cited Dec. 17, 2003]. Available at: <http://www.southcentre.org/publications/publichealth/toc.htm>.

Cukier, Kenneth N. 2003. Community property: Open-source proponents plant the seeds of a new patent landscape. *Acumen* 1(3): 54–60. <http://www.cukier.com/writings/opensourcebiotech.html>.

Doha WTO Ministerial. 2001. *Ministerial Declaration adopted 14th November* 2001 [cited March 1, 2004]. Available at <http://www.wto.org/english/thewto_e/minist_e/min01_e/mindecl_e.htm>.

Drahos, Peter, and John Braithwaite. 2002. *Information feudalism: Who owns the knowledge economy?* London: Earthscan.

EICTA (European Information and Communications Technology Industry Association). 2004. Available at <http://www.eicta.org/copyrightlevies/index.html>.

Families USA. 2003. *Out of bounds: rising prescription drug prices for seniors. Families USA Publication No. 03-106* 2003 [cited Dec. 16, 2003]. Available at: <http://www.familiesusa.org/site/DocServer/Out_of_Bounds.pdf?docID=1522>.

Ficsor, Mihály, and World Intellectual Property Organization. 2002. *Collective Management of Copyright and Related Rights*, WIPO publication *No. 855*. Geneva: World Intellectual Property Organization.

Free Software Foundation. 1989. *GNU General Public License*. [cited March 1, 2004]. Available at: <http://www.gnu.org/copyleft/gpl.html>.

————. 1996. *The Free Software Definition*. [cited March 1, 2004]. Available at: <http://www.gnu.org/philosophy/free-sw.html>.

Ed Gillespie, and Bob Schellhas, eds. 1994. *Contract with America: The bold plan by Rep. Newt Gingrich, Rep. Dick Armey and the House Republicans to change the nation*. New York: Times Books.

Henley, Don. 2004. Killing the music. *Washington Post*, February 17, 2004, A19.

Hubbard, Tim J. 2003. Human Genome: Draft Sequence. In D. N. Cooper (ed.), *Nature encyclopedia of the human genome*. London: Nature Publishing Group.

Hubbard, Tim J., and James Love. 2003. Medicines without barriers. *New Scientist* June 19: 29.

————. 2004a. A New Trade Framework for Global Healthcare R&D. *PLoS Biology* 2(2): 147–150.

————. 2004b. We're patently going mad. *Guardian*, March 4, 2004, 6. Also available at: <http://www.guardian.co.uk/life/opinion/story/0,12981,1161123,00.html>.

Kremer, Michael. 1998. Patent buyouts: A mechanism for encouraging innovation. *The Quarterly Journal of Economics* 113(4): 1137–1167.

Love, James. 2002. *Artists want to be paid: The Blur/Banff proposal. 02//:Blur, power at play in digial art and culture*. [cited March 1, 2004]. Available at: <http://www.nsu.newschool.edu/blur/blur02/user_love.html>.

————. 2003. *From TRIPS to RIPS: A better trade framework to support innovation in medical technologies*. [cited Dec. 17, 2003]. Available at: <http://www.cptech.org/ip/health/rndtf/trips2rips.pdf>.

Musgrave, Richard A. 1959. *The theory of public finance. A study in public economy*. New York: McGraw-Hill.

Raymond, Eric S. 1999. *The cathedral and the bazaar: Musings on Linux and open source by an accidental revolutionary*. Beijing and Cambridge: O'Reilly. Also available from <http://www.catb.org/~esr/writings/cathedral-bazaar/>.

Rockefeller Foundation. 2002. *Rockefeller Foundation initiative to promote intellectual property (IP) policies fairer to poor people*. [cited March 1, 2004]. Rockefeller Foundation Dialog, Bellagio, Italy, November 20–25, 2002. Available at <http://www.rockfound.org/display.asp?context=1&Collection=1&DocID=547&Preview=0&ARCurrent=1>.

Rome. 1961. International ("Rome") Convention for the Protection of Performers, Producers of Phonograms, and Broadcasting Organizations, 1961. Available at <http://www.wipo.int/clea/docs/en/wo/wo024en.htm>.

Royal Society. 2003. *Keeping science open: The effects of intellectual property policy on the conduct of science* 2003 [cited Dec. 15, 2003]. Available at: <http://www.royalsoc.ac.uk/files/statfiles/document-221.pdf>.

Shavell, Steven, and Tanguy van Ypersele. 2001. Rewards versus intellectual property rights. *Journal of Law and Economics* 44(2): 525–547.

Sulston, John, and Georgina Ferry. 2002. *The common thread: A story of science, politics, ethics and the human genome*. London: Bantam Press.

Uruguay Round Agreement. 2004. *TRIPS: Trade-Related Aspects of Intellectual Property Rights. Annex 1C of Marrakesh Agreement Establishing the World Trade Organization, signed 15th April* 1994 [cited March 1, 2004]. Available at: <http://www.wto.org/english/docs_e/legal_e/27-trips_01_e.htm>.

Wellcome Trust. 2003. *Sharing data from large-scale biological research projects: A system of tripartite responsibility* 2003 [cited March 10, 2003] Available, at <http://www.wellcome.ac.uk/en/1/awtpubrepdat.html>.

Wright, Brian D. 1983. The economics of invention incentives: Patents, prizes, and research contracts. *American Economic Review* 73: 691–707.

III

Ownership, Property, and the Commons

The first two sections of this book have shown that collaborative ownership and collaborative production are neither a new phenomenon, nor are they restricted to specific domains. Although free software may be the most widely discussed form of collaborative production today, collaborative ownership is as old as the oldest Australian Aborigine communities and as ubiquitous today as the entire world of scientific and academic research. Today, however, we live in a world where there exists a World Intellectual Property Organization, and in its temple-like headquarters in Geneva, you find freely available comics available in five languages to indoctrinate visitors' children into the belief that "everything has been invented . . . you creative people, start patenting!" or enthusiastically cheering "LET'S HEAR IT FOR COPYRIGHT"[1] (*sic*).

Does the existence of collaborative ownership in various domains and the increasing possibilities for and mechanisms of collaboration—described in part two of this book—lead to a challenge for the IPR orthodoxy, which, at least, *is* new? The chapters in this part argue for such a challenge.

James Boyle's wonderful contribution on the "Second Enclosure Movement" is a version of a previously published paper, which was, in turn, based on his lecture at the original CODE conference in Cambridge, England, April 2001. It is included in this collection partly because of its history and relationship to that conference, but mainly because it is an important work that deserves a wide readership. Boyle begins in the context of the enclosure movement of the fifteenth century onwards, where the commons disappeared as property was fenced in and private ownership strengthened and enforced, encroaching on the rights of many commoners. While this may have set the stage for the industrial revolution and economic growth that eventually spread widely, Boyle shows how a similar process is now taking place where the "information commons" is being fenced in. This time, however, the economics and technology of information suggest that enclosures will not lead to growth, and nevertheless result in a tragic loss of the "commons of the mind"—unless we do something to reverse this process.

The contribution from David Bollier and John Clippinger is good to read after Boyle, as it hopefully suggests a "renaissance of the commons." They situate this hopeful vision in a context where free-market individualism has developed from a common-sense approach rooted in particular socioeconomic circumstances into a dogma. This new orthodoxy extends beyond economics into our attitude towards social constructions, politics, and their underlying morality. They argue that such a dogma denies the worth of collaborative activity and the sense of community that often supports such activity; worse, this dogma prevents and suppresses the growth of collaborative activity that offers solutions to many of the socioeconomic problems we face today, in particular in the domain of information. However, a new renaissance, the renaissance of the commons, is an effective and growing force against this orthodoxy. The authors see the rapid acceptance of open source software in the business community as the first sign of this renaissance, and believe that this forces people to think about the effectiveness of the "commons" in situations—from software to biology—where a market of individuals may not provide optimal results. They correctly criticize the "tragedy of the commons"[2] as an example of the uncontrolled private ("individual, free-market"!) appropriation of public domain resources, quite different from a protected commons where access is available to all but under conditions that preserve the commons and prevent private appropriation. They describe how in an information commons such as the environment of free software developers, sociopolitical relationships are not alienated from economic ones, enabling better protection of the commons and thus a better environment for collaborative ownership and collaborative production than that of traditional property rights focused on individually identified owners.

Implicitly reflecting the arguments of David, Hubbard, and Love in previous chapters, Bollier and Clippinger justify their enthusiasm for a new renaissance with examples of collaborative ownership and "open" production processes in the scientific community and successful practices in academic research.

Philippe Aigrain goes further, and argues that the current Intellectual Property Rights (IPR) framework is based on a negative approach to rights— it defines ownership rights first as restrictive, i.e., wholly exclusive, and then provides exceptions that allow others to share the benefits of individually owned works. Aigrain argues convincingly for a positive approach to rights, which focuses on the conditions necessary for the widest possibilities for promoting creativity and innovation, and then defines restrictive but limited property rights that support such conditions. He suggests that the current global legislative environment—focused exclusively on strengthening apparently beyond any limits the rights of large intellectual property holders (as opposed to small or collaborative owners)—may lead to a new "tragedy of enclosures," unless the foundation of rights is redefined to acknowledge and incorporate collaborative creation, the commons, and the public domain. He starts such a redefinition by listing "positive rights" that creators may have over their creations—rights based not on restrictions for others, but on the creators' needs, what they must be able to do. Aigrain then considers different forms of creation, to which these positive rights may apply differently, and proceeds to lay out a detailed argument favoring an approach to rights that takes into account differences in types of creation and the interplay of creator, creation, and the social environment, rather than lump rather diverse instruments under the single umbrella term of "intellectual property."

Richard Stallman has said that having a national policy on Intellectual Property Rights—combining trademarks, patents, and copyrights that are all quite different from each other into one term—is akin to having a "national fluids policy" that treats oil, water, and dairy together. Although he is best known as the founder of the Free Software Foundation and creator of the GNU General Public Licence (GPL)—which has been the legal and philosophical basis for much of the free software phenomenon—Stallman's contribution to this volume goes well beyond software. Rather, he addresses the broader issues affecting collaborative ownership in any domain, and the threats posed by maximalist doctrines of copyright and patents—increasingly being promoted globally through international trade policy.

Notes

1. WIPO/INDECOPI comics—three issues, titled "Patents," "Copyright," and "Trademarks," available in the official UN languages from the WIPO headquarters building. Ironically, although these publications are dated (August 2002, October 2001, and August 2000, respectively) they do not have a copyright claim message. Can we photocopy and redistribute them freely? Perhaps under a fair use right to quote for the purposes of satire or criticism? Ask <wipo.mail@wipo.int>.

2. Garrett Hardin. "The Tragedy of the Commons." *Science* 162 (1968): 1243–1248.

13

Fencing Off Ideas: Enclosure and the Disappearance of the Public Domain

James Boyle

The First Enclosure Movement

The law locks up the man or woman
Who steals the goose from off the common
But leaves the greater villain loose
Who steals the common from off the goose.

The law demands that we atone
When we take things we do not own
But leaves the lords and ladies fine
Who take things that are yours and mine.

The poor and wretched don't escape
If they conspire the law to break;
This must be so but they endure
Those who conspire to make the law.

The law locks up the man or woman
Who steals the goose from off the common
And geese will still a common lack
Till they go and steal it back

This poem (Anon 1821) is one of the pithiest condemnations of the English enclosure movement, the process of fencing off common land and turning it into private property. (Although we refer to it as "*the* enclosure movement," it was actually a series of enclosures that started in the fifteenth century and went on, with differing means, ends, and varieties of state involvement, until the nineteenth.) The poem manages in a few lines to criticize double standards, expose the artificial and controversial nature of property rights, and take a slap at the legitimacy of state power. And it does it all with humor, without jargon, and in rhyming couplets.

Sir Thomas More went further, though he used sheep rather than geese to make his point. He argued that enclosure was not merely unjust in itself, but harmful in its consequences. It was a *cause* of economic inequality, crime, and social dislocation.

Your sheep that were wont to be so meek and tame, and so small eaters, now, as I hear say, be become so great devourers and so wild, that they eat up, and swallow down the very men themselves. They consume, destroy, and devour whole fields, houses, and cities. For look in what parts of the realm doth grow the finest and therefore dearest wool, there noblemen and gentlemen . . . leave no ground for tillage, they enclose all into pastures; they throw down houses; they pluck down towns, and leave nothing standing, but only the church to be made a sheep-house. . . . Therefore that one covetous and insatiable cormorant and very plague of his native country may compass about and enclose many thousand acres of ground together within one pale or hedge, the husbandmen be thrust out of their own.[1]

The enclosure movement continues to draw our attention. It offers irresistible ironies about the two-edged sword of "respect for property" and lessons about the role of the state in making controversial, policy-laden decisions to define property rights in ways that subsequently come to seem both natural and neutral.

Following in the footsteps of Thomas More, critics have long argued that the enclosure movement imposed devastating costs on one segment of society. Some of these costs were brutally and relentlessly "material"—for example, the conversion of crofters and freeholders into peons, seasonal wage-laborers, or simply, as More argued in *Utopia*, beggars and thieves.[2] But other harms were harder to classify: the loss of a form of life, and the relentless power of market logic to migrate to new areas, disrupting traditional social relationships, views of the self, and even the relationship of human beings to the environment.

A great many economic historians have begged to differ. As they see the matter, the critics of enclosure have fallen prey to the worst kind of sentimentality, romanticizing a form of life that was neither comfortable nor noble, and certainly not very egalitarian.

From an economist's point of view, the key fact about the enclosure movement is that it worked: this new property regime allowed an unparalleled expansion of productive possibilities.[3] By transferring inefficiently managed common land into the hands of a single owner, "enclosure" averted one aptly named "tragedy of the commons."[4] It also created incentives for large-scale investment, allowed control over exploitation, and, in general, ensured that the resource could be put to their most efficient use. Unless the feudal lord knew that the fruits of his labor would be his alone, he would not have invested in drainage schemes, the purchase of sheep, or the rotation of crops in order to increase the yield of his acreage.

Strong private-property rights and single entity control helped to avoid the tragedies of both overuse and underinvestment.[5] As a result of the enclosure movement, fewer Englishmen starved: more grain was grown, and more sheep were raised. If the price of this social gain was a greater concentration of economic power in fewer hands and despoliation of the environment, so be it. Those who weep about the terrible effects of private property should realize that it literally saved lives. Or so say the economic historians.

The Second Enclosure Movement

This is a debate of more than antiquarian interest, for we are in the midst of a new kind of enclosure movement, this one aimed at exploiting a new and intangible kind of commons—call it a "commons of the mind."[6] Once again, things that were formerly thought to be uncommodifiable, essentially common, or outside the market altogether are being turned into private possessions under a new kind of property regime. But this time the property in question is intangible, existing in databases, business methods, and gene sequences.

Take the human genome as an example. The opponents of "enclosure" have claimed that the genome "belongs to everyone," that it is literally "the common heritage of humankind." The code of life ought not and perhaps in some sense cannot be owned by an individual or a corporation. When patents have been granted for stem cells and gene sequences, critics have mused darkly about the way in which the state is simply handing over monopoly power to private parties, potentially thwarting future research and innovation. The new monopolists have names like Geron, Celera, and Human Genome Sciences, and their holdings are in the form of patent portfolios rather than oil wells or steel plants. Alongside these reports about the beneficiaries of the new property scheme run news stories about those who were not so fortunate, the commoners of the genetic enclosure. Law students across America now read *Moore* v. *Regents*, a California Supreme Court case deciding that poor Mr. Moore had no property right to a cell line derived from his spleen.[7] In this case, the court decided that giving property rights to "sources" would make it more difficult for scientists to share cell lines with fellow researchers—reading the decision, one can almost picture the Styrofoam coolers criss-crossing the country by Federal Express in an orgy of altruistic flesh swapping. Yet this fear of the pernicious effects of property rights did not last for long. In another portion of the opinion the court speaks approvingly of the patent granted to the doctors whose inventive genius created a billion-dollar cell line from Mr. Moore's "naturally occurring raw material." Like the commoners, Mr. Moore finds that his naturalistic and traditional property claims are portrayed as impediments to innovation. Like the beneficiaries of enclosure, the doctors are granted a property right to encourage efficient development of a wasted resource.

Of course, like the first enclosure movement, this new one has its defenders. To the question "should there be patents over human genes?" the answer will be "private property saves lives." Only by extending the reach of property rights can the state guarantee the investment of time, ingenuity, and capital necessary to produce new drugs and gene therapies. Private-property rights are a necessary incentive to research; economists need only worry about how to allocate these rights most efficiently. Or so say the advocates of private-property rights.

The genome is not the only area to have been partially "enclosed" in the past decade. In recent years, intellectual-property rights have been dramatically expanded in many different fields of human endeavor—from business-method patents[8] to the Digital Millennium Copyright Act,[9] from trademark antidilution rulings to the European Database Protection Directive.[10]

In 1918, the American jurist Louis Brandeis confidently claimed that "[t]he general rule of law is, that the noblest of human productions— knowledge, truths ascertained, conceptions, and ideas—become, after voluntary communication to others, free as the air to common use."[11] At the time that Brandeis made that remark, intellectual-property rights were the exception rather than the rule; it was widely agreed that ideas and facts must always remain in the public domain.[12] But that old consensus is now under attack. Long-standing limits on the reach of intellectual property—the antierosion walls around the public domain—are being eaten away each year.

The annual process of updating my syllabus for a basic intellectual-property course provides a nice snapshot of what is going on. I can wax nostalgic looking back to a five-year-old text, with its confident list of the subject matter that intellectual-property rights couldn't cover, the privileges that circumscribed the rights that did exist, the length of time before a work fell into the public domain. In each case, the old limits have recently been changed or challenged.

Patents are increasingly stretched out to cover "ideas" that twenty years ago all scholars would have agreed were unpatentable: the so-called business method patents, which cover such inventions as auctions or accounting methods, are an obvious example.[13] Most troubling of all are the attempts to introduce intellectual-property rights over mere compilations of facts.[14] If Anglo-American intellectual-property law had an article of faith, it was that unoriginal compilations of facts would remain in the public domain. This was "no mere accident of a statutory scheme," as the Supreme Court once put it: protecting the raw material of science and speech is as important to the next generation of innovation as the intellectual-property rights themselves. The system would offer a limited monopoly for an invention or an original expression of ideas, but the monopoly was to be tightly confined to the layer of invention or expression. The facts below, or the ideas above, would remain free for all to build upon. Even the stuff that could be protected by intellectual property—the drug or the poem, say—was supposed to pass into the public domain after a certain number of years. As Jefferson and Macaulay both observed, intellectual-property rights were necessary evils. They should be strictly limited in both time and extent.

Today, these traditional assumptions about intellectual-property law are under attack. Some of the challenges are subtle. In patent law, stretched interpretations of novelty and nonobviousness allow intellectual-property rights to move closer and closer to the underlying data layer; gene sequence patents come very close to being rights over a particular discovered arrangement of data—C's, G's, A's, and T's.[15] Other challenges are overt; the European

Database Directive does (and the various proposed database bills in the United States would) create proprietary rights over compilations of facts, often without even the carefully framed exceptions of the copyright scheme, such as the usefully protean category of "fair use."[16]

The older strategy of intellectual-property law was a "braided" one: thread a thin layer of intellectual-property rights around a commons of material from which future creators would draw. Even that thin layer of intellectual-property rights was limited to allow access to the material when the private-property owner might charge too much, or just refuse; fair use allows for parody, commentary, and criticism, and also for "decompilation" of computer programs so that Microsoft Word's competitors can reverse-engineer its features in order to make sure that their program can convert Word files. (Those who prefer topographical metaphors might imagine a quilted pattern of public and private land, with legal rules specifying that certain areas—beaches, say—can never be privately owned, and accompanying rules giving public right-of-way through private land if there is a danger that access to the commons might otherwise be blocked.)

From the inception of intellectual-property law in the eighteenth century until quite recently, protection of the public domain—the intangible commons—was one fundamental goal of the law in most nations. In the new vision of intellectual property, however, property rights should be established everywhere; more is better. Expanding patentable and copyrightable subject matter, lengthening the copyright term, giving legal protection to "digital barbed wire," even if it is used in part to prevent fair use: each of these can be understood as a vote of no confidence in the productive powers of the commons. We seem to be shifting from Brandeis's assumption that the "noblest of human productions are free as the air to common use" to the assumption that any human production left open to free use is inefficient, if not tragic.

How Much of the Intangible Commons Must We Enclose?

So far I have argued that there are profound similarities between the first enclosure movement and our contemporary expansion of intellectual property. Today, as in the fifteenth century, proponents and opponents of enclosure are locked in battle, hurling at each other incommensurable claims about innovation, efficiency, traditional values, the boundaries of the market, the saving of lives, the loss of familiar liberties. Once again, opposition to enclosure is portrayed as economically illiterate; the beneficiaries of enclosure tell us that an expansion of property rights is needed in order to fuel progress. Indeed, the post-Cold War "Washington Consensus" is invoked to claim that the lesson of history itself is that the only way one gets growth and efficiency is through markets; property rights, surely, are the sine qua non of markets.[17]

But if there are similarities between the two enclosure movements, there are also crucial differences. The digitized and networked "commons of the mind," circa 2002, differs greatly from the grassy and isolated common plots of land that dotted England circa 1400.[18] Some of the key differences should lead us to question whether stronger intellectual-property rights are really either necessary or desirable.

For example, consider the well-known fact that a digital text, unlike a plot of land, can be used by countless people simultaneously without mutual interference or destruction of the shared resource. Unlike an earthly commons, the commons of the mind is generally what economists call "nonrival." Many uses of land are mutually exclusive. If I am using the field for grazing, it may interfere with your plans to use it for growing crops. By contrast, a gene sequence, an MP3 file, or an image may be used by multiple parties; my use does not interfere with yours. To simplify a complicated analysis, this means that the depredations through overuse that affect fields and fisheries are generally not a problem with intellectual property. (The exceptions to this statement turn out to be fascinating; in the interest of brevity I will ignore them entirely.)

Thus, one cause of tragedy on the earthly commons generally does not arise on the commons of the mind. Overuse is normally not a problem. But what about incentives to create the intellectual resources in the first place?

Here intellectual property, especially in our digitized age, seems at first glance to pose a unique problem. It has long been relatively easy for pirates to produce unauthorized copies of poems, novels, treatises, and musical compositions. In the language of the economists, it has long been difficult, and in some cases virtually impossible, to stop one unit of an intellectual good from satisfying an infinite number of users at zero marginal cost. A familiar conclusion seems irresistible: without an ability to protect their creations against theft, creators will be unable to earn an adequate living. There will be inadequate incentives to create. Thus the law must step in and create a monopoly called an intellectual-property right.

This is the standard argument in favor of intellectual-property rights, but it has recently acquired a historical dimension, a teleology of expansion over time. After all, in our digitized age, it is easier than ever before for pirates to copy not just a book, but a film, a photograph, a recorded piece of music, a drug formula, a computer program—the list goes on. Surely the historical lowering of copying and transmission costs implies a corresponding need to increase the strength of intellectual-property rights.

Imagine a line. At one end sits a monk, painstakingly transcribing Aristotle's *Poetics*. In the middle lies the Gutenberg printing press. Three-quarters of the way along the line is a photocopying machine. At the end lies the Internet. At each stage, copying costs are lowered and goods become both less rival and less excludable.

Among some analysts, the assumption seems to be that the strength of intellectual-property rights must correspond inversely to the cost of copying. The argument goes something like this: To deal with the monk-copyist, we need no intellectual-property right; physical control of the manuscript is enough. To deal with the Gutenberg press, we need the Statute of Anne.[19] But to deal with the Internet, we need the Digital Millennium Copyright Act,[20] the No Electronic Theft Act,[21] the Sonny Bono Copyright Term Extension Act,[22] and perhaps even the Collections of Information Anti-Piracy Act.[23] As copying costs approach zero, intellectual-property rights must approach perfect control. And if a greater proportion of product value and GNP (Gross National Product) is now in the form of information, then obviously we have an independent reason to need strengthened protection. A five-dollar padlock would do for a garden shed, but not for a vault.

Like any attractive but misleading argument, this one has some truth. The Internet does lower the cost of copying and facilitates illicit copying. The same technology also lowers the costs of production, distribution, and advertising—and dramatically increases the size of the potential market.

Is the net result, then, a loss to rights-holders such that we need to increase protection in order to maintain a constant level of incentives? The answer is not self-evident.

A large, leaky market may actually produce *more* revenue than a small, tightly controlled market. What's more, the same technologies that allow for cheap copying also allow for swift and encyclopedic search engines—the best detection device for illicit copying ever invented. It would be impossible to say, on the basis of the evidence we have, that owners of protected content are better or worse off as a result of the Internet.

My intuition—as well as our historical experience with prior "dangerous" technologies such as the VCR—points strongly to the possibility that copyright holders are better off. In any case, there simply isn't enough evidence, either to support my intuition or to support the conclusion that as copy costs decline intellectual-property rights must be strengthened. Furthermore, given the known static and dynamic costs of monopolies, and the constitutional injunction to encourage the progress of science and useful arts, the burden should be on those requesting expanded intellectual-property rights to prove their value.

Another argument commonly offered in defense of granting new intellectual-property rights stresses the increasing importance of products that use, embody, or process information in today's global economy. Perhaps the commons of the mind requires enclosure because it is now such a vital sector of economic activity. The importance of agriculture to the economy was certainly one of the arguments for the first enclosure movement. (Lovers of Patrick O'Brian's novels may remember Maturin's stolid silence in the face of an admiral's increasingly vehement insistence that enclosure was essential to produce the corn necessary to fight the Napoleonic war.)

Here we come to another big difference between the commons of the mind and the earthly commons. As has frequently been pointed out, information products are frequently made out of fragments of other information products; one person's information output is someone else's information input.[24] These inputs may be snippets of code, discoveries, prior research, images, genres of work, cultural references, databases of single nucleotide polymorphisms—all can function as raw material for future innovation. And every potential increase of protection over such products also raises the costs of, or reduces access to, the raw material to create new products.

The right balance is difficult to strike. One Nobel Prize-winning economist has claimed that it is actually impossible to produce an efficient market for informational goods.[25] Whether or not it is impossible in theory, it is surely a difficult problem in practice. In other words, even if enclosure of the arable commons always produced gains (itself a subject of debate), enclosure of the information commons clearly has some potential to *harm* intellectual innovation. More property rights, even though they supposedly offer greater incentives, do not necessarily ensure greater intellectual productivity. Sometimes just the opposite may be true.[26]

Intellectual Property and Distributed Creativity

My arguments so far have taken as a given the various problems to which modern intellectual-property laws have been a response. I have discussed the extent to which the logic of enclosure works for the commons of the mind as well as it did for the arable commons, taking into account the effects of an information society and a global Internet. Remember that when I speak of enclosure, I am talking about increases in the level of rights: protecting new subject matter for longer periods of time, criminalizing certain technologies, making it illegal to cut through digital fences even if they have the effect of foreclosing previously lawful uses, and so on.

What I have not yet done is ask whether the brute fact of the Internet actually unsettles old assumptions and forces us to reconsider the need for incentives—at least in certain areas. But this is a question that cannot be evaded.

For anyone interested in the way that computer networks may embody a new mode of collaborative production, an exemplary case to study is the open-source software movement.[27] This software is released under a series of licenses, the most important being the General Public License, or GPL. The GPL specifies that anyone may copy the software, provided the license remains attached and the "source code" for the software always remains available.[28] Users may add to or modify the code, may build on it and incorporate it into their own work, but if they do so then the new program created is also covered by the GPL. Some people refer to this as the "viral" nature of the license; others find the term offensive.[29] The point, however, is that the open quality of the creative enterprise spreads; it is not simply a donation of a program or a work to the public domain, but a continual accretion in which all gain the benefits of the program on pain of agreeing to give their own additions and innovations back to the communal project.

The open-source software movement has produced software that either rivals or exceeds the productive capacities of conventional proprietary software.[30] Its adoption on the enterprise level is impressive, as are the various technical encomia to its strengths.

But the most remarkable aspect of the open-source software movement is harder to see. It functions as a new kind of social system: many of those who contribute to the movement by writing a part of the software do so as volunteers, without direct remuneration. Here, it seems, we have a classic public good—code that can be copied freely, and sold or redistributed without paying the creator or creators.

Skeptics, of course, wonder if this mode of production can be sustained. There seem to be inadequate incentives to ensure continued productivity and innovation. "*E pur si muove*," as Galileo is reputed to have said in the face of Cardinal Bellarmine's certainties—"And yet it moves."[31]

Still, there is no consensus about why the system works. Perhaps the open-source software movement is actually a contemporary form of potlatch, in which one gains prestige by the extravagance of the resources one "wastes." Perhaps it is simply a smart way for a young programmer to build a résumé that will eventually pay off in a conventional job. Or perhaps the movement is driven by what Karl Marx considered an innate aspect of our "species-being": namely, the urge to create, which drives human beings to labor out of love rather than material need.

Like Yochai Benkler and Eben Moglen, I believe that such speculation is interesting but irrelevant.[32] My own explanation for why the system works is this.

Assume a random distribution of incentive structures in different people, a global network. Assume also that the costs of transmission, information sharing, and copying approach zero. Assume finally a modular creation process. With these assumptions, it just doesn't matter why unpaid code writers do what they do; what matters is that a certain number of people will do what the unpaid code writers do. One may do it for love of the species, another in the hope of a better job, a third for the joy of solving puzzles, and so on. Each person also has his or her own "reserve price," the point at which he or she says "now I will turn off 'Survivor' and go and create something." But on a global network, there are a lot of people, and with numbers that big, and information-overhead that small, even relatively hard projects will attract a sufficient number of motivated and skilled people to sustain the communal project. For the whole structure to work without large-scale centralized coordination, the creation process has to be modular, with "units" of different size and complexity, each requiring slightly different expertise, all of which can be added together to make a grand whole. I can work on the sendmail program, you on the search algorithms. More likely, lots of people try to solve the sendmail and search algorithm problems, and their products are judged by the community and the best ones adopted. Under these conditions—an ad hoc mode of production that curiously combines anarchism and entrepreneurialism, Kropotkin and Adam Smith—we will get innovation and productivity, without having to rely on the proprietary model.

What's more (and this is a truly fascinating twist), when the production process does need more centralized coordination, some governance that guides how the modular bits are most productively associated, it is at least theoretically possible that we can come up with the control system in exactly the same way; distributed production is potentially recursive. Governance processes, too, can be assembled through distributed methods on a global network, by people with widely varying motivations, skills, and reserve prices.

Again, skeptics will have their doubts. One organization theorist I know dismisses the possibility of anarchic coordination as "governance by food fight." Anyone who has ever been on an organizational listserv, or been part of a global production process run by people who are long on brains and short on social skills, knows how accurate that description is. *E pur si muove.*

But, in the language of computer programmers, does the open-source software movement "scale"? Can we generalize anything from this limited example? How many types of production, innovation, and research fit into the model I have just described? After all, for lots of types of innovation and invention one needs hardware, capital investment, large-scale real-world data collection, stuff—in all its facticity and infinite recalcitrance. Maybe the open-source model has solved the individual incentives problem, but that's not the only problem. And how many types of innovation or cultural production are as modular as software?

My own guess is that this method of production is far more common than we realize. "Even before the Internet," as some of my students have taken to saying portentously, science, law, education, and musical genres all developed in ways that are markedly similar to the model I have described. "The marketplace of ideas," the continuous roiling development in thought and norm that our political culture spawns, is itself an idea that owes much more to the distributed, nonproprietary model than it does to the special case of commodified innovation that we regulate through intellectual-property law. It's not that copyright and patent haven't helped power the rise of modern civilization; it's just that it would be wrong to see them as the only engine of innovation. Indeed, the mottoes of free software development have their counterparts in the theory of democracy and the open society. The open-source movement describes its advantage over closed and secretive systems concisely: "given enough eyeballs, all bugs are shallow." Karl Popper would have cheered.[33]

Furthermore, I suspect that the increasing migration of the sciences toward data-rich, processing-rich models will make it likely that a greater amount of innovation and discovery could follow the distributed, nonproprietary model of intellectual production. Bioinformatics and computational biology, the open-source genomics project at <www.ensembl.org>, the possibility of distributed data scrutiny by lay volunteers that NASA used on the Mars landing data—all of these offer intriguing glances of a possible future.[34] And finally, of course, the Internet is one big experiment in distributed cultural production.

My own utopia would include modes of nonproprietary intellectual production flourishing alongside a scaled-down but still powerful intellectual-property regime. Of course, my utopia hinges on a hunch about the future. Still, there is some possibility (I might say hope) that we could have a world in which much more intellectual production is free—"free" meaning that it is not subject to centralized control, and "free" meaning that its products are available without payment. Insofar as this is at least a possible future, then surely we should think twice before foreclosing it.

Yet foreclosing this possibility is precisely what lawmakers and government regulators in America, Europe, and much of the world are now doing. The point about the dramatic recent expansion of intellectual-property rights—in database protection bills and directives that extend intellectual-property rights to the layer of facts, in the efflorescence of software patents, in the validation of shrink-wrap licenses that bind third parties, in the anti-circumvention provisions of the Digital Millennium Copyright Act or EU Copyright Directive[35]—is not merely that they hamper the nonproprietary mode of intellectual production unfairly and without justification. The point is rather that they run the risk of ruling it out altogether.[36]

Beyond Enclosure?

We have come full circle. As I have shown, we are in many ways in the midst of a second enclosure movement. The opponents and proponents of enclosure are currently locked in battle, each appealing to conflicting and sometimes incommensurable claims about efficiency, innovation, justice, and the limits of the market.

But should there be a second enclosure movement? Do we know that property rights in this sphere will yield the same surge of productive energy that they did when applied to arable land?[37]

I think the answer is a resounding no. We are rushing to fence in ever-larger stretches of the commons of the mind without convincing economic evidence that enclosure will help either productivity or innovation—and with very good reason to believe it may actually hurt them.[38]

As I have argued elsewhere, this process should bother people across the ideological spectrum, from civil libertarians to free marketeers. Researchers and scientists should be particularly worried by what is happening. Until now, the American system of science, for all its flaws, has worked astoundingly well; changing some of its fundamental premises, such as by moving property rights into the data layer, is not something to be done lightly.

The dangers are particularly acute at the moment for three reasons. First, under the conditions that currently obtain in our digitized commons of the mind, the creation of new intellectual-property rights tends, in a vicious circle, to create still further demands for new intellectual-property rights. The argument is a little too complicated to lay out here.[39] But in essence the position is this: once a new intellectual-property right has been created over some informational good, the only way to ensure efficient allocation of that good is to give the rights holder the ability to charge every user the exact maximum each consumer is willing to pay, so that the market can be perfectly segregated by price. In order to protect their ability to set prices for digital intellectual-property goods, whose marginal cost to produce and distribute in fact approaches zero, the rights holders will inevitably argue that they need even *more* changes of the rules in their favor: relaxed privacy standards, so they can know more about consumers' price points; enforceable shrink-wrap or click-wrap contracts, so that consumers can be held to the term of a particular license, no matter how restrictive; and changes in antitrust rules, to allow for a variety of practices that are currently illegal, such as resale price maintenance and various forms of "tying." Rights-holders will also claim that they need technical changes with legal backing: for example, the creation of personalized digital objects surrounded by state-sanctioned digital fences, objects that are tied to particular users and particular computers, so that reading my e-Book on your machine is either technically impossible, a crime, or a tort— or possibly all three. My conclusion: extending ever-stronger intellectual-property rights is a very slippery slope.

Second, the broader the scope of intellectual-property rights, the more the characteristics of the Internet that have made it so attractive to civil libertarians—its distributed, anonymous character, its resistance to control or filtering by public or private entities, its global nature—start to seem like vices rather than virtues. The process of trying to make the Net safe for price discrimination has already begun. Yet as Lawrence Lessig has argued, this is a fundamental political choice that ought to be made deliberately and publicly, not as a side effect of an economically dubious digital enclosure movement.[40] Because of some threats, such as terrorism, we might choose to live in a pervasively monitored electronic environment in which identity and geography, and thus regulability, have been reintroduced. (In my own view, the price is not worth paying.) But to do so on the basis of some bad microeconomic arguments about the needs of the entertainment industry and in the absence of good empirical evidence, and to foreclose some of the most interesting new productive possibilities in the process—well, that would be really sad.

Third, the arguments in favor of the new enclosure movement depend heavily on the intellectually complacent, analytically unsound assumptions of "neoliberal orthodoxy," the "Washington consensus."[41] Convinced that property is good, and that creating more property rights is better, neoliberals are primed to hand out patents on gene sequences and stem cell lines and copyrights on compilations of facts.[42] It would be ironic, to say the least, to let such neoliberal convictions determine the fate of the information commons, the one area where the pros and cons of a property regime need to be most delicately balanced, and also an area where the possible consequences for the public good ought to be vigorously and openly debated.

What is to be done, then? I cannot lay out a full answer here, but I would suggest two broad strategies. First, we ought to insist on considerably better empirical and economic evidence before signing on to the proposals of the second enclosure movement. There are a few serious comparative and historical studies of the economics of innovation, but we need a lot more. Indeed, there should be an annual audit of our intellectual-property system, perhaps, in America, by the General Accounting Office. What are the costs—static and dynamic—and the benefits of our current intellectual-property regime? With one of the largest industry subsidies given by government (through its granting of patents and copyrights), this regime deserves the same searching scrutiny that we apply to the recipients of other state subsidies. I am a firm believer in intellectual-property rights; properly balanced and judiciously applied, such rights safeguard a wonderfully decentralized system for the promotion of innovation. But this is a rational belief in particular rules based on empirical evidence, not an unquestioning faith that any increase in intellectual-property rights is automatically good.

Second, we need to make clear the current dangers to the public domain, in the same way that environmental activists in the 1950s and 1960s made visible not only particular environmental threats" but the very existence of "the environment" itself. The environmental movement gained much of its political power by pointing out that there were structural reasons why lawmakers were likely to make bad environmental decisions: a legal system based on a particular notion of what "private property" entailed, and a technological tendency to treat the world as a simple, linear set of causes and effects, ignoring the complex interrelationship among natural systems. In both of these conceptual systems, the environment actually disappeared; there was no place for it in the analysis. Small surprise, then, that lawmakers were not able to protect it properly.

We should press a similar argument—as I have done here—in the case of the public domain.[43] We should exploit the power of a concept like the public domain both to clarify and to reshape perceptions of self-interest. The idea that there is a public domain—a "commons of the mind"—can help a coalition to be built around a reframed conception of common interest. In the narrowest sense, that common interest might be the realization, spurred by greater attention to intellectual interrelationships, that the freest possible circulation of ideas and facts is important to anyone whose well-being significantly depends on intellectual innovation and productivity—that is to say, every citizen of the world.

The poem with which I began this essay contained some advice: "And geese will still a common lack / Till they go and steal it back" (Anon 1821).

I can't match the terseness or the rhyme. But if we blithely assume that the second enclosure movement will have the same benign effects as the first, we may look like very silly geese indeed.

Notes

A previous version of this article is made available by the author under a Creative Commons License at <http://www.creativecommons.org/licenses/by-sa/1.0>. A fuller version is also available at <http://www.law.duke.edu/journals/66LCPBoyle>.

1. Thomas More (1947, 32).

2. Karl Polanyi (1957, 35).

3. See generally Lord Ernle (1962).

4. Hardin (1968).

5. For an excellent summary of the views of Hobbes, Locke, and Blackstone on these points, see Hannibal Travis (2000, 789–803).

6. The analogy to the enclosure movement has been too succulent to resist. To my knowledge, Ben Kaplan, Pamela Samuelson, Yochai Benkler, David Lange, Christopher May, David Bollier, and Keith Aoki have all employed the trope, as I myself have on previous occasions. For a particularly thoughtful and careful development of the parallel between the two enclosure movements, see generally Travis (2000).

7. 793 P.2d 479, 488–97 (Cal. 1990).

8. See State St. Bank & Trust Co. v. Signature Fin. Group, 149 F.3d 1368, 1373 (D. C. Cir. 1998).

9. Pub. L. No. 105–304, 112 Stat. 2860 (1998) (codified as amended in scattered sections of 5, 17, 28 and 35 U.S.C.).

10. Directive 96/9/EC of the European Parliament and of the Council of 11 March 1996 on the Legal Protection of Databases, 1996 O.J. (L 77) 20, Available at <http://europa.eu.int/ISPO/infosoc/legreg/docs/969ec.html> [hereinafter DIRECTIVE] (last visited Dec. 19, 2002).

11. Int'l. News Serv. v. Associated Press, 248 U.S. 215, 250 (1918) (Brandeis, J., dissenting).

12. Benkler (1999: 354, 361, 424).

13. See e.g., State St. Bank & Trust Co. v. Signature Fin. Group, Inc., 149 F.3d 1368, 1373 (Fed. Cir. 1998).

14. Collection of Information Antipiracy Act, S. 2291, 105th Cong. (1998); Database Investment and Intellectual Property Antipiracy Act of 1996, H.R. 3531, 104th Cong. (1996).

15. See Rebecca S. Eisenberg, (1990, 740–744), Alexander K. Haas (2001).

16. See DIRECTIVE, above in note 10.

17. The phrase "Washington Consensus" originated in John Williamson (1990). Over time, it has come to be used as shorthand for a neoliberal view of economic policy that puts its faith in deregulation, privatization, and the creation and defense of secure property rights as the cure for all ills. See Joseph Stiglitz (1999). It has thus become linked to the triumphalist neoliberal account of the end of history and the victory of unregulated markets. See Francis Fukuyama (1992). Neither of these two results are, to be fair, what its creator intended. See John Williamson (1999).

18. The differences are particularly strong in the arguments over "desert": Are these property rights deserved or are they simply violations of the public trust and privatizations of the commons? For example, some would say that we never had the same *traditional* claims over the genetic commons that the victims of the first enclosure movement had over their commons; this is more like newly discovered frontier land, or perhaps even privately drained marshland, than it is like well-known common land that all have traditionally used. In this case, the enclosers can claim (though their claims are disputed) that they discovered or perhaps simply made usable the territory they seek to own. The opponents of gene patenting, on the other hand, turn to religious and ethical arguments about the sanctity of life and the incompatibility of property with living systems even more frequently than the farmers of the eighteenth century. These arguments, and the appeals to free speech that dominate debates over digital intellectual property, have no precise analogue in debates over hunting or pasturage, although there are common themes. For example, we are already seeing nostalgic laments of the loss of the immemorial rights of Internet users. At the same time, the old language of property law is turned to this more evanescent subject matter; my favorite title is: I. Trotter Hardy, "The Ancient Doctrine of Trespass to Web Sites" (1996).

19. 13 Ann., c. 15 (Eng.).

20. Pub. L. No. 105–304, 112 Stat. 2860 (1998) (codified as amended in scattered sections of 5, 17, 28, and 35 U.S.C.).

21. Pub. L. No. 105–147, 111 Stat. 2678 (1997) (codified as amended in scattered sections of 17 and 18 U.S.C.).

22. Pub. L. No. 105–298, 112 Stat. 2827 (1998) (codified as amended in scattered sections of 17 U.S.C.).

23. S. 2291, 105th Cong. (1998).

24. For example, James Boyle (1996, 135), Jessica Litman (2001, 91), William M. Landes and Richard A. Posner (1989, 348), Jessica Litman (1990, 1010–1011), and Pamela Samuelson and Suzanne Scotchmer (2002).

25. Sanford J. Grossman and Joseph E. Stiglitz (1980, 404).

26. For a more technical account, see James Boyle (2000a).

27. See Glyn Moody (2001), Peter Wayner (2000), and Eben Moglen (1999).

28. Proprietary, or "binary only," software is generally released only after the source code has been compiled into machine-readable object code, a form that is impenetrable to the user. Even if you were a master programmer, and the provisions of the Copyright Act, the appropriate licenses, and the DMCA did not forbid you from doing so, you would be unable to modify commercial proprietary software to customize it for your needs, remove a bug, or add a feature. Open-source programmers say, disdainfully, that it is like buying a car with the hood welded shut. See, e.g., Wayner (2000, 264).

29. See Brian Behlendorf (1999, 149, 163).

30. See Bruce Brown (2002, 28), Jim Rapoza (1999, 1).

31. E. Cobham Brewer (1898, 1111–1112).

32. See Yochai Benkler (2002–2003). For a seminal statement relying on the innate human love of creativity as the motivation, see Moglen (1999): "[I]ncentives" is merely a metaphor, and as a metaphor to describe human creative activity it's pretty crummy. I have said this before, but the better metaphor arose on the day Michael Faraday first noticed what happened when he wrapped a coil of wire around a magnet and spun the magnet. Current flows in such a wire, but we don't ask what the incentive is for the electrons to leave home. We say that the current results from an emergent

property of the system, which we call induction. The question we ask is 'what's the resistance of the wire?' So Moglen's Metaphorical Corollary to Faraday's Law says that if you wrap the Internet around every person on the planet and spin the planet, software flows in the network. It's an emergent property of connected human minds that they create things for one another's pleasure and to conquer their uneasy sense of being too alone. The only question to ask is, 'what's the resistance of the network?' Moglen's Metaphorical Corollary to Ohm's Law states that the resistance of the network is directly proportional to the field strength of the 'intellectual property' system. So the right answer to the econodwarf is, resist the resistance."

33. See Karl Popper (1945).

34. For example, NASA's "Clickworkers" experiment, which used public volunteers to analyze Mars landing data. See <http://clickworkers.arc.nasa.gov/top> (last visited September 30, 2002).

35. 17 U.S.C. § 1201 (2002); Directive 2001/29/EC of the European Parliament and of the Council of 22 May 2001.

36. This point has been ably made, inter alia, by Pamela Samuelson, Jessica Litman, Jerry Reichman, Larry Lessig, and Yochai Benkler. See Litman (1990, 2001), Benkler (1999), Samuelson (1999), Reichman and Uhlir (1999), and Lessig (2001a). Each has a slightly different focus and emphasis on the problem, but each has pointed out the impediments now being erected to distributed, nonproprietary solutions. See also Boyle (2000a).

37. That is assuming that enclosure really did produce efficiency gains for arable land, though as I pointed out earlier, economic historians are now divided about that issue. See Robert C. Allen (1982). At best, one could say that the empirical evidence is equivocal. There are certainly reasons to believe that the commons, far from being tragic, was often relatively well managed. But the case for enclosure is at its strongest with arable land; even if one gives no weight at all to the contrary evidence there, the commons of the mind is very different and most of the differences cut strongly against the logic of enclosure—at least without considerably more evidence than we currently possess.

38. Some of the legislation involved is also constitutionally dubious under the First Amendment and Copyright Clause. See Yochai Benkler (2003). This is particularly strange at a time when other government subsidies are subjected to relentless skepti-

cism and demands for empirical support. Is it really worthwhile teaching poor preschoolers to read? Where is the data?

39. The full version is given in Boyle (2000a).

40. See Lawrence Lessig (2001b).

41. See above note 17.

42. See James Boyle (2000b).

43. Boyle (1996) and James Boyle (1992). An expanded version of this argument can be found in "A Politics of Intellectual Property: Environmentalism for the Net." 47 Duke L. J. 87 (1997) <http://www.law.duke.edu/boylesite/intprop.htm>.

References

Allen, Robert C. 1982. The efficiency and distributional consequences of eighteenth century enclosures. *Economic Journal* 92: 937–953.

Anon. 1821. Anonymous poem from the eighteenth century, first referred to by Edward Birch in *Tickler* magazine (February 1821), 45.

Behlendorf, Brian. 1999. Open source as a business strategy. In: Chris DiBona, Sam Ockman, and Mark Stone (eds.), *Open sources: Voices from the Open Source Revolution*. Sebastopol, CA: O'Reilly.

Benkler, Yochai. 1999. Free as the air to common use: First Amendment constraints on enclosure of the public domain. *New York University Law Review* 74(2): 354–364, 424.

———. 2002–2003. Coase's penguin, or Linux and the nature of the firm, *Yale Law Journal* 112(3): 369–446. (A condensed version is included as Chapter 11 in this volume.)

———. 2003. Through the looking glass: Alice and the constitutional foundations of the public domain. *Law and Contemporary Problems* 66: 173–224.

Boyle, James. 1992. A theory of law and information: Copyright, spleens, blackmail, and insider trading. *California Law Review* 80: 1413–1540.

———. 1996. *Shamans, software, and spleens: Law and the construction of the Information Society*. Cambridge, MA: Harvard University Press.

———. 2000a. Cruel, mean, or lavish?: Economic analysis, price discrimination and digital intellectual property. *Vanderbilt Law Review* 53: 2007–2039.

———. 2000b. Missing the point on Microsoft. *Salon.com*, Apr. 7, 2000. Available at <http://www.salon.com/tech/feature/2000/04/07/greenspan/index.html>.

Brewer, E. Cobham. 1898. *Dictionary of phrase and fable*. Philadelphia: Henry Altemus.

Brown, Bruce. 2002. Enterprise-Level security made easy. *PC Magazine* Jan. 15, 2002, at 28.

Eisenberg, Rebecca S. 1990. Patenting the human genome. *Emory Law Journal* 39: 721–745.

Ernle, (Prothero) Lord. 1962. *English farming past and present*. 6th ed. Chicago: Quadrangle Books.

Fukuyama, Francis. 1992. *The end of history and the last man*. New York: Penguin.

Grossman, Sanford J., and Joseph E. Stiglitz. 1980. On the impossibility of informationally efficient markets. *American Economic Review* 70: 393–408.

Haas, Alexander K. 2001. The Wellcome Trust's disclosures of gene sequence data into the public domain and the potential for proprietary rights in the human genome. *Berkeley Technology Law Journal* 16: 145–153.

Hardin, Garrett. 1968. The tragedy of the commons. *Science* 162: 1243–1248.

Hardy, I. Trotter. 1996. The ancient doctrine of trespass to Web sites. *Journal of Online Law* art. 7, Available at <http://www.wm.edu/law/publications/jol/95_96/hardy.html> (last visited Dec. 19, 2002).

Landes, William M., and Richard A. Posner. 1989. An economic analysis of copyright law. *Journal of Legal Studies* 18: 325–363.

Lessig, Lawrence. 2001a. Jail time in the Digital Age. *New York Times*, July 30, 2001, at A17.

————. 2001b. *The future of ideas: The fate of the commons in a networked world*. New York: Random House.

————. 1990. The public domain. *Emory Law Journal* 39: 965–1023.

Litman, Jessica. 2001. *Digital copyright*. Amherst, NY: Prometheus Books.

Moglen, Eben. 1999. Anarchism triumphant: Free software and the death of copyright. *First Monday*, 4(8), Available at <http://www.firstmonday.dk/issues/issue4_8/moglen/>.

Moody, Glyn. 2001. *Rebel code: Inside Linux and the open source revolution*. New York: Perseus Publishing.

More, Thomas. 1947/1992. *Utopia*. New York: Alfred A. Knopf.

Polanyi, Karl. 1957. *The great transformation: The political and economic origins of our time*. Boston, MA: Beacon Press.

Popper, Karl. 1945. *The open society and its enemies*. 2 volumes New York: Routledge.

Rapoza, Jim. 1999. Open-source fever spreads. *PC Week*, Dec. 13, 1999, at 1.

Reichman, J. H., and Paul F. Uhlir. 1999. Database protection at the crossroads: Recent developments and their impact on science and technology. *Berkeley Technology Law Journal* 14: 793–838.

Samuelson, Pamela. 1999. Intellectual property and the digital economy: Why the anti-circumvention regulations need to be revised. *Berkeley Technology Law Journal* 14: 519–566.

Samuelson, Pamela, and Suzanne Scotchmer. 2002. The law and economics of reverse engineering. *Yale Law Journal* 111: 1575–1663.

Stiglitz, Joseph. 1999. The World Bank at the millennium. *Economic Journal* 109: 577–597.

Travis, Hannibal. 2000. Pirates of the information infrastructure: Blackstonian copyright and the First Amendment. *Berkeley Technology Law Journal* 15: 777–840.

Wayner, Peter. 2000. *Free for all: How Linux and the free software movement undercut the high-tech-titans*. New York: HarperCollins.

Williamson, John. 1990. What Washington means by policy reform. In John Williamson (ed.), *Latin American adjustment: How much has happened?* Washington, DC: Institute for International Economics.

————. 1999. What should the bank think about the Washington Consensus? *Institute for International Economics*, Available at <http://www.iie.com/papers/williamson0799.htm> (last visited Sept. 20, 2002).

14

A Renaissance of the Commons: How the New Sciences and Internet are Framing a New Global Identity and Order

John Clippinger and David Bollier

Cultures, like people, can run out of ideas. They can exhaust themselves in the face of events and ideas they can no longer predict, explain, or control. When they do, they revert to the repetitive assertion of the simplest and most soothing of their founding ideas. These attempts to ward off the unknown through the ritualized assertion of familiar core beliefs are what anthropologists call a "ghost dance." The name is taken from a Sioux Indian ritual dance designed to resurrect ancestors. Sioux warriors believed the dance made them impervious to the bullets of the U.S. Cavalry in the 1870s.

What may seem to be a bizarre ritual is in fact a well-documented practice of all cultures, traditional and modern. Many events in contemporary American life can be understood as a ghost dance of denial: ritualistic behavior that people hope will ward off unpleasant social and economic realities, ecological perils, and new global interdependencies that are profoundly threatening to established cultural norms. The ghost dance desperately repeats unexamined, unquestioned "truths" despite contrary evidence.

In our time, the ghost dance can be seen in a celebration of laissez-faire capitalism, radical individualism, and the alienability of all human activity and nature for market consumption. In their time, these myths were invaluable. They helped emancipate the "common man" from ancient obligations to feudal overlords by giving individuals the power not only to elect their own representatives, but to freely sell their labor in open markets. Civil freedoms would henceforth be linked with market freedoms.

Adam Smith and the American Founding Fathers were not championing a "market absolutism"; they realized that both commercial interests and individual rights depended critically upon the integrity of a shared moral and civic order. This was the idea of the "commonwealth," now a little-used term in public life. The essential principle of the commonwealth, as John Adams once put it, is that "no man, nor corporation or association of men have any other title to obtain advantage or particular and exclusive privileges distinct from those of the community, than what arises from the consideration of services rendered to the public."[1]

What was originally seen as a common-sense curtailment of the absolute powers of monarchs (read governments) and the vested rights of a ruling class, has today morphed into an all-embracing economic, cultural, and political dogma. The subtle arguments about inalienable rights and common obligations made by Jefferson, Madison, Smith and other seventeenth- and eighteenth-century philosophers, have congealed into a self-contained, ritualized belief system.

Without limitation, today's doctrine of "free markets" righteously insists that markets should govern virtually all aspects of civic, cultural and economic life. In fact, this doctrine dominates our politics, economics and public policy. Because it has become universalized, unassailable, unarguable and closed, free-market doctrine has become a dogma, or what we have called "FMD."

FMD declares that individuals maximize their self-interest by buying and selling in the "free market," and that the renowned Invisible Hand—the aggregation of these transactions—advances the public good. Believers in FMD see market activity as the supreme expression of "freedom." Any collective alternatives to the "free choices" offered by the market, especially government action, are seen as coercive and benighted.

Since FMD regards individuals as the sole originators of wealth, it follows that they alone should be entitled to own and control wealth. Government action to control property is considered inherently suspect because government is bureaucratic and wasteful, goes the thinking, while "free" individuals acting through the market are far more intelligent and innovative. Because the market is presumed to be more efficient than government, the default strategy for managing public resources is to privatize and marketize them. Attempts by government to restrict the prerogatives of ownership are often blasted as confiscatory, punitive, or unconstitutional "takings."

As for the social disruptions and environmental harms caused by market activity, FMD regards them as aberrations that markets will ameliorate over the long-term. The churn of "creative destruction"—the phrase coined by economist Joseph Schumpeter and much-touted by the *Wall Street Journal*—is said to be our best assurance of social equity and accountability. This faith is reflected in such "common sense" as "a rising tide raises all boats" and "progress through economic growth."

FMD is far more than a matter of economics, however. It is a moral calculus and foundational set of social norms. It declares price to be the best indicator of value and that market principles as the fairest way to allocate wealth and other rewards. In this sense, FMD is not just the centerpiece of conventional economics, but a catechism of our politics, economics, and culture—our American creed.

An Insurgent New Worldview

Yet even as FMD orthodoxy dictates the scope of permissible discussion in American life, a powerful new tide is rushing in to batter the citadel. Dissenting critiques are emanating from a variety of improbable sources—the hard sciences, behavioral economics, and complexity theory, robust new types of Internet-based communities, and startling new transnational social movements.

These eclectic and evolving insurgencies do not constitute a coherent response to FMD—yet. But look more closely, and with an open mind, and begin to connect the dots. A remarkable array of scientific discoveries, academic conceptualizations, and social practices are converging around some common principles. One can discern, in fact, some deep and disruptive challenges to conventional notions of property rights, free markets, organizational hierarchy, national sovereignty, and human nature.

Surely a primary exhibit is the startling growth of free and open source software, especially as exemplified by Linux. It seems nothing short of miraculous that a global network of thousands of volunteers operating via the Internet could build a highly complex operating system that could out-perform Microsoft's products. Our surprise merely suggests the limits of our mental categories, which cannot fathom how online communities harness personal identity and collaboration to produce such a sophisticated product. A number of major companies such as IBM and Hewlett-Packard, however, understand that open source is a serious business proposition, not mere idealism, and have made it a core part of their competitive market strategies.

Equally astonishing are the varieties of Internet-based networking communities that are outflanking commercial venues. Collaborative Web sites, listservs, peer-to-peer file sharing, weblogs, institutional repositories at universities, new content licensing schemes and "tagging" protocols for digital content: such tools are giving rise to entirely new sorts of creative genres, research literature, and cultural platforms. In turn, these online platforms are propelling the growth of many powerful social movements of global scope—sustainable environmentalism, human rights, socially responsible trade, affordable AIDS drugs, peace.

Within the academy, meanwhile, genetics, evolutionary biology, and brain neuroscience are challenging classical models of human brain functioning and cognitive processes. Comparative anthropologists and evolutionary psychologists are making breakthrough findings about our species' deeply embedded instincts for social cooperation. A new generation of economists is finding that neoclassical economic theories are just too rigid and abstract to do justice to the empirical realities of modern economic life. Behavioral economics is building a new intellectual edifice to explain how personal and social factors affect economic activity. Complexity theory is providing new conceptual tools for understanding the nonlinear, dynamic flows of natural and economic systems.

Predictably, the Guardians of our traditional order—neoclassical economists, the scientific establishment, the major political parties, Washington policy elite, the corporate media, and business leadership—generally have little interest in the dissenting critiques. FMD creed is, after all, comfortably entrenched and seamlessly comprehensive. Its defenders do not "need" to explain disturbances on the periphery. FMD provides a "good enough" template for explaining how things "really" work.

And in truth, most of us have so internalized the cognitive universe of FMD that it seems a bit disingenuous to rail against some external villains. The perceptual myopia that afflicts our culture—let's be frank—lies within ourselves. It is not easy to change one's sense of identity and cultural outlook, let alone cognitive habits. Psychology experiments have shown that the more a belief system fails, the more tenaciously its adherents cling to it.

This may help explain why American culture seems caught in some sort of Groundhog Day, senselessly forced to repeat the same cycles of the past ad infinitum. In our fixation on free-market dogma, we are enacting our very own ghost dance. We are stuck in an interregnum. An aging corpus of free-market dogma maintains a tight stranglehold on American life even as its explanatory power wanes in the face of new realities.

As the ghost dance intensifies, it is worth asking: Why is the old order imperiled, and how is it incompatible with emerging trends? Based on the fragmentary evidence now emerging, what are the key features of the new worldview? How might we begin to embrace a more realistic understanding the human condition and social structures in the twenty-first century?

A Renaissance of the Commons

The emerging paradigm that we see, based on the dispersed insurgencies bursting out, is the renaissance of the commons. The commons is a social regime for managing shared resources and forging a community of shared values and purpose. Unlike markets, which rely upon price as the sole dimension of value, a commons is organized around a richer blend of human needs—for identity, community, fame, and honor—which are indivisible and inalienable, as well as more "tangible" rewards.

In a commons, transactions are based on ongoing moral, social, and personal relationships, not episodic, impersonal exchanges of money. A commons is also marked by openness. This helps assure that developments affecting the community's interests can be scrutinized by all. It also helps the commoners identify and punish free-riders, preventing the so-called tragedy of the commons. (This term is actually a misnomer because it describes an open-access regime of private appropriation; a commons, by contrast, is managed by consensual rules, membership, limits on alienability, transparency, etc.)

Human societies need markets for their ability to stimulate innovation, efficiency, and growth. Price is a powerful organizing tool in this respect, facilitated by the division of resources into private property. But human societies also need things that are indivisible and inalienable, which is the essence of the commons. If the social relationships and values that constitute a commons can be bought and sold—made alienable—they are destroyed. It is hard to trust someone whose loyalty and judgment can be bought, just as we lose respect for a government corrupted by bribery and corruption. Similarly, many shared resources—parks, libraries, ecosystems, democracy—can only be sustained if they are held "in common." Their organic integrity must be protected against private exploitation, lest the shared resource be converted into a market and destroyed.

While the champions of FMD regard markets as the universal, default norm of human social organization, recent developments seem to be refuting that. Evolutionary scientists are coming to believe that many social behaviors that are crucial to the commons—social reciprocity, trust, shared values—have played a vital practical role in assuring human survival and adaptation. These human behaviors have been at least as important as the more familiar economic notions of competition and alienability.

Now, with the rise of the Internet, we are seeing a strangely appropriate convergence of the future and the past: A lightweight, high-tech infrastructure, the Internet, is enabling some primordial human impulses to come to the fore in powerful new ways. Fundamental truths that FMD has always denied—that human cooperation comes naturally, that collective action can be more efficient than markets, that the gift economy is a potent source of value-creation and human satisfaction—are being vindicated. It is still quite early in the game, but the commons may be the critical matrix for understanding many of the rebellions now underway.

It is foolish to think that the new commons will (or should) replace markets. Markets are far too necessary to human welfare to disappear. But what is likely to emerge—indeed, what is already occurring—is the rise of a hybrid without a name that will complement, and mitigate free-market dogma. This new path, the commons template, is neither laissez-faire capitalism nor state-managed collectivism. It moves beyond the antimonies of "free" versus "regulated" markets and seeks to resolve the intensifying contradictions of market capitalism. Through the commons template, one can imagine having the efficiency, flexibility, and freedom of markets on the one hand, and preserving and advancing the common good on the other.

The following sections explore the remarkable renaissance of the commons as reflected in new academic approaches, economic schools of thought, social practices, and global movements.

New Scientific Evidence vs. *Homo economicus*

One of the most potent challenges to free-market dogma—and affirmations of the commons—is coming from new scientific findings about human nature. Thanks to recent research into brain functioning, genetics, developmental and evolutionary psychology and biology, and comparative anthropology, we need no longer accept the armchair speculations of seventeenth-century philosophers such as David Hume, John Locke, and Thomas Hobbes about the actual propensities and capacities of human beings.

Although our understanding is by no means complete, recent research points to a coherent new understanding of basic aspects of human nature. The research—which is inherently nonideological and eminently testable—is almost a point-for-point refutation of the premises of free-market dogma. The implications are enormous. If the different strands of the emerging sciences could be woven together and popularized, the resulting synthesis could catalyze a sea change in our images of ourselves and human society.

While FMD conveniently offers an antiquated, highly simplified model of human nature and economic behavior, a new, more dynamic model of human agency and social identity is starting to emerge. Our history as a species reveals that social cooperation, not just brutal competition, has been a critical evolutionary factor in the survival of the human species. Unfortunately, the story of human nature continues to be told in the sound bites of seventeenth-century philosophers. A more balanced, subtle, and realistic account is long overdue.

The skeptic might ask, Why should we bother to address the vision of human nature put forward by free-market dogma? Why does it matter? Such an inquiry might be interesting and diverting, but so what if *homo economicus* is an agreed-upon fable, an abstract ideal? Isn't that more or less how the world works?

That is precisely the point: the world does not work according to the conventional representations of FMD, and those representations have incalculable sway over economics, politics, public policy, and culture. To be sure, nasty, brutish behavior still exists and flourishes. But the new sciences are showing that social reciprocity and trust are deeply engrained—indeed, biologically encoded—principles of our humanity. They are a precondition even for markets.

As Karl Polanyi (1957) described in his landmark book, *The Great Transformation*, no "free market" can survive very long without extensive social institutions and shared ethical norms. A lot of cooperation and trust is needed to devise legal regimes, establish regulatory agencies, administer a judicial system and maintain consumer confidence in markets. FMD is notably deficient in recognizing this fact, however. This was vividly demonstrated when free marketeers tried to introduce market competition to the former Soviet

Union. Predictably, the experiments floundered because the necessary institutions of civil society and cultural norms simply did not exist.

This very blind spot in the epistemology of the market has long been at work in the West as well. Without outside intervention, FMD generally doesn't recognize that social ethics, a healthy environment, product safety, and community well-being are important to the long-term vitality of markets. Its economic theories see them as distracting sideshows to the main action, market exchange. Without collective oversight (which defenders of FMD constantly seek to undermine), scandals such as Enron, Global Crossing, Worldcom, and Arthur Andersen are, sadly, inevitable.

It is here that the new insurgencies are making remarkable headway against FMD. Ingeniously, they are harnessing the forces that FMD dismisses as "exogenous variables" and leveraging them to maximum advantage. This is the most significant (and unacknowledged) achievement of the Internet—the empowerment of countless new forms of social communion, creativity, and knowledge without the ministrations of the market. The powerful psychic and social energies driving the growth of the Internet are quite inexplicable—and invisible—by the terms of FMD.

Consider it the revenge of the commons: the social context that FMD has long regarded as incidental is now surging forward as a powerful force in its own right. The emergence of the commons in cyberspace has a tantalizing correspondence with new scientific findings about the evolutionary character of the human species.

The Scientific Case for the Commons

A growing body of evidence suggests that social trust and cooperation has been the enduring theme of human evolution. The FMD model of *homo economicus*, which purports to be a universal norm, actually has very little basis in fact or history. There are three general lines of evidence.

1. Social exchange is an "evolutionarily stable strategy" (ESS) and thus the critical platform for cognitive development in humans.

In evaluating the "fitness" of an adaptation or mutation, geneticists, evolutionary biologists, and mathematical game theorists often look for evidence of an "evolutionarily stable strategy," or ESS. Such strategies are noteworthy because they are powerfully adaptive and stable; in effect they cannot be displaced by any other evolutionary strategy—or mutation or phenotype—

because there is no advantage in doing so. If an evolutionary trait can be considered an ESS by the lights of genetics or evolutionary biology, therefore, it constitutes powerful evidence that it is a deep aspect of human nature.

Recent studies have argued that the notion of "reciprocal altruism" is an ESS. So are many innate "social contracting algorithms" of the human brain.[2] What makes this evidence especially compelling is that the ESS approach can successfully predict what kind of "strategies" and even special competences will emerge in different social exchange networks. For example, many different species—vampire bats, wolves, ravens, baboons, and chimpanzees—exhibit similar social behaviors and emotions such as sympathy, attachment, embarrassment, dominant pride, and humble submission. Both ravens and vampire bats can detect cheaters and punish them accordingly—a skill needed to thwart free-riders and maintain the integrity of the group.

This indicates that "cooperative strategies" have evolved in different species and, because of the evolutionary advantages that they offer, become encoded in their genome. While much more needs to be learned in this area, evolutionary sciences appear to be identifying some of the basic principles animating the "social physics" of human behavior.[3] When different species independently "arrive at" the same ESS, it suggests that there is a unifying social physics governing complex forms of behaviors regardless of the species.

2. Reciprocal social exchange is a highly specialized brain function critical to the rise of identity, community and culture.

The fact that humans can communicate, coordinate, and carry out social exchanges so effectively stems from uniquely human social "algorithms" for doing so—patterns of instinctive response that are genetically encoded. Social contract algorithms are those innate capacities of individuals that enable human societies to function as communities. Such algorithms include a person's sense of justice and guilt, social reciprocity through gift-giving, and an ability to read social cues.

While earlier sociobiologists believed that natural selection worked almost exclusively at the individual level of gene mutation, it has become increasingly clear that many social algorithms also coevolve at the "group" level.[4] David Sloan Wilson, an evolutionary biologist who has written extensively on natural selection and cooperation, writes that "social groups become so functionally integrated that they become higher-level organisms in their own right."[5] At such a point, evolutionary pressures appear to play out at the collective level, not just at the genetic and individual level. (There is a spectrum of views about the level at which natural selection is most influential—group or individual—but not even Darwin was as radical an individualist as many contemporary scientists such as Richard Dawkins, author of *The Selfish Gene.*)[6]

Historically, many scientists and economists have relied upon rational models of self-interest to explain how organisms evolve. Game theory and "prisoner's dilemma" scenarios are often used to explore how people really behave. The presumption is that people's natural inclination is to win at the expense of their opponent or their neighbor. But neuroscientists are discovering that rational-actor models grossly misrepresent how the human organism actually functions. It seems that we as species are neurologically hardwired to be empathic and cooperative, and to connect emotionally with what is occurring in the world in general. Moreover, this occurs at a species level, not at an individual level.[7]

A species sustains itself through such cooperation. In this sense, the idea of the commons is not a cultural artifact of English history. It is a driving principle of natural selection that is literally manifested in the architecture and physiology of the brains of *homo sapiens*. It reveals itself in the kinds of effective group cooperation that humans have shown throughout two millions years, and in the development of language itself, which is thought to serve important social-bonding purposes.

Brain neuroscience is starting to confirm that we may be hardwired to empathize and cooperate. A group of neuroscientists in Parma led by Giovannia Rizzolatti and Vittorio Gallese studied how brain neurons responded in the prefrontal cortex of macaque monkeys. Scientists found that when a monkey performed a complex motor action, the same neurons would fire in other monkeys who were merely watching.[8] These neurons—"mirror neurons"—are complemented by "canonical neurons" in adjacent brain tissue, which fire when an animal sees an object of the kind normally involved in a given action. All these neurons, in turn, are connected to the portions of the brain that process emotions and govern empathy.

As linguist George Lakoff explains,

"We know from psychology professor Paul Ekman's research that configurations of facial muscles express certain emotions. Presumably, our mirror neurons fire when we see the same configurations of facial muscles on someone else that our facial muscles would make. And that firing can activate our own emotional centers. In short, that allows us to empathize—to feel someone else's pain or joy. . . . We have evolved to be empathetic (via mirror neurons and connections to the emotional centers of the brain) and to be connected to the world (via canonical neurons). Empathy and connection to the other and to the physical environment are central aspects of human nature!"[9]

Altruism is not limited to human beings, but is typical of many different social species. Experiments with monkeys have shown that monkeys would refrain from pulling a chain to deliver food if it would result in shocking other monkeys. This suggests that ethics—a sense of compassion and reciprocity—is not some kind of softheaded, idealistic, and therefore untenable evolutionary strategy of the sort dismissed by tough realists. It is, rather, a well-established fitness strategy that seems to be encoded in the behaviors of many species. The highly respected neurologist Antonio Damasio has argued in his recent book, *Looking for Spinoza*, that social emotions have an identifiable physiology and measurable role in the behavior of the human brain. Anger, fear, shame, indignation, jealousy, pride, compassion, gratitude, sorrow, and joy appear to be part of "an overall program of bioregulation."[10]

Damasio writes: "The biological reality of self-preservation leads to virtue because in our inalienable need to maintain ourselves we must, of necessity, help preserve other selves. If we fail to do so so, we perish and are thus violating the foundational principle, and relinquishing the virtue that lies in self-preservation. The secondary foundation of virtue then is the reality of a social structure and the presence of other livings organisms in a complex system of interdependence with our own organism."[11]

Evolutionary biologists have also discovered that, contrary to the precepts of free-market doctrine, people tend to act in ways that express and reinforce the social exchange rules of their group, which typically follow principles of reciprocal exchange. Social exchange—"I'll scratch your back if you scratch mine"—is the process of cooperating for mutual benefit. Sometimes called "reciprocal altruism," it is an adaptive trait that is a deeply rooted product of natural selection that benefits the collective. The history of cultures shows that social exchange is in fact a human universal; it is not a recent cultural invention.

"This mutual provisioning of benefits, each conditional on the others' compliance, is rare in the animal kingdom," write evolutionary psychologists Leda Cosmides and John Tooby (2002). "Social exchange cannot be generated by a simple general learning mechanism, such as classical or operant conditioning. . . . This strongly suggests that engaging in social exchange requires specific cognitive machinery, which some species have and others lack."[12]

Cross-cultural analysis has verified the neurobiological evidence. In a survey of fifteen very different societies, economist Samuel Bowles has shown that the celebrated *homo economicus* invoked by neoclassical economists does not exist in any recognizable form. He simply could not be found.[13]

3. The rational "free choices" that FMD considers a primary justification are in many instances reflexive social "flocking."

One of the central premises of FMD is that individuals consciously make rational choices to advance their self-interests, which a responsive market then actualizes to achieve the public good. But new findings in brain neurology are showing that a great deal of human behavior is not a matter of conscious deliberation and rationality, but of physiological and social instinct. New discoveries about cognition and thought suggest that humans are patently not "rational actors" who approach every situation free of deeply ingrained genetic predilections and cultural habits. As a species, we act in species-symptomatic ways—ways that define and perpetuate the collective (the species), not the individual. Moreover, "rationality" is but one of many capacities of the brain. Some of the most influential forces driving human behavior are autonomic reflexes that are independent, highly localized, and fragmented in the brain.

Cognitive scientists are now realizing that it is too parochial to focus exclusively on the brain if we wish to understand human intelligence. Cognition does not take place in brain tissue alone. It takes place in the context of our bodies and the external environment, both of which we constantly use to gather information, draw upon as memory aids, and conduct computations. Patients with Alzheimer's Disease, for example, rely heavily upon a highly structured environment, much of it self-created, in order to recognize things, make mental associations, and reason. Change the patients' physical environment—move them to another location—and they lose large portions of their memory and cognitive capacity. In a similar way, all of us rely critically upon an external "scaffolding" of cognitive aids—books, newspapers, computers, other people, telephones, symbols, etc.—to "think" and function intelligently.

FMD is therefore incorrect to depict conscious and rational thought as a sovereign, independent force residing within individuals. The mind is deeply intermingled with its external environment, and is particularly influenced by the cultural milieu that it inhabits. "Individual brains should not take all the credit for the flow of thoughts or the generation of reasoned responses," writes cognitive scientist and philosopher Andy Clarke. "Brain and world collaborate in ways that are richer and more clearly driven by computational and informational needs than was previously suspected."[14] Without abstract metarepresentations of language, ritual, social cues, and so forth, "rational choice" is literally impossible.

Contrary to FMD view of independent choice, human beings seem to be neurologically and genetically hardwired with many innate routines and protocols, most of which help social groups to coordinate their actions. These routines and protocols are essentially social in nature and driven more by instinct than by rationality. Because these evolutionary features of the human brain seem so deeply rooted and enduring, evolutionary game theorists believe they reflect an "equilibrium selection"—i.e., an Evolutionary Stable Strategy for human survival. At heart, we are social creatures, not rational automatons.

Beyond Determinism: A Constructivist Human Nature

The empirical findings of the new sciences do not suggest a reductionist notion of a fixed and universal "human nature" of the sort portrayed in countless "nature/nurture" arguments. Rather, they suggest a far more "spacious" model of human nature. Human nature is not "determined" by genes, as popular mythology often seems to hold. It consists of shared and specific competencies that are expressed in different ways by different societies. It is not a reductionist model, but a profoundly constructivist model. Innate propensities coevolve over time with a wide range of social and physical conditions.[15]

Seen from this perspective, we can see that FMD is a highly artificial, if not fictional, notion of humanity. The free-market dogma worldview systematically, ideologically, privileges certain attributes of human beings while disregarding other innate propensities. It ignores the crucial interdependencies that individuals have with each other, with other cultures, and with nature. It validates a normative universe of cognition that is at odds with our genetic, neurological, psychological, and social history as a species. It should not be surprising that FMD is also proving to be highly destructive of the natural environment.

It is time to recognize that our "neurocognitive architecture" has coevolved with the natural environment over millions of years, predisposing us toward certain baseline psychological, social, and cognitive behaviors. In the long sweep of human history, the values and behaviors that we take as normative in our high-technology, market-driven, media-saturated environment, are, in fact, profoundly aberrational.

The new scientific findings are not merely parlor-room curiosities. As we will see next, they could be the foundation for more enlightened public policies. Rather than privilege the unexamined tenets of free-market individualism, we could get better and more humane results if we began to leverage our deeply engrained social tendencies.

New Economic Challenges to FMD

Just as the evolutionary sciences are contesting FMD schema of human nature, so behavioral economics is questioning its core economic assumptions. Over the past generation, consumer activists and environmentalists have amassed a considerable literature documenting the chasm that separates market theory and realities.[16] A handful of prominent economists—John Kenneth Galbraith, Kenneth Arrow, and Vernon Smith come to mind—have dwelt on the serious contradictions of FMD. But now a new generation of economists is beginning to fashion a coherent alternative set of theoretical principles for understanding how markets actually work. Free-market dogma may never be the same.

The standard modus operandi for many economists is to traffic in theoretical abstractions and give short shrift to on-the-ground realities. An old joke has two economists on a desert island when a soda bottle washes ashore. One declares, "Assume a bottle opener. . . ." New schools of economic thought—especially behavioral economics and complexity theory—are moving beyond this widely accepted cop-out. While they emphasize different sets of principles, the new approaches share a contempt for three primary tenets of free-market economics—the notions of unbounded rationality, unbounded selfishness, and unbounded willpower.

The first presumes that economic actors can be perfectly informed in all their economic choices. The second presumes that economic actors necessarily act to maximize their personal and material gain. And the third presumes that economic actors have limitless determination to achieve these objectives. These axioms supposedly combine to animate the Invisible Hand, the familiar principle of Economics 101, which holds that each individual and corporation will generate the optimum public good by pursuing its own narrow self-interests without impediment. The confluence of private capital, private property, and private self-interests are said to drive us, efficiently and effectively, to new levels of innovation, wealth creation, and progress.

But this idealized model of human economic behavior is plausible only if one discounts or ignores the "externalities" that usually accompany market behavior—the social disruptions, ecological damage, health and safety hazards, and deferred costs. It is easy to understand why we might collude in overlooking these costs. Many are hard to measure and are speculative in nature. (What are the real costs of driving the snail darter into extinction?) The chief beneficiaries of FMD, investors, are usually not eager to document the full breadth of market externalities lest they be required to pay for them.

Finally, the actual inequities and costs of FMD have been tolerated for so long because the only other coherent method of wealth-creation—the centralized command-and-control system typified by the former Soviet Union—was so notoriously wasteful and inefficient. The standards for judging the success of FMD are singularly low.

And so FMD, despite its patent deficiencies, continues to be accepted as a virtual natural law of economics and the fundamental model for wealth creation and development throughout the world. Social inequities, environmental degradation, cultural homogenization, and wealth concentration are accepted with a shrug as tragic yet necessary costs of achieving "progress." Tom Friedman of *The New York Times* has approvingly called this Faustian bargain the "golden straightjacket."[17]

Behavioral economics is beginning to open up new vistas of possibility, however. By developing rigorous empirical models of the ways that markets actually behave, and by bringing market "externalities" back into the discussion, behavioral economists are pioneering radically different metrics for understanding the supposed efficiency and rationality of free markets. Their findings are undermining the largely unexamined assumption that markets are the most effective and legitimate mechanisms for collecting and allocating public resources. Using new types of on-the-ground research, behavioral economists are validating that humans actually exhibit a "bounded rationality" in their market choices. They often exhibit trust and reciprocity towards other economic players rather than selfishness. They exhibit limited motivation to maximize their "rationality" and personal gain. Social exchange theory is beginning to describe how people naturally make decisions and cooperate.

One must emphasize, again, that market activity is not going to become obsolete any time soon. It not only produces negative externalities (events beyond the market transaction itself) such as pollution and social disruption;

it often produces positive externalities. Much of the story of the transition from feudalism to mercantilism, indeed, is about how popular access to capital undermined the power and privilege of landed and titled elites, and opened the door for broader participation in the economy. The market system created new jobs, new wealth based on merit, and new economic and political freedoms.

From the vantage point of the twenty-first century, however, we can now see that there are inherent limitations to what eighteenth-century price mechanisms and property conventions can achieve. While FMD declares that the price mechanism makes all resources substitutable, for example, the real world of human beings, nature, and public resources is not always so tractable. Not all resources are, or should be, indivisible and inalienable, as FMD presumes. Progress may not really be served by letting markets decide which new species should be invented; by promoting incessant television-watching among young children; and by building functional substitutes for the melting polar ice caps. FMD is also ill-equipped to allocate resources and incentives in fair and humane ways.

Yet just as the Enlightenment and market capitalism lifted the yoke of feudalism and unleashed unimagined forms of creativity, prosperity, and civic participation, so the renaissance of the commons offers new strategies for resolving many of the paralyzing conundrums of market capitalism. The new sciences and commons-based social regimes point to new principles for coping with issues—externalities, market failure, irrational behaviors, agency costs, and public goods—that otherwise cannot be easily addressed within the terms of market theory.

Behavioral economists are not the only ones looking for new theoretical principles; others are using complexity theory to help explain nonlinear behaviors and the importance of social context in markets, among other real-life dynamics. This still-emerging critique is far more humanistic and socially oriented than the rigid, quantitative models of conventional economics. Instead of trying to come up with tidy mathematical formalities that depict a specious market equilibria, complexity theorists are far more concerned with understanding the importance of singular evolutionary pathways (for individuals, companies, and economies), the properties of self-organizing systems, and the patterns of nonlinear, dynamic change.

Taken together, these new types of economic thought are subverting some core principles of an earlier economic worldview and striding toward a postmarket economics that has yet to be named or fully described. This novel but highly cogent worldview is all but incomprehensible to mainstream economic models of the world that derive, let us recall, from the simplistic, static and mechanical concepts of seventeenth-century thought. Not surprisingly, the guardians of FMD and their critics have yet to engage in a frank, direct dialogue; their categories of understanding are so radically incommensurate!

The new sciences are attracting increasing attention, however, and for a simple reason. They are better able to explain contemporary economic phenomena. They make more sense. The growing maturity of behavioral economics can be seen in the recent Nobel Laureates given to Professor Vernon Smith of George Mason University and Professor Daniel Kahneman of Princeton University, both of whom are behavioral economists. Similarly, since its founding in 1994, the Santa Fe Institute, the leading outpost of complexity theorists, has steadily gained in stature among innovative, forward-thinking economists.

The Rise of the Internet and Global Culture

If the latest advances in evolutionary sciences and economics remain unknown to most of the public, the impact of the Internet is another matter. Its social, economic, and political repercussions are one of the most stunning developments of recent history. Here, too, the story is mostly about the surge of the commons and the limits of free-market dogma.

"We share a collective blind spot to the possibility that human beings can act together to create real value, without relying either on selfish exploitation of private property (or markets or firms) or top-down governmental action," write Internet law scholars David Johnson and Susan Crawford. "Today's political conversation ignores the potential for emergent, networked collective action. But right in front of our noses is a living example of a system that is working to produce value without visible control or rent-seeking behavior."[18]

This living system is, of course, the Internet. But because its dynamics do not fit easily into current political and economic categories, its powerful role in creating value through social collaboration remains largely unseen. Many modes of interaction occur over the Internet, but the most robust ones tend to leverage our social desires to share and collaborate. Listservs, collaborative Web sites, open source software, and peer-to-peer (P2P) file sharing technologies are among the ways that a dispersed, decentralized collective of people are coming together to create value. Scientists use P2P networks to collectively advance their research; thousands of online self-help groups host everything from genealogical research to child-adoption guidance to volunteer mapping of the craters of Mars.

Not only do these new self-organizing, "bottom-up" networks of individuals arise spontaneously without the customary "top-down" organizing apparatus of a corporation, government agency, or nonprofit, they tend to be much more innovative and efficient than market mechanisms. The kinds of leadership and coordination that once required a business enterprise—as economist Nobel Laureate Ronald Coase declared in his famous 1934 essay on the rationale for forming corporations—can now take place outside of formal boundaries of a corporation with greater efficiency and creativity.[19] This is powerfully confirmed by the flourishing open-source software movement and explained in theoretical detail by NYU law professor Yochai Benkler in his essay, "Coase's Penguin."[20] (The penguin is in the logo for Linux software.)

The efficiency claims for the commons are supported by conventional economic analysis. "The laws of network topology dictate that the more people can be connected, and the more easily those connected people can form into value-creating groups, the more easily value will be created," write Johnson and Crawford (2003).

The resulting conversation creates immense value that is not counted in economic terms nor treated as part of any governmental/political system. Yet this interwoven tapestry of collective conversation provides a large and growing percentage of the value humans collectively seek: our education, our decisions about what to do with our privately owned resources (our capital, our time, our products and services), our decisions regarding what government should do, and our social and family relationships. This new "commonwealth" has flourished precisely because, having gone unnoticed, it has had a chance to thrive.

Because FMD systematically fails to recognize the powerful influence of social context, it fails to appreciate that its own structure of property rights, contracts, enforcement, profit incentives, and so forth, are sustained by a vast social apparatus and cultural norms which entail huge agency and transaction costs. It is very expensive for a company to offer high salaries to top management, hire attorneys to draft contracts, go to court to enforce violators, and so forth. But when leadership, coordination and motivation can be achieved easily through self-synchronizing, self-enforcing means, gracefully leveraging our natural social tendencies, why should anyone be surprised that such a system of exchange will be more efficient, effective and equitable than a market system? Communities of trust and transparency can be fantastically efficient! The rise of the Internet and various software systems are so powerful precisely because they leverage people's natural desire for meaning, trust, and social belonging—traits that FMD cannot understand, but which are deeply embedded in our evolutionary history.

This is the as-yet-untold story of the commons. In the commons, price alone is not the sole arbitrator of value and property rights may actually impede the creation of value. A larger set of human values, embodied in historically unique communities, determines the meaning of value. Money is not the only meaningful currency.

Such concepts are difficult for people steeped in our current property-bounded traditions to accept. How can we collectively create valuable resources that are not owned by anyone (or that are owned by everyone, by way of government)? We assume that resources must be treated as property to make sure they are distributed, by way of the market, to those who can exploit them most efficiently. We believe that we should create "public goods" by means of government. But in the age of the Internet, these obvious propositions are not necessarily true. Intangible resources that we often treat as intellectual property increase in value as they are made available to the Internet, where others can easily find them and add value. (The rub: private companies may or may not be able to capture that increase in value for themselves alone.)

Significantly, this commons perspective is entirely supported by the findings of the evolutionary sciences. Human beings share a common genetic heritage with all forms of life, and we are therefore indivisible and interdependent with other species. Far from evolving as independent, self-actualizing, and materialistic actors, human beings emerged as a relatively small and vulnerable species 150,000 years ago because we developed a unique set of social contract algorithms based on language and cooperation. How oddly appropriate: the Internet and related technologies are simply allowing us to give fuller expression to our evolutionary legacy!

This helps account for the fledgling new forms of global culture that are coalescing around issues that must be addressed if we are going to survive as a species: preservation of ecological systems, international cooperation to assure world peace and human rights, and more socially constructive forms of global commerce. By empowering our social natures at a grassroots level, beneath the power of market institutions and nation-states, a new citizen-driven ethic is emerging on the global stage.

As David Bollier describes in his 2003 Aspen Institute report, *The Rise of Netpolitik*, the Internet is giving new global platforms to diasporic ethnic communities such as dispersed populations of emigrant Chinese and exiles from Ghana and Zimbabwe.[21] It is enabling international political movements to coordinate the work of thousands of citizens, leading to impressive public agitation to ban land mines, and clean up the Bhopal chemical disaster. Millions of citizens are bypassing the corporate media and converging around personal Web logs and independent Web sites to find information they consider more reliable or at least more overt about their biases.

In short, the commons is growing rapidly. As it becomes a less exotic and more familiar cultural category, so there is a greater prospect of creating more transparent, accountable, ecologically benign, and humane institutions. Just as the environmental movement introduced a new kind of framing rhetoric into public dialogue, so "the commons" opens up new opportunities to reframe issues. It asks us to move beyond conventional dualities of private versus public, market versus state, individual versus the group, consumer versus seller. Such dichotomies become less relevant as the new models of commons-exchange take root and proliferate.

But what might these models look like? We conclude by offering a speculative preview of how the commons perspective might alter our approach to numerous public policy questions.

Public Policy in the Age of the Commons

The resurgent notion of the commons may be most valuable in helping us reconceptualize approaches to public policy and localized modes of self-governance. One of its signal strengths is its capacity to combine social, moral, and ecological choices with serious economics in a coherent theoretical framework. The concepts that describe the commons, if elaborated, could serve as valuable building blocks for a kind of postmarket critique. Precisely because it approaches economic questions in a holistic, long-term way, it embodies a more humane and sustainable vision.

The worldview implied by the commons opens up fresh new avenues for the imagination and institutional innovation. One promising idea is a new conception of ownership rights and decision-making authority. Collective action can often lower "agency costs" within organizations through greater efficiencies of trust, reciprocity, and self-enforcing social contracts. They also tend to result in more equitable outcomes.

One way to facilitate the creation of organized commons is to develop new forms of "tags" that can "mark off" work that is developed through a commons, as opposed to a market. This is essentially what the General Public License, or GPL, does for products of free software communities. It sets the work product off from the standard market products and identifies it as legally "belonging" to the commons. This ensures that no free riders can "take private" the code that the members of the commons have created.[22]

One can also imagine new public policy vehicles for asserting direct and responsible stewardship of collective resources. Already there is a burgeoning movement seeking to use certain segments of the public's electromagnetic spectrum as a commons (instead of assigning exclusive control to commercial licensees). The State of Alaska has pioneered the use of a stakeholder trust, the Alaska Permanent Fund, to share oil revenues from drilling on state land, with all Alaskan citizens.[23] This model has inspired a Sky Trust proposal to give all citizens an equity stake in the atmosphere, so that they can reap the financial benefits of selling "pollution rights" to corporations (instead of giving away those rights for free).[24]

The essential point of such commons vehicles is to bypass the bloated overhead of traditional corporations and government bureaucracies, and to more directly empower citizens in the stewardship of resources that they legally or morally own.

The commons approach to policymaking has some deep implications for how we reconcile market activity with the natural environment. By recognizing that human beings are interdependent with all of life—rather than somehow apart, as FMD holds—we can begin to craft institutions that are more compatible with life systems. Amory Lovins and his colleagues have developed this perspective in their book, *Natural Capitalism*.[25]

Embracing the principles of the commons can also yield greater efficiencies and sustainable wealth-creation opportunities. Market theory holds that creating private property rights gives people indispensable incentives to produce new wealth. But the empirical evidence of this framework is being refuted in a growing number of wealth-creating realms. Software development, natural resource management, and online knowledge, among other areas, are showing that a commons stewardship can be more efficient, sustainable and feasible over the long-term. It turns out that the much-vaunted efficiency of material self-interest, as advanced through property rights, is often an illusion because the markets/property/contracts framework structurally ignores the significant externalized costs it displaces onto other people and nature. A commons critique also helps us get beyond some fatally deceptive assumptions of market theory, which holds that all inputs are essentially fungible and substitutable.

But this logic has catastrophic results when applied to nature—for good reason. Ecological areas tend to be unique and indivisible. FMD makes a "category mistake" in applying false analytic terms onto natural systems that are organic and interconnected. FMD presumes that parts of nature can be divided, monetized and traded without harm to the whole. The past half-century of pell-mell economic development has vividly demonstrated the ecological fallacy of this doctrine.[26]

In a similar fashion, a commons critique can help expose the dangers of surrendering the social order and its values to commercial forces. Major corporations are now exploiting brain and anthropological research to explore how humans make affective attachments from childhood through adulthood.[27] Sony's highly successful Aibo robotic dog is an early prototype of such emotionally designed products. Disney has similar aspirations in designing animation and theme-park characters.

This intent of such research is to develop emotionally irresistible products and experiences, and to intensify brand loyalties and product dependencies. The market logic is impeccable and ingenious. But the morality and cultural wisdom of exploiting children's "Darwinian buttons" in order to open up new market opportunities is dubious. The commons perspective gives one a philosophical vantage point from which to confront the problematic behavior of markets.

Yet another realm that may be invigorated by a commons perspective is international relations and globalization. Throughout most of history, human beings have divided themselves into separate tribes and relied upon force to preserve their tribal differences. But as the once-separated segments of the "family of man" inexorably comes together on the global stage, more people are beginning to realize that we must either learn to coexist with nature and with each other—or destroy nature and humanity itself.

Rather than accept our past identity as controlling and immutable, the human species must somehow, as a matter of survival, engineer a new leap in our cultural and moral evolution. We must own up to our atavisms, our propensity for reflexive, violent flocking behavior in the face of uncertainty and threat. The Holocaust, Rwanda, Kosovo, and other pogroms against The Other are not the exception but the rule of human history. But if, in the past, these were evolutionary stable strategies and contributed to the overall evolutionary success of the species, they are patently lethal in the context of a globally integrated humanity.

Neurologist Antonio Damasio has noted that innate human propensities for cooperation and trust have a dark side as well. "The nice emotions can easily turn nasty and brutish when the are aimed outside the inner circles towards which they are naturally targeted. The result is anger, resentment, and violence, all of which we can easily recognize as a possible embryo of tribal hatred, racism and war. This is the time to introduce the reminder that the best of human behavior is not necessarily wired under the control of the genome. The history of our civilization is, to some extent, the history of a persuasive effort to extend the nest of "moral sentiments" to wider and wider circles of humanity, beyond the restrictions of the inner groups, eventually encompassing the whole of humanity."[28]

This may be the story of the new global culture that seems to be emerging—a fitful movement, it would appear, that aspires to cultivate new values and social protocols. At this point, no one can simply declare anything so grand as a new identity and ethos for the emerging global culture. Yet we can start to realize that the either/or, us/them perspective that pits one closed worldview against another is a relic of the Pleistocene era. There is a dawning awareness that it is seriously maladaptive in today's highly integrated, technologically potent global culture. As weapons of mass destruction have grown smaller, cheaper and more available to everyone, we are facing a threat to humanity that is utterly unprecedented.

What may seem like a moral or cultural crusade of utopian dimensions may in fact be a pragmatic necessity, even to those with the most callous notions of self-interest. Recognizing our identity as a species and our fragile place in evolutionary history may be the first, indispensable step toward saving ourselves.

Such a collective revelation is becoming even more urgent as the lines between what is natural and humanly constructed blur. Various new technologies are enabling unprecedented comingling of biological life forms with human design—genetic manipulations of agricultural seedlines, genetic engineering of human beings and animals, and irreversible manipulations of ecological systems and the global atmosphere. These developments signal a new era in human history. Human beings are no longer the children and adversaries of nature, the abject subjects of the gods. We are nature's stewards; we have become our parents. Nature is not something outside ourselves; it is something that we are constructing—cocreating—with all forms of technology, resulting in new forms of coevolution between ourselves and nature.

Even though we are totally unprepared for this responsibility, within the next decade human societies will somehow have to confront—or evade—the inevitable problems that ensue. To the extent that many problems stem from our overweening faith in FMD, a critique that acknowledges our common humanity—and not just the competitive pursuit of private gain—could help us chart a new course.

It's Time to Start a New Conversation

It is time to get beyond the ghost dance that afflicts this moment in our history. We desperately need a new humanistic vision, one that gets us past the large flaws and dated assumptions of FMD. The archetype of the commons may provide just such a platform for building such a vision. It complements the findings of the new sciences, it cogently deconstructs free-market ideology, and it offers its own feasible alternatives.

There could not be a more apt moment for ambitious, imaginative thinking. The new sciences are yielding a rich harvest of new insights into our contemporary circumstances. The Internet is enabling rich new forms of value-creation and social exchange. Many old models of economic life and human nature, relics of the eighteenth century, are crumbling. The rudiments of a new citizen-based global culture are sprouting up.

But we must remember that the old rarely yields to the new without a struggle. The new must be actively and imaginatively built. That will require forging new networks of visionary thinkers and bringing disparate disciplines together into new conversations. It will require challenging the comfortable shibboleths of FMD and taking new risks to develop a more accurate understanding of the human species.

Could there be a more urgent task for the twenty-first century? It is a daunting challenge, to be sure, but the long-term transformations—for economics, politics, policy, and culture—could not be more needed.

Notes

1. See McCullough (2001, 222).

2. See Cosmides and Tooby (2002).

3. John H. Clippinger, "Why Routing is Better Than Sharing," November 2002 (work in progress, on file with author).

4. See Durham (1991).

5. See Sober and Wilson (1998, 176).

6. See Dawkins (1976).

7. One compelling bit of evidence that social exchange is a universal trait for all human societies is a study that compared the ability to detect deceit among the Shiwiar, a nonliterate, isolated Amazonian tribe of hunter-horticulturalists, and Harvard undergraduates. If the ability to identify cheating were the product of culture or economic development, clear differences in competence would be discernible. But the study found that "cheater detection reasoning" has been found in every developed and developing country that has been studied. See Sugiyama, Tooby, and Cosmides (2000).

8. See Rizzolatti, Fadiga, Fogassi, and Gallese (1999).

9. George Lakoff, personal communication, 2003.

10. See Damasio (2003, 162).

11. See Damasio (2003, 171).

12. See Cosmides and Tooby 2002.

13. A cross-cultural survey of fifteen societies by economist Samuel Bowles has shown that the celebrated *homo economicus* that neoclassical economists routinely invoke does not exist in any recognizable form. See Henrich, Boyd, Bowles, Camerer, Fehr, Gintis, and McElreath (2001).

14. See Clark (1997, 69).

15. The fact that there are genetically encoded innate mechanisms that predispose or shape human thought and action should not come as a surprise. But this does not imply that there is strict determinism of human activity. If anything, the complexity sciences are especially respectful of the indeterminacy and indeed unpredictability of many of seemingly simple behaviors. Geneticists also recognize that genes are not literal blueprints that strictly determine morphological development or growth over time. Hence the so-called nature/nurture dichotomy—so often seized upon by the popular press—is a false one engendering much heat and little light. See, e.g., Pinker (2002).

16. See, e.g., Mullainathan and Thaler (2001).

17. See Friedman (1999, 83–92).

18. David Johnson and Susan Crawford, private correspondence.

19. See Coase (1937).

20. See Benkler (2002–2003).

21. See Bollier (2003).

22. The General Public License is a legal innovation of the Free Software Foundation, at <http://www.fsf.org>.

23. For more on the Alaska Permanent Fund, see <http://www.apfc.org>.

24. See Barnes (2001).

25. See Hawken, Lovins, and Lovins (1999).

26. See McNeill, McNeill, and Kennedy (2001) and Flannery (2001).

27. See Thompson (2003). See also, letter from Gary Ruskin (2001), of Commercial Alert, to Emory University President James Wagner, calling for a halt to all neuromarketing experimentation on human subjects at Emory.

28. See Damasio (2003, 163).

References

Barnes, Peter. 2001. *Who owns the sky? Our common assets and the future of capitalism.* Washington, DC: Island Press.

Benkler, Yochai. 2002–2003. Coase's penguin, or Linux and the nature of the firm. *Yale Law Journal* 112(3): 369–446.

Bollier, David. 2003. *The rise of Netpolitique: How the Internet is changing international politics and diplomacy.* Washington, DC: Aspen Institute.

Clark, Andy. 1997. *Being there: Putting brain, body, and world together again.* Cambridge, MA: MIT Press.

Coase, Ronald H. 1937. The nature of the firm. *Economica* 4(NS) (16): 386–405.

Cosmides, Leda, and John Tooby. 2002. *Evolutionary psychology: A primer.* Santa Barbara: University of California, Center for Evolutionary Psychology.

Damasio, Antonio. 2003. *Looking for Spinoza: Joy, sorrow and the feeling brain.* New York: Harcourt.

Dawkins, Richard. 1976. *The selfish gene.* Oxford, UK: Oxford University Press.

Durham, William. 1991. *Coevolution: Genes, culture and human diversity.* Stanford, CA: Stanford University Press.

Flannery, Tim. 2001. *The eternal frontier: An ecological history of North America and its peoples.* Boston: Atlantic Monthly Press.

Friedman, Thomas L. 1999. *The Lexus and the olive tree.* New York: Farrar, Straus, and Giroux.

Hawken, Paul, Amory Lovins, and L. Hunter Lovins. 1999. *Natural capitalism: Creating the next industrial revolution.* Boston: Little, Brown.

Henrich, Joseph, Robert Boyd, Samuel Bowles, Colin Camerer, Emst Fehr, Herbert Gintis, and Richard McElreath. 2001. In search of *Homo economicus*: Behavioral experiments in fifteen small-scale societies. *American Economic Review* 91(2): 73–78.

Johnson, David, and Susan Crawford. 2003. The Commonwealth Project. Unpublished memo on file with authors, February 16.

McCullough, David. 2001. *John Adams.* New York: Simon and Schuster.

McNeill, J.R., John Robert McNeill, and Paul Kennedy. 2001. *Something new under the sun: An environmental history of the twentieth century.* New York: W.W. Norton.

Mullainathan, Sendhil, and Richard H. Thaler. 2001. Behavioral Economics. In *International Encyclopedia of Social Sciences*, New York: Pergamon.

Pinker, Stephen. 2002. *The blank slate: The modern denial of human nature.* New York: Viking.

Polanyi, Karl. 1957. *The great transformation: The political and economic origins of our time.* Boston, MA: Beacon Press.

Rizzolatti, Giacomo, Luciano Fadiga, Leonardo Fogassi, and Vittorio Gallese. 1999. Resonance behaviors and mirror neurons. *Archives Italiennes de Biologie* 137(2–3): 85–100.

Ruskin, Gary. 2001. Sell the naming rights to your suits, Councilman. News release Available at <http://www.commercialalert.org/index.php/category_id/1/subcategory_id/82/article_id/21>.

Sober, Elliot, and David Sloan Wilson. 1998. *Unto others: The evolution and psychology of unselfish behavior.* Cambridge, MA: Harvard University Press.

Sugiyama, Lawrence S., John Tooby, and Leda Cosmides. 2000 Cross-Cultural evidence of cognitive adaptations for social exchange among the Shiwiar of Ecuadorian Amazonia. *Proceedings of the National Academy of Science USA* 3529: 99(17): 11537–11542.

Thompson, Clive. 2003. There's a sucker born in every medial prefrontal cortex. *New York Times Magazine*, October 26, 2003.

15

Positive Intellectual Rights and Information Exchanges

Philippe Aigrain

This chapter[1] proposes a reversal in how to consider the rights associated with information, media contents, software, and other intellectual entities. Intellectual property, forgetting its original purpose, now mostly focuses on granting the ability to restrict usage of intellectual entities. It then defines a number of exceptions to cope with the adverse effects of such a restriction. On the contrary, the proposed—better?—approach is one that sets as its basis a number of positive intellectual rights, defined to enable a wide societal production and exchange of intellectual entities. Only then does it define how the granting of specific attributes of property is necessary to ensure that the positive rights are not abused to the detriment of some basic values, and are implemented in reality. Without the proposed (re-)foundation of "intellectual property," there is a risk of losing the extraordinary benefits resulting from a greater plurality of creators and information sources, from a much greater and quicker visibility and accessibility of intellectual entities, and from the possibility to build new tools and processes for creating, assessing, criticising, and analyzing intellectual productions. Beyond information technology per se, this chapter also debates intellectual rights issues for all technology that are based on the identification and manipulation of information layers in complex processes, notably modern biotechnology. In contrast to approaches that stress abstract principles and absolute rights, this chapter argues that one should derive practical features of intellectual rights by differentiating between varieties of intellectual entities (according to how they can be produced, used, and exchanged). By doing so, one is able to propose a framework that truly serves creators without restricting unduly information exchanges.

A Historical Prologue

This text is of a normative nature. It defines philosophical principles on which it is hoped that one can derive inspiration for evolving legal systems and related policies. However, this tentative norm only makes sense in a context. Many great thinkers, including key contributors to this book, have described this context in the past few years. It is however necessary to recall it in a few lines to situate the proposed approach.

Between the 1930s and the mid-1950s, the scientific and technical basis of a revolution was created. The theoretical foundations of symbolic logic and technical inventions of computers gave birth to information technology in the modern sense. In parallel, cybernetics led us to see and design physical machines as made up of information control centers connected to sensors and actuators. This view also spread into our models of the natural world, and soon, information-based models and technology revolutionized genetics and gave birth to biotechnology in all its dimensions. It took a long time before we became aware of the range of effects of this revolution. It developed in a quiet, underground way. Vast bodies of the new knowledge were for instance developed in the public domain, such as algorithmics and most of the art of programming, as well as a great deal of genetic information. Some pioneering thinkers such as Jacques Ellul (1967), Ivan Illitch (2001), Jacques Robin (1989), or René Passet (1979) described the information revolution as early as in the late 1960s and the 1970s.

However, the relevance of their analysis was not widely accepted, in part because their criticism of technology was so strong that few saw that it also opened alternative paths of development. It is only in the 1980s that it became apparent that two powerful and contradictory processes had been set into motion. The first process is the creation of a new realm of free creation and exchange of information, with extremely low transaction costs, and a huge multiplicity and diversity of contributors. The first Internet revolution (based on e-mail, newsgroup, ftp, and bulletin boards) and the birth of free software may have mobilized only specialized groups, but they nonetheless were paradigms of a new information world. Today this world is also the world of the Web, of public genomics or astrophysics data, of open scientific publishing, of free encyclopedias, of new cooperative media, and so forth. However, in parallel, the second process saw huge industries being reshaped (pharmaceuticals, agro-food, centralized media) or born (proprietary packaged software). These industries have become highly dependent on the ability to gain property or control usage of information and knowledge entities. This has led them to ask for and obtain a huge extension of the scope, duration, intensity, mechanisms, and enforcement of property on artefacts that consist wholly or largely of information. The system of intellectual property has developed into a huge machine, largely out of control, and ever more aggressive as it fails to stop the floodwater of information from breaking through the barriers it tries to erect.

In the middle, many economic players are struggling to find a difficult path. To survive, they have to fight their way in a game whose rules have been set for the benefit of a few oligopolies, while they cannot afford to be cut off from the innovation resources of free knowledge.

The Crisis and the Risk of a Tragedy of Enclosures

Information and communication technology has opened a new world of possible activities, of which we have only started to understand the potential. Information, creative works in all media, software, and other intellectual or knowledge entities are easier to put together individually and even more collectively, to the point that commons-based peer production has been described by Yochai Benkler (2002–2003) as a superior mode of production for intellectual artefacts. It is incredibly cheaper and easier to duplicate and exchange these artefacts. It is also much easier to store, locate, and access them globally, to compare or analyze them. Of course, as the new activities of the digital world are immature, some of the traditional quality of old media forms is initially lost, while new rules and know-how are only being invented. Despite this immaturity one can only feel enthusiasm at these new developments. The essential features of the new potential have been described beautifully in Paul Starr's paper (2000) on the The Electronic Commons. But the same paper and books from Lawrence Lessig (2001) and David Bollier (2002) make clear that the realization of this potential is by no means a certainty. History abounds in examples of technology and media (Hargittai 2000) for which the imagined potential never materialized. Media and technology with increasing returns have powerful trends towards concentration, vertical integration, proprietary control of access, and locking-in of funding models that can only be counterbalanced by explicit efforts to ensure diversity, freedom of choice, empowerment, and openness. The information society is by no means something that is already defined and for which the only problem would be to spread it and attain it quicker. It is a space that can be filled with very different applications, activities, and usage. The technology supporting it itself will be shaped by the interaction with the intellectual rights environment, as much as it will shape it.

There is today a deep crisis of intellectual property and of use-right restrictions as primary tools for the organization of intellectual activities. This crisis creates expectations, concerns, and uncertainty for intellectual creators. Intellectual property management-based businesses feel endangered. They try to compensate for the undermining of the property-based approach by asking for ever-increased protection, to the point of endangering basic human rights. Old forms of businesses like music publishers or broadcasters, or recent dominant players in biotechnology or software, call for longer, stricter monopolies to be embedded in the access devices themselves, to be completed by regulation outlawing circumvention, to be enforced by extreme measures, and so forth. They claim for property new domains through the extension of patentability or new interpretation of property rights such as those on photography of buildings and landscape, or by claiming a specific property right for broadcasters. They are seconded or driven in their enterprise by interest groups such as heirs of intellectual property assets and intellectual property professionals (lawyers, consultants, collecting societies) and organizations, including some public organizations such as patent offices and national intellectual property institutes.

Cooperative usage of information technology and the Internet evidently points toward a much wider diversity of producers, a greater freedom of accessing and reusing information artefacts. But as there is a great uncertainty on how this will be incorporated in an economy, the lobbies of the existing economy grasp intellectual property as a life vest, and the lobbies of the new economy try to use it to construct new vertically integrated oligopolies, from contents to networks, from seeds to pesticides. This has developed to a disease with such extreme symptoms as:

- Multinationals asking governments to put a sixteen-year-old in jail for creating software that could be used to illegally copy protected contents, though it was written and used by him for legitimate purposes,

- Patents on genetic sequences to which governments are still giving a hand despite some afterthoughts,
- "Protected" e-Books or digital TV apparatus that won't let you transfer or quote contents without risking to be charged with breaking the law,[2] or,
- Proposals to make people collectively liable for the compound virtual loss of income that may result from their disputably illicit behavior.

One could analyze this as the last effects of the old paradigm before it is replaced by a new one. But a closer look at past historical examples (in the history of writing and press for instance) shows that these last effects can cause long-lasting damage, and even lock the whole development of information exchanges in restrictive paths. If we fail to develop a positive foundation for intellectual rights, we may be witnessing a new tragedy of enclosures.[3] This time, it would be the public domain of the future that would be made the property of a few. Instead of enabling new production techniques to develop at the expense of societal damage (as in the agricultural enclosures), we would witness a restriction of innovation and its usage, together with the societal damage.

Digging the Foundations

One cannot just declare intellectual property defunct. John Perry Barlow's paper on "Selling Wine without Bottles: The Economy of Mind on the Global Net" (Barlow 1992–1993) created a salutary shock, but did not lead to a practical refoundation, because it did not set a new basis on which positive intellectual rights could be asserted, even though it provides useful concepts for the valuation of information. Many writers, creators, innovators, or policy-makers still accept to be enrolled by intellectual property lobbies in their defense. That's because they see intellectual property as the only way they know to get authorship acknowledged, ensure reward and remuneration, encourage investment, or allow redress of libel. However poorly the existing intellectual property framework achieves all of this, they will not jump in the unknown if one cannot outline how a new framework will address intellectual rights. But attempts at working out a new balance within the existing intellectual property framework are also bound to fail. I have myself supported such an approach in the past (Gonthier and Aigrain 1997), and European research programs have supported many technology projects claiming to work in this direction by enabling efficient, low-entry cost, intellectual property management. But because these well-intended efforts have been fed into a restrictive property-based regulatory environment and practice, they have failed to reach their goal. Despite their alleged good intentions, we witness even more monitoring of usage through technology, more embedding of restrictive technology into devices making innovative user functionality harder or almost impossible to implement, no clear enlargement of diversity of offer, little empowerment of authors toward producers and distributors, and a public domain that remains narrow and lacks accessibility, despite recent exciting developments. We will see next that these adverse effects derive from staying on the wrong side of an essential dividing line: whether in the information world, access and usage should remain tightly bound (including by technology) to monetary and contractual transactions, or whether one accepts to decouple these processes at the level of individual usage.

Since neither the tabula rasa nor the reform approach can work, one has to go back to the foundations: what purpose was intellectual property to fulfil? What positive rights was it supposed to give to people? We must rebuild the full edifice of intellectual rights, starting with the knowledge of its history, its aims and principles, and the concepts it has built to deal with different objects such as books, scientific ideas, journals, inventions, photographs, films, or algorithms. But we must first forget some implicit hypotheses about technical forms of production and exchange of information, and business models that are built in intellectual property legislation, since quite a few of these hypotheses have become erroneous. Let us start by an attempt at defining what an intellectual entity is. Some essential clarifications have been moved to footnotes for sake of readability of the full definition. An intellectual entity is an artefact

- constructed under control of human mind(s);[4]
- using other such constructs, and signals or information extracted from the physical world;[5]
- that can be made perceptible to other human beings, or executed to control technical processes;
- and that can be separated from the carrier or signal that embodies it.[6]

Here are a few examples of direct rights, expressed without any of the restrictions or additional rights that may prove necessary to make them enforceable or avoid perverse effects:

R1   To create[7] new intellectual entities, including by making use of preexisting ones.

R2   To make one's creation public (original meaning of publishing).

R3   To be acknowledged as creator of all or part of an intellectual entity.

R4   To obtain economic or noneconomic reward for one's creation, in proportion[8] to the interest others show for it.

R5   To access any intellectual entity that has been made public.

R6   To quote extract(s)[9] of an intellectual entity whatever its media, for the purpose of information, analysis, critique, teaching, research, or the creation of other intellectual entities.

R7   To redress mistakes, libellous statements, false information, or erroneous attributions.

R8   To give reference, link to, or create inventories of intellectual entities produced by others as soon as they have been made public.[10]

Let's consider this list only as a foundation, the first step of a thought experiment. If it were to be implemented as such, intellectual-property thinkers would announce a tragedy of the commons. They would claim it would destroy the incentive to create new entities by not setting precise schemes ensuring the remuneration of their creators. Or that it would destroy the incentive to invest into the media that ensure the accessibility and promote the quality of intellectual entities. Most moral rights defenders would claim it to kill culture itself by not including explicit rights to defend the integrity of a creation in its future usage. Even the free software license specialists might object because these licenses are based on writers of software having rights in their creation to which we have not referred directly previously here. But before we define property rights and other restrictions, it is better to fully explore mentally what can develop on the basis of positive rights. To outline this potential, one will have to differentiate between different types of intellectual entities. Here are some of the essential parameters that influence which positive rights or property-based schemes can be deployed:

C1   The size of the initial investment necessary to create an intellectual entity before it can first be used or accessed.[11]

C2   Whether the entity is created once, and then accessed without modifications, or on the contrary incrementally created and revised through sequences of usage and (re)-creation. A particular case of entities that are created once (possibly through a complex process) and then accessed without or with little modifications are those referring to a live process (such as music performance) or resulting in a real-time consumption process (such as viewing a movie in a theatre). One should note that the intellectual rights framework influences the nature of entities: if it sets freedoms of reuse, it is more likely that intellectual entities that are iteratively recreated will flower, while if it restricts rights to modify, one will see mostly created-once-and-for-all entities.

C3   Whether the creation is individual or collective.

C4   Whether the creation is or not the embodiment of knowledge about the physical world, or about society.

C5   The relation between the entity and action on the physical world ranging from intellectual designs of physical devices (machines, for instance) at one extremity to intellectual entities whose only link with physical processes arises when they are mapped into physically perceptible signals.

C6   Whether the usage of the entity is of such a nature that one needs to allow long lasting appropriation to make possible for this usage to develop in a sustainable manner.

Now that we have basic tools, let's start by putting the public domain first, and organizing the public space of intellectual exchanges on its basis.

Public Domain and Public Space

What should be in the public domain? Is the public domain truly public, is there a public space in which one can in practice freely access and reuse public domain entities?

Let's first take an historical look at this issue. In modern but predigital times, the situation was simple: some entities were considered as not appropriable[12] and fed naturally the public domain, for instance, ideas, mathematical and scientific theories, algorithms, knowledge about the physical world and society,[13] as well as of some other entities excluded from patentability in the text of the Munich Convention[14] and in U.S. practice until the 1980s. Apart from these entities, the public domain was fed by extinction of rights. Copyright stock owners[15] have successfully lobbied to prevent recorded media documents to fall into the public domain, and obtained the extension of the duration of protection to fifty and later seventy years after the death of the last right owner in most cases. In addition, the analog character of documents and the difficulty of analog telecommunication restricted accessibility to the premises of organizations caring for public domain documents. These documents consisted mostly of old books, journals, and prints, as well as of old photographs. With the advent of digital documents for all media, the birth of new digital media, and the development of free software, a new situation has arisen. The most important aspect is that extinction of rights is no longer the main source for the public domain: there is now a powerful stream of intellectual entities that people directly contribute to the public domain, as free software,[16] and as free information. In addition, some countries have enacted public access laws that put information produced by governments in the public domain. In parallel, networked digital technology has made the public domain potentially accessible to many at low cost. But potentially only, because legal,[17] or economic[18] factors and related interest group pressure still restrict it in practice. Free software is the only really flourishing and truly accessible public domain. Many are now calling for the creation of a real public space for information of various types, nonindividual genome data (sequence and structural databases of genomes of various organisms) and scientific publishing being just prominent examples of growingly successful commons.

Going back to positive right-thinking, it is worth asking oneself if there can be any valid reason to restrict voluntary contribution to the public domain? The question may seem surprising, or even obscene, but the extent of the intellectual property crisis is such that we must be ready to witness the most incredible restrictions. Intellectual property owners can imagine that the development of a public space for intellectual entities could take away from them one scarce and valuable resource: the attention time of people. Of course, studies (for instance on public libraries) seem to indicate that on the contrary, the more people access freely intellectual entities, the more they are able and willing to spend time accessing and creating valuable entities. But who knows, it may be that in the long run, the public domain will become so rich that only entities that are truly unique,[19] novel, or creative will be marketable. If this happens, so much the better, as it will lead to rewards to creation and innovation rather than to assets owners.[20] In any case, we must adopt a clear principle: the voluntary contribution of one's creation to the public domain is a right that cannot be restricted by any commercial interest.[21]

The next question concerns precisely those entities that have always been considered as naturally belonging to the public domain, because of a major societal interest at never allowing their appropriation, and because making them public domain did not result in a tragedy of the commons as sufficient incentives or schemes existed for their creation. For instance some scientific discoveries can be achieved only after huge investment. But one does not wish to grant property rights on numerical values of properties of quarks even if it is necessary to build particle accelerators to measure them or confirm them. When an intellectual entity is the embodiment of knowledge about the physical world or about society, governments or society invest in the means of creating this knowledge and making it available to all. Sometimes, the reason for this is that the value of this knowledge is so unpredictable and long-term, that even if one allowed appropriation, no private party would have interest in investing in it.[22] Most often, the reason is of a moral nature: the equitable implementation of the reuse aspect of right R1, that is the possibility for all to use such knowledge, is so binding, it is so morally unacceptable or absurd that even for a short period some parties could limit the use of knowledge to their benefit, that schemes other than property rights are needed. A new dimension has recently arisen: in some cases it is needed to limit the use of knowledge in industrial applications to prevent some unethical consequences. When this is likely, putting knowledge in the public domain is the condition of a true public debate on whether and how this limitation should occur.

It is a very sad fact that one has departed, hopefully not for long, from this wisdom, and started throwing these entities in the basket of industrial property, by removing exclusions to their patentability, for instance by allowing patents on gene sequences.[23] This process has occurred under pressure of some industries, and under the conduct of the interest groups of intellectual property consultants and organizations. The peak of this process was reached around 1998, and since then a growing and powerful opposition has built up. Europe, in particular, is a battlefield between promoters and opponents of gene-sequence patents or patenting the underlying ideas of computer programs. One must fight with utmost energy those who want to make increased patentability irreversible, for instance by pushing maximalist interpretations of the TRIPS agreement (WTO 1994). Later, discussion is devoted to the issue of which domains should fall under patentability, but for what concerns the public domain, we should remember the default rule: intellectual entities belong to the public domain, except if allowing their temporary appropriation is absolutely needed and does not result in unacceptable consequences.[24]

Extinction of rights is the general scheme that is supposed to bring everything in the public domain after some time. At the origin of copyright law, this time was defined (fourteen years) as the time needed for an intellectual entity to reach any of its potential users. It was assumed that any owner of copyright had had enough time to make value of its creation in that period. The same definition would lead today to a protection time ranging from a few days to ten years depending on the type of entities.[25] When dealing with property exceptions to positive rights, one needs to go back to the old wisdom of keeping them short enough and to further take in account the much faster accessibility of intellectual entities.

The public space is endangered not so much by explicit attempts at restricting it, than by the indirect effects of restrictive management of intellectual property. The development of "protection" technology, its embedding in access devices and telecommunication technology are a major risk in that respect. In many cases, the exigence of keeping the public space free is not included in the requirements for the design of these devices and technology. The debates on various forms of "protection technology" is now reaching its climax with Digital Right Managements Systems (DRMS) based on Trusted Computing,[26] or broadcast flag[27] systems, which we look at next. Such protection schemes that aim at universal deployment threaten to corner the public domain into a small ghetto, where a marginalized sect of adorers would be allowed to access and use it, provided that they accept to being cut from accessing any form of protected contents. So the principles stated here are not only of a declarative nature, they must be binding for future decisions on technology implementation. Circumvention that is needed for the public domain and its public space is by nature legitimate. Such decisions on technical measures must also include the consideration of the limited duration of property exceptions; that is, no technical measure can be given legal standing unless it disappears with the extinction of rights.

Finally, the public space is centered around the access of all to the public domain, but also around the access for some usage[28] to all entities. Protection technology must not block the possibility of quotation for the sake of criticism for instance, or access by the disabled.

Creator Rights

Let's now look at intellectual creation from the angle of reward for creators (right R4). Other creator rights such as attribution and integrity will be dealt with later. Positive rights enable a new synergy between a rich public space and creators' rights to be rewarded for their creations. These rights are presently very poorly served by the intellectual property framework, which favors asset owners and intermediaries with limited added-value (for instance distributors or financial investors) to the detriment of creators, editors,[29] and prescriptors (high added-value intermediaries).

When one entity does not fall naturally in the public domain under one of the conditions listed in the previous section, property rights are to be granted when the investment[30] needed to create an intellectual entity is high (C1 = big), and this high investment is needed before one can start using the end result (C2 = all at once). When only a very small investment is needed to obtain an intellectual entity (C1 = small), or when more complex ones are put together through a long series of small incremental steps (C2 = incremental), economic remuneration may still be needed or useful, but does not have, and generally cannot take the form of property rights. The reason for this impossibility of using property rights is simple: if only a small effort is needed to create an intellectual entity, then it is likely to be created at the same time by many different creators. And if it is created through a multitude of incremental steps, then the attribution and management of property rights will result in excessive transaction costs. Of course there are many intermediate situations such as software, news reporting, or photography[31] for which both property-based schemes and nonproperty-based schemes are likely to coexist and compete. In those intermediary situations, contributing such entities to the public domain can only result from a free choice by the creators. Property rights must thus be granted, but their nature and enforcement should be such that the competition between the two schemes remains a fair one: it must not be possible to abuse some property rights on critical entities (for instance a basic software, a hardware device or a telecommunication protocol) in such a way as to force the systematic usage of property-based schemes on other entities such as contents.

So we have a continuum of situations with, at one end, entities like a motion picture feature film or a complex invention in manufacturing that fall naturally in the realm of property-based rights and, at the other end, information fora that fall naturally out of property-based schemes.[32] In the latter case, reward (right R4) is granted through access to the creations of others and through the reputation, attention, or simple pleasure of doing well that one gets from contributing.

When property-based rights have to be granted for the sake of remuneration, the main choice is between granting them on some embodiment (protected by copyright) of the entity, or on a class of possible embodiments of the entity (protected by a patent).[33] The key criterion for choosing one or the other is the scope of the protection that one wants to grant. Patents can be used only if the scope of use of an intellectual entity can be assessed at the time at which it is created,[34] if this scope is not too general, and if its novelty and originality can be evaluated at a reasonable cost by examiners. In practice, this leads to reject patents as a possible intellectual property scheme for all intellectual entities that can be manipulated as pure information contents. In other terms, patents should be restricted to entities for which C5 = design, of physical devices and processes. See the next section for additional conditions on patentability.

For most entities, copyright will thus be the major intellectual property scheme. But what does copyright cover exactly? We must here fight two illusions. The first one is John P. Barlow's wine-and-bottle metaphor,[35] which sees the scope of protection by copyright only as the container. The second one is the claim often made by patent fans that copyright protects only a given expression in an extremely narrow sense, and thus can be turned around easily by counterfactors, simply by giving a different expression to a functionally identical entity. Copyright protects an equivalence class of realizations of an entity, but this is more than a container and it can be enough to reward creators. One of the effects of information and communication technology is that a precise shape is imposed on an entity later and later in its production process, most often at presentation time, and under user control or under the effect of technical parameters that are only partially controlled by the creator of the entity.

This means that the embodiment of an entity that is protected by copyright becomes more abstract and more general. The definition of the scope of protection for each medium needs some rehaul, most likely to be explored though case law and later harmonised. Provided that this adaptation is done when needed, past history has shown that copyright has an extremely adaptable scope: for instance, if we consider a given recording of a given performance of a given musical work, we can see that each of these dimensions can be covered by copyright. If we look at software, we can see that copyright can apply across languages (from source code to binary form, for instance), to a class of equivalent (for some technical context) expressions.

But is copyright enforceable in the digital era? Of course it is, if objectives are set to a reasonable level with regards to pricing and with regards to what should be enforced. If we want to understand the conditions for a possible enforcement of remuneration through copyright, we must first accept a brief detour through discussing business models. In today's (or is it already yesterday's?) situation:

- For centralized media (broadcasting for instance), many intellectual entities are made available to their end-users for free due to indirectly funded business models, with a predominance of advertising.
- For decentralized media, high prices for intellectual entities are artificially maintained through oligopolies or the organization of rarity (in particular by concentration of promotion and control on distribution channels).

Both cases lead to low diversity, and an inefficient economy of remuneration (at macroeconomical level, that is the total value distributed to creators is incredibly low if one compares it with the total time spent by users accessing these entities, for instance). Of course some specific creators can benefit from this situation. Now, when intellectual property businesses try to maintain this situation in the digital world, they will find themselves in a much weaker position to do so. The ease of copy, transmission and sharing of intellectual properties undermine the ability of anyone to maintain artificially excessive prices for licensing property rights on intellectual entities. Even more, the alternative possibility of direct production in the public domain and remuneration by service business models (including concerts for musicians, for instance) and/or reputation sets a reference point that makes evident for everyone the artificially restricted diversity and excessive pricing of the old models. Since copying, storage, and exchange of information is much cheaper,[36] the usual practice of sharing contents with others develops to a new scale, to the point at which it becomes a distribution channel of its own. When analysing this extended practice, one should carefully distinguish two forms of it, that intellectual property lobbies have a strong interest to consider as identical. Industrial piracy can seriously undermine remuneration, but there is no indication that it is harder to fight in the digital world that in the analog world.[37]

One has yet to prove that the other form, decentralized individual copying and exchange, harms the remuneration of creators globally. Recent claims for

Philippe Aigrain

instance that it would be due to it that the audio CD market would have suffered a decrease are unsupported: examples such as the Finnish market[38] show that CD sales might have suffered more (elsewhere than in Finland) from copy protection and reduction of the number of titles than directly from peer-to-peer file sharing. Of course, these claims point to an unavoidable fate for the centralized business models based on concentration of promotion on a few titles: the birth of new musical media will one day take away attention and business from CD distribution and centralized publishing. The challenge is to ensure that before it occurs, new forms of creator remuneration, such as the one suggested by Richard Stallman,[39] will have developed.

The exact form it will take is yet unknown, but there is clear evidence that copyright-based remuneration can be enforced by the assent of most to pay as to reward creators, provided they can do it simply, at a fair price or at their choice, without infringing on privacy, and obtain rights to a sufficient range of possible uses. Who will really want to do illegal copies for resale of the equivalent musical content of a CD if it sells for 2 or 3 euros?[40] Since we discuss property rights, it must of course be evident that owners of such rights are free to choose whichever licensing model they desire[41] within the limits of positive rights and consumer protection.[42] The purpose of the discussion was just to state that the practical enforceability of copyright will depend on this choice.

Right-holders are also faced with another choice. They can try to maintain in the information world the indissociable link between accessing and using contents that exists for physical carriers such as books. In the information world this can be achieved only by overturning the principle of copyright. Copyright in the physical world is something you have to decide to respect or not, and possibly face the consequences. The copyright sign in a book does not stop you physically from doing anything; it is the limits of the object that do, and the respect for the law. Keeping these limits unchanged in the information world means enforcing them a priori, making technology the judge of what is right and what is not. It is the path the majors and their technology providers seem to have chosen. One should not allow for this suicide to be also a crime against others: the implementation of possible restrictive licensing (in particular in access devices and networks) must not be of a nature to make liberal licensing more complex or impossible. More generally, protection mechanisms should always make appropriate provision for the practical implementation of rights R1, R2, R6, and R8.

Coming back to property rights, a difficult case arises for collective creations. Two approaches exist, one that consists in granting to each author rights similar to those that would be granted to the single author of the work, and the second, which is to create a special status of collective creation that basically strips all rights from the authors to give them to the producer or publisher of the entity. Both approaches have major drawbacks, at least with present licensing rules: the first one because it unduly restricts the usage of collectively created entities by making extremely complex to obtain licenses, the second one because it does not respect positive author rights.[43]

Another special case occurs when one reuses a great number of entities to such an extent that each of them no longer accounts in the final results for more than the partial of a note in a symphony. John Oswald's remix music has made fun of the maximalist interpretation of copyright protection, for which there is total protection on each microsegment of recorded music, even when this segment is mixed with hundreds of other segments from other sources, is no longer assignable to any creator (and thus cannot lead to moral damage[44]), and when the original right owner cannot claim any commercial damage from such usage. This is a useful reminder of the purpose of copyright, that is to ensure reward to creators, not to set an unlimited possibility for right owners to decide how copyrighted items can be used.

Finally, as already stated in the section on the public domain, the duration of copyright should be made much shorter. It is hard to imagine how policy makers have been convinced of the usefulness of granting copyright type of intellectual property for longer than a few years after the death of a creator.[45]

Keeping Patentability Where It Belongs

Historically, patents have been developed to stimulate and disseminate mechanical inventions that needed a complex elaboration process and for which a costly investment in production infrastructure was necessary. That is, it was designed for cases where $C1$ = big investment, $C4$ = not a discovery, and $C5$ = design of physical devices and processes, in particular when $C6$ = long lasting appropriation needed for deployment of usage.[46] Patent protection is characterized by a priori examination, and thus a relatively complex preparation and high entry cost. The exact definition of the scope of protection offered by a patent is complex. This makes it prone to litigation. All these properties led to the creation of a rich network of consultants, lawyers, and administrative offices. None of this raised major difficulties while the scope of patentability was kept in its original definition. But the birth of information technology and more generally of information-based technology[47] such as biotechnology has challenged traditional patent protection and has given rise to a drift toward extending patentability to entities that do not meet the conditions stated above.

The origin of this recent crisis can be simply understood if one examines what happens when a classical technology is reshaped by the introduction of software components, or by the introduction of layers of information entities (such as gene sequences). The information entities themselves have properties that clearly exclude them from patentability, but a physical invention including them often still meets the criteria for patentability. This tension has led to an intense pressure for an increased patentability of the information entities themselves, which has progressively introduced itself in case law and in the practice of patent offices. A number of dangerous mistakes have developed, such as the idea that a gene sequence "would represent a biological function, and its usage in a possible drug, treatment of biotechnological process" or that a computer program "would represent its execution on a generic computer, and the usage of this execution in a technical process." These statements are factually wrong,[48] and they have been used to justify the unjustifiable: patenting discoveries, human expression and ideas, when none of the criteria for patentability was met. Some now claim that because some patent gene sequences or computer programs, all should do it, to defend themselves in competition. This is what can be called the National Rifle Association argument. Not only is this unethical, inefficient economically and in terms of innovation, but it simply won't work. Unfortunately, if we are late in recognizing it, the cost of returning to common sense will be higher and higher.

One important aspect of this discussion is that one must assess what patent protection will become for technical devices and processes when larger and larger chunks of them will be accomplished under the control of software or information processes (for instance bioinformatics). As a thought experiment, let's imagine that a set of formerly mechanical processes would become one single metamechanical machine tool, where a software tool would control which of the former individual processes is accomplished by the metamachine. The metamachine itself would deserve patent protection for its technical implementation innovative aspects. But each of the individual instantiating software tools should not be covered by patents. To understand why, one can consider two aspects of this change. The first one is that the motivation to introduce it is naturally to replace a complex and rigid mechanical design process by a less costly and flexible to rearrange software development or information process. It is exactly because the software part of the new process no longer meets the criteria (C1 = big investment) for patentability that investors might want to introduce it. But in addition, contrarily to what classical patent thinkers always assume, the software components, considered in themselves, are not mechanical inventions. They are nothing but algorithms mapped though the particular semantics of an execution process into the realm of mechanical processes.

In conclusion for this rationale to keep patentability into the restricted corner of physical devices and processes, which can be absolutely enough to guarantee positive rights and investment in the domain of material inventions, one must further consider the case of what exceptions to patent protection must be allowed. We live in a world in which one waits for millions of sick people to die without receiving existing treatment before allowing ourselves to consider that there may be a dysfunction of the system of property. Only then are governments of poor countries allowed to commission the manufacturing of patent-protected drugs at production cost in their countries, or to import these generic drugs from other countries. The claimed justification is that not offering this extremely strong protection would have deterred investment that made it possible for these drugs to exist. Recent treaties and related agreements have been imposed to many developing countries that will restrict further in a few years their ability to override intellectual property for major health reasons (for instance). Isn't it time to reverse the order of steps?

Integrity, Libel, and Redress

There is a true tension between the development of new information exchanges and the moral rights of creators and more generally of any human being. Increased possibility of reuse, new intermediary and end-user empowerment on presentation—all this means that a given contents will be used in a context that is less and less under control of its original creator. Quick transmission of information and diversification of sources evidently create an environment that is prone to the propagation of false or libellous information. The possibility for all to acquire images and sounds anywhere and to make them available also threatens privacy. But the same processes that threaten integrity, or seem to call for powerful mechanism of redress, can also contribute to a much better acknowledgement of authorship, a quick correction of false information, a limitation of the damage created by libel.

In such a situation, two approaches can be followed. The first one is to reinforce a priori control on information publishing (to use a polite wording for censorship and restriction to the right to publish), to enforce strong penalties on publishers of false information or those who distribute it, to protect integrity by limiting the ability of users of intellectual entities to control how they access them (presentation for instance) or by restricting their freedom in reusing them to a degree going beyond what is needed for the sake of the remuneration of creators. In addition safeguards would be put in place to forbid the publishing of entities resulting from the capture of information associated with persons without their agreement.

The second approach is to try to constitute positive counterweights to the potentially dangerous trends. Develop formats and related standards to enable creators to define how they would like their creation to adapt to user-controlled context changes.[49] Develop and disseminate tools for information authentication and information assessment. Exploit to the largest degree the extraordinary potential of cooperative information sharing to spot and redress false or libellous information. Develop tools to enable users to build a representation of complex sets of information coming from multiple sources or complex sets of arguments.

Not all problems of integrity or libel can be solved by using the new social organisation of exchanges and the technology that contributed to create them. The publication in 2000 in the United Kingdom of names and addresses of alleged sexual offenders has provided an example of types of perverse usage that can probably be prevented only by outlawing them. But if we do not invest enough in the positive approach, one can easily imagine a situation in which we would get the worse of all worlds. Centralized media and restriction to criticism together with low-quality information, no integrity of creation (even for entities created once and for all) together with no privacy for one's image and deeds. To avoid this nightmare scenario it is worth investing as much as possible in the positive right approach of building expression and criticism tools and encouraging their usage. Not all problems will be solved in that way, but we will able to develop restrictive approaches only when they are truly necessary. We will also be surer that we develop them for the benefit of all and not just for the opportunistic defense of some particular interests.

Transition Issues

How do we get there from here? How can the positive-rights approach turn into a widespread reality? Of course, political awareness and resulting legislative action can stop the production of restrictive property-based regulation. But even assuming a strong mobilization in favor of positive intellectual rights, considering the inertia of regulation, the real feasibility of transition rests on the existence of a critical mass of exchanges that follow by choice the positive-rights approach. The free software movement has here shown the way, by successfully reaching this critical mass in a domain in which it was far from easy. It also demonstrated that some additional safeguards are necessary to ensure that an approach based on voluntary contribution is not stopped before reaching critical mass. Without these safeguards, it is too easy for opportunistic players to use the richness of what is been created and made freely available and to turn it against itself by making it proprietary through some minor additions or control on necessary environments for usage.

The copylefting schemes of the GNU General Public License are a vaccine against such misuse. When critical mass is reached, the illustration of the benefits of a positive rights approach in terms of value creation, true author benefits and user empowerment become so clear that the balance of power shifts quickly. Those players in property-based business models who have the necessary creative resources are able to re-engineer their practice, and find new opportunities based on the infrastructure of sharable intellectual entities. This process took a bit more than fifteen years for software, and we see only the premises of it for other types of intellectual entities. But these premises are those of a true Renaissance.

Acknowledgments

The author is grateful for comments and inspiration from Richard Stallman, Jean-Claude Guédon, and Philippe Quéau. The author remains solely responsible for the resulting contents of this text.

Notes

1. The original version of this text was written in 2000, to appear in this book, which was already planned at the time. An extract appeared in French as the article "Domaine

et espace publics" of the *Dictionnaire Critique de la Mondialisation* (Aigrain 2002). Intermediate preprint versions were posted, in English on the MIT site of the *Free/Open Source Research Community* (Aigrain 2001), and in French on the *Biblio du Libre* site (Aigrain 2003a). The historical prologue appeared in different formats as the introduction to the special issue "Open Knowledge" (Aigrain and Gonzales-Barahona 2003) of the *Upgrade* European magazine, and in French as a communication in the *Libre Software Meeting* (Aigrain 2003b). The author is working on an extended version, to appear as a book under the title "Les nouveaux biens communs informationnels et leur espace public."

2. Regarding restriction implemented in e-books, refer to Richard Stallman's piece "The Right to Read" (Stallman 1997). See also note 27.

3. From the sixteenth century, in most of Western Europe, the communal land freely usable by all was turned into private property. This created major social disruptions leading to powerful revolts and a related slow down of the process. This also allowed the development of much more intensive agricultural production (with related technology innovation). Refer to Karl Polanyi (1944) for a detailed analysis. The expression tragedy of enclosures has become a common counterphrase to the "tragedy of the commons" used by Garrett Hardin (1968) to claim that the management of scarce resources cannot be based on free interaction of individuals, without some correction like property or regulation implementing the constraints of necessity. Whatever one thinks of the conclusions of Gareth Hardin for physical commons, it is utmostly absurd to apply the same reasoning to information commons, that are nondepletable, and for which usage raises value instead of destroying it.

4. Is computer code generated by an automatic code generator still an intellectual entity? Yes, just as a poem generated by rules that the poet applies mechanically but has chosen with knowledge of what they were likely to produce.

5. For painters, it was already clear, at least from the Renaissance, that a technical way of recording light was one of the instruments of creation. Photography has made clear that control on that process (choice of subject and time, framing, lighting, exposure control) was in itself creation.

6. In the analog world, this separability realizes itself only through complex processes, such as the work of the copyist for manuscripts. But it is nonetheless already at the core of what defines an intellectual entity at the origin of laws on author rights, copyright, and privileges for publishers. In the digital world, it has become very easy to separate an intellectual entity from any of its particular realizations. One key general

effect of digital separability is that more and more creative functions are moved towards the final realisation/perception/usage of an intellectual entity. Media and technology are deeply reshaped by that process. But this does not mean that one can forget about the possible forms of the realisations of intellectual entities. The fact that in each medium, one can easily separate signal from carrier, or even that one can map an entity from one medium to another does not mean that entities have become "medium-less": moving image contents can be repurposed from the theater to the TV and vice versa, but within the realm of one overall perceptive medium with its rules of narration and perception; interactive music still has the real-time listening properties of music.

7. In this text, creator and create are used to refer generically to authoring, innovation, and creation in the artistic or technical sense, whether in an individual or a collective context.

8. The nature and size of this reward, or the relation it has with the number of people interested and the intensity of their interest, are out of the scope of our discussion of rights. Similarly, how this right can be transferred to investors in a creative venture instead of the creators themselves is left for future discussion.

9. This looks to be a restriction, but the distinction between reproducing an entity and quoting it (that is reproducing only part of it and making that part only a part of a newly created entity) is a valuable asset of existing intellectual rights, and it is worth including it from the start in positive rights: some restrictions that might prove necessary to the right to reproduce, use or present intellectual entities will not apply to quotation. Filmmaker Jean-Luc Godard elegantly expressed it when he answered Michelangelo Antonioni asking permission to re-use part of one of its movies: "Do what you want, there are no author rights, only duties" (original French: *Fais ce que tu veux, il n'y a pas de droits d'auteur, seulement des devoirs*).

10. This may not seem a primary right (not part of a minimal set of rights from the which all others could be derived), but as in the case of quotation, the ability to create and publish inventories pointing to creations that have been made public is at the core of the definition of what public means. It is a matter of social contract: by making something public, one accepts that it can be criticised, and referred, linking being the modern form of referring.

11. Some critics have rejected this criterion as invalid because it would favor large-monied interests to the detriment of individual creators. However, our criterion does not apply to investment by people or organizations, but to how intellectual entities

can be created. The fact that a music publisher invests huge amounts of money to promote one title will not make it eligible for strong property rights when it was possible to listen to the music without any of this promotion. However, feature films—as we understand them today—call for significant investment before anyone can view them. There is a likelihood that stronger property rights will be necessary for them, but this does not say to whom they should be granted.

12. The fact that these entities were not appropriable did not mean that their authors and creators had no rights. Rights R1, R2, R3, and R7 were fully recognized to them, and even right R4 (reward) cared for through indirect mechanisms.

13. Both physical world and society must be interpreted here in the widest sense, including entities such as plant or animal genome data, knowledge about human behavior, or societal process models for instance.

14. The Munich Convention is an intergovernmental treaty that defines the scope and rules of the European patent. With regard to exclusions, see its article 52.

15. Audiovisual media firms, and heirs of authors or composers being the most active.

16. Richard Stallman (n.d.) insists on the fact that free software is not public domain because in the existing framework, public domain means "not copyrighted." But for our discussion of the public domain, we can temporarily forget that the entities have been contributed to the public domain by people who had rights on them. Stallman adds that one needs schemes to prevent things that are contributed to the commons from being appropriated and turned against them. This makes it necessary to implement a copylefting scheme that forbids to incorporate at least some strategical freely contributed entities into proprietary products. I do not introduce such a scheme in my basic framework because it is not based on positive rights, but only a reaction to possible abuse of property. But one needs it to handle transition to the new framework. See section on transition issues.

17. For instance, legal deposit laws (where they exist) restrict access to the sites of the organizations caring for the legal deposit. Even if this applies only to nonpublic domain documents, it leads to a situation in which even public domain entities are not in practice made accessible as much as they could.

18. Pressure put in many countries on those public organizations holding public domain entities to make money out of public access by entering in partnership with private entities commercializing them.

19. For instance, live events.

20. One potential risk is that artificial or inflated events will be engineered, possibly at a large scale, to attract attention. A healthy development of public criticism is needed to keep that process under control.

21. It is the basic implementation of rights R1, R2, and R5, and there is no convincing evidence that it can seriously damage the implementation of other positive rights or societal benefits.

22. In other terms, C6 does not apply.

23. The fact that these sequences are extracted from human, animal, vegetal, or fungi genome is not the key issue here. Arguments developed by some to the effect that in reality sequences were not truly made patentable per se in Europe since they are patentable only if a related function is mentioned are not convincing—to say the least. If claims on sequences are allowed, sequences are patentable, full stop.

24. See section on patentability for examples of entities such as medical drug production processes, which have all attributes to fall under patentability, but for which exceptions must be allowed to throw them back in the public domain.

25. This does not mean that entities do not have value after this period is over, but that the justification for allowing them to be private property no longer holds.

26. A specification of the Trusted Computing Platform Alliance, whose original purpose was information security, but which is endorsed by some major players for DRMS usage.

27. Recently adopted by the FCC in the United States, and under discussion in WIPO in the frame of the preparation of a Broadcaster and Web-caster Treaty, this technology and associated legal environment tries to close entirely the full chain of distribution and usage of "casted" material, threatening—if it was indeed deployed—to make almost impossible the exercice of right R6 (quotation) for instance.

28. See, for instance, list in the definition of right R6.

29. Publishers and broadcasters today have both an editorial role, through selection, editing, packaging, and indexing, and a distribution role associated with specific business models. In a new framework, there is continued need for the editorial role, but

it will be redesigned by the new organization and economy of exchanges. For instance, selection will often be moved from being a step prior to publication, to being an evaluation of already (self)-published materials.

30. "Investment" is used here for both work or efforts and financial investment. In practice, different players are generally involved. It maybe that a particular intellectual entity can be created by a very simple action, but that considerable skills and efforts have been needed to build the ability to produce the right action at the right time. This must, of course, be taken in account: it is the full process leading to the creation of entities that defines the size or intensity of the investment.

31. There are are at least 30 billion photographs taken in the world every year, and this number will grow enormously with the further dissemination of digital photography. For Raymond Depardon (one of my preferred photographers), it may be quite natural to use property-based schemes since the value of each of his photographs is high. For myself, I would rather contribute mine to a cooking-pot where I put my photographs and get the rights of access to photographs of others. Enabling a continuum of positions in which one can move with no major barrier from the latter position closer to the former is probably one of the most important conditions for creating a positive coupling between information exchanges at-large and the economy.

32. Dan Sperber (1999) has identified this process, but he is wrong in assuming that it can be extended to all entities.

33. This chapter does not discuss intermediate regimes of protection such as utility models and trademarks, as this would lead to too complex a presentation, without real conceptual benefit.

34. This is not the case for software for instance, but only for a given use of software in a device or process.

35. Leaving aside the obvious fact that when one drinks wine, nobody else can drink it anymore.

36. Though far from free: the average cost of downloading 100 MB of MP3 contents in July 2001 was at least 0.5 euro for the best available ADSL subscription fees—counting connection at both ends. This ignores costs of hardware and time spent at both ends. This cost goes down with better telecommunication offers but remains significant.

37. Most of the fight against industrial piracy on copyright occurs at intergovernmental level, in negotiations with countries that have encouraged its development.

38. *Suomen Ääni-ja kuvatallennetuottajatÄKT ry*, statistics for music sales in Finland, January–September 2003. The Finnish music market is markedly segmented between Finnish music and international music. The music publishers have dropped use of copy protection in Finland and abstained from any action against peer-to-peer network users (in full bloom during the studied period). The result is a 10% growth in the overall market for music carriers, with only the international music singles and vinyls suffering a decrease.

39. Richard Stallman (2001) suggested a scheme based on voluntary contributions, available in context (sending $1 to the artists would be possible anytime when listening to their music) but decoupled from rights to access or any form of content "protection." If one tries to associate micropayments with rights to access contents, it creates inacceptable transaction costs and user choice overhead (Shirky 2000). This generally leads to a preference for subscription schemes for paying online contents, which in turn results into a poor remuneration of creators, and an often poor quality and diversity of contents. Stallman's scheme was disregarded by many at the time as unrealistic, but recent developments show that it may work in practice if an adequate payment infrastructure is available, as starts being the case in the United States.

40. This figure is a "guesstimate," since of course nobody has yet an idea of what will be the a fair pricing in the digital economy of various media.

41. For some specific media, licensing and rights collection are handled at the level of a profession and not individually. This has clear benefits in terms of providing an uniform licensing framework, provided that transaction costs are kept reasonable (in other terms that usage does not have to be monitored at an excessive level and that fees are indeed redistributed to creators and not used to a large extent for the functioning of collecting societies). Unfortunately, this condition is generally not met.

42. Limits that the Digital Millenium Copyright Act (DMCA), or Uniform Computer Information Transactions Act (UCITA) ignore bluntly, and the European directive on Copyright in the information society ignores in good part.

43. A typical example can be found in the leonine contracts publishers impose on writers of parts of encyclopedias. Such a scheme will not survive, as encyclopedias using free licenses develop.

44. Quite rightly, there was some debate on the cover of one of John Oswald's CDs, on which a modified photograph of Michael Jackson was recognizable as him . . . and as a woman.

45. One may wonder why it is needed to go so far, and in particular to refer the duration of protection to the life of the creator and not to the date of the creation of the entity. One motivation is to guarantee that authors can be protected against producers and publishers "freezing" distribution until protection is extinct. Similar results have been searched for by setting clauses granting recovery by creators of all rights transmitted to producers and distributors when these have not been properly exploited, but these clauses are always difficult to enforce.

46. Though this last argument is often brought up by promoters of wide patentability in fields such as biotechnology, one has to recognize that in recent history, the rise of shareholder value reasoning has made many private businesses radically incapable of investing in such long-lasting deployment. In such a situation, the exact frontier between what can be supported by private appropriation and what can be supported only though public support to deployment is yet unclear. This is made even more difficult to analyze by the fact that a great part of public support can be hidden in indirect support schemes (for instance drug reimbursement by public medical insurance, or military spending).

47. That is, technologies that are based on the isolation of information entities such as gene sequences and the modelling of the relation between this information layer and physical functional phenomena—in an organism or in a technical environment.

48. See Atlan (1999) on genetic sequences and the fact that it is the set of the sequence and the complete cellular expression machinery that constitutes a biological process. For software, people are often confused by the reference to universal computers as being equivalent one to another, which would seem to support the fact that indeed a software "represents its execution." But as early as 1948, John von Neumann developed a luminous analysis of why this theoretical equivalence was practically inoperative, and in any case it applies only to programs with predetermined input/output. In practice, a software technical effect can be understood only if its full execution environment is specified, including compilers, run-time, input-output devices, and input-output contents.

49. For instance XML-coded metadata or presentation description formats.

References

Aigrain, Philippe. 2001. Positive intellectual rights and information exchanges. Available at <http://freesoftware.mit.edu/papers/aigrain.pdf>.

———, ed. 2002. Domaine et espace publics. In GERM, *Dictionnaire critique de la mondialisation*. Paris: Le Pré aux Clercs.

———. 2003a. Droits intellectuels positifs et échanges d'information. Available at <www.freescape.eu.org/biblio/article.php?id_article=133>.

———. 2003b. Où en sont les droits intellectuels positifs? Communication at the Libre Software Meeting, Metz, France. Available at <www.sopinspace.com/~aigrain/Droitspositifs.pdf>.

Aigrain, Philippe, and Jesus Gonzales-Barahona. 2003. Ownership and terms of use for intangibles: Land grab or commons. *Upgrade* 4(3). Available at <www.upgrade-cepis.org/issues/2003/3/upgrade-vIV-3.html#presentation>.

Atlan, Henri. 1999. *La fin du tout génétique*. Versàilles, France: INRA éditions.

Barlow, John Perry. 1992–1993. Selling wine without bottles: The economy of mind on the global Net. Available at <www.eff.org/Publications/John_Perry_Barlow/HTML/idea_economy_article.html>.

Benkler, Yochai. 2002–2003. Coase's penguin, or Linux and the nature of the firm. *Yale Law Journal* 112(3): 369–446. Available at <www.benkler.org/CoasesPenguin.PDF> (a condensed version is including as a chapter in this book).

Bollier, David. 2002. *Silent theft: The private plunder of our commonwealth*. London: Routledge.

Ellul, Jacques. 1967. *The technological society*. New York: Vintage. Translation from the French original edition.

Gonthier, Dominique, and Philippe Aigrain. 1997. Perspectives pour la gestion et le négoce de la propriété intellectuelle. *Document Numérique* 1(3).

Hardin, Gareth. 1968. The tragedy of the commons. *Science* 162: 1243–1248.

Hargittai, Eszter. 2000. Radio lessons for the Internet. *Communications of the ACM* 43(1): 51–57.

Illitch, Ivan. 2001. *Tools for conviviality*. London: Marion Boyars Publishers. Ltd. Available at <www.eekim.com/ba/bookclub/illich/tools.htm>.

Lessig, Lawrence. 2001. *The future of ideas: The fate of the commons in a connected world*. New York: Random House.

Neumann, John von. 1948. The general and logical theory of automata. In *Collected Works*, Volume 5, Oxford, UK: Pergamon.

Passet, René. 1979. *L'économique et le vivant*. Paris: Payot.

Polanyi, Karl. 1994. *The Great Transformation*. Boston: Beacon Press.

Robin, Jacques. 1989. *Changer d'ère*. Paris: Payot.

Shirky, Clay. 2000. The case against micro-payments. O'Reilly Network, 19 December 2000. Available at <www.openp2p.com/lpt/a/p2p/2000/12/19/micropayments.html>.

Sperber, Dan. 1999. L'utopie communiste devient possible. *Libération*: 13–14 November.

Stallman, Richard. 1997. The right to read. *Communications of the ACM* 40(2). Available at <www.gnu.org/philosophy/right-to-read.html>.

————. 2001. Copyright and globalization in the age of computer networks. Transcription of a speech given at MIT on Thursday, April 19, 2001. Available at <www.gnu.org/philosophy/copyright-and-globalization.html>.

————. n.d. Public domain software definition. Available at <http://www.gnu.org/philosophy/categories.html#PublicDomainSoftware>.

Starr, Paul. 2000. The Electronic Commons. *The American Prospect* 11(10). Available at <www.prospect.org/archives/V11-10/starr-p.html>.

World Trade Organization (WTO). 1994. Agreement on trade-related aspects of intellectual property rights. Available at <http://docsonline.wto.org:80/DDFDocuments/t/UR/FA/27-trips.doc>.

16

Copyright and Globalization in the Age of Computer Networks

Richard Stallman

I should [begin by explaining why I have refused to allow this Forum to be Web cast], in case it wasn't clear fully what the issue is: The software they use for Web broadcasting requires the user to download certain software in order to receive the broadcast. That software is not free software. It's available at zero price but only as an executable, which is a mysterious bunch of numbers.

What it does is secret. You can't study it; you can't change it; and you certainly can't publish it in your own modified version. And those are among the freedoms that are essential in the definition of "free software."

So if I am to be an honest advocate for free software, I can hardly go around giving speeches, then put pressure on people to use nonfree software. I'd be undermining my own cause. And if I don't show that I take my principles seriously, I can't expect anybody else to take them seriously.

However, this speech is not about free software. After I'd been working on the free software movement for several years and people started using some of the pieces of the GNU operating system, I began getting invited to give speeches [at which] . . . people started asking me: "Well, how do the ideas about freedom for software users generalize to other kinds of things?"

Of course, people asked silly questions like, "Well, should hardware be free?" and "Should this microphone be free?"

Well, what does that mean? Should you be free to copy it and change it? Well, as for changing it, if you buy the microphone, nobody is going to stop you from changing it. And as for copying it, nobody has a microphone copier.

Outside of "Star Trek," those things don't exist. Maybe some day there'll be nanotechnological analyzers and assemblers, and it really will be possible to copy a physical object, and then these issues of whether you're free to do that will start being really important. We'll see agribusiness companies trying to stop people from copying food, and that will become a major political issue, if that technological capability will ever exist. I don't know if it will; it's just speculation at this point.

But for other kinds of information, you can raise the issue because any kind of information that can be stored on a computer, conceivably, can be copied and modified. So the ethical issues of free software, the issues of a user's right to copy and modify software, are the same as such questions for other kinds of published information. Now I'm not talking about private information, say, personal information, which is never meant to be available to the public at all. I'm talking about the rights you should have if you get copies of published things where there's no attempt to keep them secret.

The History of Information Distribution and the Origin of Copyright

To explain my ideas on the subject, I'd like to review the history of the distribution of information and of copyright. In the ancient world, books were written by hand with a pen, and anybody who knew how to read and write could copy a book about as efficiently as anybody else. Now somebody who did it all day would probably learn to be somewhat better at it, but there was not a tremendous difference. And because the copies were made one at a time, there was no great economy of scale. Making ten copies took ten times as long as making one copy. There was also nothing forcing centralization; a book could be copied anywhere.

Now because of this technology, because it didn't force copies to be identical, there wasn't in the ancient world the same total divide between copying a book and writing a book. There are things in between that made sense. They did understand the idea of an author. They knew, say, that this play was written by Sophocles but in between writing a book and copying a book, there were other useful things you could do. For instance, you could copy a part of a book, then write some new words, copy some more, and write some new words, and on and on. This was called "writing a commentary"—that was a common thing to do—and these commentaries were appreciated.

You could also copy a passage out of one book, then write some other words, and copy a passage from another book and write some more and so on, and this was making a compendium. Compendia were also very useful. There are works that are lost but parts of them survived when they were quoted into other books that got to be more popular than the original. Maybe they copied the most interesting parts, and so people made a lot of copies of these, but they didn't bother copying the original because it wasn't interesting enough.

Now as far as I can tell, there was no such thing as copyright in the ancient world. Anyone who wanted to copy a book could copy the book. Later on, the printing press was developed and books started to be copied on the printing press. Now the printing press was not just a quantitative improvement in the ease of copying. It affected different kinds of copying unevenly because it introduced an inherent economy of scale. It was a lot of work to set the type and much less work to make many identical copies of the page. So the result was that copying books tended to become a centralized, mass-production activity. Copies of any given book would probably be made in only a few places.

It also meant that ordinary readers couldn't copy books efficiently. Only if you had a printing press could you do that. So it was an industrial activity.

Now for the first few centuries of printing, printed books did not totally replace hand-copying. Hand-copied books were still made, sometimes by rich people and sometimes by poor people. The rich people did this to get an especially beautiful copy that would show how rich they were, and poor people did it because maybe they didn't have enough money to buy a printed copy but they had the time to copy a book by hand. As the saying goes, "Time ain't money when all you got is time."

So hand-copying was still done to some extent. I think it was in the 1800s that printing actually got to be cheap enough that even poor people could afford printed books if they were literate.

Now copyright was developed along with the use of the printing press and given the technology of the printing press, it had the effect of an industrial regulation. It didn't restrict what readers could do; it restricted what publishers and authors could do. Copyright in England was initially a form of censorship. You had to get government permission to publish the book. But the idea has changed. By the time of the U.S. Constitution, people came to a different idea of the purpose of copyright, and I think that that idea was accepted in England as well.

For the U.S. Constitution it was proposed that authors should be entitled to a copyright, a monopoly on copying their books. This proposal was rejected. Instead, a crucially different proposal was adopted which is that, for the sake of promoting progress, Congress could optionally establish a copyright system that would create these monopolies. So the monopolies, according to the U.S. Constitution, do not exist for the sake of those who own them; they exist for the sake of promoting the progress of science. The monopolies are handed out to authors as a way of modifying their behavior to get them to do something that serves the public.

So the goal is more written and published books which other people can then read. And this is believed to contribute to increased literary activity, increased writing about science and other fields, and society then learns through this. That's the purpose to be served. The creation of private monopolies was a means to an end only, and the end is a public end.

Now copyright in the age of the printing press was fairly painless because it was an industrial regulation. It restricted only the activities of publishers and authors. Well, in some strict sense, the poor people who copied books by hand may have been infringing copyright, too. But nobody ever tried to enforce copyright against them because it was understood as an industrial regulation.

Copyright in the age of the printing press was also easy to enforce because it had to be enforced only where there was a publisher, and publishers, by their nature, make themselves known. If you're trying to sell books, you've got to tell people where to come to buy them. You don't have to go into everybody's house to enforce copyright.

And, finally, copyright may have been a beneficial system in that context. Copyright in the United States is considered by legal scholars as a trade, a bargain between the public and authors. The public trades away some of its natural rights to make copies, and in exchange gets the benefit of more books' being written and published.

Now, is this an advantageous trade? Well, when the general public can't make copies because they can only be efficiently made on printing presses—and most people don't own printing presses—the result is that the general public is trading away a freedom it is unable to exercise, a freedom that is of no practical value. So if you have something that is a by-product of your life and it's useless and you have the opportunity to exchange it for something else of any value, you're gaining. So that's why copyright may have been an advantageous trade for the public in that time.

But the context is changing, and that has to change our ethical evaluation of copyright. Now the basic principles of ethics are not changed by advances in technology; they're too fundamental to be touched by such contingencies. But our decision about any specific question is a matter of the consequences of the alternatives available, and the consequences of a given choice may change when the context changes. That is what is happening in the area of copyright law because the age of the printing press is coming to an end, giving way gradually to the age of the computer networks.

Copyright, Control, and Computer Networks

Computer networks and digital information technology are bringing us back to a world more like the ancient world where anyone who can read and use the information can also copy it and can make copies about as easily as anyone else could make them. They are perfect copies and they're just as good as the copies anyone else could make. So the centralization and economy of scale introduced by the printing press and similar technologies is going away.

And this changing context changes the way copyright law works. You see, copyright law no longer acts as an industrial regulation; it is now a Draconian restriction on a general public. It used to be a restriction on publishers for the sake of authors. Now, for practical purposes, it's a restriction on a public for the sake of publishers. Copyright used to be fairly painless and uncontroversial. It didn't restrict the general public. Now that's not true. If you have a computer, the publishers consider restricting you to be their highest priority. Copyright was easy to enforce because it was a restriction only on publishers who were easy to find and what they published was easy to see. Now the copyright is a restriction on each and everyone of you. To enforce it requires surveillance—an intrusion—and harsh punishments, and we are seeing these being enacted into law in the United States and other countries.

And copyright used to be, arguably, an advantageous trade for the public to make because the public was trading away freedoms it couldn't exercise. Well, now it can exercise these freedoms. What do you do if you have been producing a byproduct which was of no use to you and you were in the habit of trading it away and then, all of a sudden, you discover a use for it? You can actually consume it, use it. What do you do? You don't trade at all; you keep some. And that's what the public would naturally want to do. That's what the public does whenever it's given a chance to voice its preference; it keeps some of this freedom and exercises it. Napster is a big example of that, the public deciding to exercise the freedom to copy instead of giving it up. So the natural thing for us to do to make copyright law fit today's circumstances is to reduce the amount of copyright power that copyright owners get, to reduce the amount of restriction that they place on the public and to increase the freedom that the public retains.

But this is not what the publishers want to do. What they want to do is exactly the opposite. They wish to increase copyright powers to the point where they can remain firmly in control of all use of information. This has led to laws that have given an unprecedented increase in the powers of copyright. Freedoms that the public used to have in the age of the printing press are being taken away.

For instance, let's look at e-books. There's a tremendous amount of hype about e-books; you can hardly avoid it. I took a flight to Brazil and in reading the in-flight magazine, there was an article saying that maybe it would take ten or twenty years before we all switched to e-Books. Clearly, this kind of campaign comes from somebody paying for it. Now why are they doing that? I think I know. The reason is that e-Books are the opportunity to take away some of the residual freedoms that readers of printed books have always had and still have—the freedom, for instance, to lend a book to your friend or borrow it from the public library or sell a copy to a used bookstore or buy a copy anonymously, without putting a record in the database of who bought that particular book. And maybe even the right to read it twice.

These are freedoms that the publishers would like to take away, but they can't do this for printed books because that would be too obvious a power-grab and would raise an outcry. So they have found an indirect strategy: First, they obtain the legislation to take away these freedoms for e-Books when there are no e-Books; so there's no controversy. There are no preexisting users of e-Books who are accustomed to their freedoms and will defend them. That they obtained with the [U.S.] Digital Millennium Copyright Act in 1998. Then they introduce e-Books and gradually get everybody to switch from printed books to e-Books and eventually the result is, readers have lost these freedoms without ever having an instant when those freedoms were being taken away and when they might have fought back to retain them.

Richard Stallman

We see at the same time efforts to take away people's freedom in using other kinds of published works. For instance, movies that are on DVDs are published in an encrypted format that used to be secret—it was meant to be secret—and the only way the movie companies would tell you the format, so that you could make a DVD player, was if you signed a contract to build certain restrictions into the player, with the result that the public would be stopped even from fully exercising their legal rights. Then a few clever programmers in Europe figured out the format of DVDs and they wrote a free software package that would read a DVD. This made it possible to use free software on top of the GNU Plus Linux operating system to watch the DVD that you had bought, which is a perfectly legitimate thing to do. You ought to be able to do that with free software.

But the movie companies objected and they went to court. You see, the movie companies used to make a lot of films where there was a mad scientist and somebody was saying, "But, Doctor, there are some things Man was not meant to know." They must have watched their own films too much, because they came to believe that the format of DVDs is something that Man was not meant to know. And they obtained a ruling for total censorship of the software for playing DVDs. Even making a link to a site where this information is legally available outside the United States has been prohibited. An appeal has been made against this ruling. I signed a friend-of-the-court brief in that appeal, I'm proud to say, although I'm playing a fairly small role in that particular battle.

The U.S. government intervened directly on the other side. This is not surprising when you consider why the Digital Millennium Copyright Act was passed in the first place. The reason is the campaign finance system that we have in the United States, which is essentially legalized bribery where the candidates are bought by business before they even get elected. And, of course, they know who their master is—they know whom they're working for—and they pass the laws to give business more power.

What will happen with that particular battle, we don't know. But meanwhile Australia has passed a similar law and Europe is almost finished adopting one; so the plan is to leave no place on earth where this information can be made available to people. But the United States remains the world leader in trying to stop the public from distributing information that's been published.

Recent Developments in Copyright Enforcement: The "Soviet Approach"

The United States, though, is not the first country to make a priority of this. The Soviet Union treated it as very important. There, this unauthorized copying and redistribution was known as Samizdat and to stamp it out, they developed a series of methods. First, guards watching every piece of copying equipment to check what people were copying to prevent forbidden copying. Second, harsh punishments for anyone caught doing forbidden copying. You could sent to Siberia. Third, soliciting informers, asking everyone to rat on their neighbors and co-workers to the information police. Fourth, collective responsibility—You! You're going to watch that group! If I catch any of them doing forbidden copying, you are going to prison. So watch them hard. And, fifth, propaganda, starting in childhood to convince everyone that only a horrible enemy of the people would ever do this forbidden copying.

The United States is using all of these measures now. First, guards watching copying equipment. Well, in copy stores, they have human guards to check what you copy. But human guards to watch what you copy in your computer would be too expensive; human labor is too expensive. So they have robot guards. That's the purpose of the Digital Millennium Copyright Act. This software goes in your computer; it's the only way you can access certain data and it stops you from copying.

There's a plan now to introduce this software into every hard disk, so that there could be files on your hard disk that you can't even access except by getting permission from some network server to access the file. And to bypass this software or even tell other people how to bypass it is a crime.

Second, harsh punishments. A few years ago, if you made copies of something and handed them out to your friends just to be helpful, this was not a crime; it had never been a crime in the United States. Then they made it a felony, so you could be put in prisons for years for sharing with your neighbor.

Third, informers. Well, you may have seen the ads on TV, the ads in the Boston subways asking people to rat on their coworkers to the information police, which officially is called the Software Publishers Association.

And fourth, collective responsibility. In the United States, this has been done by conscripting Internet service providers, making them legally responsible for everything their customers post. The only way they can avoid always being held responsible is if they have an invariable procedure to disconnect or remove the information within two weeks after a complaint. Just a few days ago, I heard that a clever protest site criticizing Citibank for some of its nasty policies was disconnected in this way. Nowadays, you don't even get your day in court; your site just gets unplugged.

And, finally, propaganda, starting in childhood. That's what the word "pirate" is used for. If you'll think back a few years, the term pirate was formerly applied to publishers that didn't pay the author. But now it's been turned completely around. It's now applied to members of the public who escape from the control of the publisher. It's being used to convince people that only a nasty enemy of the people would ever do this forbidden copying. It says that "sharing with your neighbor is the moral equivalent of attacking a ship." I hope that you don't agree with that and if you don't, I hope you will refuse to use the word in that way.

So the publishers are purchasing laws to give themselves more power. In addition, they're also extending the length of time the copyright lasts. The U.S. Constitution says that copyright must last for a limited time, but the publishers want copyright to last forever. However, getting a constitutional amendment would be rather difficult, so they found an easier way that achieves the same result. Every twenty years they retroactively extend copyright by twenty years. So the result is, at any given time, copyright nominally lasts for a certain period and any given copyright will nominally expire some day. But that expiration will never be reached because every copyright will be extended by twenty years every twenty years; thus no work will ever go into the public domain again. This has been called "perpetual copyright on the installment plan."

The law in 1998 that extended copyright by twenty years is known as the "Mickey Mouse Copyright Extension Act" because one of the main sponsors of this law was Disney. Disney realized that the copyright on Mickey Mouse was going to expire, and they don't want that to ever happen because they make a lot of money from that copyright.

The original title of the talk on which this chapter is based was supposed to be "Copyright and Globalization." If you look at globalization, what you see is that it's carried out by a number of policies which are done in the name of economic efficiency or so-called free-trade treaties, which really are designed to give business power over laws and policies. They're not really about free trade. They're about a transfer of power: removing the power to decide laws from the citizens of any country who might conceivably consider their own interests and giving that power to businesses who will not consider the interests of those citizens.

Democracy is the problem in their view, and these treaties are designed to put an end to the problem. For instance, NAFTA actually contains provisions, I believe, allowing companies to sue another government to get rid of a law that they believe is interfering with their profits in the other country. So foreign companies have more power than citizens of the country.

There are attempts being made to extend this beyond NAFTA. For instance, this is one of the goals of the so-called free-trade area of the Americas, to extend this principle to all the countries in South America and the Caribbean as well, and the multilateral agreement on investment was intended to spread it to the whole world.

One thing we've seen in the 1990s is that these treaties begin to impose copyright throughout the world, and in more powerful and restrictive ways. These treaties are not free-trade treaties. They're actually corporate-controlled trade treaties being used to give corporations control over world trade, in order to eliminate free trade.

When the United States was a developing country in the 1800s, the country did not recognize foreign copyrights. This was a decision made carefully, and it was an intelligent decision. It was acknowledged that for the United States to recognize foreign copyrights would just be disadvantageous, that it would suck money out and wouldn't do much good.

The same logic would apply today to developing countries but the United States has sufficient power to force them to go against their interests. Actually, it's a mistake to speak of the interests of countries in this context. In fact, I'm sure that most of you have heard about the fallacy of trying to judge the public interest by adding up everybody's wealth. If working Americans lost $1 billion and Bill Gates gained $2 billion, would Americans generally be better off? Would this be good for America? Or if you look only at the total, it looks like it's good. However, this example really shows that the total is the wrong way to judge because Bill Gates really doesn't need another $2 billion, but the loss of the $1 billion by other people who don't have as much to start with might be painful. Well, in a discussion about any of these trade treaties, when you hear people talk about the interests of this country or that country, what they're doing, within each country, is adding up everybody's income. The rich people and the poor people are being added up. So it's actually an excuse to apply that same fallacy to get you to ignore the effect on the distribution of wealth within the country and whether the treaty is going to make that more uneven, as it has done in the United States.

A Uniform Copyright Regime for Everything?

So it's really not the U.S. interest that is being served by enforcing copyright around the world. It's the interests of certain business owners, many of whom are in the United States and some of whom are in other countries. It doesn't, in any sense, serve the public interest.

But what would make sense to do? If we believe in the goal of copyright stated, for instance in the U.S. Constitution, the goal of promoting progress, what would be intelligent policies to use in the age of the computer network? Clearly, instead of increasing copyright powers, we have to pull them back so as to give the general public a certain domain of freedom where they can make use of the benefits of digital technology, make use of their computer networks. But how far should that go? That's an interesting question because I don't think we should necessarily abolish copyright totally. The idea of trading some freedoms for more progress might still be an advantageous trade at a certain level, even if traditional copyright gives up too much freedom. But in order to think about this intelligently, the first thing we have to recognize is, there's no reason to make it totally uniform. There's no reason to insist on making the same deal for all kinds of work.

In fact, that already isn't the case because there are a lot of exceptions for music. Music is treated very differently under copyright law. But the arbitrary insistence on uniformity is used by the publishers in a certain clever way. They pick some peculiar special case and they make an argument that, in that special case, it would be advantageous to have this much copyright. And then they say that for uniformity's sake, there has to be this much copyright for everything. So, of course, they pick the special case where they can make the strongest argument, even if it's a rather rare special case and not really very important overall.

But maybe we should have that much copyright for that particular special case. We don't have to pay the same price for everything we buy. A thousand dollars for a new car might be a very good deal. A thousand dollars for a container of milk is a horrible deal. You wouldn't pay the special price for everything you buy in other areas of life. Why do it here?

So we need to look at different kinds of works, and I'd like to propose a way of doing this.

This includes recipes, computer programs, manuals and textbooks, reference works such as dictionaries and encyclopedias. For all these functional works, I believe that the issues are basically the same as they are for software and the same conclusions apply. People should have the freedom even to publish a modified version because it's very useful to modify functional works. People's needs are not all the same. If I wrote this work to do the job I think needs doing, your idea as a job you want to do may be somewhat different. So you want to modify this work to do what's good for you. At that point, there may be other people who have similar needs to yours, and your modified version might be good for them. Everybody who cooks knows this and has known this for hundreds of years. It's normal to make copies of recipes and hand them out to other people, and it's also normal to change a recipe. If you change the recipe and cook it for your friends and they like eating it, they might ask you, "Could I have the recipe?" Then maybe you'll write down your version and give them copies. That is exactly the same thing that we much later started doing in the free-software community.

So that's one class of work. The second class of work is works whose purpose is to say what certain people think. Talking about those people is their purpose. This includes, say, memoirs, essays of opinion, scientific papers, offers to buy and sell, catalogues of goods for sale. The whole point of those works is that they tell you what somebody thinks or what somebody saw or what somebody believes. To modify them is to misrepresent the authors; so modifying these works is not a socially useful activity. And so verbatim copying is the only thing that people really need to be allowed to do.

The next question is: Should people have the right to do commercial verbatim copying? Or is noncommercial enough? You see, these are two different activities we can distinguish, so that we can consider the questions separately—the right to do noncommercial verbatim copying and the right to do commercial verbatim copying. Well, it might be a good compromise policy to have copyright cover commercial verbatim copying but allow everyone the right to do noncommercial verbatim copying. This way, the copyright on the commercial verbatim copying, as well as on all modified versions—only the author could approve a modified version—would still provide the same revenue stream that it provides now to fund the writing of these works, to whatever extent it does.

By allowing the noncommercial verbatim copying, it means the copyright no longer has to intrude into everybody's home. It becomes an industrial regulation again, easy to enforce and painless, no longer requiring Draconian punishments and informers for the sake of its enforcement. So we get most of the benefit—and avoid most of the horror—of the current system.

The third category of works is aesthetic or entertaining works, where the most important thing is just the sensation of looking at the work. Now for these works, the issue of modification is a very difficult one because on the one hand, there is the idea that these works reflect the vision of an artist and to change them is to mess up that vision. On the other hand, you have the fact that there is the folk process, where a sequence of people modifying a work can sometimes produce a result that is extremely rich. Even when you have artists' producing the works, borrowing from previous works is often very useful. Some of Shakespeare's plays used a story that was taken from some other play. If today's copyright laws had been in effect back then, those plays would have been illegal. So it's a hard question what we should do about publishing modified versions of an aesthetic or an artistic work, and we might have to look for further subdivisions of the category in order to solve this problem. For example, maybe computer game scenarios should be treated one way; maybe everybody should be free to publish modified versions of them. But perhaps a novel should be treated differently; perhaps for that, commercial publication should require an arrangement with the original author.

Now if commercial publication of these aesthetic works is covered by copyright, that will give most of the revenue stream that exists today to support the authors and musicians, to the limited extent that the present system supports them, because it does a very bad job. So that might be a reasonable compromise, just as in the case of the works that represent certain people.

If we look ahead to the time when the age of the computer networks will have fully begun, when we're past this transitional stage, we can envision another way for the authors to get money for their work. Imagine that we have a digital cash system that enables you to get money for your work. Imagine that we have a digital cash system that enables you to send somebody else money through the Internet; this can be done in various ways using encryption, for instance. And imagine that verbatim copying of all these aesthetic works is permitted. But they're written in such a way that when you are playing one or reading one or watching one, a box appears on the side of your screen that says, "Click here to send a dollar to the author," or the musician or whatever. And it just sits there; it doesn't get in your way; it's on the side. It doesn't interfere with you, but it's there, reminding you that it's a good thing to support the writers and the musicians.

So if you love the work that you're reading or listening to, eventually you're going to say, "Why shouldn't I give these people a dollar? It's only a dollar. What's that? I won't even miss it." And people will start sending a dollar. The good thing about this is that it makes copying the ally of the authors and musicians. When somebody e-mails a friend a copy, that friend might send a dollar, too. If you really love it, you might send a dollar more than once and that dollar is more than they're going to get today if you buy the book or buy the CD because they get a tiny fraction of the sale. The same publishers that are demanding total power over the public in the name of the authors and musicians are giving those authors and musicians the shaft all the time.

I recommend you read Courtney Love's article in *Salon* magazine,[1] an article about pirates that plan to use musicians' work without paying them. These pirates are the record companies that pay musicians 4% of the sales figures, on the average. Of course, the very successful musicians have more clout. They get more than 4% of their large sales figures, which means that the great run of musicians who have a record contract get less than 4% of their small sales figures.

Here's the way it works: The record company spends money on publicity and they consider this expenditure as an advance to the musicians, although the musicians never see it. So nominally when you buy a CD, a certain fraction of that money is going to the musicians, but really it isn't. Really, it's going to pay back the publicity expenses, and only if the musicians are very successful do they ever see any of that money.

The musicians, of course, sign their record contracts because they hope they're going to be one of those few who strike it rich. So essentially a rolling lottery is being offered to the musicians to tempt them. Although they're good at music, they may not be good at careful, logical reasoning to see through this trap. So they sign and then probably all they get is publicity. Well, why don't we give them publicity in a different way, not through a system that's based on restricting the public and a system of the industrial complex that saddles us with lousy music that's easy to sell. Instead, why not make the listener's natural impulse to share the music they love the ally of the musicians? If we have this box that appears in the player as a way to send a dollar to the musicians, then the computer networks could be the mechanism for giving the musicians this publicity, the same publicity which is all they get from record contracts now.

We have to recognize that the existing copyright system does a lousy job of supporting musicians, just as lousy as world trade does of raising living standards in the Philippines and China. You have these enterprise zones where everyone works in a sweatshop and all of the products are made in sweatshops. I knew that globalization was a very inefficient way of raising living standards of people overseas. Say, an American is getting paid $20 an hour to make something and you give that job to a Mexican who is getting paid maybe $6 a day, what has happened here is that you've taken a large amount of money away from an American worker, given a tiny fraction, like a few percent, to a Mexican worker and given back the rest to the company. So if your goal is to raise the living standards of Mexican workers, this is a lousy way to do it.

It's interesting to see how the same phenomenon is going on in the copyright industry, the same general idea. In the name of these workers who certainly deserve something, you propose measures that give them a tiny bit and really mainly prop up the power of corporations to control our lives.

If you're trying to replace a very good system, you have to work very hard to come up with a better alternative. If you know that the present system is lousy, it's not so hard to find a better alternative; the standard of comparison today is very low. We must always remember that when we consider issues of copyright policy.

So I think I've said most of what I want to say. I'd like to mention that tomorrow (April 20, 2001) is "Phone-In Sick Day" in Canada. Tomorrow is the beginning of a summit to finish negotiating the free trade area of the Americas to try to extend corporate power throughout additional countries, and a big protest is being planned for Quebec. We've seen extreme methods being used to smash this protest. A lot of Americans are being blocked from entering Canada through the border that they're supposed to be allowed to enter through at any time. On the flimsiest of excuses, a wall has been built around the center of Quebec to be used as a fortress to keep protesters out. We've seen a large number of different dirty tricks used against public protest against these treaties. So whatever democracy remains to us after government powers have been taken away from democratically elected governors and given to businesses and to unelected international bodies, whatever is left after that may not survive the suppression of public protest against it.

I've dedicated seventeen years of my life to working on free software and allied issues. I didn't do this because I think it's the most important political issue in the world. I did it because it was the area where I saw I had to use my skills to do a lot of good. But what's happened is that the general issues of politics have evolved, and the biggest political issue in the world today is resisting the tendency to give business power over the public and governments. I see free software and the allied questions for other kinds of information that I've been discussing today as one part of that major issue. So I've indirectly found myself working on that issue. I hope I contribute something to the effort.

Response

David Thorburn Let me offer a brief general response. It seems to me that the strongest and most important practical guidance that Stallman offers us has two key elements. One is the recognition that old assumptions about copyright, old usages of copyright are inappropriate; they are challenged or undermined by the advent of the computer and computer networks. That may be obvious, but it is essential.

Second is the recognition that the digital era requires us to reconsider how we distinguish and weigh forms of intellectual and creative labor. Stallman is surely right that certain kinds of intellectual enterprises justify more copyright protection than others. Trying to identify systematically these different kinds or levels of copyright protection seems to me a valuable way to engage with the problems for intellectual work posed by the advent of the computer.

But I think I detect another theme that lies beneath what Stallman has been saying and that isn't really directly about computers at all, but more broadly about questions of democratic authority and the power that government and corporations increasingly exercise over our lives. This populist and anticorporate side to Stallman's discourse is nourishing but also reductive, potentially simplifying. And it is also perhaps overly idealistic. For example, how would a a novelist or a poet or a songwriter or a musician or the author of an academic textbook surivive in this brave new world where people are encouraged but not required to pay authors. In other words, it seems to me, the gap between existing practice and the visionary possibilities Stallman speculates about is still immensely wide.

So I'll conclude by asking if Stallman would like to expand a bit on certain aspects of his talk and, specifically, whether he has further thoughts about the way in which what we'll call "traditional creators" would be protected under his copyright system.

Stallman   First of all, I have to point out that we shouldn't use the term "protection" to describe what copyright does. Copyright restricts people. The term "protection" is a propaganda term of the copyright-owning businesses. The term "protection" means stopping something from being somehow destroyed. Well, I don't think a song is destroyed if there are more copies of it being played more. I don't think that a novel is destroyed if more people are reading copies of it, either. So I won't use that word. I think it leads people to identify with the wrong party.

Also, it's a very bad idea to think about intellectual property for two reasons: First, it prejudges the most fundamental question in the area which is: How should these things be treated and should they be treated as a kind of property? To use the term "intellectual property" to describe the area is to presuppose the answer is yes, that that's the way to treat things, not some other way.

Second, it encourages overgeneralization. Intellectual property is a catch-all for several different legal systems with independent origins such as, copy-rights, patents, trademarks, trade secrets and some other things as well. They are almost completely different; they have nothing in common. But people who hear the term "intellectual property" are led to a false picture where they imagine that there's a general principle of intellectual property that was applied to specific areas, so they assume that these various areas of the law are similar. This leads not only to confused thinking about what is right to do, it leads people to fail to understand what the law actually says because they suppose that the copyright law and patent law and trademark law are similar, when, in fact, they are totally different.

So if you want to encourage careful thinking and clear understanding of what the law says, avoid the term "intellectual property." Talk about copyrights. Or talk about patents. Or talk about trademarks or whichever subject you want to talk about. But don't talk about intellectual property. Opinion about intellectual property almost has to be a foolish one. I don't have an opinion about intellectual property. I have opinions about copyrights and patents and trademarks, and they're different. I came to them through different thought processes because those systems of law are totally different.

Anyway, I made that digression, but it's terribly important.

So, let me now get to the point. Of course, we can't see now how well it would work, whether it would work to ask people to pay money voluntarily to the authors and musicians they love. One thing that's obvious is that how well such a system would work is proportional to the number of people who are participating in the network, and that number, we know, is going to increase by an order of magnitude over a number of years. If we tried it today, it might fail, and that wouldn't prove anything because with ten times as money people participating, it might work.

The other thing is, we do not have this digital cash payment system; so we can't really try it today. You could try to do something a little bit like it. There are services you can sign up for where you can pay money to someone—things like PayPal. But before you can pay anyone through PayPal, you have to go through a lot of rigmarole and give them personal information about you, and they collect records of whom you pay. Can you trust them not to misuse that?

So the dollar might not discourage you, but the trouble it takes to pay might discourage you. The whole idea of this is that it should be as easy as falling off a log to pay when you get the urge, so that there's nothing to discourage you except the actual amount of money. And if that's small enough, why should it discourage you? We know, though, that fans can really love musicians, and we know that encouraging fans to copy and redistribute the music has been done by some bands that were, and are, quite successful like the "Grateful Dead." They didn't have any trouble making a living from their music because they encouraged fans to tape it and copy the tapes. They didn't even lose their record sales.

We are gradually moving from the age of the printing press to the age of the computer network, but it's not happening in a day. People are still buying lots of records, and that will probably continue for many years—maybe forever. As long as that continues, simply having copyrights that still apply to commercial sales of records ought to do about as good a job of supporting musicians as it does today. Of course, that's not very good, but, at least, it won't get any worse.

Question

With regard to the functional works, how do you, in your own thinking, balance out the need for abolishing the copyright with the need for economic incentives in order to have these functional works developed?

Stallman   Well, what we see is, first of all, that this economic incentive is a lot less necessary than people have been supposing. Look at the free software movement where we have over 100,000 part-time volunteers developing free software. We also see that there are other ways to raise money for this which are not based on stopping the public from copying and modifying these works. That's the interesting lesson of the free software movement. Aside from the fact that it gives you a way you can use a computer and keep your freedom to share and cooperate with other people, it also shows us that this negative assumption that people would never do these things unless they are given special powers to force people to pay them is simply wrong. A lot of people will do these things. Then if you look at, say, the writing of monographs which serve as textbooks in many fields of science except for the ones that are very basic, the authors are not making money out of that. We now have a free encyclopedia project that is, in fact, a commercial-free encyclopedia project, and it's making progress. We had a project for a GNU encyclopedia but we merged it into the commercial project when they adopted our license. In January, they switched to the GNU free documentation license for all the articles in their encyclopedia. So we said, "Well, let's join forces with them and urge people to contribute to them." It's called "NUPEDIA," and you can find a link to it, if you look at <http:// www.gnu.org/encyclopedia>. So here we've extended the community development of a free base of useful knowledge from software to encyclopedia. I'm pretty confident now that in all these areas of functional work, we don't need that economic incentive to the point where we have to mess up the use of these works.

Notes

This is an edited transcript from a speech given at MIT in the Communications Form on Thursday, April 19, 2001, following a similar speech on April 4, 2001, (titled "Copyright vs Community in the age of Computer Networks") at the CODE conference, Queens' College, Cambridge, United Kingdom.

1. Love, Courtney 2000. Courtney Love does the math. *Salon*, June 14. Available at <http://dir.salon.com/tech/feature/2000/06/14/love/index.html>.

Contributors

Philippe Aigrain is the founder and CEO of Society for Public Information Spaces. Previously he was head of sector "Software Technology and Society" within the Information Society General Directorate of the European Commission. He was, in particular, in charge of actions related to free/open source software actions. Before that Dr. Aigrain was head of the "Media Analysis and Interaction" research group within the Institut de Recherche en Informatique de Toulouse. He has also done research on computer processing, indexing, retrieval, and interaction for audiovisual media (video, music, still images). His fields of interest further include the history, economy, and sociology of information exchanges.

Yochai Benkler is a Professor of Law at Yale Law School. His research focuses on the effects of laws that regulate information production and exchange on the distribution of control over information flows, knowledge, and culture in the digital environment. His particular focus has been on the neglected role of commons-based approaches towards management of resources in the digitally networked environment. He has written about the economics and political theory of rules governing telecommunications infrastructure, with a special emphasis on wireless communications, rules governing private control over information, in particular intellectual property, and of relevant aspects of U.S. constitutional law. Previously, Benkler had been a professor at New York University School of Law, where he was the Director of the Engelberg Center for Innovation Law and Policy and Director of the Information Law Institute.

Boatema Boateng is an Assistant Professor in the Department of Communications, University of California, San Diego. Her research focuses on issues of power as they are manifested in institutional structures and in practices around the production and consumption of cultural products including information, knowledge, and material objects. Her most recent study was on the local, national, and international power implications of the treatment of indigenous knowledge and folklore as intellectual property, taking Ghana's copyright protection of adinkra and kente textiles as a case. Dr. Boateng's upcoming research projects include an analysis of the ways in which different kinds of knowledge and cultural production become gendered in their encounter with intellectual property regulatory regimes.

David Bollier is an independent strategist, journalist, and consultant specializing in progressive public policy and the impact of digital media on democratic culture. Bollier has been an advisor to television writer/producer Norman Lear on politics, public affairs, and special projects since 1984, and is a Senior Fellow at the Norman Lear Center at the USC Annenberg Center for Communication. He is also cofounder of Public Knowledge, a public-interest policy organization dedicated to defending the commons of science, culture, and the Internet.

James Boyle is William Neal Reynolds Professor at Duke Law School, a member of the Board of Creative Commons, and the founder of Duke's Center for the Study of the Public Domain. He is the author of *Shamans, Software, and Spleens: Law and the Construction of the Information Society* and a number of law-review articles about intellectual-property law and legal and social theory. He is currently working on a book about the public domain. His work can be found at <http://james-boyle.com>.

John Clippinger has been involved in a wide array of public policy and digital technology issues over the past thirty years. He participated in the founding of the National Telecommunications and Information Administration during the Carter Administration; built one of the first corporate Intranets for knowledge management as Director of Intellectual Capital at Coopers and Lybrand; cofounded three technology companies; and was author-editor of *Biology of Business: Decoding the Natural Laws of Enterprise* (Jossey-Bass). Currently, Dr. Clippinger is Chairman of Parity Communications in Boston and a Senior Fellow at BUILDE—Boston University's Institute on Leading a Dynamic Economy. He has held research positions at Harvard, Brandeis, and the

University of Pennsylvania, and is active with the Aspen Institute and The Santa Fe Institute.

Paul A. David is Professor of Economics and Senior Fellow of the Institute for Economic Policy Research at Stanford University, where he has been a member of the faculty continuously since 1961 and was formerly (in 1977–1994) the William Robertson Coe Professor of American Economic History. From 1994 until the fall 2002 he held a Senior Research Fellowship at All Souls College, Oxford, where he has since been elected an Emeritus Fellow. In November 2002, the Oxford Internet Institute announced David's appointment as its first Senior Fellow. His research interests include the economics of technological change, demographic change, and institutional change, and other areas of theoretical and empirical research on the nature of path-dependence in economic processes; economic history, with special reference to the United States; and the North Atlantic economies in the modern era. His most current research has focused on contemporary public policy issues: the role of interoperability standards in the evolution of network industries and the changing interrelationships between "open science" and proprietary R&D activities.

Rishab Aiyer Ghosh is Founding International and Managing Editor of *First Monday*, perhaps the most widely read peer-reviewed academic journal of the Internet. He is Program Leader at MERIT/International Institute of Infonomics at the University of Maastricht, Netherlands. He writes and speaks frequently on the socioeconomics of the Internet and free/open source software. He coordinated the European Union funded FLOSS project, one of the most comprehensive studies of free/libre/open source users and developers. He is actively involved in initiatives related to government policy on open source, and is involved in research projects on related topics funded by the European Union, the Dutch government, and the U.S. National Science Foundation.

Cori Hayden is currently Assistant Professor of Anthropology at the University of California, Berkeley, on research leave at Girton College, University of Cambridge. She received her PhD in Cultural Anthropology from the University of California, Santa Cruz in 2000, and she works on the anthropology of science in the Americas and the United Kingdom. Her first research project concerned the relationship among local knowledge, public sector science, and drug companies. She is currently exploring developments in the ethics and practice of clinical research in Latin America, as well as the rise of an ethic of benefit-sharing in human genetic research.

Tim Hubbard is Head of Human Sequence Analysis at the Wellcome Trust Sanger Institute Hinxton, UK (Sanger Centre) founded to further the knowledge of genomes, particularly through large-scale sequencing and analysis. He is Joint Head of the open source genome annotation project Ensembl, a joint project between the Sanger Centre and the European Bioinformatics Institute (EMBL-EBI). He is coauthor of *SCOP, Structural Classification of Proteins Database*, and is also co-organizer of CASP, the biannual "competition" to critically assess protein structure prediction methods.

Christopher Kelty is currently Assistant Professor in anthropology at Rice University, Houston, and he received his PhD from Massachusetts Institute of Technology. His research focuses on anthropology of networks and information, intellectual property, health-care and medical technology, and science and technology studies. The current research interests include forms of property and contract in software/IT, the mechanization of thought processes, memory systems, and universal languages, information infrastructure and exchange in Europe, the United States, and South Asia.

James Leach is a Research Fellow at King's College Cambridge, and Associate Lecturer in Social Anthropology, investigating the theory and practice of description, with an emphasis on how material and social forms emerge from the processes of interdisciplinary collaboration. Leach is a social anthropologist who has conducted fieldwork in Papua New Guinea on kinship, place, myth/ritual, material culture, ownership, and intellectual property. His subsequent fieldwork in the United Kingdom has focused on issues of creativity, knowledge production, and ownership in arts/science and Free/Open Source collaborations.

James Love has worked for the Center for Study of Responsive Law in Washington, D.C., since 1990, and since 1995 has been the Director of the Consumer Project on Technology. Love is an advisor on intellectual property policies to a number of national governments, international and regional intergovernmental organizations, public health NGOs, and private sector pharmaceutical companies. He is the U.S. co-chair of the Trans Atlantic Consumer Dialog (TACD) Working Group on Intellectual Property, a member of the Médecins Sans Frontières (MSF) Working Group on Intellectual Property and the MSF Neglected Disease Group, President of Essential Inventions, Inc., and a former member of the World Business Council on Sustainable Development, Working Group on Access to Human Genetic Resources. Love was previously Senior Economist for the Frank Russell Company, a Lecturer at Rutgers University, and a researcher on international finance at Princeton University.

Fred Myers is Professor and Chair of Anthropology at New York University and currently is President of the American Ethnological Society. He was editor of Cultural Anthropology from 1991–1995. He has received grants from the John Simon Guggenheim Foundation, the National Science Foundation, National Endowment for the Humanities, National Geographic Society, American Council of Learned Societies, and the Institute of Advanced Study at Princeton. Myers does research with Aboriginal people in Australia, concentrating on Western Desert people. He is interested in exchange theory and material culture, the intercultural production and circulation of culture, in contemporary art worlds, in identity and personhood, and in how these topics are related to theories of value and practices of signification.

Anthony Seeger is an anthropologist, ethnomusicologist, archivist, record producer, and musician. His research has concentrated on the music of Amazonian Indians. He has served as Associate Professor of the Graduate Faculty of the Department of Anthropology at the National Museum in Rio de Janeiro, and he is Professor of Anthropology and Director of the Indiana University Archives of Traditional Music. Seeger established the Smithsonian Folkways record label and has produced many recordings. He accepted a position at the University of California at Los Angeles in 2000. Dr. Seeger has held executive positions in a number of professional organizations, including the Society for Ethnomusicology and the International Council for Traditional Music. He serves on the advisory boards of archives in India and the Sudan, and has consulted on archival issues in Peru, Brazil, Hong Kong, Indonesia, South Africa, and the United States.

Richard Stallman is the founder of the GNU free operating system, the principal author of the GNU C compiler and other programs. Stallman received the Grace Hopper award for 1991 from the Association for Computing Machinery. In 1990 he was awarded a MacArthur Foundation fellowship, and in 1996 an honorary doctorate from the Royal Institute of Technology in Sweden. In 1998 he received the Electronic Frontier

Foundation's pioneer award along with Linus Torvalds. In 1999 he received the Yuri Rubinski award. In 2001 he received a second honorary doctorate, from the University of Glasgow, and shared the Takeda award for social/economic betterment with Torvalds and Ken Sakamura. In 2002 he was elected to the U.S. National Academy of Engineering and in 2003 to the American Academy of Arts and Sciences. In 2003 he was named an honorary professor of the Universided Nacional de Ingenieria in Peru, and he received an honorary doctorate from the Free University of Brussels.

Marilyn Strathern is Mistress of Girton College and William Wyse Professor and head of the Department of Social Anthropology at the University of Cambridge. A fellow of the British Academy, and Foreign Hon. Member of the American Academy of Arts and Sciences, she is currently Chair of the European Association of Social Anthropologists. She has published on both Melanesia and the United Kingdom. Research in Papua New Guinea involved gender relations, feminist scholarship, dispute settlement and legal anthropology and, most recently, intellectual property. In the United Kingdom, her writings on "English" culture and society have focused on English kinship and the new reproductive technologies, and on the audit culture, as well as the area of bioethics. Strathern has also received the Viking Fund Medal in 2003 from the international Wenner-Gren Foundation for Anthropological Research, and was elected a medallist for the prestigious Huxley medal 2004. In 2001 she was presented with the Order of Dame Commander of the British Empire (DBE) in recognition of services to social anthropology.

Index